# SCHOOL EFFECTIVENESS AND SCHOOL IMPROVEMENT

# SCHOOL EFFECTIVENESS AND SCHOOL IMPROVEMENT

Proceedings of the Second International Congress
Rotterdam 1989

Edited by

Bert Creemers
Ton Peters
Dave Reynolds

SWETS & ZEITLINGER B.V. AMSTERDAM / LISSE

SWETS & ZEITLINGER INC. ROCKLAND, MA / BERWYN, PA / *PUBLISHING SERVICE*

CIP-GEGEVENS KONINKLIJKE BIBLIOTHEEK, DEN HAAG

Schooleffectiveness

School effectiveness and school improvement / ed. by Bert
P.M. Creemers, Ton Peters and Dave Reynolds. – Amsterdam
[etc.] : Swets & Zeitlinger ; Berwyn : Swets & Zeitlinger
Met lit. opg.
ISBN 90-265-1008-X geb.
SISO 450.4 UDC 371.012 NUGI 724
Trefw.: schoolorganisatie.


**Library of Congress Cataloging-in-Publication Data**

Schooleffectiveness and schoolimprovement / edited by Bert P.M.
    Creemers, Ton[y] Peters, and Dave Reynolds.
        p.   cm.
    "This volume contains a revised and rewritten selection of the
papers which were given at the Second International Congress for
School Effectiveness that was held in Rotterdam in Januari 1989"--P. 7.
    ISBN 902651008X : $57.00 (U.S.)
    1. School improvement programs--Congresses.  2. Schools-
-Evaluation--Congresses.   3. Education and state--Congresses.
I. Creemers, Bert P.M.  II. Peters, Tony.  III. Reynolds, David,
1949-  .  IV. International Congress for School Effectiveness (2nd
: 1989 : Rotterdam, Netherlands)  V. Title: School effectiveness and
school improvement.
LB2822.2.S36   1989
379.1'54--dc20                                          89-37119
                                                          CIP

Printed by Offsetdrukkerij Kanters B.V., Alblasserdam
© Copyright 1989 Swets & Zeitlinger B.V., Lisse

ISBN 90 265 1008 X
NUGI 724

Edu.

# Contents

# PREFACE AND INTRODUCTION

This volume contains a revised and rewritten selection of the papers which were given at the Second International Congress for School Effectiveness that was held in Rotterdam in January 1989. In deciding which papers to publish, we tried as far as possible to ensure that both standards of high academic quality and of relevance to policymakers and teachers were adhered to, whilst at the same time we tried to ensure that a wide range of different countries' contributions to the Congress were recognised. Some contributors who presented material to both the Rotterdam meeting and to the First Congress in London in 1988 therefore appear in only one of the conference proceedings and the activities of some country planning teams are reported in only one of the volumes in the same way. The first conference proceedings – School Effectiveness and Improvement, Proceedings of the First International Congress, London 1988 – have already been published by the University of Wales, College of Cardiff in the United Kingdom and the RION Institute for Educational Research in the Netherlands, edited by Dave Reynolds, Bert P.M. Creemers and Ton Peters.

It is perhaps important to make clear exactly what the International Congress for School Effectiveness is and exactly what it does. Originally, half a dozen people from different countries met at the American Educational Research Association in April 1987 to plan an informal meeting for perhaps ten or twenty academics and practitioners, so that people in different countries could learn from the strengths of the research and improvement enterprise internationally. At the first meeting in London in January 1988, over 120 people arrived and adopted a draft 'constitution' that pledged the organisation to work in different countries for excellence and equity amongst the students of state schools, both elementary and secondary. Each of the dozen countries involved has set up a country planning team, which is responsible for a range of activities in each country. The country planning teams themselves meet annually to plan international activities. The aim of the national and international enterprise is to exchange information, encourage links between policymakers, practitioners and researchers and to network and run conferences that will further the aims of school effectiveness and improvement.

The papers in this volume move – we hope – logically through in sequence. Section One contains the papers which were given in plenary sessions of the Congress and which between them cover most of the major disciplinary areas of the still expanding field of school effectiveness and improvement. Thomas Good outlines the bodies of knowledge on school effectiveness and on teacher effectiveness and goes on to argue for teachers to themselves conduct clasroom and school based research in order to secure both school improvement and enhanced teacher professionalism. Barry Fraser uses the large scale National Assessment in Science data base to explore the school, classroom and curriculum influences on student achievement and Desmond Nuttall outlines the ways in which the Inner London Education Authority assesses the effectiveness of their schools by adjusting schools' 'raw' achievement results to allow for the different types of intakes that the schools are getting. Rima Miller concludes this section of the book by outlining ways in which the literature on school effectiveness can be used to directly improve schools, giving two detailed case studies that show improvement in action.

Section Two contains reports on the 'state of the art' for school effectiveness and school improvement in the various different countries which were represented at the Rotterdam Congress and attempts to show the activities of researchers, policymakers and practitioners, and how they may be interrelated. The overall impression of international activity is one of rapid growth in the area (and in linked areas such as school evaluation and performance indicators) and one of increasingly strong links between school effectiveness research and its application directly in school improvement strategies (especially in countries such as the United States, Canada, Israel and Australia). Differences between countries in the within-school factors that they believe to be important are also in evidence, with Canada and Sweden utilising different models of effective school processes to those shown by research in the Netherlands for example.

Section Three covers a very wide range of school effectiveness topics based upon a large number of mostly on-going and new research studies. A number of studies have been undertaken in secondary schools (Leithwood et al, Bosker and Van der Velden, De Vries), which is helpful since the majority of effective school studies so far have been in elementary or primary schools. A high proportion of the studies (eg. Knuver and Brandsma) are utilising 'social' and affective as well as academic outcomes as their dependent measures, again a welcome departure from the past concentration in research upon only cognitive school outcomes. Turning to look at the results as to which school factors are important, it is clear that high expectations of pupils, aspirations for pupils' success and diagnostic use of tests are important factors in generating effectiveness but the educational leadership factors often noted by North American studies seem to be considerably less important in an European context (Scheerens and Creemers). To complicate matters further these factors, however, may be different in schools according to their catchment area characteristics (Teddlie et al) and it is also clear that whole educational districts can be differentially effective (De Vries), not just individual schools.

There are, as one might expect, clear differences in the substantive findings in this section as well as similarities. International data reported by Scheerens et al shows weak and/or inconsistent effects of the 'time on task' variable with achievement, whilst Teddlie et al find that 'high academic engaged time on task' is associated with effectiveness. Nevertheless, school effects appear relatively stable over time and their size, although small by comparison with the size of home background effects, may be of great importance at a policy level (Bosker and Scheerens). The overall progress that has been made in terms of our empirical understanding is perhaps illustrated by the fact that the Section can conclude with a quite sophisticated theoretical model which integrates school structure and classroom environments with various individual level variables (Scheerens and Creemers), and by the fact that at a policy level substantial gains can result from whole-school based improvement strategies (Bashi and Sass) that are based upon school effectiveness research.

Section Four on school improvement again reveals substantial growth in our knowledge base. Stringfield and Teddlie outline their programme of school effectiveness research and move away from this point-in-time 'snapshot' of schools to a detailed description of how some of their schools have self improved over the years and of how effective and ineffective schools may developmentally evolve. Other themes given attention in this section are the extra-school, district level organisational factors generating greater equity in student outcomes (Chrispeels and Pollack), the school principal as a generator of change (Andrews) and the school principal as a generator of change by means of his/her development of leadership teams (Hallinger). Following a detailed description of what is probably a typical North American school improvement programme (Young), Ackerman et al speculate about what outside-school system factors are necessary to generate school effectiveness and Renihan and Renihan outline their concerns as school improvement efforts based upon school effectiveness work begin to stretch into their second decade of existence.

Section Five outlines the concluding thoughts of two of us as we considered the whole range of paper sessions at the Congress and of papers in this volume. In research terms, we saw genuine progress reflected in the papers, but albeit with a need to understand the importance of context and cultural differences in shaping 'effectiveness'. Looking at improvement, we were more pessimistic and concerned about the use of improvement strategies that were 'recipes' unrelated to curriculum or instructional matters and which were often dropped into schools without the benefit of a school-centred review of their appropriateness. As well as more research and improvement studies, we may now need to consider the development of middle range theories of school effectiveness and school improvement in order to keep an increasingly complex body of knowledge in a shape whereby it can be easily accessed and understood.

Bert Creemers
Ton Peters
Dave Reynolds

# PLENARY
# SESSIONS

# USING CLASSROOM AND SCHOOL RESEARCH TO PROFESSIONALIZE TEACHING

Thomas L. Good *
University of Missouri, Columbia

## INTRODUCTION

The history of reform in American education has been driven by external change agents who often pose simplistic answers for complex problems. Teachers are vulnerable to external pressure for rapid change because of an inadequate knowledge base and because of citizens' lack of understanding about the complexity of teaching and how difficult it is to bring about meaningful change. The isolation under which teachers work is widely known; after they become teachers, many teachers never observe another teacher (Lortie, 1975), and many have little means to do so. Moreover, because of the putative claim of low test scores — and the domination of achievement testing in the U.S. — teachers are bombarded almost daily with information about the general inadequacy of their profession and their lack of control in establishing and monitoring their own performance (Good & Mulryan, in press).

### Crisis Orientation
A recent publication by the National Center for Educational Statistics (Stern & Chandler, 1988) that describes students' performance on achievement tests states that "all students had particular difficulty with tasks that required them to elaborate upon or to defend their judgments and interpretation about what they had read (p.16)." This same source indicates that students' computer competence is low and that their knowledge of U.S. history and litera-

---

* I acknowledge the support provided by the Center for Research in Social Behavior at the University of Missouri-Columbia and especially thank Teresa Hjellming and LeeAnn Debo for typing the manuscript and Gail Hinkel for editing it. Also, I want to thank Bruce Biddle, Jere Brophy, and Susan Rosenholtz for their valuable review of the manuscript.

3

ture is extremely uneven. However, this report and the research on which it is based do *not* describe instruction in classrooms (or in homes) in which students have developed adequate computer competence. The constant attention to a single problem (whether Sputnik in the 1950s or economic competitiveness in the 1980s) leaves administrators and teachers vulnerable to political pressure (fadism in curriculum reform and simplistic approaches to professional licensing). Educators in turn believe that quick action will enhance their credibility with the public, but it also limits careful reflection and the development of new programs based on research.

### External Pressure for Solutions

Sarason (1982) has emphasized external change agents' lack of understanding of the time and effort required of individual teachers if a new innovation is to be successful: "The proponents seem to assume that because they are convinced about the value of the change, teachers should be willing (even enthusiastic) to accept more demands on their time. Any attempt to change regularities in the classroom places the teacher in an unlearning and learning process, a fact that has obvious implications for the time perspective of those seeking change" (pp. 285-286). Unfortunately, without time to understand a "problem" and the alternative range of solutions that might be useful in correcting it (without creating new ones), the problem is often redefined by external change agents and the cycle of futility continues. Although there is some recognition by policymakers and school administrators that teachers must be part of the change process (identifying the problem) as well as simply altering their own behavior, Sarason notes that even today this recognition is often more rhetorical than actual. Ironically, most calls for reform come from people outside of schools and hence from those who are least knowledgeable about the internal dynamics and issues that may prevent meaningful change from occurring. Further, the spate of recent bureaucratic reforms aimed at teachers indicates little confidence in teachers' ability to conduct research and to become more professional. However, in contrast to the recent movement toward bureaucratic control, there is growing evidence of a body of knowledge about teaching.


## RESEARCH KNOWLEDGE

As several recent research reviews have made clear, we know much more about the relation between teacher behavior and student achievement than we did 20 years ago (Brophy, 1988; Brophy & Good, 1986; Shulman, 1986). Furthermore, in the textbook *Looking in Classrooms*, Jere Brophy and I discuss how teachers can use research linking teacher behavior to student achievement to make classroom decisions and plans. It is important to realize that knowledge of classroom instruction is interactive and must be integrated with other knowledge to be useful (i.e., content knowledge, knowledge of students, etc.). Teaching success is not defined by a few broad variables but rather many aspects of instructional process and curriculum must be coordinated if classroom learning is to be productive (Brophy & Evertson, 1976; Fraser, 1989).

Brophy and I stress that research evidence, at its best, provides only information. Some educators pursue goals that are not considered by researchers. For those educators, the research may have little if any value. Further, in all cases research information has to be interpreted with a given teacher's style and knowledge of students in a particular context. Still, the field has made notable progress in some areas.

It is beyond the purpose of this paper to review this literature in any detail (interested readers can see Brophy & Good, 1986; Good & Brophy, 1987; Richardson-Koehler, 1987; Shulman, 1986). However, I want to stress that important progress has occurred and that it is evident that new advances are occurring in basic curriculum areas such as mathematics, reading, writing, and science, and in the presentation of these subjects in the classroom (see for example Anderson & Smith, 1987; Confrey, 1987; Florio-Ruane & Dunn, 1987; Raphael, 1987). It is also clear that more attention is paid to the student as learner in a complex social environment than was the case even a decade ago (see for example Corno & Rohrkemper, 1985; Mergendoller & Marchman, 1987; Wittrock, 1986). Further, it is important to note that modern research is beginning to utilize outcome measures that are broader than the knowledge typically assessed on standardized achievement tests.

*Use and Misuse of Classroom Research*
The significance of recent research on teacher behavior is that it yields useful instructional models that are relevant to structuring learning activities so that students master lower-level content and skills. Some models based on more recent classroom research can also be applied to higher-level activities such as reading comprehension and study skills, and to certain types of scientific experimentation and mathematical problem solving. However, considering the way that the data have been collected, research on teaching, at present, does not yield information about instructional processes (debate, discovery, discussion, role play, etc.) rather than products or tasks that call for students to discover or create processes (interpretation of literature, creative writing, etc.) rather than to follow prescribed processes.

Teachers must convey information in a way that promotes student thinking and comprehension, and they must frequently conduct demonstrations. Knowledge about how to do this successfully is important, especially since there is considerable evidence that a number of teachers have difficulty managing classrooms and promoting students' comprehension of basic concepts. Despite the contributions of recent research, it is foolish and counterproductive to equate knowledge of such teaching effects with effective teaching per se (Brophy, 1988; Brophy & Good, 1986).

Overgeneralizing from research on teaching is similar to equating a good physician with only the ability to interpret an x-ray correctly, defining a competent mechanic as one who can tune a car, or reducing the definition of a successful basketball player to one who can make a 15-foot jump shot reasonably consistently (Good & Mulryan, in press). The skills, knowledge, and understanding necessary to be successful in any area are numerous and diverse (a good physician must understand cell structure, bone structure, as well as principles of physiology and pharmacology, to name but a few; a good mechanic must know about carburetors, fuel-injection systems, principles of suspension, and how to identify the cause of engine malfunctions; or a basketball player must have skills of defense, rebounding, running the court, and passing, as well as court presence). We have made progress but the knowledge base is still very limited.

# SCHOOL RESEARCH

Until recently, many individuals believed that resources invested in schools were not related to student achievement. Following the publication of the well-known Coleman et al. (1966) report, many researchers attempted to relate school inputs (e.g., number of books in the library) to school outputs (student achievement). However, this research ignored what took place in schools (e.g., do teachers take advantage of libraries by allowing students to use them?). It is now clear that the *utilization* of resources is far more important than the level of resources available. There is now considerable research showing that the school students attend can make a substantial difference in their education (Brookover et al., 1979; Edmonds, 1983; Good & Brophy, 1986a; Good & Weinstein, 1986; Purkey & Smith, 1983; Rutter, 1983). It is beyond the purpose of this paper to review this literature in detail; however, it is appropriate to consider briefly some of the broad findings from this research.

*General findings.* Edmonds (1983) contends that the characteristics of effective schools are (a) leadership of the principal reflected by continuing attention to the quality of instruction; (b) a pervasive and broadly understood instructional focus; (c) an orderly, safe climate conducive both to teaching and learning; (d) teacher behaviors that convey an expectation that all students are to achieve at least minimum mastery; (e) the use of measures of pupil achievement as the basis for program evaluation. Rutter (1983) reports that the correlation between the combined measure of overall school process and each of the outcome measures (attendance, achievement, student conduct) was much stronger than was the correlation between any single process variable and outcome measure. This empirical finding implies that various social factors may combine to create a school ethos, or a set of values and behaviors that characterizes a school.

Rosenholtz (1985), in examining the evidence for making a claim that some schools are more effective than others, placed heavy emphasis on the notion of explicit organizational goals. She notes that the locus of school excellence can be found in rational planning and certainty of action because principals and teachers are combined in their attempts to combat a "solvable" problem ... low student achievement. Because of the certainty of success and commitment, in effective low-SES schools, responsive principals were found to provide teachers with clear and common objectives, provided them with the opportunity to develop detailed teaching strategies that in part were further developed through collaborative effort with other teachers, and given other technical resources and the necessary time for planning improvement efforts.

*Context*. Although comparatively little research has been conducted on school context, existing evidence illustrates that the social context in which schools operate has important influences on what behaviors, organizational strategies, and beliefs constitutes effectiveness (see e.g., Hallinger & Murphy, 1986; Teddlie & Stringfield, 1985; Teddlie, Stringfield, Wimpleberg, & Kirby, 1989). Such data make it clear that some of the simplistic prescriptions that result from school effects research can have unfortunate consequences if literally applied. That is, techniques that are effective in one setting may not be effective in other settings.

*Theory*. Rosenholtz (1989) recently completed a theoretically guided study that provides an authoritative analysis of differences in functioning between schools that are changing and improving ("moving" schools) and those that are not ("stuck"). Most previous work on effective schools has described only single variables of schooling (e.g., communication of expectations, goal setting, leadership) without an analysis of how the variables might combine in important ways (Good & Weinstein, 1986).

Rosenholtz found several dimensions useful in characterizing how "moving" schools differed from those in which teachers were "stuck." In moving schools teachers and principals tended to agree on the definition of teaching and assigned high priority to instructional goals. Teachers appeared to work toward shared school goals because the goals reflected their own opinions and were also supported by many of their colleagues who had similar opinions.

Teacher collaboration was another important aspect of life in moving schools. In too many schools, norms of self-reliance discourage teachers from asking for or giving help. In contrast, in moving schools, teaching was seen as inherently difficult and thus colleagues held the view that many minds work better than one. In such settings, requests for and offers of advice were commonplace.

7

Teachers' learning opportunities were another important characteristic of moving schools. Rosenholtz notes that in stuck or learning-impoverished schools there was a numbing sameness to school routine and teachers did not have the opportunity to interact with one another in a meaningful fashion. She argues that norms of self-reliance encouraged teachers to view their work as easy to learn; "teaching is easy"; one either grasped it or not. In moving schools, there seemed to be a pervasive ethos that no one ever stopped learning to teach. Here, principals provided frequent and useful evaluation of teaching and arranged opportunities for teachers to collaborate with one another.

### Abuses of Research on Schools

Rosenholtz (1989) notes that although research on successful school practices offers clear evidence that schools affect student achievement, not enough comprehensive evidence is available to form a base for policy changes. The success of any given strategy for enhancing student performance depends largely on the context in which schooling occurs, and there is no easy formula for school improvement — only guidelines and concepts that educators can use in planning improvement programs. She argues that the issue is not how to put more power into bureaucratic hands but how to get more power into the hands of teachers and principals. However, despite careful critiques pointing out the limitations of school research (see, for example, Good & Brophy, 1986a; Good & Weinstein, 1986), many districts are attempting to apply the results of school-effectiveness research in order to improve student performance. Unfortunately, many of the prescriptions and formulae for effective schools are exceedingly narrow and undermine rather than enhance teacher creativity. It is the case that many school reform plans appear to be uninformed by recent evidence suggesting that the social context of a school is a key factor when reflecting upon planning school reform (e.g., Hallinger & Murphy, 1986).

### Common Weaknesses in Classroom and School Research

Most studies of the effects of classroom and school processes on student achievement are atheoretical. Research at both levels has yielded general and practical findings suggesting that there are important differences between both teachers and schools in terms of their effects on student achievement. Unfortunately, because of the atheoretical nature of the research, it is not possible to describe how school and classroom characteristics are related and interact (Good & Weinstein, 1986). Considering that in the early 1970s many social scientists, educators, and citizens raised important questions about whether school processes affected student achievement, the empirical research that attempted to verify that teachers and schools could affect student achievement was probably justifiable. However, because researchers have now clarified that schools and teachers make a difference, it is important to explain more completely how processes at both levels operate and how they can be combined in additive ways. Researchers should not only examine school practices (e.g., school rules) or classroom assignments (e.g., the extent to which instruction emphasizes rote learning or meaningful learning) but should also study how the effects of one teacher can be combined with the effects of other teachers in ways that do not threaten teacher autonomy yet make schooling more coordinated and effective for all concerned. For example, in this spirit one might ask how the second-grade experience can be designed so as to take advantage of first-grade experiences and to prepare students for the third grade (Good & Weinstein, 1986).

Another common weakness of research at both the school and classroom levels is that the relations examined involve student achievement as measured by standardized achievement tests. However, as Rhona Weinstein and I argue, research on the effects of instruction cannot be limited simply by what is currently taught in the majority of the nation's schools (Good & Weinstein, 1986). Considering that in the future computers will simplify access to information, the instructor's role will likely shift from providing students with authoritative conceptualization and information toward helping them develop analytical skills for critically evaluating information.

## TEACHING AS PROFESSIONAL ACTIVITY

It is beyond the scope of this paper to provide a detailed discussion of the organizational and institutional behaviors that distinguish a profession from an occupation or from "work." However, in many schools teachers do not function as professionals, and they may be unable to do so until the structure of schools changes in order to allow teachers more time for peer association and reflection. It is also unlikely that teachers as a group will function as professionals until teacher education programs change to provide teachers with appropriate dispositions, knowledge, and skills to act as professionals. I want to emphasize that some schools and teacher education programs do provide prerequisite conditions for professional behavior, although these appear to be the exception rather than the rule (Lanier & Warren-Little, 1986).

Goode (1957) argues that a profession is a "community," a group with a common experience and a shared identity that has a long tradition, a distinct public image, and a reasonably homogeneous system of professional training and socialization. In a sense, then, a profession is not *sharply* differentiated from an occupation by role specialization (an administrative elite who make all policy decisions, and professional workers who carry out all of the day-to-day activities of the profession). Perhaps the hallmark of a profession is its ability to claim specialized knowledge and to have that claim generally supported by the larger public. As is well known, legislators and parents themselves have been "students" for many years, and there appears an easy base upon which citizens can and do "debate" specialized knowledge about educational settings in ways that they do not in other areas, even those about which they possess much practical experience and knowledge. For example, affluent and informed patients tend not to debate issues of nutrition with physicians, even though physicians often have little knowledge of nutrition and other issues, such as the role of exercise in rehabilitating a knee injury. Hence, a *technical culture* and its *perceived legitimacy* are at least two of the requirements for professional status. By "technical culture" I imply a set of findings, concepts, and specialized knowledge that those who are not members of the profession do not possess.

Certain role behaviors and use of technical knowledge also define a profession. Professionals strive for a balance between original thinking and individual judgment, and conformity to a shared norm about appropriate professional behavior. Describing professional behavior in complex organizations is difficult. Freidson (1984) notes that a large literature discusses the putative conflict between bureaucratic administration and professionalism. The basic argument is that professionals are committed to peers and to the profession. They are motivated to control their own professional work, with attention to peer standards, and resist taking orders from bureaucratic superiors who assert the primary aims of the organization. However, according to Freidson, despite this common argument, empirical data and organizational theory challenge the simple assumption that large organizations are necessarily organized along bureaucratic lines to order and control the behavior of professionals who work within them. Thus, one cannot assume that professionals who work in large organizations are subjected to the same constraints that industrial workers experience on their jobs (close supervision, little discretion in work performance, etc.).

Freidson contends that it is not necessary to speak of deprofessionalization as long as the formulation and direction of professional work remain in the hands of members of the profession. However, in certain professions in which workers make the putative claim to be professionals, this issue of control is extremely problematic. Increasingly, the control of education is in the hands of members of state boards of education or state departments of education, although their formal connection to university faculty members, public school teachers, and educational researchers is often remote at best. The argument that members of the education profession are controlling the direction of the profession is therefore extremely problematic and in many cases erroneous.

Decisions about standards of curriculum and pupil performance are increasingly made by individuals who have little understanding of student cognition and development, formal knowledge of subject matter, and insight into instructional process linking students and subject matter in integrative

10

ways (i.e., sophisticated decisions about what subjects and instructional methods are appropriate for particular students). Even though our technical knowledge of teaching is expanding and it is the case that we understand better the degree of integration of knowledge that must occur if teachers are to enact curriculum meaningfully (e.g., Doyle, in press), teachers' and schools' capacity for decision making is being diminished by external influences.

Despite external influences that strive for control of the school curriculum, the message in some school districts is that teachers must be learners, and that principals must actively support and strive to improve the instructional capacity of their schools. The literature on effective schools (Rosenholtz, 1989) illustrates that some schools become communities of scholars where knowledge (of teaching, students, subject matter) is valued and where learning flourishes because of identifiable collegial norms and activities. If schools are to become more productive, it will be necessary both that *technical knowledge become more advanced* and that *norms for professional behavior be enhanced* so that teachers play a more important role in the development and use of technical knowledge.

### Inadequate Opportunity for Teacher Control

There is clear — and growing — evidence that teachers have too little opportunity to define and to improve their conditions of work. For example, the recent study, "The Conditions and Resources of Teaching," conducted by the National Education Association (1988), found that teachers perceive that they lack the basic conditions necessary to do their jobs. Of the 2,000 teachers surveyed in this national sample, 60% indicated that they have no say over staff development opportunities. In addition, half of the teachers indicated that the quality of administrative supervision creates problems for them in doing their jobs, and 40% of teachers reported inadequate equipment, supplies, and materials. Teachers reported dissatisfaction with the decision-making power provided to them. Teachers, in too many cases, are treated as workers, not professionals.

Various educators and professional groups have started to assert that the workplace conditions of teaching are often difficult and unrewarding (see, for example, the Holmes Group Report, *Tomorrow's Teachers*). Teachers teach the entire day with little or no time for lesson preparation, lesson analysis, or exchange of ideas with peers. Growing teacher dissatisfaction associated with these conditions poses a serious threat to the attractiveness of teaching as a profession (talented youth are not considering teaching as a career; capable teachers leave the profession after only 1 or 2 years). Many argue that until teaching becomes more of a profession, it is unreasonable to expect the field to attract a sufficient number of talented individuals to public schools (e.g., Schlechty & Vance, 1983).

### Increasing Teachers' Opportunities for Research

Although countless questions and issues could form an agenda for professional development, in this paper I want to discuss teacher research as one area where concerns with classroom and school processes could form a focus for involving teachers in professionally stimulating activities and enhancing their capacity to direct instructional programs.

I stress teachers' involvement in research because it seems to me that their participation in the production and analysis of technical information is at the core of professional activity. Further, changing the structure of schooling to allow teachers more power and autonomy to influence the production of specialized information is a means of helping teachers to obtain more professional status. This assumes, of course, that sufficient attention is given to assisting teachers in developing specialized competencies that help them to conduct research in a meaningful way.

It should be clear that by advocating that teachers conduct research, I do not mean their simply discussing research by others or conducting a series of treatments in their classrooms that do not yield defendable conclusions or insights. Rather, teachers who conduct research should read and synthesize relevant literature and know how to select an appropriate research methodology. Unfortunately, students at the master's level in teacher education programs are often exposed to sophisticated — and sometimes esoteric research designs and statistics but do not receive a firm grounding in research designs that they can use to conduct research in their own classrooms (e.g., case studies, single-subject designs, etc.). Some teachers may not want to conduct research and prefer to use their time to design curriculum and integrate curriculum units in innovative and useful ways. Further, some teachers who are interested in research will not want to conduct careful comparative research and may instead prefer to study topics such as what other teachers do in their classrooms; or to explore research that has been developed by other researchers (e.g., Billups & Rauth, 1987).

However, I would be remiss if I left the impression that the only advantage of involving teachers in research is to influence the structure of schooling and to enhance the professional activities of teachers (even though these are extremely important outcomes). I want to stress that large substantive gains can occur from allowing teachers to jointly conceptualize classroom phenomena and to share insights about ways in which problematic conditions of teaching can be improved through innovations in instruction and curriculum. Teachers possess viable knowledge of practice that can be enhanced when it is shared with peers and interested others (e.g., classroom researchers).

Obviously, there are countless ways that teachers could work together on significant topics such as improving the curriculum in computer technology and students' competence in using the computer, developing and testing strategies for working more effectively with parents (especially parents of students who are having academic difficulty), studying and exchanging information about research on teaching, and observing and giving feedback to peers about their performance in the classroom. Along these lines, Jere Brophy and I note in our book, *Looking in Classrooms* (1987), the advantages of study groups in which teachers share information and resources and analyze teaching in collegial settings. We believe that teachers can often use regularly scheduled in-service time or release time during the school day to plan and work in study groups. This procedure can be especially beneficial for small groups of teachers who share common problems or interests (see Good & Brophy, 1987 for more details and examples). In combining the study of classrooms and schools, the topic of teacher inquiry is not important. Rather, the major issue is that teachers be allowed to pursue topics as part of teams that examine implications of research and share strategies that inform practice across grades or classrooms. That is, teachers deal with issues that are directly related to their own classrooms but that are broader as well.

Although collaborative programs can be organized for many purposes, I use teachers as researchers as an example here. As various educators note, there is too little classroom observational research, and teachers are isolated in terms of knowledge of what other teachers do and of alternative ways to approach various topics that they teach (e.g., Good & Biddle, 1988). However, there is no reason why teachers cannot conduct classroom research themselves and certainly no reason why they should not have the necessary resources to do so in their own schools (e.g., secretarial support; release time to observe their own students while someone else teaches; or the opportunity to observe other teachers). It also seems important that teachers have access to videotape technology so that they can observe their own teaching and to have access to video libraries that allow teachers to observe other teachers as they present ideas. Part of the focus on teacher-researcher might involve opportunities for teachers to study, to discuss, and to consider the applications of research results. For example, teachers might study various recommendations that have been made about teaching in a particular subject (e.g., mathematics), consider the alternative conceptualizations of teaching and learning in the literature, and discuss how best to benefit from the diversity in the literature (e.g., Bauersfeld, 1988; Carpenter, Fennema, Peterson, Chiang, & Loef, 1988; Confrey, 1987; Good & Grouws, 1987; Hoyles, 1988). Teachers would not be expected to implement someone else's approach but to consider strategies and ideas and to use those to reflect on teaching. Research findings would be used to stimulate thinking and would be integrated with teachers' general knowledge and with knowledge of their classrooms. Such an approach underlies the belief that effective schools represent a nonroutine technical culture in which teaching professionals reflect on problems of practice and adapt research information and information from their own experience in an intelligent, thoughtful fashion (e.g., Good & Brophy, 1986b; Good & Brophy, 1987; Rosenholtz, 1989).

13

Weinstein (1988) reports findings from a cooperative intervention program that features collaboration between university researchers and teachers from an urban high school. The initial project data show positive effects on students and illustrate how a team of teachers can collaborate to enhance the curriculum and learning climate for low-achieving students in ways that are "richer" than the usual interventions in individual classrooms. Although this particular collaboration involved university and school personnel, there is no reason that meaningful collaboration cannot be conducted by teachers without outside assistance. Although I believe that collaboration between universities and public schools holds rich potential, I want to stress that teacher-conceived and conducted research is a viable model that can increase the professional role of teachers.

The conceptualization of teacher research groups and the value of teacher-controlled research have been documented elsewhere (e.g., Fraser, 1986; Kyle & McCutcheon, 1984). Furthermore, the procedures for allowing teachers to form study groups and to share ideas generally or to examine research specifically have also been discussed elsewhere (Billups & Rauth, 1987; Good & Brophy, 1987). The intent here is to argue the need for active teacher collaboration concerning both classrooms and school concerns.

# THE ROLE OF RESEARCH IN SCHOOL IMPROVEMENT

Teachers who collaborate to conduct research should realize that research does not yield rigid prescriptions that apply to all situations. It can, however, provide a better understanding of practice, alternate conceptions of practice, a range of behaviors that might be appropriate in a situation, and a better conceptualization of an issue (e.g., Good & Power, 1976). Three teachers working together might derive different benefits from a research project or from a review of research.

Biddle and Anderson (1986) argue that the role of classroom research is to generate and test plausible theory concerning teaching. Such work identifies classes of observable events and provides propositions that summarize observed relations among variables studied. However, they argue that in their more advanced form, theories or beliefs that result from classroom research include explanations for the observed events (did students respond one way in one situation but in different ways under other conditions?). That is, simply noting differences is not as important as explaining the patterns that are obtained.

### Structural Elaboration versus Personal Elaboration
Fenstermacher (1983) distinguishes the structural elaboration from the per-

sonal elaboration of research. By structural elaboration he suggests that administrators, teachers, or policymakers use research findings as answers or prescriptions. If, for example, researchers found that 10 minutes of homework were effective in a particular program, structural elaboration would advocate that all teachers use 10 minutes of homework. In contrast, when research is used for personal elaboration, the decision about how to apply research and about its value resides with the individual teacher, who thinks about the needs of his/her students. It is vital that teachers have access to recent research-based knowledge particularly knowledge derived from observation of classrooms — but it is important that teachers reflect and form their own ideas about the value of the knowledge and its relevance to their contexts. Fenstermacher argues that the key question is whether teachers will discover what research reveals or whether they will simply accept someone else's (administrators') opinion of the implications of research. This question applies to research by teachers as well as by others.

### Teacher Evaluation of Research
The key argument here is that teachers must consider research in terms of the problems and potentials inherent in their own classrooms. It is important to help teachers to develop dispositions to be careful users of research. It is unfortunately the case that too many teachers who use research look for simple answers. An orientation for quick and external solutions will lead to poor results.

As an example of a simplistic orientation, assume that teachers in a study group have read two books: *Active Mathematics Teaching* (Good, Grouws, & Ebmeier, 1983) and *Teachers' Workplace* (Rosenholtz, 1989). Table 1 depicts the effects of research information as a function of teachers' views of research. Using Fenstermacher's concepts, a structural interpretation of research results is likely to lead to a different explication of results than is a personal interpretation. The conclusions that individuals make after reading a book, of course, are problematic, but in this example we assume that the teachers focus on meaning/student understanding and improving the development phase of the lesson as the most important points made by the researchers who conducted the mathematics study. After teachers discuss their conclusions and obtain a consensus within the group, the action resolution resulting from a structural interpretation might be to use more teacher-directed instruction (the quality of dialogue and the role of students might be ignored) and to adhere more closely to the textbook, leaving less opportunity for students to explore mathematical ideas. These changes in instruction would reduce the range of action that teachers consider to be appropriate and *reduce reflection* on the part of teachers. Their interpretation of research might move them to define mathematical teaching more narrowly.

Teacher study groups who explore the same book but who have a personal-interpretation perspective might interpret the research in the same way.

Table 1. Application of Research Findings as a Function of Teachers' Views of Research

| Research Program | Perspective | Perceived Focus | Action Resolution | Outcome |
|---|---|---|---|---|
| Active mathematics teaching | Structural interpretation | * Meaning/student understanding<br>* Improve development phase of lesson | * More teacher talk<br>* Greater adherence to textbook/less exploration of ideas | * Reduced range of action; less reflection |
| Active mathematics teaching | Personal interpretation | * Meaning/student understanding<br><br>* Improve development phase of lesson | * Teacher exploration of criteria for thinking about the quality of development<br>* Chance for teachers to observe/exchange ideas with peers | * Greater range of action; more reflection |
| Teachers' Workplace | Structural interpretation | * More feedback<br>* Shared goals | * More principal evaluation<br>* Less chance to determine focus of observation<br>* Less opportunity for reflection | * Less interest in feedback; increased self-reliance |
| Teachers' Workplace | Personal interpretation | * More feedback<br>* Shared goals | * Variety of feedback opportunities<br>* Frequent peer observation<br>* Teacher control of resources | * Enhanced teacher knowledge; increased interest in peer feedback |

However, because of their interest in discussing, explaining, and thinking about the research, the resulting action resolution might be quite different. In this example, teachers might be led to discuss with one another more fully the criteria for thinking about what constitutes development (what represents quality?). In the quest for more personal information and greater understanding, they might agree to observe one another during the teaching of development. Hence, reading the book, *Active Mathematics Teaching* might enhance these teachers' range of action and lead to *more reflection*. Of course, it is possible that because of different perceptions of research, the perceived focus of research might also differ between groups that take a structural-interpretation stance and those that use personal interpretation.

The same processes illustrated in Table 1 can be demonstrated with Susan Rosenholtz's book, *Teachers' Workplace*. Teachers might conclude from reading this book that they need more feedback about their performance and that schools ought to have shared goals around which this feedback can be organized. Acting upon this perceived focus, the action resolution of a group that uses structural interpretation might involve a perceived need for more principal evaluation of teaching, less opportunity for individual teachers to define the focus of the observation (the shared goals of the school define what should be observed), and less opportunity for teachers to reflect on various aspects of the lessons that they design and implement. Hence, the outcome from this interpretation might be reduced interest in feedback and *withdrawal from collegial interaction* (not asking other teachers questions, etc.). In contrast, teachers who have a personal-interpretation stance might enact the perceived focus in quite different ways. Extended discussion of alternative ways in which teachers might benefit from the ideas that have been presented might lead to the need for a variety of feedback opportunities. Further, the need for frequent peer contact might be established and the idea that teachers need to control resources (e.g., teachers identify classroom behaviors that they would like information about, their interpretation of the shared goal is being acted upon). Hence, in these settings the outcome might be enhanced teacher knowledge of instruction, *increased interest in peer feedback* and the opportunity to share ideas in other ways as well.

### Toward Integrative Knowledge
From the perspective argued here, when teachers begin to study research collectively and/or to collect research data, it is important that they attend to dimensions that are a bit broader than their own classrooms. Teachers should participate voluntarily in such groups; individual commitment and interest in the topics being pursued and the agenda of inquiry are a bit broader than in the individual classroom. In this way, the opportunity for teachers to engage in research or to examine research yields a perspective that not only enhances their own classrooms but provides the basis of a dialogue with other teachers in their own schools or with teachers in other schools. This discussion helps

them to address the coherence of the school curriculum and the effects of various instructional strategies on students. For example, teachers might explore what can be done in first and third grades in order to facilitate more active classroom participation by sixth-grade students. Here teachers begin to examine creatively the strategies that they have been using, what is known about student passivity from the literature, (e.g., Good, Slavings, Harel & Emerson, 1987; Good & Slavings, 1988; Good, Slavings, & Mason, 1988), and discuss viable strategies that might enhance students' capacity to generate their own questions and to pursue those questions. Similarly, teachers might inquire how the formal evaluation process in their schools might be improved so that both teachers and administrators learn more. The intent here is not to reduce the focus on individual thinking and the autonomy of individual teachers but rather to enhance teachers' understanding and to offer teachers a greater set of resources that they can utilize in order to improve and to make decisions. According to Rosenholtz (1989), "By rejecting the idea that task autonomy and school quality are necessarily opposed to each other, professional educators would make it much more difficult for policymakers to dismiss their moral authority in the name of devotion to excellence" (p. 220). It appears that in successful schools, the conflict between individual teacher autonomy and community responsibility is creatively negotiated. She argues, "Our own research suggests that though the premium on individual effort is never lost, a communal choreography of the school eventually takes over" (p. 220).

### Constraints on Use of Teachers as Researchers
In arguing for increased teacher collaboration in using research knowledge and/or conducting research, I have purposefully ignored several practical concerns that lie outside the scope of this paper. For example, it is clear that some (perhaps many) teacher education programs do not equip teachers with the technical skills necessary for reading and evaluating research nor do they train teachers to conduct original research. Although graduates of teacher education programs in the 1990s and beyond should be able to understand and produce research knowledge, many teachers who wish to participate in collaborative discussions of research would need to acquire these skills.

Another practical concern is that the costs to schools for teacher collaborative time are extremely high. However, as Bird and Warren-Little (1986) argue, to ignore these needs and to neglect this investment in human resource development would be more costly in the long run. Further, norms in many schools mitigate against collaborative sharing, and the risks associated with professional interaction in some schools are relatively high. Undoubtedly some (perhaps many) teachers do not believe in a technical culture (i.e., teaching is only an art) or the value of collegial exchange. However, as I argue in this paper, collegiality, self-regulation, and specialized knowledge are at least some of the dimensions of professional activity. Although there are other ways in which teachers' professionalism can be enhanced (e.g., work on curriculum issues), conducting research is one way in which teachers can more directly influence how teaching is conceptualized, examined, and altered.

Not all teachers will want to – or necessarily should – participate in research groups. However, in every school a few core members of the teaching staff should have a continuing concern with classroom research and scholarship that are relevant to their school's context.

### Expanding the Professional Image of Teaching

The proposal for increasing teachers' involvement in research also seems consistent with broader events occurring in teacher education. For example, Doyle (in press) argues that research on teaching should be expanded to examine not only how instruction affects students' learning but also how a given practice or method represents substantive meaning to teachers and students in a particular context (i.e., Why do teachers behave as they do?). As the field attempts to examine more systematically how teachers conceptualize difficult instructional issues as well as how teachers' decisions affect students (e.g., what concepts to emphasize, how fast to go through material, etc.), it seems essential to include teachers in the conduct of such research.

Hence, the notion of teachers in the 1990s as a community of scholars who have joint responsibilities for examining and extending extant knowledge, and also for using that knowledge wisely in their own classrooms, is both exciting and important. The challenge to all of us (teachers, administrators, teacher educators, researchers, policymakers, and citizens) is enormous as we work toward professionalizing the role of teachers.

In closing, I argue that increasing teachers' professionalization is a necessary step if we are to improve both the conditions and outcomes of schooling. I have used research groups as one example of how a philosophy of teachers as scholars and as professionals might be implemented. In my opinion, the advantage of collaboration that combines both school and class concerns is that it may enhance the performance of schools (for teachers and administrators as well as students) without eroding teacher autonomy.

# REFERENCES

Anderson, C., & Smith, E. (1987). Teaching science. In V. Richardson (Ed.), *Educators' handbook: A research perspective*, (pp. 84-111). White Plains, NY: Longman.

Bauersfeld, H. (1988). Interaction, construction, and knowledge: Alternative perspectives for mathematics education. In D. Grouws & T. Cooney (Eds.), *Perspectives on research on effective mathematics education*, (pp. 27-46). Hillsdale, NJ: Erlbaum.

Biddle, B., & Anderson, D. (1986). Theory, methods, knowledge, and research in teaching. In M. Wittrock (Ed.), *Handbook of research on teaching* (Third Ed.), (pp. 230-252). New York: Macmillan.

Billups, L., & Rauth, M. (1987). Teachers and research. In V. Richardson (Ed.), *Educators' handbook: A research perspective*, (pp. 624-639). White Plains, New York: Longman.

Bird, T., & Warren-Little, J. (1986). How schools organize the teaching occupation. *Elementary School Journal, 86*, 493-511.

Brookover, W., Beady, C., Flood, P., Schweitzer, J. & Wisenbaker, J. (1979). *School social systems and student achievement: Schools can make a difference*. New York: Praeger.

Brophy, J. (1988). Research on teacher effects: Uses and abuses. *Elementary School Journal, 89*, 3-22.

Brophy, J. (Ed.) (1989). Teaching for meaningful understanding and self-regulated learning. *Advances in research on teaching* (Vol. 1). Greenwich, CT: JAI Press.

Brophy, J., & Evertson, C. (1976). *Learning from teaching: A developmental perspective*. Boston: Allyn & Bacon.

Brophy, J., & Good, T. (1986). Teacher behavior and student achievement. In M. Wittrock (Ed.), *Handbook of research on teaching* (3rd Ed.), (pp. 328-375). New York: Macmillan.

Carpenter, T., Fennema, E., Peterson, P., Chiang, C., & Loef, M. (1988, April). Using knowledge of children's mathematical thinking in classroom teaching: An experimental study. Paper presented at the annual meeting of the American Educational Research Association, New Orleans.

Coleman, J., Campbell, E., Hobson, C., McPartland, J., Mood, A., Weinfield, F., & York, R. (1966). *Equality of educational opportunity*. Washington, DC: U. S. Government Printing Office.

Confrey, J. (1987). Mathematics learning and teaching. In V. Richardson (Ed.), *Educators' handbook: A research perspective*, (pp. 3-25). White Plains, NY: Longman.

Corno, L., & Rohrkemper, M. (1985). Self-regulated learning. In R. Ames & C. Ames (Eds.), *Research and motivation in education* (Vol. 2). Orlando, FL: Academic Press.

Doyle, W. (1986). Classroom organization and management. In M. Wittrock (Ed.), *Handbook of Research on Teaching* (3rd ed.), (pp. 392-431). New York: Macmillan.

Doyle, W. (in press). Themes in teacher education research. In W. R. Houston (Ed.), *Handbook of research on teacher education*. New York: Macmillan.

Edmonds, R. (1983). Search for effective schools: The identification and analysis of city schools that are instructionally effective for poor children (Final Report). East Lansing: Michigan State University.

Fenstermacher, G. (1983). How should implications of research on teaching be used? *Elementary School Journal, 83*, 496-499.

Florio-Ruane, S., & Dunn, S. (1987). Teaching writing: Some perennial questions and some possible answers. In V. Richardson (Ed.), *Educators' handbook: A research perspective*, (pp. 50-83). White Plains, NY: Longman.

Fraser, B. (1986). *Classroom environment*. London: Croom Helm.

Fraser, B. (1989). Instructional effectiveness: Processes on the micro-level. This Volume, pp. 23-37.

Freidson, E. (1984). The changing nature of professional control. *American Review of Sociology, 10,* 1-20.

Good, T., & Brophy, J. (1986a). School effects. In M. Wittrock (Ed.), *Handbook of research on teaching* (3rd ed.), (pp. 570-602). New York: Macmillan.

Good, T., & Brophy, J. (1986b). *Educational psychology: A realistic approach* (3rd ed.). New York: Longman.

Good, T., & Brophy, J. (1987). *Looking in classrooms* (4th ed.). New York: Harper & Row.

Good, T., & Grouws, D. (1987, June). Developing inservice training programs for increasing understanding of mathematical ideas. *Phi Delta Kappan,* 778-783.

Good, T., Grouws, D., & Ebmeier, H. (1983). *Active mathematics teaching.* New York: Longman.

Good, T., & Mulryan, C. (in press). Teacher ratings: A call for teacher control and self-evaluation. In J. Millman & L. Darling-Hammond, *Handbook of teacher evaluation* (2nd ed.). Beverly Hills, CA: Sage.

Good, T., & Power, C. (1976). Designing successful environments for different types of students. *Journal of Curriculum Studies, 8,* 45-60.

Good, T., & Slavings, R. (1988). Male and female student question-asking behavior in elementary and secondary mathematics and language arts classes. *Journal of Research and Childhood Education, 3,* 5-22.

Good, T., Slavings, R., Harel, K., & Emerson, H. (1987). Student passivity: A study of student question asking in K-12 classrooms. *Sociology of Education, 60,* 181-199.

Good, T., Slavings, R., & Mason, D. (1988). Learning to ask questions: Grade and school effects. *Teaching and Teacher Education, 4,* 363-378.

Good, T., & Weinstein, R. (1986). Schools make a difference: Evidence, criticisms, and new directions. *American Psychologist, 41,* 1090-1097.

Goode, W. J. (1957). Community within a community: The professions of psychology, sociology, and medicine. *American Sociological Review, 25,* 902-914.

Greeno, J. (1989). A perspective on thinking. *American Psychologist, 44,* 134-141.

The Holmes Group (1986). *Tomorrow's teachers.* East Lansing, MI: The Holmes Group Inc..

Hoyles, C. (1988). From fragmentation to synthesis: An integrated approach to research on teaching of mathematics. In D. Grouws & T. Cooney (Eds.), *Perspectives on research on effective mathematics teaching,* (pp. 143-168). Hillsdale, NJ: Erlbaum.

Kyle, D., & McCutcheon, G. (1984). Collaborative research: Development and issues. *Journal of Curriculum Studies, 16,* 173-179.

Lanier, J., & Warren-Little, J. (1986). Research on teaching education. In M. Wittrock (Ed.), *Handbook of research on teaching* (3rd ed.), (pp. 527-569). Washington, DC: American Educational Research Association.

Lortie, D. (1975). *School teacher.* Chicago: University of Chicago Press.

Mergendoller, J., & Marchman, V. (1987). Friends and associates. In V. Richardson-Koehler (Ed.), *Educators' handbook: A research perspective,* (pp. 297-328). White Plains, NY: Longman.

Mortimore, P., Sammons, P., Stoll, L., Lewis, D., & Ecob, R. (1988). *School matters.* Berkeley: University of California Press.

National Education Association Survey (1988, December). Are you treated like a professional or a tall child? *NEA Today, 7,* 4-5. Washington, DC.

Pearson, P. (Ed.) (1984). *Handbook of reading research.* White Plains, NY: Longman.

Porter, A., & Brophy, J. (1988). Synthesis of research on good teaching: Insights from the work of the Institute for Research on Teaching. *Educational Leadership 45*(8), 74-85.

Purkey, S., & Smith, M. (1983). Effective schools: A review. *Elementary School Journal, 83,* 427-452.

Raphael, T. (1987). Research on reading: But what can I teach on Monday? In V. Richardson (Ed.), *Educators' handbook: A research perspective,* (pp. 26-49). White Plains, NY: Longman.

Resnick, L. (1983). Toward a cognitive theory of instruction. In S. Parls, G. Olson, & H. Stevenson (Eds.), *Learning and motivation in the classroom.* Hillsdale, NJ: Erlbaum.

Richardson-Koehler, V. (Ed.) (1987). *Educators' handbook: A research perspective.* White Plains, NY: Longman.

Rohrkemper, M. (in press). Self-regulated learning and academic achievement: A Vygotskian view. In D. Schunk & B. Zimmerman (Eds.), *Self-regulated learning and academic achievement: Theory, research, and practice.* New York: Springer-Verlag.

Rohrkemper, M., & Corno, L. (1988). Success and failure on classroom tasks: Adaptive learning and classroom teaching. *Elementary School Journal, 88,* 299-312.

Rosenholtz, S. (1985). Effective schools: Interpreting the evidence. *American Journal of Education, 93,* 353-387.

Rosenholtz, S. (1989). *Teachers' workplace: The social organization of schools.* White Plains, New York: Longman.

Rutter, M. (1983). School effects on pupil progress: Research findings and policy implications. In L. Shulman & G. Sykes (Eds.), *Handbook of teaching and policy,* (pp. 3-41). New York: Longman.

Sarason, S. (1982). *The culture of the school and the problem of change* (2nd ed.). Boston: Allyn & Bacon.

Schlechty, P., & Vance, B. (1983). Recruitment, selection, and retention: The shape of the teaching force. *Elementary School Journal, 83,* 469-487.

Shulman, L. (1986). Paradigms and research programs in the study of teaching: A contemporary perspective. In M. Wittrock (Ed.), *Handbook of research on teaching* (3rd ed.), 3-36. New York: Macmillan.

Slavin, R. (Ed.) (1989). *School and classroom organization.* Hillsdale, NJ: Erlbaum.

Stern, J., & Chandler, M. (1988). *1988 Education Indicators.* Washington, DC: National Center for Education Statistics.

Teddlie, C., & Stringfield, S. (1985). A differential analysis of effectiveness in middle and lower socioeconomic status schools. *Journal of Classroom Interaction, 20,* 38-44.

Teddlie, C., Stringfield, S., Wimpleberg, R., & Kirby, P. (1987). *Contextual differences in models for effective schooling in the U.S.A.* Paper presented at the annual meeting of the American Educational Research Association, Washington, DC.

Weinstein, R. (1988). An expectance model for improving the motivational climate of classrooms in schools. In *Expectations and high school change: Teacher-researcher collaboration in preventing school failure.* Paper presented as part of a symposium conducted at the 1988 annual meeting of the American Educational Research Association, New Orleans.

Wittrock, M. (Ed.) (1986). *Handbook of research on teaching.* (3rd ed.) New York: Macmillan.

Wittrock, M. (1986). Students' thought processes. In M. Wittrock (Ed.), *Handbook of research on teaching,* (3rd ed.) (pp. 297-314). New York: Macmillan.

# INSTRUCTIONAL EFFECTIVENESS: PROCESSES ON THE MICRO LEVEL

BARRY J. FRASER

Curtin University of Technology, Perth

Over the last decade or so, considerable research effort concerning effective schools has led to the identification of common characteristics of effective schools and the establishment of criteria for measuring school effectiveness. Reviews of this literature, however, clearly reveal that several conceptual and methodological shortcomings have plagued some of the past research (Purkey & Smith, 1982), and that there is no consensus on the definition of an effective school and that the research is characterized by the use of a variety of methods and measures (Frederick, 1987; Reynolds, 1985). For example, in our own most recent research on exemplary or effective science and mathematics teaching, we used qualitative, ethnographic methods and effective teaching was operationally defined using a process in which peers nominated teachers whom they considered to be exemplary (Tobin & Fraser, 1987, 1988).

For the purposes of this paper, a quite limited definition of school effectiveness is adopted and attention is restricted to studies which have used one specific set of research methods. The measure of student effectiveness is student achievement and this is defined predominantly in terms of cognitive outcomes only. The type of research considered here is restricted to quantitative, empirical studies of factors associated with the school which are empirically linked with student achievement. Clearly, these empirical studies of student achievement, although certainly important, cannot provide a complete picture of the schooling process and, therefore, other research methods and other criteria for school effectiveness are equally important and worthwhile.

The research described here - that is, research into the factors which predict student achievement - recently has been labelled educational productivity research (Fraser, Walberg, Welch, & Hattie, 1987). This research clearly is relevant to school effectiveness because its central aim is to identify through educational research those factors which lead to improved student achievement so that, in turn, schools can be changed to optimize the factors which will enhance the performance of students.

Educational productivity work has involved two main methods. First, rather than drawing on the enormous number of past individual studies, the many dozens of meta-analyses conducted during the 1980s have been used as a basis for attempting to identify generalizable patterns. Second, the technique of secondary analysis has been used with large, national data bases to test models of educational productivity (i.e., models of the factors which predict student learning). It is the second of these methods, secondary analysis, which forms the major focus in this paper.

# MODELS OF EDUCATIONAL PRODUCTIVITY AND PAST RESEARCH SYNTHESES

## Walberg's Model

According to Walberg (1981, 1983, 1986), nine factors require optimization to increase affective, behavioral, and cognitive learning. These nine factors are potent, consistent, and widely generalizable. The proposed theory of educational productivity has the following groups of factors:

Student aptitude variables
1. *Ability* or prior achievement, as measured by the usual standardized tests;
2. *Development*, as indexed by chronological age or stage of maturation;
3. *Motivation*, or self-concept, as indicated by personality tests or the student's willingness to persevere intensively on learning tasks;

Instructional variables
4. *Quantity of instruction* (amount of time students engage in learning);
5. *Quality of instruction*, including psychological and curricular aspects;

Educationally stimulating psychological environment
6. *Home* environment;
7. *Classroom* or school environment;
8. *Peer group* environment outside the school;
9. *Mass media* environment, especially amount of leisure-time television viewing.

Each aspect appears necessary for learning in school because, without at least a small amount of each, the student can learn little. Large amounts of instruction and high degrees of ability, for example, could count for little if students are unmotivated or if instruction is unsuitable. Also correlations among the productivity factors in the model are to be expected because "Mathew effects" (Walberg, & Tsai, 1983) abound in education. For example, those advantaged on one factor such as home environment are likely also to be advantaged on other factors, such as ability and motivation, and attend schools with better instruction and more positive classroom environments.

The four remaining factors in the model are environmental variables. Three of these environmental factors - the psychological climate of the classroom group; enduring affection and academic stimulation from adults at home; and an out-of-school peer group with its learning interests, goals, and activities - influence learning in two ways. Students learn from peers directly; and these factors indirectly benefit learning by raising student ability, motivation, and responsiveness to instruction. In addition, about 10 (not the more typical 30) weekly hours of television time seem optimal for learning, perhaps because more television time than this displaces homework and other educationally and developmentally constructive activities outside school.

The productivity theory converges on the least number of factors that consistently and powerfully predict or explain cognitive, affective, and behavioral learning. Thus, from Walberg's view, economic, political, and sociological characteristics of the school and district are less relevant to learning because their influences are less alterable, direct, and observable. They are not substitutes for the nine factors, but more distant forces that can support or interfere with them. The educational productivity theory itself is admittedly simplified because learning is clearly affected by school and district characteristics as well as by many economic, sociological, and political forces at the school, community, state, and national levels. Yet these characteristics and forces - such as the sex, ethnicity, and socioeconomic status of the student, the size and expenditure levels of schools and districts, and their political and sociological organization - are less alterable in a democratic, pluralistic society; are less consistently and powerfully linked to learning; and appear to operate mainly through the nine factors in the determination of achievement.

Because no single educational research study, no matter how large or widely publicized, can be taken by itself as definitive, tests of Walberg's model have drawn on past quantitative research syntheses or meta-analyses (Glass, McGaw, & Smith, 1981; Hedges, & Olkin, 1985; Walberg, 1986). In fact, about two dozen quantitative syntheses of over 2,500 individual empirical studies of the effect of particular factors on learning (e.g., Frederick, &Walberg, 1980; Graue, Weinstein, & Walberg, 1983; Iverson, & Walberg, 1982; Uguroglu, & Walberg, 1979; Williams, Haertel, Haertel, & Walberg, 1982) have been undertaken.

Walberg's findings were surprisingly generalizable in that studies yielded similar results in national and international samples of students of different characteristics such as sex and age, in different subjects such as civics and science, and using different research methods such as surveys, case studies, and experiments. That is, the more powerful factors appeared to benefit all students under all conditions, although of course some students benefitted somewhat more than others under some conditions.

Collectively, the various meta-analyses (Fraser, Walberg, Welch, & Hattie, 1987; Walberg, 1986) suggested that the three groups of aptitudinal, instructional, and environmental factors are powerful and consistent in influencing learning. The first five essential factors in the educational productivity model (ability, development, motivation, quantity of instruction, quality of instruction) appear to substitute, compensate, or trade off for one another at diminishing rates of return. Immense quantities of time, for example, could be required for a moderate amount of learning if motivation, ability, or instructional quality is minimal. Thus, no single essential factor overwhelms the others; all appear important.

### Hattie's Model

Hattie has reviewed and synthesized numerous models of student learning in order to come up with another model of educational productivity which incorporates most of the factors in Walberg's model (see Fraser, Walberg, Welch, & Hattie, 1987). The seven main classes of factors in Hattie's model are *school* factors, *social* factors, *instructor* factors, *instructional* factors, *student* factors, *method of instruction* factors, and *learning strategy* factors. In order to test this model, 134 meta-analyses that had related some facet of the model of school learning to student outcomes were identified. As expected, most were related to achievement outcomes. Table 1 presents a summary of the meta-analyses relating to achievement grouped according to the seven factors in Hattie's model. (The number of correlations occasionally is less than the number of studies as only those relationships to achievement outcomes are presented.) For comparison purposes, all meta-analysis effect sizes were converted to correlations.

Altogether the 134 meta-analyses were based on 7,827 studies and 22,155 correlations. These figures are approximate as some studies have been used in more than one meta-analysis. Only a crude estimate of sample size can be suggested as the majority of meta-analyses report neither the sample size nor the number of unique persons. However, the 134 meta-analyses are based on somewhere between 5 and 15 million persons (Fraser, Walberg, Welch & Hattie, 1987).

An attempt is made in Table 1 to synthesize the 134 individual meta-analyses. The bottom of this table shows that the average correlation with achievement for all factors is 0.20 (sd = 0.15), the average weighted by the number of studies is 0.18, and the average weighted by the number of correlations is 0.19. Overall, 75 per cent of the correlations were positive. Thus with large samples any facet that has a correlation with achievement of greater than 0.2 (or where the effect size is greater than 0.40 standard deviations) is well worth pursuing and any correlation greater than 0.3 (0.62 student deviations) should be of much interest. It could be a mistake to

Table 1. Summary of Meta-Analyses Relating Factors to Achievement

| Factor | No. of Meta-Analyses | No. of Studies | No. of Relation-ships | Average r |
|---|---|---|---|---|
| School | 16 | 781 | 3313 | 0.12 |
| Aims & Policy | 6 | 307 | 542 | 0.12 |
| Physical Attributes | 5 | 372 | 1850 | -0.02 |
| Class Environment | 5 | 102 | 921 | 0.2 |
| Social | 4 | 153 | 1124 | 0.19 |
| Peer | 1 | 12 | 122 | 0.19 |
| Mass Media | 1 | 23 | 274 | -0.06 |
| Home | 2 | 118 | 728 | 0.31 |
| Instructor | 9 | 329 | 1097 | 0.21 |
| Background | 1 | 65 | 22 | 0.29 |
| Style | 8 | 264 | 1075 | 0.20 |
| Instruction | 31 | 1854 | 5710 | 0.22 |
| Quality | 1 | 41 | 22 | 0.47 |
| Quantity | 4 | 110 | 80 | 0.38 |
| Methods | 26 | 1763 | 5668 | 0.17 |
| Science | 11 | 730 | 1562 | 0.18 |
| Mathematics | 6 | 416 | 1713 | 0.16 |
| Reading | 8 | 557 | 2333 | 0.24 |
| Others | 1 | 60 | 60 | 0.13 |
| Pupil | 25 | 1455 | 3776 | 0.24 |
| Affective | 8 | 355 | 1882 | 0.12 |
| Cognitive | 8 | 484 | 896 | 0.44 |
| Physical | 6 | 551 | 905 | 0.10 |
| Disposition to Learn | 3 | 65 | 93 | 0.29 |
| Methods of Instruction | 37 | 2541 | 6352 | 0.14 |
| Individualization | 5 | 467 | 630 | 0.07 |
| Simulation/games | 2 | 151 | 111 | 0.17 |
| Computer-assisted | 11 | 557 | 566 | 0.15 |
| Programmed Instruction | 4 | 285 | 220 | 0.09 |
| Tutoring | 2 | 218 | 125 | 0.25 |
| Learning Hierarchies | 1 | 15 | 24 | 0.09 |
| Mastery Learning | 3 | 106 | 104 | 0.25 |
| Team Teaching | 1 | 41 | 41 | 0.03 |
| Homework | 2 | 44 | 110 | 0.21 |
| Instructional Media | 6 | 657 | 4421 | 0.14 |
| Learning Strategies | 12 | 714 | 783 | 0.28 |
| Reinforcement | 3 | 76 | 139 | 0.49 |
| Advance Organizers | 5 | 430 | 387 | 0.18 |
| Behavioral Objectives | 1 | 111 | 111 | 0.06 |
| Remediation/feedback | 3 | 97 | 146 | 0.30 |
| Grand Total or Mean | 134 | 7827 | 22155 | 0.20 |

assume that correlations of 0.2 or 0.3 are very small and are of little practical usefulness.

# USE OF NATIONAL SURVEY DATA IN TESTING WALBERG'S MODEL OF EDUCATIONAL PRODUCTIVITY

Descriptions were given above of how quantitative syntheses of prior bivariate studies were used to identify variables consistently correlated with student learning and to test models of educational productivity. While consistent evidence of bivariate associations between learning and individual productivity factors is valuable, it is desirable also to probe the validity of productivity models through multivariate research in which most of the productivity factors are incorporated into the same study of student outcomes. This section describes such a multivariate study of factors linked to the science achievement of students at several different age levels. In fact, Walberg's nine-factor model was tested with data collected from large samples of 17-, 13-, and 9-year-old students involved in the National Assessment in Science in the USA in 1981-82.

Few prior intensive experiments and quasi-experiments are national in scope, and most analyse only one or two of the productivity factors and sample limited populations within a school or community. They are often strong on observational technique, measurement, verification, and random assignment to treatments (in short, internal validity), but they are often weak in generalizability or external validity since they do not sample rigorously from large, well-defined populations. Survey research has complementary strengths and weaknesses: it often draws large, stratified, random samples of national populations and measures more factors but sacrifices internal validity since the factors are usually measured cross-sectionally and perhaps superficially with only a few items. Also, survey research can control statistically to some extent for multiple causes and can be more causally convincing than quasi-experiments controlled only for one or two covariates. The complementarity of intensive and extensive studies, however, is important. In principle, the consistent and powerful effects which emerge from the syntheses of bivariate studies also should emerge from survey research.

### National Assessment in Science
The National Assessment of Educational Progress (NAEP) was established in the USA in 1969 to assess periodically students' knowledge of various school subject areas. In science, national assessments were conducted by NAEP in 1969-70, 1972-73, and 1976-77. But, because of legislative decisions and financial constraints, the National Institute of Education postponed

the next fully-fledged NAEP science assessment until the late 1980s, thus causing an anticipated gap of approximately 13 years between successive assessments. Many science educators were concerned that this hiatus would permit emerging problems to go unchecked. Consequently, during 1981 and 1982, the National Science Foundation funded a science assessment known as the National Assessment in Science (Hueftle, Rakow, & Welch, 1983).

This National Assessment in Science involved a national random sample of approximately 18,000 students of ages 17, 13, and 9 in about 700 schools in the USA. In order to minimize testing time per student, the total test battery for 17- and 13-year-olds was divided into four separate test booklets, each containing nearly 100 separate items. In the case of 9-year-old students, there was only one booklet and this was responded to by all students in the sample. To ensure a broad sample of schools, an average of 16 students in any school answered a particular test booklet. The size of the subsample responding to any given test booklet was approximately 2,000 students. In fact, the exact sample sizes for the analyses reported in this paper are 1,955 17-year-olds, 2,025 13-year-olds, and 1,960 9-year-olds.

## Operationalizing Outcomes and Productivity Factors

As the National Assessment in Science data included items which could be interpreted as measures of most of the factors in Walberg's educational productivity model, secondary analyses were conducted for the purpose of probing the validity of the productivity model. The first step in the secondary analyses involved using the data base to operationalize two measures of student outcomes and at least one measure of seven of the nine productivity factors in the model. Fraser, Walberg, Welch, & Hattie (1987) provide detailed descriptions and operational definitions of each of the variables involved at each of the three age levels.

The cognitive achievement measure used with both the 17- and 13-year-old samples consisted of 49 multiple-choice items covering content topics, inquiry skills, and understanding of societal issues (alpha reliability = 0.87 for 17-year-olds and 0.80 for 13-year-olds). For the 9-year-old sample, science achievement was measured with 29 multiple-choice items covering content topics, inquiry skills, and an understanding of societal issues (alpha reliability = 0.79).

Ability among 17- and 13-year-old students was assessed with a self-report item asking about students' previous grades in school. In the case of the 9-year-old sample, ability was measured with 5 multiple-choice items assessing classification and mapping abilities (alpha reliability = 0.61). Age was excluded because each of the three samples consisted of students all of the same age (namely, either 17, 13, or 9 years) and therefore age exhibited limited variability. Motivation for the 17- and 13-year-old samples was assessed with 8 items asking about the frequency of voluntary participation in science-related activities (alpha reliability = 0.82 for 17-year-olds and 0.78

29

for 13-year-olds). For 9-year-olds, motivation was assessed by 21 items measuring whether students had ever been involved in a variety of science-related activities and experiments (alpha reliability = 0.71).

Quality of instruction was assessed by two different variables. First, for all three age groups, the average science teaching budget per pupil (as reported by the school principal) was used. Second, for the 17- and 13-year-old samples only, students' attitudes toward their science teacher were assessed by 5 Likert-type items with an alpha reliability of 0.72 for 17-year-olds and 0.66 for 13-year-olds; similar items were not available for 9-year-olds. The quantity of instruction also was assessed by two variables, namely, the amount of science and the average number of hours of homework per day. The amount of science was defined for 17-year-olds in terms of the total number of semesters of different science courses taken in Grades 9-12, for 13-year-olds in terms of whether the student took 0, 1, or 2 science courses over a two-year period, and for 9-year-olds in terms of the average number of hours per week for which science was taught as reported by the principal. The amount of homework was assessed simply with an item requesting the student to indicate the average amount of time spent on homework per day on all school subjects.

The class environment for 17- and 13-year-olds was measured by 6 items asking students how they felt during science classes (alpha reliability = 0.78 for 17-year-olds and 0.68 for 13-year-olds). A similar 5-item questionaire with an alpha reliability of 0.60 was used to assess class environment with the 9-year-old sample.

For all age groups, home environment was assessed in terms of the higher of the ratings for father's and mother's education coded on a scale of 1 to 6. The items included in the National Assessment in Science did not permit the peer group environment to be assessed at any age level. The mass media environment for each age group was assessed in terms of the number of hours of television watched during the previous day. In addition to the above factors in the productivity model, the present study involved the two extra variables of gender and race (white vs non-white) because they had been found to be good predictors of learning among science students in past research. Of course, should these extra variables of gender and race prove to be significant independent predictors of learning, this would suggest an omission in the original productivity model at least as it applies specifically to outcomes in science education.

The above descriptions of variables show that several of the productivity factors are incompletely, crudely, or unreliably indexed by the questionnaire items available as part of the National Assessment in Science. Also, the multiple-choice achievement measures used in this study are not without controversy. For example, they emphasize recognition more than recall of the best answer and students who achieve high scores on such tests are not necessarily able to apply their knowledge in the real world or to create new knowledge.

## Analyses and Results

Table 2 reports the results obtained when the effect of each productivity factor on student achievement was investigated. Because of collinearity among predictors, multiple regression analysis was used to provide a multivariate test of the joint influence of the set of all factors on an outcome and an estimate of the effect of each individual factor when all other factors were held constant. The multiple regression results in Table 2 are those obtained for the full model when the whole set of 11 predictors was regressed on achievement. The information reported for each productive factor is the raw regression weight, b, together with the significance level obtained from a t test of whether the magnitude of the regression weight is greater than zero. The bottom of Table 2 also shows that the multiple correlations for the whole of a set of predictor variables ranged from 0.50 to 0.59 for different age groups for different outcomes.

Raw regression weights are reported because they indicate the change in the number of points on an outcome measure associated with a one-unit increment in each independent variable when all other independent variables are held constant. For example, Table 2 shows that, for 17-year-old students' achievement and with other factors held constant, an increase of one hour per day in the time spent on homework was associated with 3.11 points increase, while a decrease of one hour of television-viewing per day was associated with 0.23 of a point increase. Also, for the binary variables coded 0 and 1, regression weights can be interpreted directly as group differences. For instance, for 13-year-olds' cognitive achievement, Table 2 shows that males scored 1.56 points higher than females and whites scored 4.12 points higher than non-whites when the other productivity factors were held constant. That is, with other factors fixed, 13-year-old white males scored 5.68 (about five-sixths of a standard deviation) higher than non-white females on the science achievement test.

## Consistency of Results Across Age Groups

In interpreting the consistency across age groups of the multiple regression results in Table 2, it should be remembered that certain differences exist between the three age levels in the definition of some of the variables. Whereas all variables except amount of science instruction are defined identically for 17- and 13-year-olds, several variables were defined in a different way for 9-year-olds. These differences are present for the achievement outcome and for ability and motivation. Also, minor differences exist between 9-year-olds and the other two age levels in the way that amount of science instruction and class environment was measured.

The results for 17-year-olds in Table 2 show that, of the 11 predictors of science achievement, all 11 were found to have statistically significant regression weights. In the case of 13-year-olds, 10 of these predictors (with the exception being attitude to the teacher) again were significant independent

Table 2. Effect of Each Productivity Factor on Achievement for Three Age   Levels

| Productivity Factor | Regression Weight at Age | | |
| --- | --- | --- | --- |
| | 17 | 13 | 9 |
| Ability | 1.49** | 0.81** | 1.44** |
| Motivation | 1.04** | 1.09** | 2.22** |
| Quality of Instruction | | | |
| . Science Teaching Budget | 0.06* | 0.04* | -0.05 |
| . Attitude to Teacher | 0.55* | 0.00 | - |
| Quantity of Instruction | | | |
| . Amount of Science | 0.57** | 1.66** | 0.02 |
| . Homework | 3.11** | 2.05* | -0.03 |
| Class Environment | 0.66** | 1.14** | 0.20** |
| Home Environment | 0.83** | 0.51** | 0.33** |
| Media (television-viewing) | - 0.23** | -0.17** | -0.13** |
| Gender | 2.30** | 1.56** | 0.74** |
| Race | 4.88** | 4.12** | 2.60** |
| Multiple Correlation: | 0.59** | 0.50** | 0.57** |

* $p<0.05$,  ** $p<0.01$
Sample consisted of 1,955 17-year-olds, 2,025 13-year-olds, and 1,960 9-year-olds.

predictors of achievement. Of the 10 predictors of 9-year-olds' achievement, Table 2 shows that 7 were significant when other independent variables were held fixed. The three variables which were found not to be significantly related to achievement were science teaching budget, amount of science, and amount of homework (and the attitude to teacher variable was not measured among the 9-year-old sample). Overall, then, there is quite high consistency of achievement results across the three different age groups since statistically significant regression weights were found for all three age groups for as many as seven of the productivity factors, namely, ability, motivation, class environment, home environment, television-viewing, gender, and race.

### Results for Each Individual Factor

*Ability.* As expected, ability is among the strongest and more consistent predictors of both science achievement and attitude. In fact, when all other factors were held constant, ability was found to be significantly related to achievement for the 17-, 13-, and 9-year-old samples.

*Motivation.* Similarly, as would be anticipated from reviews of the effects of motivation and achievement (Uguroglu, & Walberg, 1979), motivation also was found to be a significant independent predictor of achievement at all three age levels.

*Quality of Instruction.* The first measure of quality of instruction, namely, science teaching budget, turned out to be a relatively weak predictor of student outcomes when other variables were held constant. Science teaching budget was found to be a significant independent predictor of achievement ($p<0.05$) for 17- and 13-year-olds, but not for 9-year-olds. The regression weights for achievement suggest that, with other factors fixed, an increase of $1 per pupil in the science teaching budget is associated with an increase in achievement of only 0.06 points for 17-year-olds and 0.04 points for 13-year-olds. The second variable assessing quality of instruction, namely, student attitude to the teacher, was a significant independent predictor of achievement among 17-year-olds only. Some caution needs to be exercised in interpreting these findings for instructional quality, however, because the present study's two measures of quality (namely, science teaching budget and attitude to teacher) are not ideal indicators of quality of instruction.

*Quantity of Instruction.* It is salient that either or both of the variables measuring quantity of instruction - namely, the amount of science studied at school and the amount of homework - turned out to be significant independent predictors of achievement among 17- and 13-year-olds, but not among 9-year-olds. For 17-year-olds, an increase of one semester in the amount of science taken was associated with an increase of only 0.57 of a point on the science achievement test when other factors were held constant, whereas an increase of one hour of homework per night was associated with an increase of over three points (over one-third of a standard deviation).

*Class Environment.* It is noteworthy that the nature of the classroom psychosocial environment emerged as a significant predictor of science achievement to science at all three age levels when other factors were held constant. The simple outcome-class environment correlations of 0.14 to 0.25 for achievement at different ages are among the larger correlations found for any of the productivity factors. These findings are consistent with Haertel, Walberg, and Haertel's (1981) meta-analysis and Fraser's (1986, 1989) recent comprehensive reviews.

*Home Environment.* Table 2 shows that home environment was significantly related to science achievement at all three age levels when other factors were fixed. The simple correlations between home environment and cognitive achievement of between 0.16 and 0.27 are somewhat weaker than in some past research, possibly due to the fact that home environment was assessed in terms of parental education and not directly in terms of measures of intellectual stimulation by adults in the home which have been found to correlate 0.37 on average with achievement (Graue, Weinstein, & Walberg, 1983; Iverson, & Walberg, 1982).

*Television Viewing*. The results in Table 2 suggest that the amount of television viewing was significantly and negatively related to science achievement at all three age levels when other predictors were held constant. The negative simple correlations of -0.09 to -0.16 between science achievement and amount of television viewing at different ages are generally consistent with the negative correlation found at different age levels in a variety of content areas in a meta-analysis of 274 correlations from 23 studies, surveys, or reviews (Williams, Haertel, Haertel, & Walberg, 1982). The regression weights in Table 2 suggest that a one-hour decrease in television viewing per day is associated with an increase on the achievement test of 0.23 points for 17-year-olds, 0.17 for 13-year-olds, and 0.13 for 9-year-olds.

*Gender*. Prior research generally has revealed gender differences in science achievement, with boys scoring higher than girls on both criteria (Keeves, 1973). The results of the present research in Table 2 indicate that these gender differences were replicated for science achievement at each of the three age levels. Table 2 shows that, on the science achievement test, boys outscored girls by 2.30 points at age 17, by 1.56 points at age 13, and by 0.74 points at age 9.

*Race*. Table 2 shows that race was a significant independent predictor of science achievement for all these age groups. The interpretation of these results for the binary coded race variable is that the science achievement of whites was superior to that of non-whites by 4.88 points (over half a standard deviation) among 17-year-olds, by 4.12 points (almost two-thirds of a standard deviation) among 13-year-olds, and by 2.60 points (over half a standard deviation) among 9-year-olds.

## CONCLUSIONS AND IMPLICATIONS

The results of the secondary analysis show that a number of factors, previously revealed to be consistent correlates of achievement in the syntheses of small-scale bivariate research, were found also to be significant predictors of students' achievement when mutually controlled for each other in a large national survey. This suggests that national achievement is jointly influenced by a number of factors rather than by a single dominant one. The secondary analyses reported in this paper generally support the validity of Walberg's model of educational productivity. In the present research which involved at least one measure of seven of these productivity factors - namely, ability, motivation, quality of instruction, quantity of instruction, class environment, home environment, and the mass media environment - it is noteworthy that each of the seven factors emerged as a statistically significant predictor of science achievement at one or more of the three age levels when other factors were held constant. However, the two variables of gender and race also emerged as significantly related to cognitive achievement at all age levels. These findings, if replicated in other studies, would suggest that the two variables of gender and race omitted from the original productivity model could be included in the model to improve the prediction of achievement in the area of science.

The present research has identified four relatively unalterable factors - namely, ability, home environment, gender, and race - which are significant independent predictors of science achievement at one or more of the three age levels. Still, five relatively school-alterable factors were significant independent predictors of science achievement and attitudes among at least one age group. These alterable factors are motivation, quality of instruction (indexed by science teaching budget per pupil and/or attitude to the teacher), quantity of instruction (assessed in terms of amount of science and/or amount of time devoted to homework), the class environment, and the amount of television-viewing (negative relationship). It is encouraging to find that the present results suggest that there are numerous school-alterable factors which teachers can work on if they wish to improve the achievements and attitudes of their science students.

This paper's findings clearly lead to important implications for improving educational productivity and school effectiveness. Generally, the secondary analysis and the meta-analyses provide considerable support for Walberg's nine-factor model of educational productivity and highlight the need to attempt to raise several of the factors if appreciable improvements in achievement are to be accomplished. We should not expect any 'single factor' to have an enormous impact on student learning; rather, the key to improving student learning lies in simultaneously optimizing several different factors each of which bears a modest relationship to achievement.

Not all of the factors in the productivity model are readily alterable by educators. For example, the length of the school day and the proportion of time devoted to different school subjects is partly a political decision outside the control of individual schools. Motivation is likely to be determined in part by parental influence and attitudes, as so too is the home environment (in terms of academic stimulation) and the amount and nature of television-viewing. On the other hand, schools are likely to be able to take steps to improve quantity of instruction, quality of instruction, and the classroom environment (although the variables of ability, development, and the peer environment are likely to prove more difficult to alter). Because schooling occupies only about 13 per cent of the waking hours of the first 18 years of life (which is smaller than the amount of time some children spend watching television), schools cannot be blamed fairly for all our educational problems.

Educational experiences in the home, among peers, and in the community also make a contribution toward student learning. For example, studies show that families differ markedly in terms of how much time parents spend with their children to encourage and help them in relation to their schoolwork. These major differences in parental investment of time and concern could go a long way in accounting for children's varying capacities to profit from schooling and other educational experiences. Because children spend so much time at home with their parents, it is likely that altering home conditions and partnerships between home and school could have a favorable influence on student learning.

The findings emerging from the work reported in this paper refute several claims made in relation to school learning and assumptions made in educational research. First, although much prior research has been bivariate in nature, this work clearly illustrates that no single factor alone can produce marked increases in achievement. Improving all the productive factors using scarce resources, including human time and effort, as efficiently as possible would seem a more advisable policy than improving only one. Second, the results are at variance with another commonly held view that school learning is too complex to be understood in terms of a relatively small number of underlying factors. The third notion dispelled by the present findings is that the only important factors in predicting student outcomes are those that cannot be altered by teachers or the school. In particular, the results here do not support the view expressed in the Coleman, Jencks, and Plowden reports that school factors are of little importance relative to home factors in determining students' school achievement.

# REFERENCES

Fraser, B.J. (1986). *Classroom environment*. London: Croom Helm.

Fraser, B.J. (1989). Twenty years of classroom environment work: Progress and prospect. *Journal of Curriculum Studies*. (in press)

Fraser, B.J., Walberg, H.J., Welch, W.W., & Hattie, J.A. (1987). Syntheses of educational productivity research. *International Journal of Educational Research, 11*, 145-252.

Frederick, J.M. (1987). *Measuring school effectiveness: Guidelines for educational practitioners* (TME Report 93). Washington, DC: ERIC Clearinghouse on Tests, Measurements, and Evaluation.

Frederick, W.C., & Walberg, H.J. (1980). Learning as a function of time. *Journal of Educational Research, 73*, 183-194.

Glass, G.V., McGaw, B., & Smith, M.L. (1981). *Meta-analysis in social research*. Beverly Hills, CA.: Sage.

Graue, M.E., Weinstein, T., & Walberg, H.J. (1983). School-based home instruction and learning: A quantitative synthesis. *Journal of Educational Research, 76*, 351-360.

Haertel, G.D., Walberg, H.J., & Haertel, E.H. (1981). Socio-psychological environments and learning: A quantitative synthesis. *British Educational Research Journal, 7*, 27-36.

Hedges, L.V., & Olkin, I. (1985). *Statistical methods for meta-analysis*. New York: Academic Press.

Hueftle, S., Rakow, S., & Welch, W. (1983). *Images of science: A summary of results from the 1981-82 National Assessment in Science*. Minneapolis: Minnesota Research and Evaluation Center, University of Minnesota.

Iverson, B.K., & Walberg, H.J. (1982). Home environment and school learning: A quantitative synthesis. *Journal of Experimental Education, 50,* 144-151.

Purkey, S., & Smith, M. (1983). *School reform: The policy implications of the effective schools literature*. Paper presented for National Institute of Education, Washington, DC. (ERIC ED 245 350)

Reynolds, D. (Ed.) (1985). *Studying school effectiveness*. London: Falmer Press.

Tobin, K., & Fraser, B.J. (Eds.) (1987). *Exemplary practice in science and mathematics education*. Perth: Curtin University of Technology.

Tobin, K., & Fraser, B.J. (1988). Investigations of exemplary practice in science and mathematics teaching in Western Australia. *Journal of Curriculum Studies, 20,* 369-371.

Uguroglu, M.E., & Walberg, H.J. (1979). Motivation and achievement: A quantitative synthesis. *American Educational Research Journal, 16,* 375-389.

Walberg, H.J. (1981). A psychological theory of educational productivity. In F.H. Farley and N. Gordon (Eds.), *Psychology and education*. Berkeley, CA: McCutchan.

Walberg, H.J. (1983). Scientific literacy and economic productivity in international perspective. *Daedalus, 112,* 1-28.

Walberg, H.J. (1986). Synthesis of research on teaching. In M.C. Wittrock (Ed.), *Handbook of research on teaching* (3rd ed.). Washington, DC: American Educational Research Association.

Walberg, H.J., & Tsai, S.-L. (1983). Mathew effects in education. *Review of Educational Research, 20,* 359-373.

Williams, P.A., Haertel, E.H., Haertel, G.D., & Walberg, H.J. (1982). The impact of leisure-time television on school learning: A research synthesis. *American Educational Research Journal, 19,* 19-50.

# HOW THE INNER LONDON EDUCATION AUTHORITY APPROACHES SCHOOL EFFECTIVENESS

Desmond L. Nuttall

Inner London Education Authority, London

## INTRODUCTION

The Inner London Education Authority (ILEA) has two major objectives: improving the quality of education in its schools and colleges, and making opportunities more equal for every pupil and student regardless of sex, race or social class. In pursuit of both these aims, it is vitally concerned with the equality of education in each institution and therefore seeks ways of judging that equality in a regular, systematic and cost-effective manner. At the same time, it seeks to identify the factors that contribute to improved quality and greater equality, and to disseminate its findings to institutions and the providers of in-service education and training.

As a consequence it has been in the vanguard of school effectiveness research in the United Kingdom. The sample of schools used in *15,000 Hours* (Rutter et al., 1979) were all ILEA schools and Peter Mortimore, one of Rutter's team, became Director of Research and Statistics for the ILEA shortly thereafter. There he directed the Junior School Project (Mortimore et al, 1988) which set new standards for the breadth of measures used (of input, process and outcome) and for the analytical techniques employed, as well as yielding findings that are being applied all over the world.

This work had the aim of identifying the factors that contributed to some schools' effectiveness and to others' comparative lack of effectiveness, where effectiveness is defined in terms of the relative progress made by the pupils at each school or the 'value added' by the school. With the diversity of the economic and social conditions in different parts of inner London, coupled with the ethnic and cultural diversity of the population, it is essential to consider the characteristics of the group of pupils attending each school as well as their achievements on leaving the school if a fair judgement of its effectiveness is to be made. But what this work did *not* aim to do was to judge the effectiveness of individual institutions, and another strand of the work of the ILEA's Research and Statistics Branch has therefore been to work with the Authority's Inspectorate and Schools to identify effective and ineffective schools so that appropriate action can be taken to improve the quality of education.

### The ILEA's Work on Examination Results

To make school effectiveness a routine topic of study risks simplifying it and, at worst, trivialising it since the range of measures available about every institution will inevitably be less than the batteries of instruments and observations used in research on a sample. The common outcome measures available for junior schools in the ILEA have been reduced recently to just one, a test of reading attainment, and only exploratory work has been done using this measure. Among secondary schools, though, common outcome measures are universally available in the form of public examination results.

Public examinations in England are taken at two main ages: the General Certificate of Secondary Education (GCSE) at 16, when about 90 per cent of the age group sit examinations in a range of different subjects, and the General Certificate of Education Advanced level (GCE A-level) at 18, primarily for those planning to enter higher education, usually in three subjects. Entry to many vocational training courses and to employment is also dependent upon performance in these examinations, and they are therefore highly valued by parents and pupils and are regarded as the most important outcome of secondary education. The GCSE was taken for the first time in 1988 and replaced a dual system of examinations; it is administered by five different examining groups who are all required to adhere to the same standards of assessment but are in competition for entries from schools all over the country. GCE A-level is administered by eight examining boards, most of which are linked with universities.

The 1980 Education Act requires each school to publish its examination results in a standard form, but considerable detail has to be produced and the information is not easily summarized or interpreted by parents. The heads and staff of schools use these results to investigate relative strengths and weaknesses of different departments (e.g. the group of teachers teaching History or Mathematics) and to some extent of different teachers. Many local education authorities (the bodies responsible for maintaining and running most schools) use examination results as one measure of the performance of different schools. A number of agencies exist to process data (which can come from a variety of different examining bodies) and to summarise them. The Inner London Education Authority, which is the largest local education authority in England and Wales, collects computer tapes of results from the ten or so bodies involved and  matches the records for the 25,000 pupils taking examinations to create a single record of examination results for each pupil. It then aggregates the GCSE results to form a single numerical examination score for each pupil, and averages these across the age cohort within each school to provide a single score for each school. Other summary measures for each school include the proportion of students achieving five or more specified grades in the GCSE examination, or two or more specified grades at GCE A-level.

These measures vary between schools, but is not appropriate to make comparisons without taking into account differences in the intake, that is, the characteristics of the pupils in each school. In order to reduce educational inequality between social classes and ethnic groups, the ILEA provides resources to schools according to their educational need. On the basis of its research into the social, economic and other factors associated with low educational achievement (for details, see ILEA Research and Statistics, 1982 and 1983), the ILEA has considerable information about the characteristics of the pupils attending each of its schools, for example about family structure, economic deprivation, type of work undertaken by male and female parent/guardian, and the ethnicity of the pupil.

ILEA takes account of differences in schools' intakes using multiple regression, having found that three factors consistently appear as the most important in accounting for variation in GCSE examinition performance between schools: the percentage of pupils in the cohort eligible for free school meals (a measure of family poverty), the percentage in VR Band 1 (that is, in the top 25 per cent of ability at age 11 as a measured using heads' ratings of verbal reasoning) and the percentage of girls (as girls consistently do better in public examinations than boys). These factors are largely outside the control of the school; the school examination score adjusted to reflect the influence of these factors can be regarded as a measure of the value added by the school in the five years of secondary education, and thus a reasonable measure of the effectiveness of the school in relation to its academic performance. The adjusted scores are published and made widely available - London's principal evening newspaper, *The Evening Standard*, published the results in full. The methods and results are described in ILEA Research and Statistics (1986 and 1987a).

An investigation is currently under way to see if the publication of these figures has had a detectable effect on parental preferences for particular secondary schools; preliminary results suggest that publication has not had a significant effect, suggesting that parents are sophisticated judges of a school's suitability for their children.

The information about schools' academic performance is valued by inspectors and officers. All schools that appear to be doing worse than might be expected given the characteristics of their pupils are visited and the results discussed in detail. Schools doing better than might be expected are congratulated and studied to detect factors contributing to this success that might be copied by other schools. The results of these informal investigations bear

41

out the findings of more systematic and detailed studies of school effectiveness.

### Limitations

There are numbers of limitations to the use of examination results to judge the effectiveness of individual schools. First, examination results are only a partial measure of the success of education; they do not reflect other contributions of the school, for example to students' personal and social development. Data Envelopment Analysis (DEA) is currently being used to explore the presentation of multiple educational outcomes in quantitative form (e.g. examination results, attendance rates, and the rate of staying on in education beyond the end of compulsory schooling) in the light of inputs of the kind used by the ILEA in adjusting examination results. Jesson and his colleagues (1987) indicate how DEA can be used to study the performance of different local education authorities. Others have used the technique to investigate the performance of other public sector institutions (for example, District Health Authorities) but its use to evaluate performance of different schools is still at the trial stage, and a matter of some controversy (Woodhouse and Goldstein, 1988).

Secondly, the measures are somewhat flawed: the examining bodies may have slightly different standards, and some subjects may be harder than others. Moreover, the measures analysed are incomplete since they do not take account of performance in newer pre-vocational examinations taken at school (though the scoring of these new examinations on the same measurement scale is being investigated). Finally, there are a number of technical limitations in the statistical analyses; in particular, aggregated rather than individual data are used (though ILEA now has some information for individual pupils and are doing exploratory analyses using multi-level statistical methods, as decribed by Goldstein, 1987). Information on the ethnicity of individual pupils has allowed a study of the examination performance of different ethnic groups, which has revealed wide and disturbing differences which ILEA is trying to reduce (ILEA Research and Statistics, 1987b). Multi-level analysis has particular power in allowing the simultaneous study of differences between ethnic groups, between sexes and between schools.

### Future Developments

Despite these limitations, the analysis of examination results in this manner is generally acceptable to professionals and the public alike, though there is rightly pressure to include more comprehensive measures of educational outcomes. The 1988 Education Reform Act will require in future the assessment of children at ages 7, 11 and 14, in addition to 16, with the aggregated results of these assessments to be published for each school. Detailed proposals for this new system of National Curriculum Assessments are set out in the Reports of the Task Group on Assessment and Testing (TGAT, 1988a and b).

In particular, the Task Group proposed that the aggregated results should *not* be statistically adjusted but presented in the context of "a general report for the area, prepared by the local authority, to indicate the nature of socio-economic and other influences which are known to affect schools. This report should give a general indication of the known effects of such influences on performance."

The reasons why the Task Group rejected statistical adjustment of the results are not wholly clear. Part of the reason is thought to be their belief that there was no agreement among experts about the best way of making such adjustments. It is true that there has been controversy about methods; indeed, the ILEA temporarily suspended its publication of adjusted examination scores of individual schools while it investigated how some of the limitations described above could be overcome and while it explored other statistical approaches. It has now been decided that multi-level modelling should be used in future since there is a general consensus among statisticians that the use of such models is to be preferred whenever possible.

Another part of the reason why the Task Group did not advocate the use of statistical judgement is suggested by their argument that the publication of results and the use of them to compare schools' performance "would be liable to lead to complacency if results were adjusted, and to misinterpretation if they were not". The ILEA certainly takes the view that there is a danger that the results would be misinterpreted if no adjustment were made. There are schools in London whose examination results appear on the surface to be good but, when the characteristics of the pupils attending those schools are taken into account, the results look poor in comparison with those of similar schools. This suggests that such schools are failing in their duty to educate their pupils to the fullest extent possible; many young people attending those schools would be receiving worse examination results than they should. On the other hand, there is a danger of complacency if results are adjusted, but it is equally true that there is a danger of complacency if the results are not adjusted: a school with good results could nevertheless be failing its students since their results should be even better, as argued above. That form of complacency is insidious, and such a school might well be shaken out of its complacency if its results were shown to be less good than they appear on the surface.

A school with modest results before adjustment might well have comparatively good results after adjustment. Such a school could well become complacent, feeling that the published results suggested that they were doing as well as might reasonably be expected. While there is no evidence that such schools in ILEA do become complacent, there is a general belief that too many teachers, in London and elsewhere, have too low expectations of many pupils, particularly those of low socio-economic status, those from ethnic minorities and those for whom English is not the first language of the home. The research on school effectiveness, discussed above, shows that some schools can raise the levels of achievement of all pupils, including the disadvantaged, higher than other schools and no schools can therefore ignore its responsibility to raise the levels of achievement even higher. The same argument is true about differences between the sexes; there is a danger that adjustment for sex differences in examination performance, using the statistical procedures of the ILEA, reduces the motivation of teachers of boys to consider educational ways of closing the achievement gap. In summary, there are dangers of complacency whether or not statistical adjustment is made, and it is the job of inspectors to challenge schools and teachers to improve the quality of education.

A more fundamental criticism, not stated by the Task Group, is that statistical adjustment conceals the actual level of functioning of a school. The level of performance is of great interest to the provider and the consumer, and can give an indication of the ethos and aspirations of the school, even if it is not a fair indicator of the effectiveness of the school. It would therefore be desirable to find some method of presenting the results which combine both the actual results and the adjusted results. An alternative method might be to publish the actual results in a variety of different ways, for example presenting the results of schools with pupils of similar characteristics to provide an appropriate context, or by showing the performance of different groups (e.g. the sexes or ethnic groups) within the school.

The most appropriate methods of presenting the results of examinations and assessment for individual schools therefore remains a topic that is likely to be controversial for many years to come as National Curriculum Assessments are introduced from 1992. Meanwhile, another provision of the Education Reform Act 1988 abolishes the Inner London Education Authority, and the future of its Research and Statistics Branch, which has pioneered the statistical adjustment of examination results of individual schools on a regular basis, is therefore in jeopardy.

# REFERENCES

Goldstein, H. (1987), *Multilevel models in educational and social research*. London: Charles Griffin & Company Ltd.

ILEA Research and Statistics (1982), *Education Priority Indices - a new perspective*, (RS 858/82). London: ILEA Research and Statistics.

ILEA Research and Statistics (1983), *The Effect of the 1983 Educational Priority Indices on the Allocation of AUR*, (RS 899/83). London: ILEA Research and Statistics.

ILEA Research and Statistics (1986), *Looking at School Performance*, (RS 1058/86). London: ILEA Research and Statistics.

ILEA Research and Statistics (1987a), *Actual and Predicted Examination Scores in School*, (RS 1129/87). London: ILEA Research and Statistics.

ILEA Research and Statistics (1987b), *Ethnic Background and Examination Results - 1985 and 1986*, (RS 1120/87). London: ILEA Research and Statistics.

Jesson, D., Mayston, D., & Smith, P. (1987). Performance assessment in the educatior sector: educational and economic perspectives, *Oxford Review of Education, 13 (3)*, 249-266.

Mortimore, P. Sammons, P., Stoll, L., Lewis, D., & Ecob, R. (1988) *School Matters*. London: Open Books.

Rutter, M., Maughan, B., Mortimore P., & Ouston, J. (1979). *Fifteen Thousand Hours*. London: Open Books.

Task Group on Assessment and Testing (1988a), *A Report*, Department of Education and Science and the Welsh Office, London and Cardiff.

Task Group on Assessment and Testing (1988b), *Three Supplementary Reports*, Department of Education and Science and the Welsh Office, London and Cardiff.

Woodhouse, G., & Goldstein, H. (1988). Educational performance indicators and LEA league tables, *Oxford Review of Education, 14 (3)*, 301-320.

# SCHOOL EFFECTIVENESS TRAINING: RESEARCH INFLUENCING PRACTICE*

Rima Miller
Research for Better Schools, Inc., Philadelphia

## INTRODUCTION

The relationship between research and practice has often been an awkward one, with researchers and practitioners viewing each other as different species. Seymour Sarason (1972) captures this dilemma when he describes practitioners as people who understand the real world and see themselves as people of action, while the theoreticians or academics are "not noted for their immersion in the real world" (p. 247).

Educational research, in the eyes of the practitioner, is often removed from day to day reality. Research provides important information, but what good is that information if practitioners can't figure out how to use it? A research/practitioner conundrum exists with one result being a gap in the two professional communities at a time when our industry can least afford such division. School Effectiveness Training (SET) is an effort to bridge that gap and bring the worlds of research and practice together.

## SCHOOL EFFECTIVENESS TRAINING

Traditionally, in America, teachers work alone, trying to improve their own classrooms themselves, their social relations characterized by poor communication and isolation (Lieberman, 1986). SET, an improvement process developed by a regional educational laboratory and a state affiliate of a national teachers' association, attempts to exchange those norms of isolation for new norms of cooperation by inviting all staff to participate in analyzing

---

* This publication is based on work sponsored, wholly or in part, by the Office of Educatioal Research and Improvement (OERI), Department of Education. The content of this publication does not necessarily reflect the views of OERI, the Department, or any other agency of the US Government.

47

their school and identifying commonly perceived problems. Once identified, the problems can be attacked collectively by administrators and teachers.

SET combines the findings from research on effective schools with intensive team building and priority setting techniques found in other staff development strategies (NJEA, 1981). The objective of the SET program is to create a more effective school by building commitment to a building-level action plan that meets the needs of students, staff and parents. The content framework of the action plan is shaped by the research conducted primarily by Ron Edmonds and others. However, the plan's activities are based on the belief that the greatest resource for improving any school is the staff already working there, especially when their experiences and knowledge can be harnessed and directed (NJEA, 1981). SET introduces staffs to the effective schools research, at the same time as it presents an implementation process through which school change can occur.

Thus, three research bases have contributed to the design of SET: effective schools research; school change research; and research on productive organizations (Bassin & Gross, 1978; Beckhard, 1969; Brown, 1976; Clark, Lotto & Astuto, 1984; Edmonds, 1978; Edmonds & Frederiksen, 1979; Schmuck & Runkel, 1985).

### SET in Action

The SET program is organized around three major groups of activities: the pre institute, the institute, and the post institute components.

*Pre Institute.* The Pre Institute component informs people about SET, generates interest, gains a commitment and prepares staff for the institute. The formal orientation program provides an overview of the effective schools research and a description of the school improvement process. Staff have the opportunity to raise questions and discuss their concerns. Following the orientation, a vote is taken to see if there is enough interest on the part of the staff to continue. It is recommended that two-thirds of the staff be interested since unanimous support for SET is not vital, but there does need to be a critical mass of support. If a majority of staff are interested in continuing, planning commences for the SET Institute.

*The Institute.* The Institute is a two-day retreat for school staffs to lay the foundation for the SET program. There are four major activities that must be accomplished during the institute:

- participants receive a rigorous exposure to the factors associated with effective schools
- participants are taught a problem solving and planning process to facilitate school improvement activities
- the framework for a comprehensive school improvement plan is developed

48

• participants are organized into an implementation structure to facilitate school improvement.

During the institute, all participants immerse themselves in reviewing the effective schools literature through specially prepared position papers which discuss six school effectiveness factors in some depth. These factors include positive school climate, monitoring and assessment, parent involvement, basic skills, high expectations and leadership. In addition, school staffs listen to lecturettes and participate in structured small group discussions where they discuss each factor and begin to apply the research information to their own school situation.

While participants are absorbing the effective schools research, they also are learning problem solving techniques for defining problems, generating solutions, assessing alternatives, selecting a solution, and planning action steps. They develop these techniques further by applying them to their own school problems within each effectiveness factor.

As staff members work together to understand the research, engage in problem solving, and study school data, the content for their own improvement plan begins to emerge. They begin to better understand their school's strengths and see more clearly areas that need improvement. As a result, the staff is able to identify priorities, set preliminary improvement goals, and begin to develop improvement strategies.

As the institute progresses, school staffs learn more about the roles they will play in the improvement process through participating on the Coordinating Council and task groups.

The hub of the SET process is the Coordinating Council, a school based leadership team. The Council is a representative group of staff working with the building principal to lead the day to day improvement activities. It is a formal structure consisting of the building principal and a cross section of school staff. Linked to the Coordinating Council are six task groups, one for each school effectiveness factor. Task groups are problem solving groups that are made up of volunteers and recruits who develop specific projects within each effectiveness factor while the Coordinating Council leads the overall improvement effort. During the institute, staff begin volunteering or agreeing to serve on one of these teams.

Participants usually leave the two day institute feeling tired but optimistic. They have learned some important research about what may make a school more effective and they have used that research to systematically begin a process of planning for change.

*Post Institute.* Post Institute activities include setting up standard operating procedures for Coordinating Council operations and task groups, completing the action plan, and encouraging ongoing staff participation. Participants consider some of the following implementation related issues.

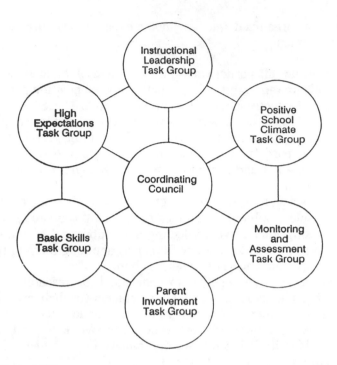

*Figure 1: School Effectiveness Training*

- Council and task group meetings need to be scheduled, preferably on school time. Schools are encouraged to schedule these meetings on the master schedule to let everyone know when they are occurring but also to make the symbolic point that these are important activities.
- Overtures need to be made to the people who did not choose to participate in the institute. Not only do they need to be informed about what occurred, they need to be encouraged to become involved.
- A public relations program needs to be started that keeps SET on the fore-front of school business and also keeps people up to date on progress, up-coming events, etc.
- Forums for sharing new ideas and brushing up on old ones need to be planned, as well as future staff development programs. Ongoing training in problem solving and school innovations will provide people with the tools they need to be able to fully participate in the improvement activities.
- Every school that participates in SET is asked to carefully document its progress and the impact of its action plan. Areas of success need to be reported and areas where things did not go as expected need to be studied.
- Celebrations for success need to be organized.

A most important post institute activity is the establishment and operation of the Coordinating Council and task groups. While membership on these committees will change, their basic functions do not.

It is the job of the Coordinating Council to help set improvement priorities, review task group recommendations, develop the school wide improvement plan, monitor implementation activities, evaluate progress, and make progress reports to the school community. Its members may be elected or appointed. They may represent department, grade level or teaching teams. The Council, while convened by the building principal, must be made up in such a way that no one feels left out; every work group must feel as though they have access to representation. The Council has the responsibility for coordinating the work of the related task groups.

It is the job of the task groups to review and define specific problems within each effectiveness factor, to explore solutions, to make recommendations for solutions, and to assist with implementation. Projects within task groups are short-term and sharply defined, focused around the accomplishment of very specific objectives. The task groups themselves should be organized to cut across organizational structures so as not to reflect any special interest bias.

It is during the post institute phase of SET that the real challenges of driving the research into practice surface. Implementation issues such as time, resources, and incentives to participate emerge. How these issues are treated will either support or hinder improvement efforts. Schools that are serious about their improvement activities will build systems that support implementation.

Thus, SET puts into action a continuous cycle of assessment, problem solving and planning. It is a process which looks to research to provide an improvement framework but it relies on an understanding of change and implementation issues in order to be successful.


# TWO CASE DESCRIPTIONS

Two school cases are presented below which describe the interaction of research and practice. The first case, Yorkshire Junior High School, describes a medium sized school in a small urban community (D'Amico & Presseisen, 1985). The second case describes Jackson Senior High School, a large secondary school in a rapidly changing community (D'Amico & Miller, 1985).

### Yorkshire Junior High School
Yorkshire Junior High School, a medium sized school in a small urban community, enrolls 770 ethnically diverse students in its seventh, eighth and

ninth grades and is staffed with 50 teachers and two administrators. Prior to participation in the SET program, despite its calm surface, the school was filled with tension and dissent. Teachers felt in conflict with the values of students and parents, and saw the students as, "just getting by," as one teacher puts it. Discipline, even enforcement of rules, and classroom management were seen as a major problem. Teachers voiced a great deal of hostility toward the school's administrator whom they saw as authoritarian, arbitrary, unsupportive and insincere. In addition, survey data showed that teachers were at odds with each other as well.

The principal was very concerned that Yorkshire maintain its reputation as a good school in the community. It was this concern plus the superintendent's strong support of SET and the promise of resources that led to the decision to implement SET at Yorkshire Junior High School. SET was also strongly supported by the teacher's union in the district. The teachers were skeptical, concerned about issues of control and accountability, but were anxious to improve the situation in their school.

During their institute, skeletal plans in four factor areas were discussed: school climate, high staff expectations, academic press and leadership. They adopted an open ballot election process for selecting Coordinating Council members, and planned for task group formation.

Following the institute, the Coordinating Council met and organized itself. It elected officers and planned task group formation by identifying Council members to serve as liaisons to each task group. Task groups were asked to meet and finish the plan that was begun during the institute.

The task groups developed fairly specific action plans that focused in on:

- school climate with an emphasis on improving staff communication and management skills, developing more specific discipline policies and procedures, and revising the program for students in the discipline room
- expectations emphasizing the development of behavioral standards and a student reward system
- leadership with an emphasis on consistent and equitable enforcement of rules, allowing teachers more say in duty assignments, and reviewing the student behavior code
- academic press with emphasis on developing a concentrated program to help students improve study skills.

SET was well launched in Yorkshire Junior High School. Teachers were enthusiastic and optimistic. Central office administration was contributing resource support. The building principal was working hard to utilize SET principles of cooperation and shared decisionmaking, which enhanced communication. The Coordinating Council met regularly, on school time, and groups also were given school time to plan and implement their activities. By the end of the first year, approximately 50 percent of the staff were involved with SET activities.

SET continued to flourish through year two. District initiatives were incorporated into the SET structure; council and task groups continued to meet regularly, now involving well over 50 percent of the staff; and the principal appeared to have changed his management style from what had been described the year before. Teachers now saw him as cooperative, open, helpful and sincere about working to make SET work. Published accomplishments ranged from planned morale boosters to an orientation for seventh graders, improved discipline policies and procedures, a merit reward system for students, an instructional improvement program, and more effective teacher involvement.

The following year (year 3) SET continued to run smoothly. Many of the programs developed through SET became institutionalized, including council and task group meetings. As old projects reached their conclusion, new projects were developed, including a uniform homework policy, a study skills program, a writing across the subject areas program, and plans for a new gymnasium.

In spite of these accomplishments, two problems emerged during this third year. First, school staff actively involved with SET began to resent those staff not involved and teachers not involved began to see the involved staff as an elitist group. A rift began to grow among the teachers. The principal, aware of this growing rift, instituted policies that mandated some sort of school improvement activity for everyone. Second, after three years, essentially the same staff constituted the Coordinating Council and the task groups; no plans had been made for renewal and participants were beginning to show signs of fatigue and continued impatience with non-participants. However, their commitment to ongoing school improvement remained genuine. And, today, five years later, SET continues to be the umbrella for ongoing improvement activities at Yorkshire Junior High School.

Yorkshire is a good example of a successful merging of research and practice. Equal attention was paid to both the content of their improvement plans and a process for implementation which allowed for genuine participation and involvement.

### Jackson Senior High School

Jackson Senior High School, grades 9 to 12, has a racially diverse student body of approximately 2,200 with a faculty of 126 and an administration of one principal and four vice principals. The building is 50 years old, with narrow hallways, small classrooms with poor lighting and often furnished with original desks and cabinets. Observers noted that "many rooms in Jackson High look like museum exhibits" (D'Amico & Miller, 1985). The students come from the city of Jackson and seven districts in nearby communities with no high schools. According to building administrators, as many as 60 percent of the students go on to college, many of them receiving scholarships and academic honors.

53

Despite these assets, Jackson also suffers from many of the characteristics of the large urban school in America: drug and alcohol abuse, high dropout rate, low level of parent involvement, teacher frustration, and overall mediocre academic performance.

There is a fair amount of tension between the administration and the teaching staff who are convinced the school's mediocrity is due to the principal's lack of organization. Even though the principal is well liked, he is criticized for his sloppy management and non existent leadership. The superintendent receives the same treatment from the teachers who hold him responsible for the principal's shortcomings.

Up to the time when SET was introduced to Jackson, school improvement activities were conducted through different academic departments which were strongly supported by the principal. There had not been much attempt to organize a school wide improvement effort because it was seen, hopefully, as something that would come and go.

SET was introduced through the efforts of the local teacher's union which was interested in initiating teacher decisionmaking programs. The introduction of SET also was supported by the school administration who saw SET as a way to involve teachers. However, teachers were not excited about the prospects and there was some feeling that SET was being handed down from above.

After a series of orientation sessions and a period of data collection, a coordinating council institute was planned for the members of the council who were hand picked by the principal. During this retreat, the council identified seven major issues on which they would focus. These were:
• reduction of paper work related to keeping attendance
• student discipline
• classroom management
• student scheduling
• staff manual
• equity in non-teaching assignments
• condition of facility related to cleanliness and safety.

Following the retreat, a newsletter was distributed among the faculty describing the retreat, and the focus areas and asking for volunteers to serve on task groups. An extraordinary 60 percent of the faculty responded. The program was off and running.

The second year got off to a good start. Several committees had been paid to work over the summer and many of their recommendations were implemented at the start of the school year. The coordinating council was meeting regularly as were most of the task groups. Faculty participation was dropping off slightly but the principal established a policy mandating participation in either SET or a curriculum writing project which was occurring simultaneously. As a result, participation remained fairly stable.

In spite of the first flush of success, activities began to slack off. The council chairperson who was earlier able to mobilize the staff became tired of feeling responsible for other staff's productivity or lack of it. The council lost its focus and energy. A special mini council retreat was called and members attempted to analyze what was happening. They decided to reorganize themselves and formed a committee to write a council charter outlining council's purpose, meeting structure, membership guidelines and officer selection. The structure provided by this charter gave the council a boost and renewed their energies.

For the next two years, a similar pattern reoccurred, a period of accomplishment would be followed by a period of disorganization. Despite this rocky course, leaders still identified major accomplishments:
• more equitable non teaching assignments
• new computer attendance program which reduced teachers' paperwork
• a major facility clean up
• new facilities design
• proposals written and effective school grant received.

After five years of numerous short term activities, primarily centered around school climate, and because of the results of state mandated high school proficiency testing, instructional issues have finally emerged as an improvement priority. Today, SET is the process through which Jackson Senior High School addresses its basic skills improvement program.


## CONCLUDING REMARKS

In the cases presented and in other schools studied, schools engaged in improvement programs often experience ongoing battles to balance the content of the program (school effectiveness) and the process (implementation strategies), with the content often taking a back seat as school staffs struggled with the implementation issues. What has been learned is that the success of research driven programs, no matter how valid, useful, or beneficial, rests not always with the quality of the research but with a carefully thought-out implementation and follow up strategy.

Where schools and districts have paid attention to such issues as time, availability of resources and incentives for participation (Corbett & D'Amico, 1987), the programs flourish. For example, in Yorkshire Junior High School, time was clearly allocated for SET activities and funds made available. The principal and the teaching staff took the time to work out some of the differences between them, with both making efforts to change some of their behaviors. Thus, a trust developed that allowed them to work collaboratively.

Where attention has not been paid, the programs tend to flounder. Jackson Senior High School thought it could mandate participation. The mandate got people in the room, but that was not enough to really develop participation. SET survived because a small group of stubborn staff members maintained their commitment to it and the laissez faire style of the principal allowed them to do as they pleased. When they wrote a proposal and received external funding, school administrators and staff took more notice.

A great deal of information about school change has been acquired over the past ten years. That information must be used to create strategies that will enable the results of research to impact practice. And those strategies must pay attention to process issues such as commitment, participation and trust (Woods-Houston & Miller, 1988). Leaders and program planners must demonstrate their commitment by putting their money where their mouth is, and "walk what they talk." Participation must be genuine and involvement encouraged and rewarded. And, finally, in order to focus on common issues, barriers that separate must be broken down and trust built.

The task is to wed theory to practice. As in any relationship, new lessons and new skills must be learned. "People of action," the practitioners must "think" differently, while our "theoreticians" must "act" differently (Sarason, 1972).

# REFERENCES

Bassin, M., & Gross, T. (1978). Organization development: A viable method of change for urban secondary schools. Paper presented at the meeting of the American Education Research Association, Toronto.

Beckhard, R. (1969). *Organization development: Strategies and models.* Reading, MA: Addison Wesley.

Brown, L. D. (1976). Organizational change from the bottom up. *Education and Urban Society, 8(2),* 159-171.

Clark, D. L., Lotto, L. S., & Astuto, T. A. (1984). Effective schools and school improvement: A comparative analysis of two lines of inquiry. *Educational Administration Quarterly, 20(3),* 41-68.

Corbett, H. D., & D'Amico, J. (1987). *Context and change: A training program for school improvement.* Philadelphia: Research for Better Schools, Inc.

D'Amico, J., & Miller, R. (1985). *Jackson high school: A case study of a collaborative process for school improvement.* Philadelphia: Research for Better Schools, Inc.

D'Amico, J., & Presseisen, B. Z. (1985). *Yorkshire junior high: A change process turned around.* Philadelphia: Research for Better Schools, Inc.

Edmonds, R. R. (1978, July). *A discussion of the literature and issues related to effective schooling.* Paper presented at the National Conference on Urban Education, St. Louis, MO.

Edmonds, R. R., & Frederiksen, J. R. (1979). *Search for effective schools: The identification and analysis of city schools that are instructionally effective for poor children.* Cambridge, MA: Center for Urban Studies.

Lieberman, A. (1986). Collaborative work. *Educational Leadership, 43(5),* 4-8.

New Jersey Education Association. (1981). *School effectiveness training program manual*. Trenton, NJ: Author.

Sarason, S. B. (1972). *The creation of settings and future societies*. San Francisco: Jossey Bass.

Schmuck, R. A., & Runkel, P. J. (1985). *The handbook of organizational development in schools, 3rd edition*. Palo Alto: Mayfield Publishing Company.

Woods-Houston, M. A., & Miller, R. (1988). *Labor management cooperation in schools: An idea whose time has come*. Philadelphia: Research for Better Schools, Inc.

# COUNTRY
# REPORTS

# AUSTRALIA

## Judith Chapman and Jeffrey Dunstan

### Major Trends

Since the last Congress a number of developments of interest have occurred. In general in this period the issue of school effectiveness in Australia has been considered mostly from the point of view of accountability. The key question of the moment could be said to be "How do we know that our education provision is effective, or not?"

There has been a significantly increased interest, at both national and state levels, in the accountability of public education systems of all types from primary schooling through to tertiary provision. Education has come under public scrutiny with considerable media and political attention. In this time the national and state elections were held and these placed accountability in education firmly on the agenda of public policy.

### National Initiatives

At the national level the Conference of Director Generals of Education and the Commonwealth Schools Commission have mounted a national project entitled "Reporting on Educational Progress, performance indicators in education". This project has produced a series of information and discussion papers, and a national conference, which have attracted much interest. (Contact address: Directorate of Special Programs, N.S.W. Department of Education, Box 33 GPO, Sydney 2001, Australia.)

The Commonwealth Curriculum Development Centre has published in its series National Curriculum Issues a paper entitled "Indicators, Information and Education. A discussion of possibilities and problems".

### State Initiatives

Different approaches have been taken in the different states addressing the issue. Some states are considering student testing programs. Some are looking to the reporting relationships embedded in the organisational structures of their education departments to provide for monitoring of schools' effectiveness.

In the state of Victoria a great deal of work has been conducted in this area. There the general framework of government education policy, as expressed since 1982 in a key series of Ministerial Papers, has paid particular attention to matters of school improvement and participative decision-making involving the school community. Within this context the past year has seen the issue of school effectiveness and accountability receive especially wide-ranging attention.

The State Board of Education has mounted a project, "Monitoring the Achievements of Schools", to consider and consult with the education community on the issues involved in systems' and schools' accountability for student outcomes. (Contact address: State Board of Education, Rialto Towers, 525 Collins Street, Melbourne, Victoria 3000, Australia.)

Within the restructured Ministry of Education a School Improvement Branch, with an Evaluation and Development Section, has been created. Its brief is to respond to an identified need for explicit, mainstream attention to school improvement and to provide a new focus on planning and coordinated policy development. It is required to develop an evaluation and accountability framework for the 2065 government schools and their system across the state. Four elements of such a framework have been noted for discussion and development work:
* Regular reporting by schools and agencies
* A cyclical process of program planning and evaluation for schools and agencies
* The collection of data by education systems in the key areas of contexts, inputs, processes and outcomes
* A mechanism to examine evaluation processes and report on systemwide issues including the support provided to schools and the success of policy initiatives.

The first two elements have now been incorparated in developmental work on a planning approach to be used by schools. A decision-making approach comprising a cycle of phases of review, planning, implementation, evaluation and reporting, and involving the participation of school communities is being considered.

Projects of interest in this area include a project considering management information systems and the issues involved in developing them; a project on teacher stress and managing student behaviour which involves schools in conducting the decision-making cycle noted above to examine and plan for their response to this difficult issue; and a project developing descriptive profiles of students' achievements in subject areas which are standards based but which offer a full range of diagnostic information rather than simple numerical scoring. Thus accountability for quality in general management, issues management and in student outcomes is being considered in detailed projects to inform the broader discussion of accountability mechanisms and processes. (Contact adress: School Improvement Branch, Ministry of Education, Rialto Towers, 525 Collins Street, Melbourne 3000, Australia.)

# BOPHUTHATSWANA

### J.M. Noruwana

At the time of the London Conference in January 1988, plans to establish ICSE as a movement in the region were at a very initial stage. Contacts had been made with two Departments of Education (Transkei and Bophuthatswana) and discussions involving the three parties - policymakers, practitioners and researchers - had taken place with the Transkei regional group.

To date, these discussions have continued and have been extended in both regions. In the Transkei region planning for implementation has reached an advanced stage, and both the Ministry of Education and the Teachers' Association have accepted in principle the idea of implementing school improvement strategies in the school system as well as being involved as members in the ICSE movement.

In June 1988 the Transkei Teachers' Association organised their twenty first Annual Conference around the theme: "Effective schools in deprived communities: an agenda for action in the nineties." I was invited to deliver the keynote address at this conference on June 27, 1988.

Further meetings with policymakers and practitioners have been held in Transkei. At these meetings preliminary plans for possible implementation of effective school strategies were discussed and an agreement was reached on the need to base our implementation strategies on sound research strategies. The following areas of research and implementation were thus identified:

1. *Research to establish how effective our schools are*
   There was, however, no finality about the best research stategy to tap this information.

2. *Small pilot study versus system-wide study*
   A system-wide study was discounted in favour of a limited small-scale study of a few effective and ineffective schools to indentify the differentiating characteristics.

3. *Classroom observation studies versus self-reports*
   It was noted that, while ideally the best way of acquiring "valid" information, classroom observations can be both time consuming and financially draining. Questionnaires and interviews with selected key participants (principals, teachers and other leaders) in the school setting were indentified as the main information gathering techniques. Classroom observation would be used to follow-up a limited number of selected cases.

4. *The role of principals* as key instructional leaders was highlighted. Research on principals is targeted as one of the first research projects. (To this end, two questionnaires - one for principals and the other for teachers - have been developed for use early next year).

Seminars on the Principal's role in school improvement will be conducted by the regional organiser in conjunction with the local university some time in 1989. The target group, initially, will be those schools in the pilot study.

5. *Conference*

Emanating from informal discussions the regional organiser has had with other professional educators in the region in September this year, a two-day conference will be called for some date in 1989, at which Black educational leaders will reminisce about the "good old days" of effective schools. It is hoped that this forum will enable old leaders to share with us some of their observations about what made their schools effective. It is our belief that the effective schools of the fifties used effective schools strategies, and that, therefore, a lot can be learned from what they did. The added advantage in this strategy is that it would indicate to project participants that the envisaged changes aimed at making our schools effective are not a totally new phenomenon in our school seetings.

With all these plans in the pipeline, hopefully 1989 is going to be a busy time for one region in the South African context. Naturally there are limitations to what we are likely to achieve. But we are all looking forward to making a start, no matter how small, in making our schools effective.

The lack of movement in some parts of this region has been a cause for great concern to the regional organiser. Some concerted effort will be made in 1989 to increase commitment to the ideals and activities of ICSE in the South African region.

# CANADA

## Larry Sackney

It is my distinct pleasure to again report to the International Congress for School Effectiveness further developments on the Canadian scene. The intent of this report is to briefly outline new initiatives undertaken since the last report.

In last year's report I had outlined the context within which education takes place in Canada. Education is a provincial responsibility, and consequently, there are considerable variations in emphasis across the country.

The previous report also outlined how the school effectiveness movement had taken hold as well as the models being used. In particular, the Calgary, Edmonton, Saskatchewan, Manitoba and Halton models were described. Additionally those in attendance at last year's Congress had the opportunity to hear Craig Melvin describe the Saskatchewan School Improvement Program (SSIP), Bev Priftis the Calgary model, and Dean Fink the Halton Model.

It should be noted that many of the models use the school effectiveness research as the basis for school improvement. Moreover, many of the models utilize a developmental perspective. Consequently the models tend to incorporate the teacher effects, staff development and change literature.

What have we learned from our efforts? We know that making schools more effective is a difficult, slow and often frustrating experience. Additionally, making schools more effective also requires a sustained and committed effort. Initially there is considerable enthusiasm which wanes over time. The difficulty of the 'implementation dip' as known in the change literature is a very real concern and one that is hard to overcome.

### Recent Developments

At the provincial levels no new initiatives were undertaken during 1988. Perhaps the province that was most active was Saskatchewan as it went about developing the CORE Curriculum. Much of the research on school effectiveness continues to be done by individuals within the university setting.

Research methods tend to utilize both quantitative and qualitative approaches. Most of the studies have tended towards the small or case study approaches.

Examples of quantitative studies include the work being conducted by Douglas Willms at the University of British Columbia wherein he is estimating school effects and their stability using a longitudinal hierarchical linear model. During 1988 he also was involved in a study on school and classroom contextual effects on the basis of ethnic and social class segregation in elementary schools.

Pandora Johnson completed a study of effective secondary schooling and the factors affecting academic outcomes in the Commonwealth of the Bahamas. Her research methodology was similar to the "outlier" school studies and confirmed many of the factors found in the elementary studies.

At the Ontario Institute for the Studies of Education (OISE), Ken Leitwood and Steve Lawton have been reviewing the characteristics of exemplary secondary schools as part of a larger study on retention and transition. Their framework is shown in Figure 1. Moreover, Leithwood and associates continue their studies on the principalship. In large part this work is being coordinated through the Principalship Centre.

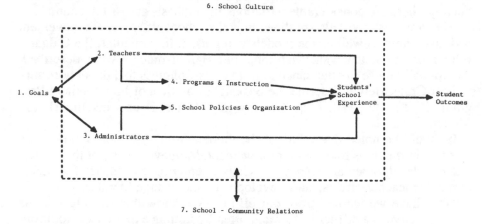

*Figure 1: A framework showing the categories of characteristics associated with exemplary secondary schools*

On the qualitative side, using the naturalistic case study approach, John Orora examined cultural assumptions of a rural, boys boarding secondary school in Kenya.

A number of Saskatchewan studies using the model of school effectiveness variables (see Figure 2) have been conducted. Three of these studies have focused on the cultural aspects of schools. Freda Trew's study, for example, examined the relationships between aspects of organizational culture and organizational commitment. In a similar vein, Wes Prosser using the Kilmann-Saxture Culture-Gap Survey examined aspects of culture in a rural school division.

A number of cultural studies are also in progress (e.g. Bodnar, Sackney and Wilson) using Schien's cultural model. These are intensive case studies that

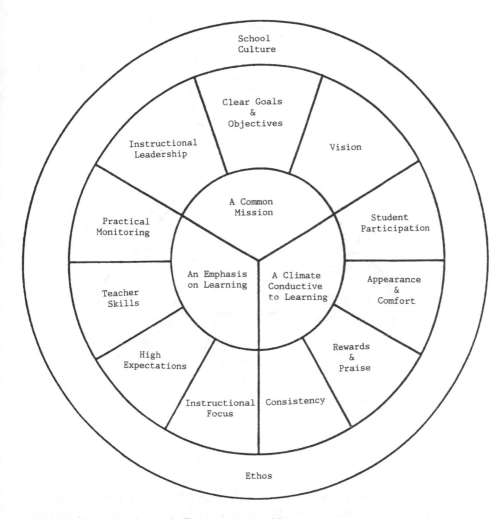

*Figure 2: A model of school effectiveness variables*

attempt to ascertain the basic norms, values and beliefs that operate in the schools. To date a highly effective and an ineffective school have been identified using the attributes of school effectiveness. Extensive field work has been initiated.

A number of quasi-experimental research designs are also being undertaken. Using a school profile concept, schools are collecting baseline data on various aspects of effective schooling. After a three year period the baseline data will be examined to see if the change strategies have made a difference on a number of variables (e.g. attendance, drop-out, achievement, behavior, etc.). Figure 3 shows the planned stages of school improvement.

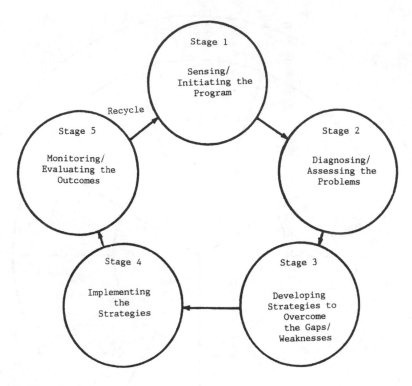

*Figure 3: The planned stages of school improvement*

## Process Activities

As reported last year, numerous school divisions have, and have continued to, implement the effective schools research. A survey of 250 larger school divisions across Canada indicated that over three-quarters of them were implementing aspects of the effectiveness research. Moreover, many were providing staff development activities that focused on effectiveness.

The Halton Board of Education under the guidance of Dean Fink hosted a national conference entitled "Beyond School Effectiveness" in May of 1988. Also in May of 1989 the Moose Jaw board will be hosting a conference entitled "Achieving Excellence". Thus interest in school effectiveness is high.

In my estimation, the drive to make our schools more effective will not be lost in the near future. The move to strengthen the national network is strong. Practitioners, policy makers and researchers all see the need to continue fostering the original school effectiveness enthusiasm. Hopefully the International Congress in part meets this need.

# REFERENCES

Bodnar, B. (1988). *A study of the basic cultural assumptions of a school.* University of Saskatchewan, Saskatoon (in progress)

Johnson, P. (1988). *Effective secondary schooling: Factors affecting academic acheivement in the Commonwealth of the Bahamas.* Unpublished doctoral dissertation, University of Toronto, Toronto.

Leithwood, K.A. (1987). *A review of research concerning the characteristics of examplary secondary schools.* A working paper prepared for the student retention and transition project. Toronto: OISE.

Leithwood, K.A. & Montgomery, D. (1982). The role of the elementary school in principal in program improvement: *Review of Educational Research, 52* (82), 309-334.

Orora, J. (1988). *School culture and the role of the principal: A study of basic cultural assumptions and their influence on the principal's role.* Unpublished doctoral dissertation, Dalhousie University, Halifax.

Prosser, W. (1987). *An examination of the culture-gaps of a rural school division.* An unpublished masters thesis, University of Saskatchewan, Saskatoon.

Sackney, L. (1988). *A school improvement model: developmental and cultural perspectives.* A paper presented at Principal's training program. Vancouver, British Columbia.

Trew, F. (1987). *Analyses of relationships between aspects of organizational culture and organizational commitment.* Unpublished masters thesis, University of Saskatchewan, Saskatoon.

Willms, D. & Raudenbush, S. (1988). A longitudinal hierarchical linear model for estimating school effects and stability. *Journal of Educational Measurement.* In press.

Willms, D. & Raudenbush, S. (1988). *School and classroom contextual effects: A study of ethnic and social class segregation in Israeli elementary schools.* A paper presented at AERA, New Orleans.

# ENGLAND AND WALES

Dave Reynolds

Few countries can be involved in such rapid educational changes as are England and Wales currently. The Conservative Government's Education Reform Act of 1988 has introduced the principles and practices of market competitiveness into the educational system, by which schools are assessed on their performance in tests of ability in Science, English and Mathematics. Schools, from this year, are also responsible for their own resource and financial management, since local education authorities now have to devolve their educational resources to individual schools. Indeed, the whole drift of the new policy arrangements is to marginalise the local education authorities or educational districts and to create a situation in which central government lays down the criteria by which schools are evaluated, parents choose their children's schools on the basis of those criteria and the schools try - unhelped by any outside-school authority - to compete in their effectiveness on the attainment of the criteria.

Given these major policy changes which are likely to increase the differences between schools in their levels of effectiveness greatly, the research and practice areas of school improvement and school effectiveness are clearly also affected by the dramatic scale of the changes.

Looking firstly at school effectiveness, it is clear that all existing research studies (e.g., Rutter et al., 1979; Mortimore et al., 1988; and Reynolds & Sullivan, 1987) are now out of date because the settings in which schools find themselves have changed so dramatically. Whilst the picture of the effective school that is found in British research of the 1980s (see Rutter, 1983; and Reynolds, 1982, 1985) may not be completely inappropriate in the 1990s, it is clear that effectiveness in a 'market economy' based educational system is going to require a large range of additional competencies and skills from such schools if they are to remain effective. Whilst there is new research planned into the area of educational leadership by Peter Mortimore at the University of Lancaster and new research into school effectiveness beginning in thirty secondary schools conducted at the University of Wales College of Cardiff, it is clear that the research base in England and Wales is no longer expanding as rapidly as in the past. The research to study an expanded definiton of 'effectiveness' is therefore partially absent.

If we look at school improvement, secondly, the situation is probably even more worrying. The direct translation of school effectiveness research into school improvement programmes has been very rare indeed and there has been none of the explosion of effective schools programmes that is so evident in North America for example. Also, the actual number of school improvement programmes themselves has been very small by comparison with other countries (see Reynolds, 1988 for a discussion). This current situation in England and Wales whereby we know more about 'good' schools than we do about how to make schools 'good' will now be rapidly worsened because of a number of factors. Schools' attention is now firmly fixed upon the short-term needs of responding to the new legislative framework, and school improvement or development programmes that are not very closely related to a narrow set of concerns are likely to be regarded as irrelevant. Also, virtually all the North American and the limited British school improvement research is likely to be completely obsolescent, since much of it was based on the need for schools to generate and manage internally generated change. Since educational change is now *externally* produced and driven, the models of successful change of the last fifteen years are now frighteningly obsolescent. The obsession with the 'bottom up' change that has been necessary to build any desire for change and any coalition of support for change in schools is no longer relevant in an age when schools know that they must either improve themselves or, like businesses in a market, simple shut down.

There are some potentially positive signs in the current England and Wales educational situation though. The policy squeeze upon schools to be effective and the large financial resources that are now available to individual schools is leading to a rapid growth in the numbers of educational consultancies and management consultants. England and Wales had only one of these in 1980 - informed guesswork suggests there were to be at least a dozen by 1990, and it is highly likely that the result will be a rapid improvement in the quality of the school improvement literature in England and Wales.

A further potentially positive aspect in England and Wales is the rapid growth of forms of teacher appraisal, in which it is planned that all teachers will be evaluated from the 1989/90 school year. Both to secure teacher participation and to make the exercise educationally valid, it is clear that there will need to be developmental aspects of any scheme that will involve helping individuals overcome any areas of weakness that appraisal may have revealed. If schools are having to get involved with staff development activities with a large proportion of their staff, then it is likely that they will have to embrace *school* development activities also, thus again increasing our knowledge of school functioning.

A last positive aspect of the current policy scene in England and Wales is connected with the greatly increased scale of formal assessment information that will become available over the next six or seven years. This information, if it is externally moderated to be comparable across different schools as is likely, represents a potentially huge data base with which to pursue issues of concern to school effectiveness researchers. One may have substantial doubts as to the extent to which the raw school test results as they will be published will actually reflect the varying effectiveness levels of different schools, since there will be a clear need to context the raw results against the various non-school, environmental influences that affect children's development. However the data itself, however limited in value, is bound to be a positive encouragement to schools and researchers interested in school effectiveness because its very existence removes one of the blocks on effectiveness research, namely the size and scale of the data collection processes required.

Overall, then, the situation for school effectiveness and improvement research may not be as bleak in the 1990s as it has been in the 1980s. A new generation of effectiveness research may be generated by the educational policy changes and a new body of knowledge on externally generated school improvement may develop also. It would be rather ironic if a government that is antagonistic to educational research in general was creating the conditions for major advances in knowledge in the specific areas of school improvement and effectiveness.

# REFERENCES

Mortimore, P., Sammons, P., Ecob, R., & Stoll, L. (1988). *School Matters: The Junior Years*. Salisbury: Open Books.
Reynolds, D. (1982) The search for effective schools. *School Organisation, 2* (3), 215-237.
Reynolds, D. (Ed.) (1985). *Studying School Effectiveness*. Lewes: Falmer Press.
Reynolds, D. (1988) British school improvement research: the contribution of qualitative studies. *International Journal of Qualitative Studies in Education, 1* (2).
Reynolds, D., Sullivan, M. & Murgatroyd, S.J. (1987). *The Comprehensive Experiment*. Lewes: Falmer Press.
Rutter, M. (1983). School effects on pupil progress - findings and policy implications. *Child Development, 54* (1), 1-29.
Rutter, M. et al. (1979). *Fifteen Thousand Hours*. London: Open Books.

Note: Futher details of research and practice in the area of school effectiveness and improvement in England and Wales can be obtained from:David Reynolds, University of Wales College of Cardiff, School of Education, 42 Park Place, Cardiff CF1 3BB, Wales, United Kingdom, Tel: (c code) 222 874000 extns. 5144 / 5333.

# HUNGARY

Gabor Halasz and Atilla Horvath

The educational system in Hungary has traditionally been centralized, so the question of effectiveness has been raised mainly at the level of the entire system and sometimes at the level of individual schools. However, recently the question of school level effectiveness came into prominence as the consequence of a policy of administrative reform increasing the autonomy of individual schools. Teaching staffs were given considerable freedom to determine how they work, and, parallel with this, clients (parents and local communities) were given new participatory rights. The interest in how to evaluate the work of individual schools has been growing.

## Initiatives at Different Levels
Initiatives to improve school level effectiveness have been taken at different levels. At *national level* regulations concerning the internal life of schools have been loosened. Measurement programs permitting the evaluation of schools have been promoted. School level curriculum innovations and experiments have been encouraged, and the elaboration of alternative programs to be choosen by schools has been supported. A new legislation establishing the legal framework of institutional autonomy has been adopted.

At *regional level* the supervisory power of administrative agencies has been restricted. Supervisors lost their right to tell schools how to teach. At the same time new advisory centers have been created in order to provide schools with the counselling service they need.

At *institutional level* the enlarged freedom of staffs has been accompanied with new responsibilities. Every school has to elaborate its own statute and pedagogical program based on the evaluation of its actual situation.

## Difficulties and Perspectives
The present situation is characterized by the coexistence of the old and the new mechanisms. While the earlier mechanisms of central control have been removed, the new ones supporting school level improvement are not yet working. Schools do not get the external support they need to improve their internal activity.

However, the first results of the new policy of school autonomy may be observed. The greater freedom given to teacher staffs meant a challenge to them in a sense that they felt a need to re-think what they are doing and what they had to do. As a consequence of this a number of schools started experimental programs, chose alternative curricula and textbooks which they thought to be better adapted to their clientele. Differences between schools, which earlier had been hidden, became visible, and this made it possible to identify the special problems of every school and to elaborate particular strategies to solve these problems.

It is expected that in Hungary the question of school effectiveness will gain a major importance in the near future. This means the need for new values, research priorities and school oriented services.

# ISRAEL

## Joseph Bashi and David Gordon

Up to the mid 1960's it would have been impossible to talk about effective schools in Israel.

The waves of mass immigration which poured into the State of Israel from its inception in 1948, forced Israel's society to adopt a melting pot approach, the aim of which was to create the *unity* and *cohesiveness* of the society. This approach to assimilation ensured that the emphasis would be placed on *commonalities* rather than differences.

Thus the Israeli education system created a common curriculum and standard unified operating regulations for schools. If school effectiveness is linked to an accountability ethos and the idea of helping each child add to what he/she knows (on the assumption that children bring *differential* entry behavior to the learning situation) then the assumptions in this era in Israeli education would never have countenanced the thinking which characterizes the effective school movement.

Changes in the direction of increased pluralism began to filter into the system in the early 1970's. The Ministry of Education began to allow greater degrees of freedom for school principals (not exploited much at the beginning, however).

Today there is an acceptance of the need to encourage school autonomy, albeit of a limited sort and of ideas like: diagnoses of children's needs and achievements, adapting and varying materials to different classrooms, the need for monitoring and feedback, and so on, all these indicating increased tolerance for diversity among schools.

This trend is encouraged today in one of two ways: (1) the Ministry implements school improvement intervention programs directly; (b) intervention programs are implemented by public bodies, academic and others, that operate with the support and approval af the Ministry.

Two particularly comprehensive projects are:
1) a project run by a special Ministry unit for the last decade which encourages "active learning" (as conceived originally in the British open learning movement in the 1960's) and helps schools adopt and implement an active learning ideology. This project today encompasses about 10% of Israel's elementary schools.
2) a project entitled "individualized teaching" run within the framework of the Institute for Educational Technology. This project also encompasses about 10% of Israel's elementary schools, and of late has begun working

with junior high schools too. The Institute prepares learning materials for differentiated, individualized classroom learning. These materials are sold on the open market and are thus also bought and used by schools not connected directly with the Institute.

These two projects were the two foci of school improvement activity in Israel in the 1970's. Neither related directly to quantitative measures of student achievement, their reports normally being formulated at the impressionistic-naturalistic level.

From the early 1980's the concept of accountability filtered into the system, and schools are beginning to be aware of the need for accountability and of variance between students.

This new atmosphere leads us to expect an increased drive towards effective schools.

### Activities During 1988/1989

During the last year there has been an impressive increase of activity related to school improvement. The activity has been of two sorts: (1) particular "private" initiatives for school improvement projects; (2) official decisions, reached in the Ministry of Education itself, that are related to school improvement.

(1) A year ago a holistic accountability-based intervention project in most of the elementary schools in two towns in southern Israel was completed. This project was coordinated jointly by an agency known as Project Renewal and the Ministry of Education, and was run under the auspices of the Van Leer Institute. (Project Renewal is a philanthropic organization based on funds supplied by Jewish communities outside Israel who "adopt" twin cities and support social development projects in problematic areas in these cities). The success criterion for the project was improved student achievement.

The results were encouraging and acted as a major incentive for discussion in the Ministry of the school effectiveness approach and decisions reached in this regard which we will explain further on in this report.

During the last year systematic follow-up of this project was begun which focuses on the maintenance of the project's positive effect on student achievement.

A project to improve all the schools in an average-size town in the south of Israel began operation this year. This is a similar project to that described above, and is the largest of its kind yet attempted in Israel, because it encompasses all the stages of formal education – elementary, junior and senior high. This is again a project in which Project Renewal and the Ministry are involved. The intervention team is from the Education Department of the Ben-Gurion University of the Negev.

(2) During 1982, the office of the chief scientist of the Ministry of Education sponsored an examination of achievement levels in basic skills in all 3rd grade classrooms in Israel. The tests were built on the basis of an absolute criterion. Their main purpose was to identify ineffective schools or town or area ineffective "pockets" in which the percentage of pupils that have not reached a satisfactory level in basic skills is relatively high. Approximately 10% of elementary schools were labelled, and during 1983-87 about two thirds of them were given help by a special unit in the Ministry.

In 1988 it was decided to deal with these schools far more intensively. Also a further 5% of schools will be involved in the project. This year the project will concentrate on preparing a field agent training program, identifying potential field agents and training them. Here again the criterion for evaluating results will be student achievement in basic skills, and also a comparison of the relative position of these schools vis-à-vis normative standardized tests.

The above-mentioned Van Leer Institute project has served as an incentive for discussion of school improvement in general. In October 1988 the Directorate of the Ministry of Education decided to attempt to improve schools (in the effective schools sense) in two urban areas in each of the six provincial districts in Israel.

A further decision reached, a highly significant one in our view, was that the school *as a whole* is to be regarded as the basic unit for school improvement in this particular program, and not a particular curriculum or teaching method in a particular subject, etc.

Another important decision: up till now various different units of the Ministry supply resources (budgetary or otherwise) to schools in order to promote the tasks or objectives for which these units are responsible. Thus in order that a school principal could get the resources available from a particular source, he/she needed to pledge to adopt particular projects in his/her school, whether the school needed them or not! Now, the schools in the two urban areas in each province will be provided with resources that have all been lumped together and these will reach the school without the usual regulations and by-laws for their use being tagged on.

The school staff itself will decide how to use these resources. This is a huge improvement in the way resources are conceived, used and adapted to the needs of the individual school.

A further change in Ministry policy is the decision to mandate the application of operationally defined criteria for success and failure of field projects. This approach, which attempts to increase school accountability, will become a norm that schools will have to conform to.

In addition we would like to mention two large conferences on effective schools held this year, one at the Bar-Ilan University, the other, under the auspices of the Van Leer Institute, catered mainly to school principals and teachers, in order to try to increase awareness of the school effectiveness issue. In addition, a first book on effective schools in Hebrew, an extensive review of the literature, was published this year (Y. Friedman, T. Horowitz and R. Shaliv, *Effectiveness, Culture and Climate of Schools,* Szold Institute).

In the light of the above, we can see 1988 as a year in which there was a considerable push forward with regards to school effectiveness and improvement.

# THE NETHERLANDS

Bert P.M. Creemers and Anja W.M. Knuver

## 1. POLICY

A few months ago a note of the Ministry of Education was published about "the Dutch school on its way to 2000". In this note the policy of the government appears to be directed to the development of more autonomy for schools in the Netherlands for the coming years. Schools will be made more autonomous in deciding how to distribute a specific budget. The budget allocated to the schools is dependent on the amount of pupils and the amount of low-SES and ethnic minority pupils. Schools themselves can decide whether or not to take effective school features into special account for their own school policy. Furthermore the government finances a large scale evaluation of educational priority areas (OVB evaluation). In this evaluation much attention will be given to the effectiveness of the means which are applied in these areas. The ultimate aim of this project is to get children attending schools within the educational priority area (many children from a lower family background) to an achievement level which is equal to that of schools in other parts of the country. Van de Werf and Tesser (1989) report on the first findings of the evaluation in these proceedings. A small amount of variance between schools could be found and explained. Only high expectations, aspirations and structured lessons seem to have an impact on the average recommendation for secondary school type.

In two notes of the advisory body for primary education a special interest towards school effectiveness and school improvement has been shown (ARBO, 1988a, 1988b). In these notes it is stated that effective schools research, although it can be criticized, shows that school matters. Special attention has been given to effective school characteristics which provide better opportunities for children from ethnic minorities or lower background families. The body advises the government, but also schools and school support services to take notice of these findings and apply them in school practice.

## 2. SCHOOL PRACTICE AND IMPLEMENTATION

A special interest in school effectiveness can also be noted in educational practice (teacher training centres, school support services and more specifically teachers themselves). In educational journals there is attention for developments and research findings with respect to school effectiveness. An example is the special issue on effective schools of the journal "School en begeleiding".

The implications on school practice of school effectiveness has also been shown by the starting of school improvement projects. For example in the near future Van der Grift in co-operation with school support services will start a school improvement program in Utrecht, a province in the middle of the Netherlands. The project got financial support from the Dutch government. Several research studies are directed at school practice and implementation. An experimental study conducted by Snippe (1988) showed that the highest implementation of a new math curriculum in primary schools will be reached when teachers receive classroom consultation. A classroom consultant who observes their lessons provides them with feedback on their behaviour. The learning results of the pupils were also the highest in the consultation group. Thus classroom consultation appears to be an effective strategy to influence curriculum implementation as well as learning outcomes of pupils.

# 3. RESEARCH

### 3.1. Looking for School and Class Characteristics.

Several research projects in the Netherlands study the effectiveness of schools. Attention was paid to the school and class characteristics that contribute to this effectiveness. In a sample of 250 primary schools Brandsma and Knuver (1988) found about 8% of variance in language and about 12% of variance in arithmetic which could be connected to differences between schools (when pupil background variables were controlled for). Part of these variances could be explained by some school and class organizational factors. Another study was conducted by Van der Hoeven-van Doorum and Jungbluth (1988). In 53 schools they studied the effect of aspiration levels set by teachers for their pupils learning achievement. The effects of school and teaching factors on learning achievement appeared to be small. Higher aspiration levels, however, tended to lead to higher test scores for children. Some 7% of the variance in test scores could be explained by the aspiration level of the teacher as a direct or interaction effect.

In secondary education Bosker and Van der Velden (1989) found cohesive schools (i.e. democratic decision making, strong relationship with parents, etc.) with a positive school climate to be effective in terms of efficiency and educational prospectives. It is important to note that none of the research findings reported here seems to be totally in accordance with previous international findings where some five effective school characteristics were accepted to be of major influence on pupil achievement. However, the setting of high expectations, which points at features of class and teacher, shows effects on pupil achievement.

## 3.2. Methodological Studies

One of the methodological studies in school effectiveness is the study of Blok and Eiting (1988) about the size of school effects in primary schools. The results show that real differences between schools (after correction for differences which occurred by chance) as far as pupil achievement in language is concerned are very small. In this research the intra class correlation coefficient rho has been used to estimate school differences as compared to individual differences. Although rho was small for most schools, some school factors could influence this measure. Especially the effect of being a "stimulated" school appeared to be present. Another methodological issue is the stability of school effectiveness. In former studies the effectiveness of schools over the years or between forms did not seem to be very stable. Recent research conducted by Bosker et al. (1988) shows that, for the data they analyzed, school effects seemed to be quite stable between school years and cohorts. A recent study by Hofman and Oorburg (1988) shows the same trend. The correlation between residual scores of two successive school years was .73. It was also shown that this correlation drops when these school years are more distant from each other, which was also the case in the Bosker et al. research. Van der Eeden and Koopman (1988) studied the problem of outliers in random coefficient models for multi level analysis. Their conclusion is that in interpreting the outcomes of analyses when using a random coefficient model, outliers have to be considered because they can influence the estimated parameters.

## 3.3. Expanding Models for Schools Effectiveness.

An important subject in school effectiveness research is the impact of class and teacher characteristics on achievement. Reezigt and Weide (1989) reported on a study regarding the effect of individualization in the classroom on pupils' achievement. Hofman and Groen (1988) tried to investigate the impact of Dutch school boards on the effectiveness of schools. It is important to note that the dependent variable in this case is 'school effectiveness producing factors', which points at factors that appeared to be effective in other research. It seems that about 17% of the variance in school effectiveness producing factors can be explained by schoolboard activity. Schoolboard activity itself is highly affected by the organizational complexity of the board. Finally we want to mention the effort of Scheerens and Creemers (1989) to synthesize school organizational research and effective schools research. Special attention is paid to research founded on a perspective of contingency theory and the way this can be linked to school effectiveness research.

# LITERATURE

Blok, H., & Eiting, M.H. (1988). De grootte van schooleffecten: hoe verschillend presteren leerlingen van verschillende scholen? *Tijdschrift voor onderwijsresearch, 13 (1)*, 16-30. [The size of school effects: how differently do pupils from different schools perform?].

Bosker, R.J., Guldemond, H., Hofman, R.H. & Hofman, W.H.A. (1988). *De stabiliteit van schoolkwaliteit.* In: J. Scheerens & J.C. Verhoeven (Eds.), Schoolorganisatie, beleid en onderwijskwaliteit. Lisse: Swets & Zeitlinger. [The stability of school quality].

Bosker, R.J. & Velden, R.K.W. van der (1989). *The effects of secondary schools on the educational careers of disadvantaged pupils.* This volume, pp. 141-155.

Brandsma, H.P., & Knuver, J.W.M. (1988). *The typology of school organisations: effects on pupil achievement.* Paper presented on the British Educational Research Association conference. Norwich.

Creemers, B.P.M., & Lugthart, E. (1988). *School effectiveness and school improvement in the Netherlands.* Paper presented at the International Congress for School Effectiveness, London, United Kingdom.

De adviesraad voor de basisonderwijs, speciaal onderwijs en voortgezet onderwijs (1988a). *Voorrang aan achterstand.* Advies over een intergraal beleid ter voorkoming en bestrijding van onderwijsachterstand. Zeist. [The advisory body for primary education. Advice for an integral policy to prevent and fight educational inequality].

De adviesraad voor het basisonderwijs, speciaal onderwijs en voortgezet speciaal onderwijs (1988b). *Een boog van woorden tot woorden.* Advies over het onderwijs aan leerlingen uit etnische minderheden. Zeist. [The advisory body for primary education. Advice for the education of pupils from ethnic minorities].

Eeden, P. van den, & Koopman, P. (1988). *De invloed van outliers op de schattingen van groepsparameters.* Paper presented on the Dutch Educational Research conference, Leuven, Belgium. [The influence of outliers on the estimates of group parameters].

Hoeven-van Doornum, A.A. van der, Jungbluth, P., & Voeten, M.J.M. (1988). *De betekenis van streefdoelen voor leerprestaties aan het einde van leerjaar 8 van de basisschool.* Paper presented on the Dutch Educational Research conference, Leuven, Belgium. [The effect of aspiration levels set by teachers on achievement at the end of primary education].

Hofman, R.H., Brouns, L., & Groen, A.G. (1988). *Schoolbesturen en schooleffectiviteiten.* Paper presented on the Dutch Educational Research conference, Leuven, Belgium. [School boards and school effectiveness].

Hofman, R.H., & Oorburg, G.H. (1988). *Schoolwerkplangebruik en schooleffectiviteit: selectie van outliers.* Interimrapport, RION, Groningen. [The use of school curricula and school effectiveness: selection of outliers].

Reezigt, G.J., & Weide, M.G. (1989). *The effectiveness of adaptive instruction in Dutch primary schools.* Paper presented at the International Congress for School Effectiveness, Rotterdam, The Netherlands.

Scheerens, J., & Creemers, B.P.M. (1989). *Towards a more comprehensive conceptual model of school effectiveness.* This volumwe, pp. 265-278.

Snippe, J. (1988). Effecten van klasseconsultatie op curriculumimplementatie en leerresultaten. *Tijdschrift voor onderwijsresearch, 13 (3)*, 141-150. [Effects of class consultation on curriculum implementation and achievement].

Werf, M.P.C., & Tesser, P. (1989). *The effects of educational priorities on children from lower income families and ethnic minorities.* Paper presented at the International Congress for School Effectiveness, Rotterdam, The Netherlands.

# NORTHERN IRELAND

## Peter Daly

Northern Ireland, although under the direct rule of the British Goverment at Westminster, has experienced some degree of variation in school organisation compared to mainland Britain. The executive influence of Northern Ireland's Department of Education together with that of the five Education and Library Boards, which exercise some of the powers of local education authorities in Great Britain, are of particular importance. In general terms the region has retained a form of competitive selection for alternative forms of post-primary schooling.

The partnership between the state and voluntary/religious bodies providing education is very significant. Pupils from the two main ethno-religious communities are, largely, educated in separate schools. However, recent financial incentives suggest that goverment is keen to encourage the growth of the present small-scale development in 'integrated' schooling (DENI, 1988). Research and policy analysis related to school segregation and integration have been considered by Darby and Dunn (1987), Spencer (1987) and Loughran (1987). Reid and Salters (1989) have been investigating the views of parents whose children attend integrated schools.

### School Improvement
There has been considerable interest on the part of Goverment in the promotion of a range of school improvement programmes at both secondary and primary school levels. The secondary school programme which has achieved the most widespread attention is the 11-16 Curriculum Development Programme (DENI, 1984; O'Shea, 1987). The programme was launched in 1984 as a partnership arrangement between the Department of Education for Northern Ireland, the Education and Library Boards and the voluntary sector. The main aim is

"to improve the quality and relevance of education for all pupils in the age 11-16 but particularly for those young people who do not relate positively to secondary education and who currently achieve little from it" (O'Shea, 1987).

The overall approach of its regional co-ordinator reflects the influence of ideas associated with the International School Improvement Project (O'Shea, 1987). Participation, on the part of secondary schools, was on a voluntary opting-in basis, initially. Currently the number of participating schools is approaching 200. The programme's future is now somewhat uncertain in the light of the proposed variant of the national curriculum for Northern Ireland (DENI, 1988). Evaluation has been problematic since each school was encouraged to set its own targets within a general framework. However, developments were reviewed regularly from the beginning, on a school, area and regional basis through the involvement of area field workers under a regional co-ordinator.

Part of the regional co-ordinator's brief was to maintain close contact with a range of parallel initiatives – notably the European Community Transition from School to Adult Working Life (TRAWL) Project, the secondary Science Curriculum Review and the Fourth and Fifth Year Curriculum Project which was targeted at low achievers in secondary schools. These projects have been under the general supervision of the Northern Ireland Council for Educational Development (NICED). The Council was set up in 1980 – along somewhat similar lines to those already indicated in relation to the 11-16 Programme. However its responsibilities were extended to include primary school pupils and pupils beyond the age of 16. It has provided support and co-ordination for a wide range of more specific subject-based and 'cross-curricular' initiatives, having inherited some projects from the former Northern Ireland Schools' Curriculum Committee and the Northern Ireland Council for Educational Technology. Summative evaluations of NICED secondary programmes have been carried out by small teams with a strong 'in-house' (NICED) representation.

NICED's work in regard to primary school improvement has received much attention. Its Primary Programme Committee was instrumental in the production and dissemination of a series of subject-based curriculum guidelines. They were designed particularly to provide head-teachers with support for whole-school curriculum review, at individual school level, in an atmosphere of collegial responsibility, without prescription (McCavera, 1987).

It now remains to be seen to what extent work initiated through the 11-16 Programme and through NICED will continue to develop in the context of a much more centrally directed approach to curriculum planning and pupil assessment, as Northern Ireland comes partly into line with national curriculum arrangements already enshrined in legislation for Great Britain (DENI, 1988). NICED will be replaced by a statutory body, the Northern Ireland Curriculum Council which is unlikely to be directly involved in developmental work. The future of the government-sponsored Centre for Education Management, which provides courses for head-teachers and other senior members of school staffs is also unclear. Teachers' Centres under the control of local Education and Library Boards may be expected to take on this work.

The Northern Ireland Council for Educational Research (NICER) has been involved in investigating the school experiences of teachers and pupils in the context of a change in the secondary school selection (transfer) procedure and its impact on school curricula at both primary and secondary stages

(Wilson, 1986; Teare & Sutherland, 1988). Gardner and D'Arcy (1988) have studied the uptake of information technology programmes in Northern Ireland classrooms.

## School Effectiveness

If we consider the distinction made by Clark et al. (1984) between school effectiveness research as involving measures of pupil achievement, however defined, rather than 'measures of the adoption of an innovation' – a typical concern in studies of school improvement – then school effectiveness studies in this sense have received limited attention in Nothern Ireland. The bulk of school effectiveness studies have been carried out by Wilson (1985, 1988) and his associates at the Northern Ireland Council for Educational Research (see Martin et al., 1989, for a brief overview of these studies). A major focus of research interest has been the performance of pupils in different sectors of a predominantly selective school system i.e. system level effectiveness. Daly (1987) has reanalysed NICER data in a school level comparative analysis.

The influence of the Northern Ireland Schools' Examinations Council with responsibility for co-ordinating new assessment procedures for pupils aged 8, 11, 14, and 16 years, may emerge as dominant in relation to future developments in all schools. Grammar schools will continue to select pupils partly on the basis of achievement in these tests at age 8 and at the age 11 (DENI, 1988). The Council has also been co-ordinating a project on Records of Achievement in a small number of post-primary schools since 1985:

"These developments in Northern Ireland are in line with stated DES policy that by 1990 all students will be able to take with them, when they leave school, a record of achievement which shall contain evidence of a wide range of the student's experience, capabilities and interests" (Northern Ireland Schools' Examination Council).

The influence of the Government's own Policy Planning Unit (PPRU), within the Department of Finance and Personnel, must not be overlooked as it provides specialist advice for a range of government departments including the Department of Education. Members of PPRU staff have been working on a cohort study of young people's choices of transition routes from school to work after reaching the age of 16 (McWhirter et al. 1987). PPRU also commissioned the independent Policy Research Institute (jointly funded by the two local universities) to provide a report on performance indicators in relation to Northern Ireland's schools with a view to updating management information services (Osborne et al. 1988).

There is evidence of continuing differences in overall attainment and in patterns of subject choice between Catholic and Protestant school leavers (Livingstone, 1977; Osborne & Cormack, 1989). Protestants tend to achieve better results in public examinations. Catholics are less likely to choose predominantly science-based subjects - although this pattern is changing. Attainment differences may be partly explained by the slightly disproportionate

Protestant representation among selective grammar school pupils and by socio-economic background differences. Catholics are more than twice as likely as Protestants to experience unemployment (Osborne & Cormack, 1986)

Gender differences in school achievement have been examined by Johnston and Rooney (1987) and Osborne and Cormack (1989). Girls' access to science subjects in single sex and co-educational grammar schools has been investigated by McEwen and Curry (1987) while Morgan and Dunn (1989) studied gender-related issues in infant and nursery classrooms.

As we move into a new era characterised by much greater government control of school curricula, closer monitoring of pupil and teacher performances, increased school level involvement in budgetary and other forms of resource management and a purported increase parental choice of school, the voices of classroom teachers, clamouring for greater support, are likely to attract widespread attention.

# REFERENCES

Clark, D.L., Lotto, L.S., & Astuto, T.A. (1984). Effective schools and school improvement: a comparative analysis of two lines of inquiry. *Educational Administration Quarterly, 20,* (3), 41-68.

Department of Education for Northern Ireland (DENI) (1984). *Secondary Schools: A New Development for 11-16 year olds.*

Department of Education for Northern Ireland (1988). *Education Reform in Northern Ireland: The way Forward.*

Gardner, J., & D'Archy, J. (1988). Learning from teachers: Teachers' perspectives of relevant courseware and training provision. *Computer Education, 12,* (2), 321-26.

Loughran, G. (1987). The rationale of Catholic education. In R.D. Osborne et al. (eds.), pp. 115-122.

McCavera, P. (1987). Aspects of change in primary education. *CORE-NICED, Autumn 1987 ,* p.4-5

McEwen, A., & Curry, C. (1987). Girls' access to science: single sex versus co-educational schools. In R.D. Osborne et al. (eds.), pp. 137-149.

McWhirter, L., Duffy, U., Barry, R., & McGuinness, G. (1987). Transition from school to work: cohort evidence. In R.D. Osborne et al. (eds.), pp. 167-190.

Martin, M., Hannon, D., & Daly, P. (1989). School Effectiveness in Ireland. *Proceedings of the First International Congress for School Effectiveness.*

Morgan, V., & Dunn, S. (1989). Gender differentiation in infant and nursery classroom. *Education North, 1,* (1), 21-24.

Northern Ireland Schools' Examinations Council, (undated). *Records of Achievement in Northern Ireland.*

Osborne, R.D., & Cormack, R.J. (1986). Unemployment and religion in Nothern Ireland. *The Economic and Social Review, 17,* (3), 215-225.

Osborne, R.D., Cormack, R.J., & Miller, R.L. (Eds.) (1987). *Education and Policy in Northern Ireland.* Policy Research Institute, The Queen's University of Belfast and the University of Ulster.

Osborne, R.D., Cormack, R.J., & Daly, P.G. (1988). Performance Indicators for Northern Irish Schools. Policy Research Institute, The Queen's University of Belfast and the University of Ulster.

Osborne, R.D., & Cormack, R.J. (1989). Gender and religion as issues in education, training and entry to work. In J. Harbison (Ed.), *Growing Up in Northern Ireland,* pp. 42-65. Belfast: The Universities Press.

O'Shea, A.T. (1987). Planning to institutionalize a programme of curriculum review and development for 11-16 year olds in Northern Ireland. In: M.B. Miles, M. Ekholm, & R. Vandenberghe (Eds.), *Lasting School Improvement: Exploring the Process of Institutionalization.* OECD, ACCO, pp. 289-316.

Spencer, A.E.C.W. (1987). Arguments for an integrated school system. In R.D. Osborne et al. (Eds), pp. 99-133.

Wilson, J,A., (1985). *Secondary School Organisation and Pupil Progress.* Belfast: NICER.

Wilson, J.A. (1986). *Transfer and the Structure of Secondary Education.* Belfast: NICER.

Wilson, J.A. (1988). *Educational Performance 1978-1987.* Belfast: NICER.

# SCOTLAND

## Peter Cuttance

### Completed Research
Recent research related to the effectiveness of schools has addressed a range of topics, including:
- variation in attainment between Catholic and secular schools;
- variation in attainment between Victorian, Edwardian, and modern schools;
- school process factors that explain variation in attainment among the above sectors;
- variation in the effectiveness of post-compulsory schooling;
- change in school performance over time.

A discussion of the research on these topics is reported in a paper entitled *The Effectiveness of Scottish Schooling* published in the proceedings of the 1988 ICSE Conference.

### Current Research
Current research related to school effectiveness is focussing on:
- the relationship of school effectiveness research to performance indicator systems for schooling.
- variation in pupil learning strategies in secondary schools.

### Educational Reforms
The above work is being undertaken against a backdrop of substantial reforms to schooling. Although the Scottish legislation is still to be presented to parliament the minister has indicated that it will be similar to the reforms for England and Wales. The main features of these reforms are:
- The devolution of a substantial degree of fiscal and managerial responsibility to locally elected school boards.
- The provision for greater choice of schools through the removal of formal catchment zones and the opportunity for schools to opt-out from LEA control, in which case they will receive their funding directly from central government.
- The introduction of a National Curriculum at both the primary and secondary level. The National Curriculum will specify in considerable detail the skills and material in a range of subjects that pupils should be able to master by specified stages (at ages 7,11, and 14 years).
- The introduction of a system of National Assessment to assess pupil attain-

ment in terms of the specified curriculum. The tests to be employed in this will be aligned with the National Curriculum, and they will be designed to provide formative and diagnostic information, in addition to summative assessments of pupil attainment.

## Synopsis of Current Research
The work on pupil learning strategies is being undertaken by Professor Entwistle in the Department of Education, at the University of Edinburgh. It is a development of earlier work that studied learning strategies among students in higher education. A pilot study to develop instruments has been completed with pupils in secondary schools. This work has been undertaken in collaboration with Professor B. Kozeki of the University of Budapest who is conducting a parallel study with a sample of Hungarian pupils.

The work on the development of a performance indicator system for schools draws heavily on the school effectiveness and school improvement literature. The work aims to develop indicators that could be employed in self-evaluation procedures by schools. It focuses on four categories of school activities at both the primary and secondary school levels:
– quality of learning and teaching
– pupil, teacher and parent satisfaction and school ethos
– management
– staffing and use of resources.

# SWEDEN

Lennart Klintestam, Lennart Grosin and Philip Holmberg

## SURVEY

So far there has not been any systematic evaluation of school development and improvement and student outcomes from which firm conclusions could be drawn on the effects of the introduction of the comprehensive school system. There is, however, a growing interest within the Swedish school system and among researchers in measuring school effects. A program for nation-wide evaluation is now being developed by the National Board of Education in cooperation with several researchers from different universities all over the country.

## ONGOING RESEARCH

There are also projects going on using methods for meta-analysis to investigate the contributions of different factors to pupil outcomes.

Up till now in school research in Sweden the concept school climate has been used only in a narrow sense, focusing mainly on the relationship between teachers and students. Also worth mentioning in this context is the research within Educational Sociology on school Codes conceptualized mainly as a result of influence from the catchment area and socioeconomic composition of the student body.

Research in Sweden on Effective Schools with the emphasis on school ethos and school climate in the more developed sense is conducted by Dr Lennart Grosin, Department of Education, University of Stockholm and funded by the University of Stockholm, the National Board of Education and the Swedish Save the Children Fund.

At the present time Dr Grosin is conducting three interrelated studies. They are at the same time a preparation for, and part of, a longitudinal investigation of the relationships between background factors, school climate and cognitive and noncognitive student outcomes.

1. The first study is a pilot investigation by means of case studies of four schools. The data consist of interviews with a large number of teachers

and students as well as with school leaders and student welfare personnel. The purpose of this study is to describe the pedagogical and social climate of the schools and to develop a frame of reference for further studies relevant to the Swedish school system.
2. In connection with this project a separate study on school leadership is being conducted.
3. The aim of the third project is to develop a less strenuous method to investigate the pedagogical and social climate in a school with the results of the case study as a starting point. Questionnaires to teachers and students have been developed for this purpose.

# EFFECTIVE SCHOOLS PROJECTS

The Effective Schools Program going on in Norrköping is described during the ICSE conference by Mr Lennart Klintestam, Superintendent of schools, presenting the paper "Norrköping Effective Schools Program: Implementation Strategies". It is to be noticed that the above-mentioned questionnaires to teachers and students have been used in Norrköping as part of the development and testing of the assessment instrument.

Two schools take part in the program: a lower and middle section school (grades 1 through 6) with 350 students, and a junior high school (grades 7 through 9) with 480 students. The project plan for the program focuses on the following six factors:

* school climate
* instructional leadership
* high expectations
* clear goals
* parental involvement
* evaluation

The following types of data are collected:

* student achievement
* student school climate questionnaire
* student self-appreciation
* attendance

It is quite clear that the process of starting up an effective schools program takes serious time and effort. Even if you can see some tangible effects after a relatively short time, the changes of attitudes to the teaching process demand an investment of time and energy sustained over several years. We have just started.

# POLICY ON SCHOOL EFFECTIVENESS

During 1988 the Ministry of Education has shown a great interest in the research on Effective Schools. The Ministry of Education also pays attention to the Norrköping Program. In a recent Government Bill you can find some suggestions influenced by effective schools research findings. Important points in this bill are:

* increased local responsibility on the commune level
* the need for an instructional leader at the building level is stressed
* goal setting
* evaluation

# SCHOOL
# EFFECTIVENESS
# RESEARCH
# REPORTS

# THE RELATIONSHIP BETWEEN SELECTED CHARACTERISTICS OF EFFECTIVE SECONDARY SCHOOLS AND STUDENT RETENTION[1]

Kenneth A. Leithwood, Stephen B. Lawton and J.Bradley Cousins
The Ontario Institute for Studies in Education, Toronto

In his recent review of research, Rumberger (1987) summarizes the personal, economic and school-related reasons why high school dropouts leave school. Special emphasis is awarded to school-related factors. Many such factors are manipulable and, even after controlling for differences in student population, schools differ widely in their retention rates.

Research on school-related factors, however, has focused largely on student behaviours in school on the implicit assumption that it is the student who must change to fit the school. Hence, interventions to reduce dropout rates often take the form of counselling and the like. But as Catterall (1987) points out, over the past 20 years in the U.S. a fourth of high school students consistently have abandoned school before graduating and many more are barely engaged (see, for example, Powell, Farrar & Cohen, 1985; McNeil, 1986). This suggests that interventions to reduce the number of dropouts ought to assume that it is the school rather than, or in addition to, the student which needs to change.

If schools must change in order to retain a larger proportion of their students, specifically what is the nature of that change? Research to date provides few clues to the answer. As Rumberger (1987) suggests, little attention has been devoted to understanding the influence of school organization, leadership, and teachers on students' decisions to leave school. What is needed, he argues, "is a more comprehensive, causal model of the dropout process" (p. 111). The objective of this study was to develop, empirically test, and refine such a causal model of school-related factors influencing the dropout rate. What follows is a description of (a) the procedure used to develop the model and the model itself, (b) methods used to test the model and the results, and (c) interpretations of results and suggestions for refining the model.

# DEVELOPMENT OF A CAUSAL MODEL OF SCHOOL RELATED FACTORS INFLUENCING DROPOUTS

School related factors influencing the dropout rate used in the development of our causal model were identified through a review of research on exemplary secondary schools. Such a starting point is justified on two grounds. First, addressing the primary reasons for leaving school (Rumberger, 1987) given the dropouts (poor performance, expulsion, negative attitude toward school concern for physical safety) are among the central objectives associated with schools identified as effective in the research literature. Characteristics of such schools ought to provide relevant insights for dropout intervention, as a consequence. Second, should characteristics of schools identified as effective in responding to their overall educational mission prove useful in explaining variations in dropout, greater coherence could be brought to school improvement efforts. That is, comprehensive efforts to improve schools could be pursued with the need – at least, in the long term – to treat dropping out as a separate problem requiring additional resources and effort. Because schools are characteristically overburdened with multiple change initiatives, the possibility of bringing greater coherence to school improvement efforts deserves serious attention until systematic evidence suggests that it is not productive.

### Method

Model development involved (a) identifying and selecting empirical studies of exemplary secondary schools to be reviewed; (b) estimated the level of confidence that was justified in knowledge claims resulting from a synthesis of the results of these studies; (c) generating categories of results to serve as components of the model and hypothesizing relationships among these components; and (d) describing the specific attributes of an effective school within each component of the model.

*Selecting Studies for Review.* Twenty original studies of effective secondary schools provided the primary data for model development. These studies were identified through a process of Education Resources Information Center (ERIC) searches, bibliographic follow-up, and prior knowledge of the researchers. Studies of effective secondary schools on which to draw were quite limited in number. For this reason, the relatively rigorous criteria often used in screening studies for review were relaxed. To be included in this review, a study only had to be concerned about exemplary secondary school practices, report original data, and provide sufficient methodological detail to be described, as in Table 1.

Table 1. Methodological Characteristics of Studies of Effective Secondary Schools.

| Authors | Categories of of Dependent Variables[a] | Design and Procedures | Sample: Nature Instruments and | Data Collection Procedures |
|---|---|---|---|---|
| 1. Arehart (1979) | S.ach. | Pre-experiment | Volunteer: 23 teachers, 26 classes | Achievement tests, class observations Q-sort |
| 2. Coleman & Hoffer (1987) | S.ach., SB | Survey | Random: approximately 25,000 students | Achievement tests, indices of student achievement |
| 3. Ford Foundation (1984) | Other | Multiple case studies | Selected: staffs in 110 schools | Interviews, observations |
| 4. Frederick, Walberg & Rasher (1979) | S. ach | Survey | Selected (convenience): 175 classrooms in 26 schools | Achievement tests, class observations |
| 5. Goodlad (1984) | | Survey case studies | Selected: 38 schools, 8,624 parents, 1,350 teachers, 17,163 students | Interviews questionnaires, class observations |
| 6. Gunn & Holdaway (1986) | Other | Survey | Population: 133 principals | Questionnaire, interviews with 10 principals |
| 7. Harnisch (1987) | S. ach | Survey | Stratified cluster: 800 schools, 18,684 students | Secondary analysis of data collected by Coleman, et al., (1982) |
| 8. Huddle (1986) | SB,T, Others unknown | Multiple case studies | Selected: 571 schools | Interviews, observations |
| 9. Keith & Page (1985) | S. ach | Survey | Random: 3,922 black students, 3,146 Hispanic students | Secondary analysis of data collected by Coleman, et al., (1982) |
| 10. Lightfoot (1983) | Other | Multiple case studies | Selected: 6 schools | Interviews, observations, documents |
| 11. Lipsitz (1984) | S. ach., SB, P, Other | Multiple case studies | Selected: 4 schools | Observation |
| 12. Little (1982) | S. ach., Other | Multiple case studies | Selected: 3 secondary 3 elementary schools, 28 administrators, 105 teachers | Interviews, observations achievement tests |
| 13. Madaus, Kellaghan, & Rakow (1976) | S. ach. | Survey | Random: 38 schools, 49 classes, 900 students | Achievement tests |
| 14. McNeil (1976) | T, SA | Multiple case studies | Selected: 4 secondary schools | Interviews, observations, document analysis |

Table 1 (cont.). Methodological Characteristics of Studies of Effective Secondary Schools.

| Authors | Categories of of Dependent Variables[a] | Design and Procedures | Sample: Nature Instruments and | Data Collection Procedures |
|---|---|---|---|---|
| 15. Morgan (1979) | SA | Multiple case studies | Selected: 3 schools, 15 classes | Class observation, interviews, questionnaires |
| 16. Murphy & Hallinger (1985) | Other | Survey | Selected: principals in 18 "effective" schools | Questionnaires |
| 17. Rossman, Corbett & Firestone (1985) | S.ach., SB | Multiple case studies | Selected: 35 schools | Interviews, observations, records, arh. tests |
| 18. Roueche & Baker (1986) | Other | Survey | Selected: 154 schools, 34 principals, 89 teachers | Questionnaire, rating scales |
| 19. Rutter, et al. (1979) | SB, S.ach. | Comparative survey | Selected: 12 schools | Pupil character- istics, school processes outcome (SB; S.ach.) battery |
| 20. Walberg & Shanahan (1983) | S.ach. | Survey | Random: 24,159 students | Secondary analysis of data collected by Coleman, et al., (1982) |

[a]Key: S. ach. - student achievement; SA - student attitude; SB - student behaviour; T - teaching and teachers; curriculum; PA - parental attitude; Other - other school features.

---

*Estimating Level of Confidence in Results.* Three methods were used to assess the status of knowledge claims resulting from a synthesis of results of the 20 studies: analysis of their methodological characteristics; a consideration of their number in comparison with the number of studies available for synthesis in related fields of inquiry; and a comparison of substantive results with results of research on exemplary elementary schools.

Only modest levels of confidence in knowledge claims are warranted, based on an analysis of the methodological characteristics of the studies reviewed: this is a consequence of variation in how effectiveness was defined, and relatively weak research designs. Among the 20 studies included in the review, some 26 specific criteria (or dependent variables) were used to operationally define the meaning of "effective" or "exemplary". These 26 criteria can be clustered into 7 categories: student achievement, student attitude, student behavior (including dropping out), teaching and teachers, curriculum quality, parental attitudes, and other school related features (e.g., self-defined school purposes). Several studies used a large number of specific criteria in making judgments of effectiveness; for example, Coleman and Hoffer (1987) used 7 criteria; Madaus, Kellaghan and Rukow (1976) used 12 criteria; Goodlad (1984) used 10 criteria; and Lipsitz (1984) used 7 criteria. In contrast, only one criterion was used by Lightfoot (1983), Morgan (1979), Roueche and Baker (1986), Gunn and Holdaway (1986) and Murphy and Hallinger (1985). Direct measures of student achievement, attitude, or behavior were used in 13 studies whereas rather global impressions of effectiveness were used in five. Dropout rates were used as a criterion of effectiveness only by Huddle (1986) and Coleman and Hoffer (1987). The studies as a whole, then, demonstrated great variation in their treatment of the dependent variable; only small numbers of studies provided evidence concerning any selected criterion of effectiveness. Furthermore, procedures used to describe the dependent variable ranged widely in their rigor from standardized achievement testing through impressions of a school's reputation by professionals outside the school.

Research designs and other relevant methodological characteristics are summarized in Table 1. Multiple case studies (8) and several different types of surveys (11) encompass most of the variation in study designs. Arehart's (1978) study can be classed as a pre-experiment, Goodlad (1984) used both surveys and case studies and Rutter, Maughan, Mortimore and Ouston (1979) labelled their own design as a "comparative survey". Neither of the dominant designs provides strong evidence of cause and effect relationships. The presence of more than one design could have increased confidence in the claims contained within the studies to the extent that such claims were similar across studies of different design. As it turned out, there was considerable variation across studies in the characteristics associated with effective schools.

A second basis for assessing the confidence to be placed in the claims made by this research concerns the relative number of studies included in the review. Most social science research is poorly controlled for a variety of ethical, economic, and other practical reasons. Confidence, as a result, develops as similar results emerge from a relatively large corpus of research. The question is: How should a corpus of 20 studies be judged?

The answer is necessarily norm-referenced and can only be suggestive. For example, Slavin's (1987) review of mastery learning strategies included 17 studies rigorously screened to provide "best evidence"; Leithwood and Montgomery's (1982) review of effective elementary school principals included 39 studies; Cousins and Leithwood's (1986) review of evaluation utilization encompassed 65 studies. By these standards, the 20 studies in this review provide a small body of evidence from which to describe effective secondary schools. This reinforces the earlier admonition to treat the results as tentative and with some skepticism.

Comparing the results of research on effective secondary schools with comparable research on elementary schools was the final method used for estimating the level of confidence to be placed with the results of this review. There is some debate about whether the characteristics of effective elementary and secondary schools ought to be similar. As compared with elementary schools, it has been suggested that secondary schools are usually larger, have greater role differentiation, and pursue more diverse outcomes, for example. These differences make communication more difficult, complicate the process of arriving at a consensus about instructional goals, and reduce the possibility of principals exercising direct instructional leadership (Firestone & Herriot, 1982; Farrar, Neufeld & Miles, 1984). Murphy and Hallinger (1985), however, argue that these differences are more apparent than real in terms of their consequences for effective schooling. Furthermore, (especially with school size factored out), little evidence is available to support claims for differences and, in any event, similarities ought to be significant. For these reasons, we considered evidence from studies of effective elementary schools which identified traits in common with those appearing in the 20 secondary school studies reviewed to be corroborating and thus contribute to confidence in their results.

Five reviews of research on effective elementary schools were used for the comparison (Weil et al., 1984; Edmonds, 1979; Cohen, 1982; Duckett et al., 1980; MacKenzie, 1983). This was a "convenience" sample of reviews for which no special justification is offered. Considerable variation among the reviews was evident in the rigor with which they were carried out methodologically and the detail in which they reported characteristics of effective elementary schools. Duckett, et al. (1980) was exemplary on both counts, offering an analysis of over 1200 studies combined with expert opinion and original case study data. Cohen (1982) provided the briefest review – in fact, an article intended to set the stage for more precisely focused and detailed reviews to follow. A major limitation of the comparison, as a whole, was the lack of detailed reporting of results in the reviews and the difficulty that presented in drawing comparisons.

Nevertheless, support was found in the reviews of effective elementary schools for at least some aspect of 23 of the 34 characteristics of effective secondary schools identified in the review of the 20 original studies.

*Generating Categories and Relationships.* Seven categories of factors within which secondary schools appear to vary in effectiveness were evident in the studies reviewed. These dimensions and the relationships among them are summarized in Figure 1: they include the goals given priority by the school, the attributes and practices of teachers and administrators, the nature of school programs and classroom instruction, school policies and organization features, school culture, and the nature of school-community relations. These categories of factors are conceptualized as having either direct and/or indirect influences on students' school experiences; these experiences, in turn, determine such outcomes of interest for students as academic achievement, types of attitudes and behaviors such as vandalism, attendance, dropping out, and the like.

The seven categories of factors identified in Figure 1 were developed through an initial reading of not only the original empirical studies eventually included in this review but theoretically-oriented discussions, as well. Once identified, the categories served as the basis for analyzing the studies reviewed and for developing the causal model. All characteristics of effective schools reported in the review studies were readily classified using these categories. Through a review of the literature which is available at present, however, it is not possible to argue strongly for the validity of the relationships among categories of characteristics suggested by the lines and arrows in Figure 1. It represents a hypothetical set of relationships with a least surface plausibility but requiring much further exploration.

*Describing specific attributes of effective schools.* A content analysis of the results of the 20 studies reviewed yielded 34 specific attributes of effective secondary schools, most identified in two or more studies. We summarize these attributes here; they are described in considerably more detail in Lawton, Leithwood, Batcher, Donaldson and Stewart (1988).

Goals included both short and long term outcomes considered important for students to achieve; they also included the conditions in the school that would be necessary to accomplish such outcomes (the term "vision" was

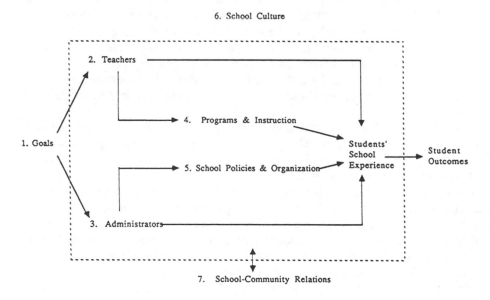

*Figure 1: A Framework Showing the Categories of Characteristics Associated with Exemplary Secondary Schools.*

101

used in reference to a combination of student outcomes and school conditions). Four studies[2] explicitly identified aspects of the school's goals as an explanation of differences in secondary school effectiveness including clarity, academic emphasis, use in decision-making, and use in creating a sense of affiliation within the school.

Nine studies[3] identified qualities of teachers found in exemplary secondary schools. These qualities addressed five aspects of the teacher (several of which overlap with aspects of "Programs and Instruction") including relevant personal qualities, view of a teacher's role, disposition toward students, and disposition toward collaboration with other teachers.

The seven studies[4] describing the nature of school administration in exemplary schools identified five clusters of phenomena: basic beliefs of administrators; the nature and use of administrators' goals; emphases among and knowledge about factors in the school influencing students' experiences, strategies used by administrators to influence factors (the studies reviewed provided most information about this cluster); and administrators' decision-making processes.

Seven studies[5] identified school policies affecting students and teachers, as well such other organizational features as school size, the use of time, the amount of school level discretion, and district support for school initiatives. Thirteen[6] of the twenty studies identified some aspect of programs and instruction as explaining the exceptional impact of effective secondary schools. For these purposes, the term "program" included the curriculum content presented to students, the degree of choice among courses available to students, and the extent of "articulation" among program components. Among the features of programs and instruction attributed greatest importance were an academic emphasis, core curriculum requirements, a relatively rich array of curriculum offerings, program coherence, and carefully planned instruction based on sound learning principles. Also, of importance were the efficient use of instructional time and the systematic monitoring of student progress.

Rossman, Corbett and Firestone (1985) define "culture" as a "unique sets of core norms, values and beliefs that are widely shared throughout the organization" (p.5). Rutter et al. (1979) use the term "ethos" in reference to "a climate of expectations or modes of behaving" (pp. 55-56), suggesting that in many cases individual actions are less important in their own right than in the accumulated impact they have on what it feels like to be a member of the school organization. Although an abstract dimension of schools, effective schools research (whether elementary or secondary oriented) has given culture, ethos or climate prominence as an explanation for differences among schools. Effective school cultures were described in the 11 studies which addressed this dimension[7] as shared and student centered.

School-community relationships were identified in three studies[8] as an important discriminator among schools which varied in effectiveness. Unlike the case in elementary schools, such relationships were not with parents directly but were instead with non-parents who had a direct contribution to make to the school and with the community at large. Effective secondary schools, it was reported, made effective use of such community resources as volunteers and student tutors. Such schools also developed solid working relationships with local business and industry (for career training, for example) and with colleges and universities (for assistance to academically talented students, for example). Effective schools were responsive to their particular social and political milieus and generated high levels of community support.

## TESTING THE MODEL OF SCHOOL-RELATED FACTORS INFLUENCING DROPOUT RATE

### Method

Descriptive information about the status of each of the categories of factors in the model in a sample of schools was provided through the responses of the schools' administrators and teachers to a questionnaire. Several means were used to obtain information about dropout rates in these same schools. Two forms of path analysis were conducted to test the model using this information.

*Sampling Procedure.* The achieved sample for the study included 58 secondary schools drawn from six school boards in the province of Ontario. Questionnaire responses were analyzed from 2,085 principals, vice principals, department heads, assistant department heads, and teachers. The number of questionnaires from schools varied from 13 to 54 per school, with an average of 36. The six school boards were selected from ten boards which had originally been nominated by the research team and were willing to participate in the study. Variation in geographical location, size of student population, wealth, and administrative structure were the criteria for choice of boards.

*Instruments.* Each school received a preliminary questionnaire during the first week of December 1987 (usually completed by the principal) in which descriptive information was collected about grades taught, student population, program characteristics, and three of five estimates of dropout rate. This instrument was developed and revised several times, once based on pilot testing with five principals.

The five measures of dropout rate or related variables included:

(a) Attendance rates: based on the number of students absent on October 5, 1987, as reported in the preliminary questionnaire;

(b) Suspension rates: based on the number of suspensions since September 8, 1987, as reported in the preliminary questionnaire;

(c) Self-reported dropout: based on the number of students who had been dropped from the rolls since September 8, 1987, as reported in the preliminary questionnaire;

(d) Ministry of education reported dropout rate calculated as the proportion of students enrolled in the school on October 1, 1986 who had left school between that date and September 30, 1987 without a diploma or certificate and not continuing their education elsewhere.

(e) Refined dropout rate: this measure, developed specifically for the study, was a response to what Williams (1987) identified as five key dimensions essential to developing meaningful data on dropout rate. These dimensions and their operational definition (Lawton et al., 1988) in this study were as follows.

*Grade levels used in the baseline population:* In this study the baseline population for a school included students classified by the school as being in grades 9 through 12 who were within the defined age range;
*Age range of students who can be classified as dropouts:* Only students between the ages of 14 and 21 were included in the baseline population;
*Length and dates of the accounting period for which rates are calculated:* The accounting period in this study was the 12 month period from October 1 through September 30 of the following year, credits earned for grade classifications were therefore as of September 1, so that summer school credits could be used for graduation in the academic year just completed;
*Allowable time period for unexplained absences:* In this study a dropout was a student belonging to the baseline population who left school without receiving a diploma and for whom no other publicly funded school was requested his or her academic records. In Ontario, a student who has been absent without excuse for 20 consecutive school days is dropped from the roles.
*Setting used to identify acceptable alternative eduction:* Only transfers as full-time students to other publicly funded diploma granting schools, counted as transfers; excluded were evening school programs, adult continuing education centres, entering the armed forces, and marriage. Those who had moved to other provinces of countries, or who moved to private schools, were counted as still enrolled in school since it was not possible to determine their exact status. Their numbers were very small relative to the numbers who left school altogether and who remained in Ontario.

Information about the attributes of each school needed to test the model of school-related factors influencing dropout rates was collected using a questionnaire developed for the study. This questionnaire included 34 closed items which sampled the attributes of effective schools identified in the literature review (it also included 19 additional items relevant to the purposes of the larger project).

*Data Analysis.* All data were keyed into a data file for computer analysis using the Statistical Package for the Social Sciences-X (SPSS-X) and LER-TAP. The latter program was used to calculate Hoyt estimates of reliability for all measurement scales. Varying from 0.0 to 1.0, the Hoyt estimate provides an index of a scale's internal consistency. SPSS-X was used to aggregate data to the school level and to calculate means, standard deviations, percentages, and path coefficients. To calculate scale scores at the school level, item means were calculated for valid responses within items. Subsequently, item means were summed. By this process, maximum use was made of all available information and complete data sets were available at the school level for all independent variables.

Path analysis was selected to analyze the relationships among process and output variables because it provides a method of testing the validity of causal inferences for pairs of variables while controlling for the effects of other variables. In addition, path diagrams provide heuristic portrayals of systems of relationships which are well suited to the systems framework used to organize the variables in this study.

Data were analyzed using the LISREL VI analysis of covariance structure approach to path analysis and maximum likelihood estimates (Jöreskog & Sörbom, 1981). Using LISREL, path models can be specified and the influence of exogenous variables corresponding to independent constructs on endogenous variables (influenced by other variables in the system) corresponding the the dependent construct can be estimated. Parameters (regression coefficients) can be estimated to assess the extent to which specified relations are statistically significant. Limitations on the meaningfulness of parameters are offset by the extent to which models can be shown to fit the data. A given model is said to fit the data if the pattern of variances and covariances derived from it does not differ significantly from the pattern of variances and covariances associated with the observed variables.

### Results

Table 2 reports Hoyt estimates of reliability and descriptive statistics for each of the seven constructs in the model used to explain dropping out. Variables were constructed by computing the average of questionnaire item scores for each school. The number of items included in the questionnaire to measure each construct also appears in Table 2. Acceptable levels of reliability (i.e., Hoyt estimate $\geq$ .50) were obtained for the constructs Goals, Teachers, Administrators, and School Culture. Measures of Programs and Instruction and School-Community Relations yielded reliability coefficients that

105

were very low and the measure of school policies and organization was found not to be reliable. However, the model developed to explain dropping out and the questionnaire used to collect the data were used in this study for the first time. Furthermore, items designed to measure each category of factors only sampled attributes of effective schools encompassed by each category. For these reasons, it seemed appropriate to explore the reasons for the unreliable measures, as is done below, rather than reject the measures.

Table 2: Reliability of Measures of Factor Categories

| Category of Factors | Number of Items | Hoyt Estimate of Reliability | Mean | S.D. | Range |
|---|---|---|---|---|---|
| Goals | 5 | .70 | 2.65 | .19 | 1 - 4 |
| Teachers | 5 | .53 | 3.16 | .16 | 1 - 4 |
| Administrators | 5[a] | .69 | 2.91 | .30 | 1 - 4 |
| School Policies and Organization | 5 | .00 | 2.85 | .12 | 1 - 4 |
| Programs and Instruction | 5 | .36 | 3.03 | .15 | 1 - 4 |
| School Culture | 5[b] | .52 | 2.85 | .21 | 1 - 4 |
| School-Community Relations | 4 | .31 | 2.99 | .19 | 1 - 4 |

[a] Counting sub-items increases the total to 14 items.
[b] Counting sub-items increases the total to 11 items.

Figure 2 presents the path diagram used to assess the effects of the model's factor categories on student dropout rate. The refined measure of dropout rate was used as the dependent variable because it was considered conceptually more valid than other measures; also, much more of its variation was explained by predictor variables than was that for most of the alternative dropout measures (see Table 3). School Culture and Goals were treated as exogenous variables in the analysis whereas all other constructs were treated as endogenous variables. Direct relationships between a factor category and dropout rate, reported as a negative path coefficients, means that the effect of the category is to reduce the dropout rate. That is, higher category scores (e.g., Teacher Effectiveness) are associated with lower dropout rates. Of the five categories directly affecting dropout, three were negative and statistically significant. School-community relations (-.30), Teachers (-.30), and Programs and Instruction (-.29). Together, the direct and indirect effects of variables in the model (see Table 4) explain 62 percent of the variation in dropout rate.

Beginning at the left of the model, with the exogenous variables, Goals and School Culture, there are two dominant influences on dropout rate. The

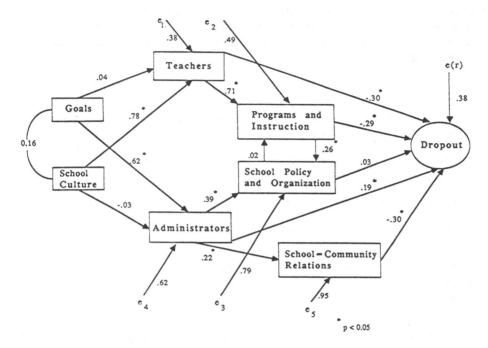

*Figure 2: Path Analysis Model for Explaining Dropout Rate (n = 58; LISREL path model using Maximum Likelihood Estimates)*

strongest path suggests that School Culture has a positive influence on Teachers (.78). Teachers, in turn, affect dropping out both directly (-.30) and through their influence on Programs and Instruction (.71). The second dominant path influencing the dropout rate begins with Goals: these have a strong influence on School Administrators (.62). The primary influence of Administrators appears to be through School-Community Relations (.21) which, in turn, was found to be a negative predictor of dropout rate (-62). Administrators also have some influence on School Policies and Organization (.39) but this variable did not predict dropout rate. The direct effect of Administrators on dropout rate was significant and positive, implying a tendency for schools with "more effective" administrators to have higher dropout rates.

As Figure 2 suggests, most of the variance in dropout explained by the model is attributable to the direct and indirect effects of Teachers and Programs and Instruction, the indirect effect of School Culture, and the direct effect of School-Community Relations. Goodness of fit indices suggest the need to continue to improve the model (GFI = .756; AGFI = .325; RMSR = .236; see Joreskog & Sorbom, 1981) although such further analysis is beyond the scope of the paper.

Table 5 displays the intercorrelations among the five alternative measures related to dropping out used in the study. All correlations were positive and, except the correlation between absence rate and the self-reported dropout rate, all were statistically significant. The highest correlates were between the refined dropout measure and suspension rates (.77) and Ministry student retirement rates (.65).

Table 3: Path Coefficients (Direct Effect) for Five Dropout Measures[a]
(Regression Coefficients; n=58)

| Alternative Paths | Refined Dropout | Absence Rate | Suspension Rate | Self-Reported Dropout Rate | Ministry Reitrement Rate |
|---|---|---|---|---|---|
| 1. From Teachers | -.43 ** | .54 ** | -.11 | -.34 * | -.31 ** |
| 2. From Programs and Instruction | -.32 ** | .04 | -.28 * | -.32 ** | -.14 |
| 3. From School Policies and Organization | -.16 | -.37 ** | -.09 | -.19 | .10 |
| 4. From Administrators | .18 | .31 ** | -.05 | .14 | .00 |
| 5. From School-Community Relations | -.62 ** | .36 ** | -.25 * | -.50 ** | .26 * |
| Unexplained Variation | .45 ** | .61 ** | .85 ** | .60 ** | .77 ** |

* $p \leq .05$;          ** $p \leq .01$

Table 4: Estimates of Direct and Indirect Effects of Model Constructs on the Refined Measure of School Dropout Rate
(Maximum Likelihood Estimates; n = 58)

| Model Constructs | Direct Effects | Indirect Effects | Total Effects | Total Variance Explained |
|---|---|---|---|---|
| Goals | - | .06 | .06 | .001 |
| School Culture | - | -.40 | -.40 | .16 |
| Teachers | -.30 | -.20 | -.50 | .25 |
| Administrators | .03 | .00 | .14 | .02 |
| School Pol./Org. | .03 | .00 | .03 | .001 |
| Prog. & Instruction | -.29 | .01 | -.28 | .08 |
| School-Comm. Rel. | -.30 | - | -.30 | .09 |

Table 5: Intercorrelations Among Alternative Dropout Measures
        (Pearson product-moment correlation coefficients; n=58)

| Measure | Absence Rate | Suspension Rate | Self-Report D/O Rate | Ministry Ret. Rate |
|---------|-------------|-----------------|---------------------|--------------------|
| Refined D/O Rate | .59 ** | .77 ** | .48 ** | .65 ** |
| Absence Rate | | .57 ** | .18 | .31 ** |
| Suspension Rate | | | .21 * | .57 ** |
| Self-Reported D/O Rate | | | | .29 ** |

\* p ≤ .05   \*\* p ≤ .01

Table 6 reports correlations between the scores on individual items measuring each construct in the model and the refined dropout measure. The overall Pearson correlation for each set of items and dropout is reported as well. Negative correlations indicate a positive relationship with reduced dropout rates. These correlations provide more specific information about the particular attributes within each component of the model sampled in the questionnaire that contribute most to school retention (i.e., components having a statistically significant, negative correlation with dropout). These attributes included:

| 1. Goals | - the importance attributed to intellectual goals for students |
|---|---|
| 2. Teachers | - the amount of time teachers spend with students outside regular classes<br>- high expectations for all students by staff<br>- high levels of collaboration among teachers in making curriculum and instructional decisions |
| 3. Administrators | - (no items significantly related to reduced dropout rates) |
| 4. School Policies and Organization | - a high proportion of the school day devoted to instructional (vs. procedural) matters<br>- an orientation in the school not preoccupied with simply "running a smooth ship" and "keeping the lid on" |
| 5. Programs and Instruction | - a strongly academic curriculum<br>- a relatively large proportion of class time spent on instruction vs. procedural matters |
| 6. School Culture and Ethos | - a low incidence of physical accidents and injuries and verbal disputes<br>- a high level of respect for the personal possessions of others |

- a shared sense of ownership in the school building
- a priority for the development of academic as opposed to athletic, social or work skills

7. School-Community Relations — a positive image of the school in the community

Table 6: Correlations Between Individual Items and Refined Measure of Dropout Rate
(Pearson product-moment correlation coefficients; n=58)

| Model Construct | Individual Items[a] | | | | Overall | |
|---|---|---|---|---|---|---|
| | 1 | 2 | 3 | 4 | 5 | |
| Goals | .33 ** | -.67 | .21 | .48 ** | .34 ** | .15 |
| Teachers | -.13 | -.58 ** | .71 ** | -.38 ** | .01 | -.62 ** |
| Administrators | -.06 | .05 | .20 | .15 | .06 | .12 |
| School Pol. & Org. | .49 ** | .14 | -.50 ** | -.32 ** | .05 | -.09 |
| Prog. & Instruct. | -.67 ** | .16 | .17 | -.50 ** | -.24 * | -.65 ** |
| School Culture | -.69 ** | -.52 ** | -.17 | -.28 * | -.66 ** | -.73 ** |
| School-Comm. Rel. | -.64 ** | -.09 | -.08 | -.03 | —[b] | -.62 ** |

[a] *p ≤ .05;   ** p ≤ .01
[b] This scale has 4 items

# SUMMARY AND CONCLUSION

The retention of students in secondary school until graduation has been justified as a worthwhile goal on individual, social and economic grounds (Wetzel, 1987; William T. Grant Foundation, 1988). Most efforts to increase retention rates, however, assume that students must change: their valuing of the school experience, relationships with adults, orientation toward the experiences offered by the school, and the like. Perhaps this is due in part to an assumption implicit in much of the literature on dropping out: that student retention is a problem of the individual student (Axumi, 1987; Bryk & Thum, 1989; Rumberger, 1983; Sinclair & Ghory, 1987). Indeed, variables such as race, socio-economic status, attitudes, behaviors, ability and self-discipline have been identified as and tested predictors of student retention in many studies of dropping out.

Recent efforts to study the dropout phenomenon have shifted from an almost exclusive focus on student variables toward explanatory frameworks based on school organization (e.g., Bryk & Thum, 1989; Coleman & Hoffer, 1987; Wehlage & Rutter, 1986). Bryk and Thum conclude, for example, that "internal organization features of schools can have significant educative consequences for all students, especially at-risk youth" (p. 28). A presupposition of this theoretical orientation is that at-risk students confer a negative evaluation to their schools by leaving them.

Our study accepts this premise. We inquired into the ways in which schools might change in order to be a more engaging environment from the point of view of at-risk students. By "engaging" we did not mean "entertaining". We hypothesized that schools which were unusually effective in achieving the full range of academic and other goals characteristic of secondary schools would also be considered sufficiently meaningful to students to cause larger than usual proportions of them to stay through graduation.

To test this hypothesis, a model of the characteristics of an effective secondary school was developed from a synthesis of 20 original empirical studies. The model was based on several attributes, each associated with one of seven categories of factors; relationships among the categories were specified in the model. Teachers and administrators in 58 schools responded to a questionnaire inquiring about the status of the effective school factors in their schools. Results of a path analysis carried out with the data suggested that the model explained about 60 percent of the variation in dropout rate across the 58 schools.

While these results provided support for our hypothesis, several unresolved problems limit the confidence that can be placed in the results and argue for further refinement of instruments. First, of the seven sub-scales in the questionnaire used to measure categories of school effectiveness, two had low reliabilities and one was manifestly unreliable. Individual item analysis identified the sources of this unreliability. Second, the questionnaire only sampled attributes of effectiveness identified in the literature review. Attributes not measured by the instrument may change sub-scale reliabilities, alter the amount of variation in dropout explained by the model and/or alter the path coefficients estimated for the model.

Another unresolved problem evident in the results concerned the category of factors called Administrators. The weak contribution of this category of factors directly and through School Policies, suggested in the path analysis, invites some form of explanation; these results are contrary to what was to be expected based on previous research. Taken as a whole, the attributes of administrator effectiveness measured involve active and highly visible intervention in the way the school is run, as well as in the nature of classroom curricula and instructional practices. Such intervention may not be warranted in schools that have achieved high levels of effectiveness, as reflected perhaps by high pupil retention. Indeed, such an interventionist image of administrative effectiveness has emerged largely from studies of principals faced with the task of "turning a school around" or improving a school serving disadvantaged students often with inadequate resources. As well, it may be that school systems have placed principals capable of the type of intervention upon which the survey was based in schools perceived to have the greatest need for improvement. While these explanations are clearly speculative, they are similar to those suggested in recent research reviewed by Hechinger (1988). This research finds little effect of administrators and bureaucratic structures on schools with high achieving students but important effects on schools with low achieving students.

Results of the study, in combination with its limitations, suggest several useful directions for future research. One such direction involves continued research on the characteristics of effective secondary schools. The present study supports the potential of "school improvement" to provide a coherent focus for secondary school reform efforts. Such coherence, however, depends on developing a richer, more detailed model (or models) of effective secondary schools than is presently available; it also depends upon a knowledge base in which more confidence can be placed than the current knowledge base warrants. This view suggests the value of a research strategy which combines qualitative case studies of secondary schools known to be exemplary with large scale, quantitative studies of a confirmatory nature.

There are several, alternative definitions of the dependent variable in studies of effective secondary schools. The annual dropout rate was the definition used in the present study. Our strongest pattern of results showed that teachers, as carriers of the school culture, impact favorably on the school dropout rate both directly through their disposition toward students and collaboration with peers and indirectly through their influence on programs and instruction. Similar variables were found to predict dropout rate by Bryk and Thum (1989) but there are few other studies that have made the link between such predictors and this specific outcome variable. Other definitions of outcome incorporate the academic, vocational, social and emotional goals aspired to for students. Subsequent research ought to be sensitive to which attributes of an effective schools model(s) contribute most to which outcomes. Previous studies have not provided this discrimination.

Results of the present study begin to provide a "... causal model of the dropout process" called for by Rumberger (1987, p. 111). However, it is not clear how much of the variance in dropout rate is explained by school-related factors as compared with other factors (e.g., student and family characteristics). Indeed, recent Canadian surveys of students and graduates (Sullen, 1988; Karp, 1988) point to a mix of student centered (e.g., frustration, work attraction, family and personal problems) as well as school-based (e.g., lack of relevancy in curriculum, teacher indifference) factors discriminating dropouts and non-dropouts. Expanding the model, through further research, will be necessary if a comprehensive explanation of dropout is to be provided.

Finally, results of this study and future research which has been suggested are of little practical consequence without parallel knowledge about school improvement processes. This is an area of knowledge expanding rapidly at the present time (see, for example, Louis & Dentler, 1988) but worthy of support in parallel with continued research on effective secondary schools.

# NOTES

1. The research reported in this paper, part of a larger study, was funded under contract by the Ministry of Education, Ontario. The paper reflects the views of the authors and not necessarily those of the Ministry. The larger study is reported, in its entirety in Lawton, et al. (1988).
2. See Huddle (1986), Lightfoot (1986), Ford Foundation (1984), and Lipsitz (1984).
3. See Huddle (1986), Murphy & Hallinger (1985), Roueche & Baker (1986), Lipsitz (1984), Rutter, et al. (1979), Ford Foundation (1984), Goodlad (1984), Madaus et al. (1976), and Lightfoot (1983).
4. These studies were Roueche & Baker (1986), Huddle (1986), Lightfoot (1983), Lipsitz (1984), Coleman & Hoffer (1987), Ford Foundation (1984), and Rutter, et al. (1979).
5. Studies providing data concerning these issues were Harnisch (1987), Huddle (1986), Ford Foundation (1984), Lipsitz (1984), McNeil (1986), Goodlad (1984), and Rutter, et al. (1979).
6. See Lipsitz (1984), Roeche & Baker (1986), Huddle (1986), Lightfoot (1983), Coleman and Hoffer (1987), Keith & Page (1985), Arehart (1979), Goodlad (1984), Walberg & Shanahan (1983), Harnisch (1987), Murphy & Hallinger (1985), Morgan (1979), and Frederick, et al. (1973).
7. See Lipsitz (1984), Roueche & Baker (1986), Huddle (1986), Murphy & Hallinger (1985), Goodlad (1984), Rossman, et al. (1985), Rutter, et al. (1979), Coleman & Hoffer (1987), Lightfoot (1983), Ford Foundation (1984), and Gunn & Holdaway (1987).
8. See Huddle (1986), Ford Foundation (1984), and Lipsitz (1984).

# REFERENCES

Arehart, J.E. (1979). Student opportunity to learn related to student achievement of objectives in a probability unit. *Journal of Educational Research, 72* (5), 253-259.

Bryk, A.S., & Thum, Y.M. (1989). *The effects of high school organization on dropping out: An exploratory investigation.* New Brunswick, NJ: Center for Policy Research in Education.

Catteral, J.S. (1987). An intensive group counseling dropout prevention intervention: Some cautions on isolating at-risk adolescents within high schools. *American Educational Research Journal, 24* (4), 521-540.

Cohen, M. (1982, October). Effective schools: Accumulating research findings. *American Education, 18* (1), 13-16.

Coleman, J.S., Hoffer, T., & Kilgore, S. (1982). *High school achievement.* New York: Basic Books.

Coleman, J.S., & Hoffer, T. (1987). *Public and private high schools.* New York: Basic Books.

Cousins, J.B., & Leithwood, K.A. (1986). Current empirical research on evaluation utilization. *Review of Educational Research, 56* (3), 331-364.

Duckett, W.R. (1980). *Why do some urban schools succeed?* Bloomington, IN: Phil Delta Kappa.

Edmonds, R. (1979). Effective schools for the urban poor. *Educational Leadership, 37*, 15-24.

Farrar, E., Neufeld, B., & Miles, M.B. (1984). Effective school programs in high school: Social promotion or movement by merit. *Phi Delta Kappan, 65* (10), 701-706.

Firestone, W.A. & Herriot, R.E. (1982). Prescriptions for effective elementary schools: Don't fix secondary schools. *Educational Leadership, 40* (3), 51-53.

Ford Foundation. (1984). *City high schools: A recognition of progress.* New York: Ford Foundation.

Frederick, W.C., Walberg, H.J., & Rashe, S.P. (1979). Time, teacher comments and achievement in urban high schools. *Journal of Educational Research, 73* (2), 63-65.

Goodlad, J.I. (1984). *A place called school.* New York: McGraw-Hill.

Gunn, J.A., & Holdaway, E.A. (1986). Perceptions of effectiveness, influence and satisfaction of senior high school principals. *Educational Administration Quarterly, 22* (2), 43-62.

Harnisch, D.L. (1987). Characteristics associated with effective public high schools. *Journal of Educational Research, 4* (80), 233-241.

Hechinger, P. (1988). Does school structure matter? *Educational Researcher. 17* (5), 10-12.

Huddle, E. (1986). Creating a successful secondary school. *NASSP Bulletin, 70* (491), 64-69.

Jöreskog, K.G., & Sörbom, D. (1981). *Lisrel: Analysis of linear structural relations by the method of maximum likelihood. Versions 5 & 6*, Chicago: National Education Resources.

Karp, E. (1988). *The dropout phenomenon in Ontario secondary schools.* Toronto: The Queen's Printer for Ontario.

Keith, T.Z., & Page, E.B. (1985). Do Catholic high schools improve minority student achievement? *American Educational Research Journal, 22* (3), 337-349.

Lawton, S.B., Leithwood, K.A., Batcher, E., Donaldson, E., & Stewart R. (1988). *Student Retention and Transition.* Toronto: The Ministry of Education, Ontario.

Leithwood, K.A., & Montgomery, D. (1982). The role of the elementary school principal in program improvement. *Review of Educational Research, 52* (82), 309-334.

Lightfoot, S.L. (1983). *The good high school.* New York: Basic Books.

Lipsitz, J. (1984). *Successful schools for young adolescents.* New Brunswick, NJ: Transaction Books.

Little, J.W. (1982). Norms of collegiality and experimentation: Workplace conditions of school success. *American Educational Research Journal, 19* (3), 325-340.

Louis, K., & Dentler, R. (1988). Knowledge use and school improvement. *Curriculum Inquiry, 18* (1), 33-62.

Mackenzie, D.E. (1983). Research for school improvement: An appraisal of some recent trends. *Educational Researcher, 12* (4), 5-16.

Madaus, G.F., Kellaghan, T., & Rukow, E.A. (1976). School and class differences in performance on the learning certificate examination. *The Irish Journal of Education, 10* (1), 41-50.

McNeil, L.M. (1986). *Contradictions of control.* New York: Routledge & Kegan Paul.

Morgan, E.P. (1979). Effective teaching in the urban high school. *Urban Education, 14* (2), 161-181.

Murphy, J., & Hallinger, P. (1985). Effective high schools - what are the common characteristics? *NASSP Bulletin, 69* (477), 18-22.

National Opinion Research Center. (1980). *High school and beyond information users: Base year (1980) data.* Chicago: The Center.

Powell, A.G., Farrar, E., & Cohen, D.K. (1985). *The shopping mall high school.* Boston: Houghton Mifflin Co.

Rossman, G., Corbett, A., & Firestone, W. (1985). *Professional cultures, improvement efforts and effectiveness: Findings from a study of three high schools.* Philadelphia: Research for Better Schools.

114

Roueche, J.E., & Baker, G.A. (Eds.) (1986). *Profiling excellence in America's schools.* Arlington, VA: American Association of School Administrators.

Rumberger, R.W. (1983). Dropping out of high school: The influence of race, sex, and family background. *American Educational Research Journal, 20* (2), 199-220.

Rumberger. R.W. (1987). High school dropouts: A review of issues and evidence. *Review of Educational Research, 57* (2), 101-121.

Rutter, M., Maughan, B., Mortimore, P., & Ouston, J. (1979). *Fifteen thousand hours: Secondary schools and their effects on children.* Cambridge, MA: Harvard University Press.

Sinclair, R.L. & Ghory, W.J. (1987). *Reaching marginal students: A primary concern for school renewal.* New York: McCutchan.

Slavin, R.E. (1987). Mastery learning reconsidered. *Review of Educational Research , 57* (2), 175-214.

Sulliran, M. (1988). *A comparative analysis of dropouts and non-dropouts in Ontario secondary schools.* Toronto: The Queen's Printer for Ontario.

Walberg, H.J., & Shanahan, T. (1983). High school effects on individual students. *Educational Researcher, 12* (7), 4-9.

Watson, C. (1977). *Focus on dropouts.* Toronto: The Ontario Institute for Studies In Education.

Wehlage, G.G. & Rutter, R.A. (1986). Dropping out: How much do schools contribute to the problem? In G. Natriello (Ed.). *School dropouts: Patterns and policies.* New York: Teachers College Press.

Weil, M., Marshalec, B., Mitman, A., Murphy, J., Hallinger, P., & Pruyn, J. (1984, April). *Effective and typical schools: How different are they?* Paper presented at the annual meeting of the American Educational Research Association, Chicago.

Wetzel, J. R. (1987). *American youth: A statistical snapshot.* Washington, D.C.: William T. Grant Foundation Commission on Work, Family and Citzenship.

William T. Grant Foundation (1988). *The forgotten half: Non-college youth in America.* Washington, D.C.: William T. Grant Foundation Commission on Work, Family and Citzenship.

Williams, P.A. (1987). *Standardizing school dropout measures.* New Brunswick, NJ: Center for Policy Research in Education, Rutgers University.

# CONTEXTUAL DIFFERENCES IN MODELS FOR EFFECTIVE SCHOOLING IN THE USA

Charles Teddlie
Louisiana State University, New Orleans

Sam Stringfield
Northwest Regional Educational Laboratory, Denver

Robert Wimpelberg and Peggy Kirby
University of New Orleans, New Orleans

## CONTEXTUAL DIFFERENCES IN MODELS FOR EFFECTIVE SCHOOLING IN THE USA

Effective schools research has become a popular basis for a large and increasing number of school improvement models and studies (Clark & McCarthy 1983; Levine 1982; McCormack-Larkin & Kritek 1982). The need of school administrators to respond to accountability pressures has led to uncritical adoption of some of the well-publicized school effectiveness findings.

There is consensus among many school administrators and school effectiveness advocates on five correlates of school effectiveness popularized by Edmonds (1981): basic skills acquisition, high expectations for student achievement, strong instructional leadership, frequent monitoring of student progress, and orderly environment. School effectiveness consultants are earning lucrative fees assisting school administrators in improving their schools' performance on these widely recognized correlates of school effectiveness.

This activity in school improvement is occurring despite numerous criticisms of school effectiveness research and its methodology (Cuban 1984; Good & Brophy 1986; Purkey & Smith 1983). Purkey and Smith concluded that there is no consensus on what constitutes the salient characteristics of effective schools. Similarly, D'Amico (1982) concluded that the effectiveness characteristics cited in four major studies of school effectiveness

117

(Brookover & Lezotte 1979; Edmonds & Frederiksen 1979; Duckett et al. 1980; Rutter et al. 1979) do not match. In fact, D'Amico concluded that each effective school may be one-of-a-kind or idiosyncratic.

In response to this criticism, Lezotte (1982) contended that a general framework for improving schools was available based on the extant school effectiveness research. He also noted that, since alternative research-based approaches to school improvement are not available, administrators may adopt the effective schools framework because it is the "only game in town."

The problem with this "only game in town" is that it is based on a body of research that was conducted primarily in low socioeconomic status (SES), urban schools (Good & Brophy 1986; Purkey & Smith 1983). Good and Brophy concluded, therefore, that the implications of the effective schools literature for suburban schools, for example, are uncertain.

Two related issues need to be addressed by school effectiveness researchers and school improvement advocates: Are the characteristics that define effective schools in one context the same as those that are found in others? Are techniques that produce an effective school in one context the same as those that should be employed in other contexts? Context can be defined along a number of dimensions, including SES of student body, different grade level configurations, geographical distinctions, public versus private schooling, etc.

Fortunately, we no longer have to speculate regarding variations in effectiveness correlates based on school context. Led by the oft-repeated suggestion that researchers should study schools in different contexts, at least three recent research efforts (Hallinger & Murphy 1986; Miller & Yelton 1987; Teddlie et al. 1984) have examined school effectiveness across different SES levels. As noted by Wimpelberg, Teddlie and Stringfield (1989), results from studies sensitive to context factors outside the rubric of school effectiveness research (i.e., Benson 1982; Thomas et al. 1982) may also be applicable.

This article will concentrate on SES as a context variable, since more research has used this variable than any other. Additionally, sociologists, psychologists, and educators (e.g., Blumberg 1972; Curtis & Jackson 1977) have long recognized the importance of different SES groups.

It is widely accepted that SES has a variety of measurable effects on the behavior of individuals within groups. For instance, Cohen and Hodges (1972) found that individuals from lower SES groups feel powerless, deprived and insecure. Perhaps, as a result of these characteristics, their social activity tends to be oriented toward family and away from participation in voluntary organizations. Within schools, it has been demonstrated that students from different SES groups have different dropout rates (Hess 1986).

A reading of the general research literature on SES and behavior indicates that much behavioral research has been undertaken with the assumption that middle class behavior is the standard against which the behavior of other classes is to be judged. Yando, Seitz, and Zigler (1979) refer to this as a

118

"deficit" model in which low-SES groups are considered inferior to middle-SES groups.

Yando, Seitz, and Zigler (1979) reject this deficit model. They state that we should

> adopt in its place a difference approach in which no group is considered superior to any other....A commitment to such a difference approach would urge behavioral scientists, and ultimately laymen, to deal with the central question of how human variation can be exploited for the enrichment of all members of society. (p.2)

Implicit in this position is the idea that different methods may be needed to optimize outcomes for groups from different social contexts.

The remainder of this article will be divided into three sections: (1) a brief summary of methods from recent studies of school effectiveness in Louisiana; (2) a listing of the contextually sensitive characteristics of effective schools from different SES levels; 3) a discussion of context issues that should be addressed in future school effectiveness research.

### Methods from the Second and Third Phases of the Louisiana School Effectiveness Study (LSES-II and LSES-III)

The findings presented here are based on two phases of the Louisiana School Effectiveness Study (LSES). Since many of the results referred to in this article are from the LSES, a brief description of the methods used in that study will be given. More detailed descriptions of the methods for LSES-II (Teddlie et al. 1984) and LSES-III (Stringfield et al. 1985; Teddlie & Lauricella 1986) can be found elsewhere.

The LSES consists of five phases ranging from a pilot study (1980-82), to a macro-level study of 76 randomly selected schools (1982-84), to micro-level case studies of 16 schools (1984-86), to a proposed school improvement study, and finally to a model building phase. The results referred to here are from the macro- and micro-level studies.

Data for LSES-II were collected during the 1982-83 school year in the third grade of 76 schools from 12 school districts. The study sample was drawn to be highly representative of the statewide population. The 12 participating districts included urban, suburban, and rural areas from northern, central, and southern regions of Louisiana. All schools from the districts were stratified on two dimensions: average percent correct on the language test of the Louisiana Basic Skills Test and average educational level of students' mothers.

A multivariate analysis of variance design was employed to analyze part of the LSES-II data. Two independent variables were utilized: (1) whether the student body of the school came from middle or low SES backgrounds, and (2) whether the student body scored above, at, or below how well they were predicted to score on a norm-referenced test (Scholastic Testing Service 1983). This design allowed for the comparison of six groups of schools: (1) middle-SES effective schools, (2) middle-SES typical schools, (3) middle-SES ineffective schools, 4) low-SES effective schools, 5) low-SES typical schools, and 6) low-SES ineffective schools.

In addition to the norm-referenced test, the researchers gathered social psychological data from 76 principals, 250 teachers, and more than 5400 students. These social psychological data were gathered from questionnaires adapted from the Brookover et al. (1979) study of effective schooling in elementary schools in Michigan.

As indicated in Table 1, there were large SES differences between the low- and middle-SES schools in LSES-II. As indicated in Table 2, students in the effective low-SES schools were able to outscore students from the ineffective middle-SES schools on the norm-referenced test that was utilized in the study.

Table 1: Selected Means for Student's Parents' Socioeconomic Characteristics for Six Types of Schools

A. Average Education of Mothers

| | | Socioeconomic Characteristics of Students' Parents | |
| --- | --- | --- | --- |
| | | Middle SES | Low SES |
| School's Performance Relative to Expectation | Effective | 3.35 | 2.70 |
| | Typical | 3.38 | 2.74 |
| | Ineffective | 3.28 | 2.87 |

B. Percentage of Students with Professional Fathers

| | | Socioeconomic Characteristics of Students' Parents | |
| --- | --- | --- | --- |
| | | Middle SES | Low SES |
| School's Performance Relative to Expectation | Effective | 33% | 11% |
| | Typical | 43% | 12% |
| | Ineffective | 33% | 10% |

*Note.* For mother's educational level: 2 = attended high school; 3 = graduated from high school

Table 2: Performance on EDS Basic Skills Tests for Six Types of Schools

| | | Socioeconomic Characteristics of Students' Parents | |
| --- | --- | --- | --- |
| | | Middle SES | Low SES |
| School's Performance Relative to Expectation | Effective | 108.13 | 97.06 |
| | Typical | 103.70 | 91.53 |
| | Ineffective | 93.75 | 85.61 |

LSES-III followed in part the general design of LSES-II. However, two major differences existed: 1) whereas LSES-II consisted mainly of quantitative data collection and analyses, LSES-III focused on a case study approach by including qualitative data collection and analyses, and 2) LSES-III incorporated a classroom level teacher effectiveness study within a general school effectiveness study. Field research and data collection for LSES-III were conducted during the 1984-85 school session.

At the onset of LSES-III, the research team decided to select nine matched pairs of schools. The study population included all schools with third grades from the same 12 districts used in LSES-II, as well as a large urban district. The total study population consisted of 345 schools.

Regression models similar to those from LSES-II were used to select schools for LSES-III. Two testing years (1982-83, 1983-84) were used. A school was considered for inclusion in the study based on three criteria. A school became a candidate for study if the school scored above prediction (+ residual score) both testing years or below prediction (- residual score) both testing years. Consideration was also given to any school that scored substantially above or below prediction at least one testing year. Finally, a school become a study candidate if a matching outlier having an opposite direction residual score and similar SES composition could be identified within the specific school system (or in a contiguous system consisting of small rural districts).

Based upon the previously mentioned selection criteria and constraints, nine pairs of schools were chosen for the study sample. Upon observation, the third grade status in one school proved to be anomalous within the school and it, along with its concomitant opposite, was omitted from the sample, leaving eight matched pairs.

## Characteristics Associated with Effectiveness in Middle- and Low-SES Schools

Data from many studies indicate that there are a number of characteristics of effective schools that should be found regardless of the SES of the school.

121

These include:
  (1) clear academic mission and focus,
  (2) orderly environment
  (3) high academic engaged time-on-task, and
  (4) frequent monitoring of student progress.

Results from the LSES confirm that these attributes are characteristic of effective schools across SES groups ( Stringfield & Teddlie, 1988; Teddlie, Stringfield, Wimpelberg, & Kirby 1987).

While there are definite similarities between effective middle- and low-SES schools, there are a number of very interesting differences between the two groups of schools. Our (Teddlie & Stringfield, 1985; Stringfield & Teddlie, 1988) research indicates that effective schools have implemented somewhat different strategies, depending on the SES context of the particular school under examination. Characteristics associated with effectiveness in middle- and low-SES schools are found in Table 3.

LSES results indicated a difference in future educational expectations by teachers in effective middle- and low-SES schools. Teachers in effective middle-SES schools held very high future and present educational expectations for their students, while teachers in effective low-SES schools held high present, but more modest future educational expectations. While teachers in effective low-SES schools had modest long-term expectations for their students' achievement, they held firm academic expectations for their students while at their schools.

Results from research in California (Hallinger & Murphy 1986) confirm these differences with regard to teacher expectations. The teacher expectations results are particularly interesting since previous school effectiveness models (Brookover & Lezotte 1979; Edmonds 1981) call for uniformly high expectations as a cornerstone for effective schooling.

To further illustrate this point, the pattern of means from LSES-II for one question dealing with teachers' expectations is presented in Table 4. There is an exaggerated difference in teacher expectation for the ineffective middle-SES group as opposed to the effective low-SES group. The teachers of students in the ineffective middle-SES group think their students will go much further in school than do teachers from the effective low-SES group. This occurs despite the fact that the effective low-SES group actually outachieved the ineffective middle-SES group.

Even though teachers from the low-SES effective group didn't believe their students would go as far in school as other groups, they managed to instill the belief in their students that they could achieve. The students in the low-SES effective group not only believed they could achieve well at the third grade level, but also that they could do well in later schooling. The teachers in the low-SES effective schools apparently got the message to their students that they could achieve by concentrating on present, rather than

Table 3: Characteristics Associated with Effectiveness In Middle- and Low-SES Schools

| Middle-SES Schools | Low-SES Schools |
|---|---|
| 1. Promote both high present and future educational expectations. | 1. Promote high present educational expectations. Make sure that the students believe that they can perform well at their current grade level. Allow high future educational goals to develop later. |
| 2. Hire principals with good managerial abilities. Increase teacher responsibility for and ownership of instructional leadership. | 2. Hire principals who are initiators, who want to make changes in the schools. Encourage a more active role for the principal in monitoring classrooms and providing overall instructional leadership. |
| 3. De-emphasize visible external rewards for academic achievement. Such rewards should be unnecessary if an adequate orientation is found at home. | 3. Increase the external reward structure for academic achievement. Make high achieving students feel special. |
| 4. Expand curricular offerings beyond the basic skills. | 4. Focus on basic skills first and foremost with other offerings after they have been mastered. |
| 5. Increase contact with the community. Encourage parents with high educational expectations to exert a press for school achievement. | 5. Carefully evaluate the effect of the community on the school. If the community does not exert a positive press for school achievement, create boundaries to buffer the school from negative influences. |
| 6. Hire more experienced teachers. | 6. Hire younger, possibly more idealist teachers. Give the principal more authority in selecting her/his own staff. |

Table 4: Teacher Expectations for Likelihood of Students Attending College

|  |  | Socioeconomic Characteristics of Students' Parents | |
|---|---|---|---|
|  |  | Middle SES | Low SES |
| School's Performance Relative to Expectation | Effective | 2.81 | 4.12 |
|  | Typical | 3.43 | 3.50 |
|  | Ineffective | 3.19 | 3.95 |

*Note.* Smaller numbers indicate a higher expectation for the students. The specific values for the scale are as follows: one = 90% or more, two = 70 to 89%, three = 50 to 69%, four = 30 to 49%, and five = less than 30%.

future success in school. If the students were told they could achieve at the third grade level, they extrapolated that they could achieve in later schooling.

A second difference between effective low-SES and middle-SES schools in LSES-II revolves around principals' characteristics. As was the case with teachers, principals exhibited significantly different opinions regarding their students' academic future in low- and middle-SES effective schools.

Principals in the effective low-SES schools projected that a smaller percentage of their students would finish high school than any of the other groups. They also indicated that fewer parents from their schools believed that their children would obtain college degrees. This occurred in spite of the facts that their students were scoring well above expectation and that their students believed they would go far in school.

The principals, like their teachers, see students in these low-SES effective schools making modest gains through the hard work of the school, almost in spite of the parents and local community. In contrast, the principals in effective middle-SES schools projected that a larger percentage of their students would finish high school and that a higher percentage of the students' parents believed their children would graduate from college than any of the other groups.

These differences in attitudes on the part of the middle- and low-SES principals were reflected in their behavior at their schools. Teachers reported that principals in low-SES effective schools observed their classes an average of 2.4 hours per semester. Teachers in effective middle-SES schools reported only 1.4 hours of observation per semester. Additionally, teachers in effective low-SES schools reported the greatest frequency of principal assistance in academic matters, while teachers in effective middle-SES schools reported less assistance. Principals in effective middle-SES schools allow teachers greater responsibility for and ownership of instructional leadership. Principals in effective low-SES schools tend to be initiators regarding academic programs within the schools, while those in effective middle-SES schools tend to be managers of the academic programs to use Hall and Griffin's (1982) terminology.

Again, Hallinger and Murphy (1986) confirmed these context differences in instructional leadership. They concluded that low-SES effective principals "tended to take a very directive role in the selection, development, and implementation of curriculum and instructional programs," while high-SES principals "exercised less direct control over classroom instruction."

The third difference between middle- and low-SES schools concerns the visibility and importance of the external reward structure of the schools. In several of the effective, low-SES schools in LSES-III (Stringfield et al. 1985), public displays of individual academic achievement were encountered repeatedly. The principals in these effective low-SES schools spent a great proportion of their time developing and maintaining external rewards.

A major difference between effective low-SES and middle-SES schools on this reward structure dimension has to do with the overtness of the display. In one effective low-SES school observed in LSES-III, there were academic slogans on signs throughout the building. Examples of the slogans included: "The only thing more expensive than education is IGNORANCE" and "The smaller your education, the smaller your paycheck." Such overt symbols were typically not found in middle-SES schools, partially because principals and staff there knew rewards for academic achievement were more likely to be found at home.

A fourth difference between effective low-SES and middle-SES schools has to do with curricular offerings. Hallinger and Murphy (1986) found a narrower focus on basic skills in the effective low-SES schools and a broader curricular emphasis in the effective higher-SES schools in their study. Observations from effective low-SES and middle-SES schools in LSES-II and -III tend to confirm these conclusions. On the other hand, our observations indicate that the narrow focus on basic skills in effective low-SES schools was also found at typical and ineffective low-SES schools. Emphasis on basic skills alone does not result in higher achievement for students in low-SES schools.

A fifth difference between effective low-SES and middle-SES schools has to do with the contact between the school and the community. In LSES-II, teachers in effective middle-SES schools were in frequent contact with parents and perceived the parents as being highly concerned with quality education. This was not the case in effective low-SES schools where teachers and principals perceived parents not to be very involved with the education of their children. The students in these effective low-SES schools saw their teachers as the adults who were pushing them very hard to succeed.

Results from Hallinger and Murphy's (1986) research confirm this difference between effective low- and high-SES schools in California. The principals in effective low-SES schools in their study tended to protect the

125

boundaries of their schools from the intrusions of the low income community surrounding them. On the other hand, principals in effective high-SES schools were more informal and less concerned about controlling and monitoring instruction.

A sixth difference between effective low-SES and middle-SES schools has to do with the principals' authority in selecting staff and with the characteristics of the staff s/he selects. Data on this issue from LSES-II are found in Table 5. Principals in effective low-SES schools were the most likely of any group to say that they had major input in hiring their own teachers. Twenty-three percent of the principals in this group said that they hired their own teachers. Only eight percent of the principals in effective middle-SES schools reported this authority.

Table 5: Percentage of Principals Who Perceive that They Make Hiring Decisions on Teachers

|  |  | Socioeconomic Characteristics of Students' Parents | |
|  |  | Middle SES | Low SES |
| --- | --- | --- | --- |
| School's Performance | Effective | 8% | 23% |
| Relative to Expectation | Typical | 0% | 9% |
|  | Ineffecative | 0% | 0% |

Additionally, the teachers in the low-SES effective schools were the least experienced of the groups of low-SES schools; that is, they had less experience teaching third grade and teaching in their school than did the typical low-SES or ineffective low-SES groups. This indicates that principals with hiring authority in low-SES schools might seek out younger, possibly more idealistic teachers for their schools. The opposite holds true for the middle-SES schools where the least experienced group of teachers were found in the ineffective schools.

## DISCUSSION

It was noted in the introduction that two questions related to contextual differences needed to be addressed: Are the characteristics that define an effective school in one context the same as those found in other contexts? Are techniques that would produce an effective school in one context the same as those that should be employed in other contexts?

126

With regard to the first question, the results of studies investigating SES as a contextual variable indicate that there are some correlates of school effectiveness that are the same regardless of SES context. If one chooses from the five correlates popularized by Edmonds plus time-on-task, common characteristics include an orderly environment, frequent monitoring of student progress, and high engaged academic time-on-task. Nevertheless, studies indicate that low- and middle-SES schools differ on the other three Edmonds' correlates: basic skills emphasis, high expectations for student achievement, and strong instructional leadership. These and other differences were summarized in Table 3.

With regard to the second question, new evidence suggests that school improvement models or techniques should be contextually sensitive. While each effective school is not purely idiosyncratic, neither are the simple and uniform school effectiveness frameworks popularized in the early 1980's adequate for all schools. The particular techniques for creating the most efficient and effective schools (Wimpelberg et al. 1989) or of maximally exploiting human variation (Yando et al. 1979) will differ depending on context.

One of the most promising aspects of the extant research is that so many of the results found in the LSES and in the Hallinger and Murphy research were congruent despite differences in methodologies and study populations. These differences between correlates of effectiveness in low- and middle-SES schools may be "stubborn facts" that "speak for themselves", which have dependability greater than the fluctuating environments in which they are examined (Cook & Campbell 1979).

As for a future research agenda, there appear to be three directions: (1) there need to be more studies of the relationship between school effectiveness and SES; (2) there need to be well-controlled school improvement studies utilizing differential models such as those proposed in this article; and (3) context variables in addition to SES need to be examined.

Even though some research investigating SES and school effectiveness has been conducted, there is an obvious need for more studies. Hopefully, new studies will have increased external validity through utilization of a variety of methodologies and populations (Cronbach 1982). Additionally, existing research from areas outside the school effectiveness field should be more thoroughly utilized as investigators develop contextually sensitive models.

There is a need for well-controlled change studies that employ contextually sensitive school effectiveness models. The most simple study might involve change in four schools: (1) one middle-class school utilizing a school effectiveness model designed for middle-SES schools; (2) one middle-class school utilizing a model for low-SES schools; (3) one lower-class school utilizing a model for low-SES schools; and (4) one lower-class school utilizing a model for middle-SES schools. While utilization of any school improvement model would likely produce increases in student achievement, schools that are matched with appropriate models should produce greater gains.

Why should any school improvement model produce student gains? First, the common elements that any school effectiveness model would incorporate (high engaged time-on-task, etc.) should result in higher achievement for any school. Second, the well-known Hawthorne effect should come into play. Stimulating any environment should make people more productive. Thus, any school improvement model should create more effective schools, but contextually sensitive models should give one a much greater rate of return.

Other school context variables will undoubtedly have an effect on school improvement efforts. Teddlie and Virgilio's (1988) research indicates, for instance, that variance in teacher behavior at the elementary grade levels is greater than that found in the secondary grade levels. This research indicated that time-on-task in elementary schools decreases from effective to typical to ineffective schools, yet such an orderly decrease in time-on-task was not found across those categories of secondary schools. In fact, research regarding factors that produce effective secondary schools (with the exception of Rutter et al. 1979) is woefully missing.

# REFERENCES

Benson, C.S. (1982). Household Production of Human Capital: Time Uses of Parents and Children as Inputs. In *Financing Education: Overcoming Inefficiency and Inequity*, edited by W.W. McMahon and T.G. Geske, pp. 52-77. Urbana, IL: University of Illinois Press.

Blumberg, P. (Ed.) (1972). *The Impact of Social Class*. New York: Thomas Y. Cromwell Co.

Brookover, W.B., & Lezotte, L.W. (1979). *Changes in School Characteristics Coincident with Changes in Student Achievement*. East Lansing, MI: Institute for Research on Teaching, College of Education, Michigan State University.

Brookover, W., Beady, C., Flood, P., Schweitzer, J., & Wisenbaker, J. (1979). *School Social Systems and Student Achievement: Schools Can Make a Difference*. New York: Praeger.

Clark, T.A. & McCarthy, D.P. (1983). School Improvement in New York: The Evolution of a Project. *Educational Researcher 12*, 17-24.

Cohen, A. & Hodges, H. (1972). Characteristics of the lower blue collar class. In: *The Impact of Social Class*, edited by P. Blumberg. New York, Thomas Y. Cromwell Co.

Cook, T. & Campbell, D. (1979) *Quasi-experimentation: Design and Analysis Issues for Field Settings*. Boston: Houghton Mifflin Co.

Cronbach, L. (1982). *Designing Evaluations of Educational and Social Programs*. San Francisco: Jossey-Bass.

Cuban, L. (1983). Effective Schools: A Friendly But Cautionary Note. *Phi Delta Kappan 64*: 695-696.

Curtis, R. & Jackson, E. (1977). *Inequality in American communities.* New York: Academic Press.

D'Amico, J. (1982). Each Effective School May Be One of A Kind. *Educational Leadership 40:* 61-62.

Duckett, W., Park, D., Clark, D., McCarthy, M. Lotto, L., Gregory, L. Herlihy, J. and Burleson, D. (1980). *Why Do Some Urban Schools Succeed? The Phi Delta Kappa Study of Exceptional Urban Elementary Schools.* Bloomington, IN: Phi Delta Kappa.

Edmonds, R. (1981). *The Characteristics of Effective Schools: Research and Implementation.* Unpublished manuscript, Michigan State University.

Edmonds, R. & Frederiksen, J. (1979). *Search for Effective Schools: The Identification and Analysis of Schools that are Instructionally Effective for Poor Children.* Cambridge, MA: Harvard University, Center for Urban Studies.

Good, T. & Brophy, J. (1986). School Effects. In *Handbook of Research on Teaching,* edited by M. Wittrock. (3rd ed.), (pp. 570-602). New York: Macmillan.

Hall, G.E., & Griffin, T. (1982). Analyzing Context/Climate in School Settings – Which is Which? Paper presented at the annual meeting of the American Educational Research Association, New York.

Hallinger, P. & Murphy, J. (1986). The Social Context of Effective Schools. *American Journal of Education 94:* 328-355.

Hess, A. (1986). Educational Triage in an Urban School Setting. *Metropolitan Education 2:* 39-52.

Levine, D. (1982). Successful Approaches for Improving Academic Achievement in Inner-City Elementary Schools. *Phi Delta Kappan 63:* 523-526.

Lezotte, L.W. (1982). A Response to D'Amico: Not a Recipe but a Framework. *Educational Leadership 40:* 63.

McCormack-Larkin, M. Kritek, W. (1982). Milwaukee's Project RISE. *Educational Leadership 40:* 16-21.

Miller, S. & Yelton, B. (1987). Correlates of Achievement in Affluent Effective Schools. Paper presented at the meeting of the American Educational Research Association, Washington, DC.

Purkey, S. & Smith, M. (1983). Effective Schools: A Review. *Elementary School Journal 83:* 427-452.

Rutter, M. Maugham, B., Mortimore, P., Ouston, J. with Smith, A. (1979). *Fifteen Thousand Hours: Secondary Schools and Their Effect on Children.* Cambridge, MA: Harvard University Press.

Scholastic Testing Service. (1983). *Educational Development Series, Lower Primary Level, Form S, Special Louisiana Edition, Teachers' Manual of Directions.* Bensonville, IL: Scholastic Testing Service.

Stringfield, S. & Teddlie, C. (1988). A Time to Summarize: The Louisiana School Effectiveness Study. *Educational Leadership 46:* 43-49.

Stringfield, S., Teddlie, C., & Suarez, S. (1985): Classroom Interation in Effective and Ineffective Schools: Preliminary Results from Phase III of the Louisiana School Effectiveness Study. *Journal of Classroom Interaction 20:* 31-37.

Teddlie, C., Falkowski, C., Stringfield, S., Desselle, S., & Garvue, R. (1984). *The Louisiana School Effectiveness Study: Phase Two, 1982-84.* Baton Rouge, LA: Louisiana State Department of Education.

Teddlie, C., Kirby, P. & Stringfield, S. (1989). Effective versus Ineffective Schools: Observable Differences in the Classroom. *American Journal of Education* (in press).

Teddlie, C., & Lauricella, A. (1986). *Quantitative results from the Louisiana School Effectiveness Study.* Paper presented at the meeting of the American Educational Research Association, San Francisco.

Teddlie, C. & Stringfield, S. (1985). A Differential Analysis of Effectiveness in Middle and Lower Socioeconomic Status Schools. *Journal of Classroom Interaction 20:* 38-44.

Teddlie, C., Stringfield, S., Wimpelberg, R. & Kirby, P. (1987). *Contextual differences in effective schooling in Louisiana.* Paper presented at the annual meeting of the American Educational Research Association, Washington, DC.

Teddlie, C. & Virgilio, I. (1988). *School context differences across grades: A study of teacher behaviors.* Paper presented at the annual meetings of the American Educational Research Association, New Orleans, LA.

Thomas, J.A, Kemmerer, F., & Monk, D.H. (1982). Efficiency in Educational Finance: The Classroom Perspective. In *Financing Education: Overcoming Inefficiency and Inequity,* edited by W.W. McMahon and T.G. Geske. Urbana, IL: University of Illinois Press.

Wimpelberg, R., Teddlie, C., & Stringfield, S. (1989). Sensitivity to Context: The Past and Future of Effective Schools Research. *Educational Administration Quarterly 25:* 82-107.

Yando, R., Seitz, V., & Zigler, E. (1979). *Intellectual and Personality Characteristics of Children: Social-class and Ethnic-group Differences.* New York: John Wiley and Sons.

# PUPILS' SENSE OF WELL-BEING AND CLASSROOM EDUCATIONAL FACTORS *)**)

Anja W.M. Knuver and
Hennie P. Brandsma

RION: Institute for Educational Research
University of Groningen

## INTRODUCTION AND RESEARCH PROBLEM

Within the framework of school effectiveness research some major studies have been conducted in the recent years (e.g. Brookover, Beady, Flood, Schweitzer, & Wisenbaker, 1979; Rutter, Maughan, Mortimore, Ouston, & Smith, 1979; Mortimore, Sammons, Stoll, Lewis, & Ecob, 1988; Brandsma, & Knuver, 1988). The concept of school effectiveness is usually defined in terms of cognitive pupil achievement; some schools are more capable than other schools in reaching higher levels of pupil achievement when student background characteristics are taken into account. It has been concluded in these studies that the between-school differences in achievement can vary from subject to subject (e.g., arithmetic, reading and language), and that they amount to some 10 to 15 percent of the total variance in pupil achievement. Some school characteristics (e.g., leadership and organizational factors) can explain part of these between-school differences (cf. Mortimore et al., 1988; Brandsma, & Knuver, 1988). Less attention, however, has been given to possible between-school differences in the non-cognitive domain, e.g., affective pupil functioning and pupil behaviour. Although the importance of cognitive skills must not be underestimated, the ultimate aim of education encloses both the cognitive and non-cognitive domain and it is shown that schools which appear to be effective in the cognitive domain are also effective in the non-cognitive domain (Hofman, & Hofman, 1987; Rutter et al., 1979). On the other hand there seems to be doubt on the part of parents and teachers that too strong an emphasis on the cognitive aspects of learning may have a negative influence on the affective development of pupils as may be indicated by high levels of truancy, demotivation and school drop out (Stoel,

---
* This research has been made possible thanks to a subsidy granted by SVO-Institute for Educational Research in the Netherlands (SVO-project nr. 6009).
** With thanks to Arnaldo Gomes and Anje Ros for their assistance.

131

1980). Little is known about the possible influence of school and classroom characteristics on non-cognitive pupil functioning. For instance, how large are these between-school differences and are the school characteristics that can explain some of the between-school differences in cognitive achievement the same or different for the affective domain? For these reasons it is important to give attention to the relationships that may exist between affective pupil functioning and school or classroom characteristics. The affective domain contains concepts like pupils' selfconcept, achievement motivation and attitudes towards schooling. Part of these aspects within the affective domain can be measured by using a concept developed by Stoel (1980), which is called "pupils' sense of well-being" with regard to school and education.

In this paper we will examine the relationships that exist between pupils' sense of wellbeing at school (as the dependent variable), student achievement scores and student background characteristics (as possible covariates at the individual level) and classroom organizational factors and teacher characteristics (as possible explanatory variables).

In Figure 1 a graphical representation is given of these expected relationships.

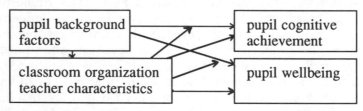

*Figure 1: Hypothesized model of (causal) influences*

In this model all the expected relationships are represented with to the right the dependent variables and to the left the explanatory and control variables. It is expected that there are direct relationships between classroom and teacher variables and pupils' sense of well-being. Furthermore teacher and classroom variables can possibly exert an influence on the relationships that exist between pupil background variables and pupils' sense of wellbeing. These are the indirect or so called interaction effects. The same relationships are expected with regard to pupil cognitive achievement. A mutual influence of pupil cognitive achievement and wellbeing is also anticipated. The emphasis in this study is on pupils' sense of wellbeing, where pupil background factors and cognitive achievement are considered as covariates and classroom and teacher factors as explanatory variables.

In the next paragraph some attention is given to the way in which these direct and indirect effects can be estimated by making use of a random coefficient model.

# THEORETICAL FRAMEWORK

## The Concept and Modelling of School Effectiveness

In this paragraph some attention is given to the way in which the concept of school effectiveness can be used to help us understand the hypothetical relationships given in Figure 1. It is believed that school effectiveness can be regarded as being composed of two dimensions, which need to be investigated separately in order to test both the hypothesized direct and indirect effects of classroom and teacher characteristics on pupil achievement or well-being. Cuttance (1987) suggests a conceptual model of school effectiveness in which two dimensions of effectiveness are distinguished, the 'quality' and the 'equity' dimension. The quality dimension refers to the differences between schools in mean scores after controlling for differences in pupil intake (e.g., SES, IQ). The equity dimension refers to the degree in which schools can compensate for differences in school intake. A regression can be estimated for each school separately. The quality dimension is then represented by the school-specific intercept $\alpha$, whereas the equity dimension is represented by the school specific slope estimate $\alpha$ for each co-variate.

Recently random coefficient models for explaining school effects have been proposed (Raudenbush & Bryk, 1986, 1987). In these models the estimators for quality ($\alpha$) and equity ($\beta$) are considered as random variables both with a proportion of 'true' variance and a proportion of 'sampling' variance. With these models school effects can be estimated more efficiently and they also make it possible to generalize the results to the total sampling population of schools (De Leeuw & Kreft, 1985; Kreft, 1987).

A random coefficient model will be used for the analysis to follow. With regard to our research problems this random coefficient model can be used to detect possible between-school differences in quality and equity. The magnitude of these between-school differences in quality and equity can be estimated. The direction and magnitude of the hypothesized direct effects (quality) and indirect effects (equity) of classroom and teacher variables on pupil well-being can be measured as well.

## Pupils' Sense of Wellbeing at School

Pupils' sense of well-being can be defined as the presence or absence of specific positive and/or negative attitudes and experiences vis à vis school and education. This broad concept encompasses several components that are believed to constitute the major part of the affective domain. These components are: pupils' self- concept, attitudes towards school and learning, motivational aspects, social interactions with fellow pupils and teachers, and contentment with their position at school.

Empirical knowledge regarding the hypothesized relationships between cognitive achievement, pupil-background and school and classroom factors on the one hand and the affective domain on the other are by no means conclusive. For instance, some report a positive relationship between cognitive and non-cognitive functioning (Brookover et al., 1979), whereas others (Mortimore et al., 1988) state that the two dimensions are largely independent.

# RESEARCH DESIGN

## Sample
In 1987 a random sample of 250 Dutch primary schools out of a population of approximately 8000 was drawn. Within these schools all pupils from grade 7 were selected (age groups 10/11). Information was gathered through the school-principal, the classroom teacher and the pupil. Both school and classroom level data were obtained by means of questionnaires. All relevant information regarding the pupil was gathered at the pupil level by means of standardized tests and questionnaires. In 1988 the same sample of schools and pupils were contacted again in order to obtain classroom organizational and teacher data from group 8 and pupil data regarding language and arithmetic achievement and pupils' sense of well-being. The 1988 sample on which the following analyses are conducted contains data of 3,475 grade-8 pupils and 196 grade 8 teachers.

## Selected Variables
With regard to the dependent variable "pupils' sense of well-being" a Likert-type scale was developed. The original scale has been constructed by Stoel (1980) and was validated for secondary school pupils. An adapted version of this scale was constructed in order to obtain reliable information from primary school pupils. The total scale contains 47 items and has a high reliability coefficient alpha of .92. For pupil attainment scores in language and arithmetic an adapted version of the 1988 Cito standard achievement test is used. The reliability coefficients for language ($\alpha=.86$) and arithmetic ($\alpha=.88$) are highly sufficient. The covariates at the pupil level which are believed to exert an influence on both achievement and well-being are socio-economic status of parents (SES), intelligence, gender, age and nationality.

As for the predictor variables classroom factors and teacher variables are taken into account, because these are expected to exert a larger influence on well-being as compared to factors on the school level. An inventory of these variables is given in the appendix. A full account of the reliability and measurement procedures of all these variables is given in Brandsma and Knuver (1989).

All continous variables are transformed to Z-scores (mean = 0, s.d. = 1) in order to be able to compare the estimates of the effects.

# ANALYSIS AND RESEARCH RESULTS

The analyses were carried out using the VARCL multi-level programme, that makes use of the random coefficient model described in section 2.1. In analyzing the data the following strategy was undertaken. The first step in the analysis was to decide which covariates at the pupil level should be modelled as having random or fixed effects (different or the same slope estimators between schools). This analysis gives insight in the question if a modelling of both equity and quality differences is appropriate for (some) covariables or that a modelling of quality differences only (differences in intercept between schools) is sufficient.

Table 1: Estimates of both fixed and random effects for 7 covariates with pupils' sense of wellbeing as the dependent variable

| Covariates | Fixed effects | | Random effects | |
| | estimate | st. error | sigma | st. error for sigma |
| --- | --- | --- | --- | --- |
| Nationality:foreign | .18 | .08* | .08 | .33 |
| Gender:female | .21 | .03* | .36 | .04* |
| Language score | .22 | .02* | .05 | .06 |
| Arithmetic score | .15 | .02* | .13 | .03* |
| SES | .04 | .02* | .02 | .06 |
| Age | .00 | .02 | | |
| Intelligence | -.01 | .03 | | |

*: $p < .05$

From the fixed effects part of Table 1 it can be concluded that 5 covariates at the pupil level show a significant effect on pupils' sense of well-being. The impact of age and intelligence is small and non significant. The estimate of SES is significant but small. Non-Dutch pupils and girls tend to have a higher sense of well-being, compared to Dutch pupils and boys. Also scores on arithmetic and language achievement tests show a positive relationship with well-being.

From the random part of Table 1 it can be seen that two covariates show significant differences in slopes between schools. Especially there are pronounced differences in slopes for gender. This means that in some schools the effect of gender on well-being is stronger than in other schools. This is also, but to a lower degree, the case for the relationship between arithmetic achievement and pupil well-being.

On the basis of the information given in Table 1 it can be concluded that 5 out of the 7 original control variables at the student level need to be modelled as covariates. Two (gender and arithmetic achievement) out of these five should also be modelled as having random effects. For these two covariates equity differences between schools exist. The other three covariates (nationality, SES and language achievement) can be modelled as fixed effects. The influence of these three covariates on well-being is approximately the same from school to school.

The next step in the analysis includes the modelling of the class organizational and teacher variables. At first all the variables described in the appendix are modelled as direct effects. On a step by step basis (backward removal) the variables that show the least promising (small, non-significant estimates) are excluded from the model. These direct effects can explain part of the between school variance in means (the quality dimension).

The same procedure was carried out by modelling interaction terms for the classroom factors with the two random-covariables (gender and arithmetic achievement). These interactions possibly explain some of the between-school differences in slopes (the equity dimension). A full account of this modelfitting procedure is given in Table 2. Only significant direct and interaction effects are given in this table.

Table 2: Variance component analysis on students' sense of wellbeing

| Model | 1. empty model | 2. covariates model | 3. classfactors direct and interaction effects |
|---|---|---|---|
| **Covariates** | | | |
| nationality:foreign | | .15 (.08)* | .15 (.07) |
| gender:female(random) | | .22 (.04) | .21 (.04) |
| language | | .22 (.02) | .22 (.02) |
| arithmetic(random) | | .14 (.02) | .13 (.02) |
| SES | | .04 (.02) | .04 (.02) |
| **Classfactors-direct effects** | | | |
| same pupils as last year | | | .11 (.06) |
| age teacher | | | -.10 (.03) |
| refresher courses | | | -.12 (.04) |
| rules set by teacher | | | -.14 (.03) |
| feedback | | | .00 (.04) |
| **Interaction effects** | | | |
| feedback x gender | | | .12 (.04) |
| refresher courses x gender | | | .10 (.04) |
| rules x arithmetic | | | .05 (.02) |
| **Variance-component** | | | |
| pupil | .835 | .681 | .681 |
| intercept:class | .151 | .148 | .111 |
| slopes:arithmetic | | .018 | .016 |
| slopes:gender | | .106 | .082 |
| **Deviance** | 9505.8 | 8975.1 | 8911.3 |

* estimates of effects with standard error of estimates within brackets.

In model 3 (see Table 2) it can be seen that five classroom and teacher variables can explain a part of the between-group variance (differences in intercepts). The amount of variance connected with the classroom level was about 15% in the empty model, about 15% in the covariates model and drops to 11% in the model with classfactors included. Thus, about 4% of the total variance in pupils' sense of well-being, which is some 25% of the between-group variance, can be explained by these four classroom and teacher variables. These variables are: 'same pupils as last year in the group', the age of the teacher, amount of refresher courses and rules set by teacher while executing a task.

Next to the between-class variance there is also about 13 percent of the total variance that can possibly be explained by interactions between classroom variables and the random covariates arithmetic and gender. Table 2 shows that the variance in slopes for gender drops from 11% to 8%. Thus about 3% of the total variance, which is about 25% of the variance in slopes for gender, can be explained by two class-variables: feedback and refresher courses in interaction with gender. The variance in slopes for arithmetic drops from .018 to .016 when the variable 'rules set by teacher while executing a task' is brought into the model in interaction with the pupil covariate achievement in arithmetic. This drop in variance is significant but hardly relevant.

Model 3 is the final model, the model which explains the maximal amount of variance both in intercept (quality) and in slopes (equity) for pupils' sense of well-being by means of a minimal amount of classroom variables.

## DISCUSSION

From the results of the analyses it can be derived that about 84 percent of the total variance in pupils' sense of well-being can be connected to the pupil level. The remaining percentage of variance is on the level of the class. These percentages do not differ much when compared to the distribution of variance for the cognitive attainment variables language and arithmetic (Brandsma & Knuver, 1988).

When modelling the pupil covariates it can be noted that girls, as expected from previous research, have a more positive sense of well-being towards education in general and their school. It also can be noted that the attainment of pupils in arithmetic and language is positively correlated with pupils' sense of wellbeing. This is also in accordance with some previous research findings. The relationship between socio-economic status and well-being is small, but positive. The relationship between nationality and well-being is positive for foreign students and rather large.

After modelling the pupil covariates there remains about 15% of the variance on the classroom level and about 13% variance in slopes. Part of these variance components can be explained by class factors directly or in interaction with pupil covariates. It can be noted that putting the covariates into the analysis does not affect the between class variance, as distinct from the results of previous analyses concerning cognitive dependent variables (Brandsma & Knuver, 1988). The amount of variance in slopes for gender is remarkably high. Not more than 3 percent was found in previous multi-level research, and this 3 percent was variance in slopes for gender and arithmetic attainment (cf. Brandsma & Knuver, 1988). This large amount of variance in slopes for gender may point to the fact that different teachers and/or classroom practices have differential effects on especially the affective functioning of boys and girls as measured by well-being. Boys and girls may not prefer the same treatments or circumstances in their classroom.

Four class-factors can be indicated, which explain some 25% of the variance between classes (this is about 3% of the total variance in pupils' sense of well-being). To be under the same teacher for more than one year appears to have a positive influence on pupils' sense of well-being. The amount of feedback the teacher gives to the pupils about their achievement has no effect in general, but this variable can explain much more in interaction with gender. Girls tend to appreciate the amount of feedback the teacher gives them about their tasks much more than boys do. The age of the teacher, the amount of refresher courses the teacher has taken and the rule-setting of the teacher when pupils are performing their tasks have a negative overall impact on pupils' sense of well-being. It is not clear if these features are consistent with findings in other research. Class factors mentioned in other studies that have an impact on non cognitive pupil output, like the grouping of pupils within the classroom, showed no significant effect in our analyses. In interaction with gender the amount of refresher-courses the teacher has taken shows a positive effect. This means that, even while the overall effect is negative, the effect of refresher courses on pupils' sense of well-being for girls is more positive (less negative) as compared to boys.

The slope differences between classes for arithmetic are rather small (about 1.5 percent of the total variance). A small part of this variance can be explained by the interaction of rule-setting by the teacher and achievement in arithmetic. The effect is positive, which means that the overall negative effect of stringent rule-setting of the teacher has less negative impact on the well-being of pupils who achieve well in arithmetic.

APPENDIX   Classroom factors expected to influence pupils' sense of well being at school and/or the relationship between wellbeing and covariates.

Age of the teacher
Gender of the teacher
Experience of teacher
Stand in or regular teacher
Same pupils as last year
Jobsharing
Refresher courses followed
Contentedness of teacher
Subscription to educational magazines
Size of the group
Average SES of group
Importance of societal goals
Rulesetting by teacher
Differentiation by gender
Differentiation by achievement

Allocation of homework to different groups
Planning of instructing by means of a schedule
Time spent on other than basic subjects
Number of hours teaching
Group combination with other groups
Curriculum for arithmetic and language
Feedback on achievement
Ordering of pupils in groups or rows
Changing groups for arithmatic and language

# REFERENCES

Aitkin, M., & Longford, N. (1986). Statistical Modelling Issues in School Effectiveness Studies. *Journal of the Royal Statistical Society*, Series A (General), *149* (1), 1-43.

Brandsma, H.P., & Knuver, J.W.M. (1988). Organisatorische verschillen tussen basisscholen en hun effect op leerlingprestaties. *Tijdschrift voor Onderwijsresearch, 13,* (4), 201-212.

Brandsma, H.P., & Knuver, J.W.M. (1989). *Basisschoolkenmerken als determinanten van het functioneren van leerlingen*. Deelrapport II. Instrumentontwikkeling. Interne publikatie, concept. Groningen: RION.

Brookover, W., Beady, C., Flood, P., Schweitzer, J., & Wisenbaker, J. (1979). *School social systems and student achievement: schools can make a difference*. New York: Bergin Publishers Book.

Cuttance, P. (1987). *Modelling variation in the effectiveness of schooling* (draft).

Hofman, R.H., & Hofman, W.H.A. (1987). Definiëring van onderwijseffectiviteit. Kanttekeningen vanuit het onderwijsonderzock. In Creemers et al. (red.), *Handboek Schoolorganisatie en Onderwijsmanagement*. Alphen a/d Rijn: Samsom.

Kreft, G.G. (1987). *Models and methods for the measurement of school effects*. Dissertation. University of Leiden.

Leeuw, J. de, & Kreft, I. (1985). *Random coefficient models for multilevel analysis*. Leiden.

Longford, N. (1986). *Variance Component Analysis: manual*. University of Lancaster.

Mortimore, P., Sammons, P., Stoll, L., Lewis, D. & Ecob, R. (1988). *School Matters. The junior Years*. Somerset: Open Books.

Raudenbush, S.W., & Bruk, A.S. (1986). A hierarchical model for studying school effects. *Sociology of Education, 59,* 1-17.

Raudenbush, S.W., & Bryk, A.S. (1987). *Quantitative models for estimating teacher and school effectiveness.* Paper for the invitational Conference of the Center for Student Testing, Evaluation and Standards. Princeton (NY).

Rutter, M., Maughan, B., Mortimore, B., Ouston, J., & Smith, A. (1979). *Fifteen thousand hours. Secondary schools and their effects on children.* London: Open Books, Publishers Ltd.

Stoel, W.G.R. (1980). *De beleving van de school door leerlingen in het voortgezet onderwijs. De ontwikkeling van een schoolbelevingsschaal.* Haren: RION.

# THE EFFECTS OF SECONDARY SCHOOLS ON THE EDUCATIONAL CAREERS OF DISADVANTAGED PUPILS*

Roel J. Bosker and Rolf K.W. Van der Velden**

RION, Institute for Educational Research, University of Groningen.

## INTRODUCTION

In the Dutch literature on school careers in secondary education, 'school success' has mostly been operationalised in terms of efficiency. That is, most scales for school success assume that school success is greater when:
(1)  a student is enrolled in a higher type of education (for details on the Dutch educational system we refer to the appendix)
(2)  a student reaches a higher class or grade (cf. Cremers, 1980; Kreft & Bronkhorst, 1985; Tesser, 1986; Roeleveld et al., 1985; Bosker & Van der Velden, 1985).

Using only this operationalisation of school success is unsatisfactory, since differences between boys and girls, for example, seem to consist largely of differential choices in subject combinations rather than on efficiency (e.g. Dekkers, 1985). These paths or tracks offer differential opportunities for further education, as further studies have specific subject prerequisites.
In this article, we will concentrate on both dimensions of school success. We will refer to the former dimension as 'efficiency' and to the latter as 'educational perspective'. We address the following questions:
(1)  How should these school success dimensions be operationalized?
(2)  Where should we locate the origin of SES-specific school success?
(3)  What is the influence of school characteristics on school success, and are these effects different for low and high SES pupils?

---

*   This research was financially supported by the SVO (Institute for Educational Research, project 4229).
**  Correspondence should be directed to R.J. Bosker, RION, P.O. Box 1286, 9701 BG Groningen, Holland.

141

The analyses will be carried out on the 'Groningen-cohort'. Detailed information about this cohort has been published earlier (Meijnen, 1977; Bosker et al., 1985). Suffice it to say that a group of more than 700 children has been observed since 1972, when they entered primary education. In 1984, when they reached the age of 18, information concerning their secondary education careers was gathered. The total experimental loss between 1972 and 1984 was 23%.

## THE TWO DIMENSIONS OF SCHOOL SUCCESS

### School Success as the Rungs of an Educational Ladder

In the Dutch educational system pupils choose at the age of 12 which type of education they will follow. The following main forms can be distinguished, ranging in decreasing order of difficulty:
1. VWO : pre-university education, duration 6 years
2. HAVO: higher general education, duration 5 years
3. MAVO: intermediate general education, duration 4 years
4. LBO : junior vocational education, duration 4 years.

These four streams might be interpreted as curriculum tracks, with little mobility between them except for graduate pupils (LBO certificate gives access to MAVO grade 4 and so on).

Because students in secondary education are not subjected to the same national school-performance test, it is difficult to determine their educational position after entering secondary education. A solution to this problem is that all educational positions, that is every specific combination of achieved educational form and grade, can be described as a certain distance (in years) to the top of the educational system.

If we define 'reaching university' as the top of the Dutch educational system, the different positions in VWO can easily be traced back: pupils entering the first grade of VWO differ 6 years from the top; pupils entering e.g. the fifth grade of VWO differ only 2 years. Because the Dutch system is strictly hierarchical, the differences between different forms of education can also be described in years. As a rule, students gain one year when going directly to a higher form of education, they lose one year when going to a lower form. For example, a student who goes to HAVO, lags one year behind the student who immediately goes to VWO. Using these principles we can construct an 'educational ladder' on which the different educational positions can be represented (for details we refer to Appendix 1).

The efficiency of a school career can now be operationalised as the ratio of the distance covered on this ladder and the time that was needed to do this. E.g. starting in the first grade of LBO and finishing in MAVO-4 after five

142

years results in an efficiency score of 100%, whereas the career VWO-1 to VWO-4 in five years results in 80% efficiency although in the latter case the final school success should be rated higher.

## *Educational Perspectives: Opportunities for Further Education*
In analyses on the choice of paths or tracks, the dependent variable (path, track) is mostly treated as a nominal or a dichotomous variable. For example, a distinction is often made between science, socio-economic and language subject combinations (e.g. CBS, 1980; Bosker et al., 1985); in vocational education the main distinction is between domestic, economic-administrative and technical tracks; and in some analyses a dichotomous variable is used: the choice (or not) of mathematics for instance (f.e. Dekkers, 1985; Kuyper & Van der Werf, 1987). Although this manner of operationalisation clearly shows the segregation between boys and girls, it does not make clear what the implications of these different choices are, nor is it clear whether choosing a specific combination of subject has the same implications for each type of education.

By defining educational perspective in terms of opportunities for further education, we create a variable at interval level with which we can analyse school careers within as well as between different types of education. These opportunities for further education are a function of the prerequisites of further studies in terms of level of education (type of education, A, B, or C-level), sector of education (subject, path or track chosen), grade (mostly last grade reached) and performance level (e.g. graduation, number of sufficient passes). For a complete overview of these prerequisites we refer to the Appendix.

In calculating the scores we use the last known path or track chosen by the students. Additionally we apply the following rules:
(1) If students leave secondary education without graduating, they obtain the score '0', unless they have succesfully completed grade 4 which gives access to some training courses in MBO (this is only the case for students in HAVO and VWO)
(2) Students from VBuO (special secondary education) and IBO (junior vocational education, individualized track) always get the score '0'.

The resulting perspective score can be considered as the sum of two partial scores:
(1) A structural score, related to the type of education. That is, the successful completion of a certain type of education gives access to a certain number of further studies, regardless of the specific path or track chosen. For example, graduation from HAVO gives access to 83 training possibilities in HBO regardless of the specific path chosen.

(2) An individual score, related to the specific path or track chosen. That is, the specific choice of certain subjects offers a student access to an additional number of training possibilities. For example, the choice of mathematics and physics gives a student from VWO access to 21 additional training possibilities at university.

In Table 1 we present an overview of the maximum perspective scores for each type of education, divided in a structural and an individual part.

Table 1: Range of perspective scores per type of education.

|  | Structural | Individual | Maximum perspective score |
|---|---|---|---|
| Type of education |  |  |  |
| VWO | 201 | 93 | 294 |
| HAVO | 166 | 51 | 217 |
| MAVO | 29 | 54 | 83 |
| LBO | 1 | 77 | 78 |
| IBO/VBuO | 0 | 0 | 0 |

From this table and the information presented in the appendix, we can draw the following conclusions:
(1) Differences in perspective scores are dominated more by structural differences (i.e.: differences between types of education) than by individual variations in the specific choice of a path or track.
(2) In MAVO and especially in LBO, the individual part, that is the choice of specific subjects, is relatively more important than in HAVO and VWO.
(3) Mathematics and physics play a crucial role in the determination of the additional number of further studies, especially in MAVO and LBO where the choice of mathematics and physics offers access to three quarters of the additional further studies. In HAVO, the choice of mathematics and physics gives access to only half of the number of additional further studies.

## THE ORIGIN OF SES-SPECIFIC SCHOOL SUCCESS

Our second research question is: Where should we locate the origin of SES-specific school success? We need to know the answer to this question to verify if and how much SES affects selection processes in secondary education. For if this figure is near zero, we might as well draw the conclusion that school effects are only relevant for the explanation of SES-specific school success in primary education. To find the answer to this question, we will have to try to split up the relation between SES and school success into stages. Analytically we can do this by separating direct SES effects from indirect effects (through former educational positions). Therefore we construct a longitudinal pathmodel. The different educational positions are depicted on a timepath and in a rather bookkeeping-like manner we then assess the direct and indirect effects of SES on the different stages of the educational career. The analysis is carried out in LISREL VI (Jöreskog and Sörbom, 1984).

Let us begin by noting that SES explains about a quarter of the total variance in school success. Furthermore we see that primary education indeed appears to be crucial in the origin of SES-specific school success, since half of the SES-bound variance can be located in this stage of our model.

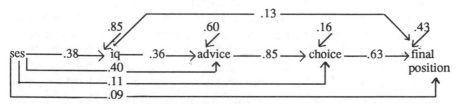

*Figure 1: Simple longitudinal pathmodel for final educational position (chi²=3.67, df=2, p=.16).*

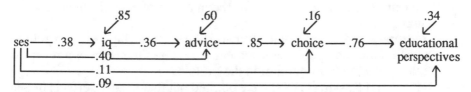

*Figure 2: Simple longitudinal pathmodel for educational perspectives (chi²=4.77, df=3, p=.19).*

Table 2: Decomposition of SES-effects on schoolsucces

|  | final educational position | educational perspectives |
| --- | --- | --- |
| pre-school period | 25% | 17% |
| primary education | 43% | 50% |
| transition to secondary school | 14% | 16% |
| secondary education | 18% | 17% |
| total effect of SES | .49 | .52 |

Relevant for this study is the fending that secondary education outweighs the pre-school period. This is even more true when we realize that half of all transitions from primary to secondary education are carried into effect in secondary education, since half of the secondary schools are comprehensive in their first grades. So it seems worthwhile to find out if secondary schools differ in their contribution to this societal problem.

# SCHOOL CHARACTERISTICS AND SCHOOL SUCCESS

### The Construction of School Configurations

None of the existing school effect models (see for an overview: Cuttance (1980) and Brutsaert (1986)) pays explicit attention to the effect of schools on educational opportunities, nor to the relationship of the schools' organisational characteristics to one another. Meijnen points out with respect to the first point of criticism (Meijen, 1986) that it seems likely that privileged pupils are less sensitive to variations in school organisation, because of the family support, than low SES pupils. Positive variations in school organisation are profitable for children in minority groups and low SES pupils, without being prejudicial to the other children.

With respect to the second point of criticism, it seems appropriate to reject simple linear statistical techniques for the analysis of school effects for the following reasons:
(a)  As Brophy and Good (1986) remark, the relationship between school characteristics and pupil achievement often takes the form of a reversed U: there is a kind of optimum in the middle.
(b)  Bidwell and Kasarda (1988) have pointed out that positive effects in one layer of the organisation may be counterbalanced by negative effects in other layers

When attempting to determine the effects of schools on educational perspectives of pupils, it is therefore better to construct a typology of schools. In this section we do this by means of cluster analysis. The cluster analysis enables us to create groups of schools which can be compared. Whether or not one configuration is more effective than another will be tested in the last section. We will construct two typologies.

The first typology is constructed to depict the school organisation in general with emphasis on the early grades. The second typology is constructed on the basis of variables which measure the organisation of the school in the final grades.

146

Table 3: Results: cluster analysis general and early grades (z-scores)

| | Clusters | | | |
|---|---|---|---|---|
| | 1 N=19 | 2 N=11 | 3 N=36 | 4 N=2 |
| Collection of intake data | -.13 | .38 | .57 | -1.05 |
| Collective decision making | .13 | .68 | -.12 | - .27 |
| Limited teacher autonomy | .74 | .87 | -.54 | - .21 |
| Collective curriculum construction | .13 | .19 | .29 | - .70 |
| School climate | .67 | - .45 | -.22 | .01 |
| Academic pressure | .84 | -1.05 | .10 | - .38 |
| Discipline pressure | .96 | -1.38 | .18 | - .46 |
| Appreciation of self-direction | -.64 | .73 | -.03 | .24 |

First of all we perform a cluster analysis on the school variables that measure the organisation in general and the early grades in particular. The resulting typology seems to be successful. 19 schools form the first type. Decision-making in this type of school is collective, that is to say decisions about the school organisation, curriculum goals, innovations, extracurricular activities and so on are made according to a majority of votes. In accordance with this is the fact that in this type teachers have limited autonomy in lesson preparation. Decisions about schoolbooks, method, work forms, teaching materials, grouping of pupils, content and so on are taken at the section level by the subject teachers. Moreover there is some consultation on these matters in other organisational units (grade-commitees, counselling groups and so on). Striking is that this type of school is not-well informed about the pupils' backgrounds, as they collect relatively little intake data. School climate characteristics are the most outstanding feature for this type of school. School climate as perceived by the teachers seems to be very positive and stimulating, and teachers attach great value to academic achievement and discipline. Notable is the result that in this type of school teachers advocate less self-direction for pupils (independency, sound judgement, critical attitude, insight) than teachers in other schools.

The eleven schools that form the second constructed type have outstanding scores for organisational features and the appreciation of self-direction. The school climate on the other hand seems to be less favourable: less academic pressure, a less stimulating environment (according to the teachers) and less attention to discipline problems. The third type contains 36 schools and is rather heterogeneous. There is a great deal of consultation, but decision-making is centralized and teachers are autonomous in their lesson preparation. Academic and discipline pressure is above average, but the school climate is viewed negatively. The fourth type of 21 schools seems to have the least favourable configuration of school characteristics. In general, there is little cohesion in the school organisation and in the decision-making processes, and relatively little attention is paid to cognitive and discipline pressure.

As to predicting effects, we hypothesize positive effects on the perspective scores for the schools in the first group. The effects might be most favourable for the disadvantaged pupils.

The next typology is constructed on the basis of the variables for the upper grades of the schools. Again we found four different types. The first type consists of 23 departments and is characterized by a relatively high degree of pupil participation in decision-making as far as school rules, daily affairs and so on are concerned. Striking is the result that the head of the department does not choose a priori the teacher's side in case of conflicts between teacher and pupil. Much attention is paid to informing parents about school rules and selection procedures. There are many extracurricular activities organized by the department, such as discos, informative lectures, hobby-clubs and instructive films. Less favourable is the score on the school rules variable, indicating that rules concerning truancy, selection procedures, marks and so on are less formalized than in the other types of schools.

Table 4: Results cluster analysis for the upper grades (z-scores)

|  | Clusters | | | |
| --- | --- | --- | --- | --- |
|  | 1<br>N=23 | 2<br>N=12 | 3<br>N=23 | 4<br>N=50 |
| Pupil participation | 1.06 | -.75 | -.13 | -.25 |
| Informing of parents | .66 | .97 | -1.09 | -.04 |
| Extracurricular activities | .96 | -.04 | .73 | -.77 |
| School rules | -.33 | -.45 | .89 | -.15 |
| Teacher-pupil conflicts | .88 | -1.18 | -.49 | .11 |

The second type contains twelve departments. The informing of parents is well organized, but on the other characteristics negative scores are the rule. The third type with 23 departments pays much attention to extracurricular activities and the formalization of school rules. On the other hand parents are less well informed, and the head of the department does not pay much attention to conflicts between teachers and pupils. The fourth type might be depicted as modal, as 50 departments form this type and all scores, except for the negative score on extracurricular activities, are close to the average.

Once again our hypothesis is that the first type should produce the most positive perspective scores, primarily for low SES pupils.

## The Analysis of School Effects

As can be deduced from our theory and hypotheses, relationships are investigated between units of different levels: schools and pupils. As far as overall school effects are hypothesized, contextual statements are involved: school effects on pupil behaviour. In as far as our hypothesis predicts differential school effects for pupils with different background characteristics it concerns macro-micro interactions (c.f. Tacq, 1986). Following the suggestion of Kreft (1987) we will use random coefficient models for the investigation of these kinds of multi-level phenomena.

Our design is seriously unbalanced: in some schools there is only one pupil. Therefore we perform seperate analyses for low and high SES pupils to test our hypotheses about the interaction effect of school and SES on school success. This way we can interpret different parameter values as interaction effects. To ensure the power of our tests we use significance levels at the pupil level of 1 percent and 10 percent at the school level (two-tailed for covariates, 5 percent one-tailed for the hypothesized effects).

As covariates in the design we have sex, SES, IQ at age 7, achievement at age 12, teachers advice at age 12 (advising the choice of LBO, MAVO, HAVO or VWO), future plans (indicating male or female profession plans) and the school choice at age 12 (LBO, MAVO, HAVO or VWO). Furthermore, we have school covariates as well: schooltype (LBO, MAVO, HAVO, VWO; LBO being the contrast-group), selective versus non-selective comprehensive schools (scholengemeenschappen) and public versus private schools.

As there are large structural effects we standardize our perspective score to a mean of '0' and a variance of '1' per type of education. For the same reason we also do not use the final position variable, but the efficiency variable instead. For the analyses we use the variance component analysis software (VARCL) developed by Longford (1986).

# RESULTS

## Introduction

We perform six analyses. First we analyse the relationships for the total sample to detect overall school effects. Then we split our sample in two parts, low versus high SES pupils, and then repeat our analyses. This way we can detect SES-specific school effects. This procedure is carried out twice, once for efficiency and once for the educational perspectives. Our strategy for analysis is as follows. First we fit a pupil-level regression model. Next, we enter the school covariates, and try to find a better fitting model. And finally we add the dummy variables for our typologies and try to find the most economical and best fitting model. The results are presented in table 5.

## The Efficiency Dimension

### General effects

First of all we have to explain why IQ and SES effects are contained in the table even though these are not significant. When following our fitting strategy it is possible that in the first stages pupil-level covariates appear to be significant, although in latter stages their effect may shrink because of multicollinearity: eg. if low SES pupils prefer LBO schools the SES effect will disappear once we use schooltype as covariate at the school level. When this is the case we still use the pupil level covariate in the model, to detect these selectivity problems. Actually the VWO and private schools' advantage is due to this kind of selectivity process. As for the predicted effects: School type 1 indeed produces the best efficiency scores, although only the difference with type 4 is significant. This result suggests that cohesive schools, with a positive climate and academic and disciplinary pressure, are the most efficient schools. Unfortunately this is not the case for our department typology, since none of the constructed configurations seems to produce more efficient school careers.

### SES-specific effects

There are some striking differences between the two SES groups. Efficiency for low SES pupils is simply a function of their cognitive level at age 12, whereas for high SES pupils it is a function of school choice and cognitive talent (did they choose the right school according to their cognitive level; if not then their efficiency score is worse). We must remark however that we should not emphasize this point to strongly, because of restriction of range and multicollinearity problems. Secondly, the private schools' advantage only exists for high SES pupils, which result supports our conjectures about selectivity processes at the intake of secondary schools. None of the configurations seems to produce outstanding efficiency for one of the two groups. So all in all (surprisingly), schools matter more for the privileged children. We will discuss this finding later on.

## Educational Perspectives

### General effects

In the general model we find effects of the pupil covariates 'intelligence at age 7' (1 standard deviation shift in IQ leads to approximately .14 standard deviation shift in perspective score) and 'sex' (boys scoring one half of a standard deviation above girls). None of the school level covariates proved to be significantly related to the perspective scores. As far as our hypotheses about the effects of the constructed school types are concerned, we indeed find some evidence suggesting that cohesive schools, with a positive climate

Table 5.: Regression coefficients for school success scores on pupil and school variables

| | educational perspectives | | | efficiency | | |
|---|---|---|---|---|---|---|
| | total group | high SES | low SES | total group | high SES | low SES |
| CONSTANT | **-.347** | **.590** | **-.960** | **50.797** | **64.320** | **100.934** |
| PUPIL LEVEL | | | | | | |
| IQ 1972 | **.009** | | **.012** | .060 | **.237** | |
| achievement tests 1978 | | | | | | |
| teachers advice 1978 | | | | | | **-12.906** |
| future plans 1978 | | | | | | |
| school choice 1978 | | | | | **-10.676** | |
| sex | **-.604** | **-.547** | **-.628** | | | 1.108 |
| ses | n.a. | n.a. | n.a. | **.409** | n.a. | |
| SCHOOL LEVEL | | | | | | |
| LBO | | | | .000 | .000 | .000 |
| MAVO | | | | 1.579 | **14.415** | **10.035** |
| HAVO | | | | 4.712 | **21.374** | **19.041** |
| VWO | | | | **20.601** | **46.914** | **47.350** |
| Selective schools | | | | | | |
| Non-selective schools | | | | | | |
| Public schools | | | | .000 | .000 | |
| Private schools | | | | **3.734** | **8.238** | |
| Department type 1 | .000 | | .000 | | | |
| type 2 | **-.398** | | -.057 | | | |
| type 3 | -.016 | | .491 | | | |
| type 4 | .102 | | .198 | | | |
| School type 1 | .000 | .000 | | .000 | | |
| type 2 | **-.489** | **-.510** | | -2.507 | | |
| type 3 | **-.333** | -.162 | | -.073 | | |
| type 4 | **-.397** | **-.437** | | **-5.933** | | |
| VARIANCE EXPLAINED | | | | | | |
| Total | 15.7% | 11.1% | 15.6% | 14.5% | 27.9% | 24.2% |
| School variables only | 6.2% | 3.9% | 2.0% | 11.4% | 18.3% | 11.1% |

*only bold coefficients are significant (pupil level <.01, school level <.10)

and academic and disciplinary pressure, have the better perspective scores for their pupils (net effect about .4 standard deviation). The first department type also has a better mean perspective score, but this only holds true in contrast with type 2.

*SES-specific effects*
Comparing the second and third column of Table 5 we find that intelligence only has an effect for the low SES pupils. Contrary to our predictions is the result that school type 1 only has significant effects for high SES pupils.

Somewhat unexpected is the result that department type 3 outperforms the other types when we analyse low SES data. It is tempting to explain this result in terms of the difference in formalization of school rules between group 1 and 3. But univariate linear analysis did not show a significant effect on educational perspectives resulting from this variable alone. So it must be the complete configuration (lack of involvement of parents and children, but clear-cut rules and many extracurriculur activities) that brings about this result for the low SES pupils.


# DISCUSSION

We first summarise our principal findings. First of all, the division of pupils after primary education into four types of education with different prestige levels has an enormous effect on future educational perspectives. But different perspectives also occur within types of education as a result of different choice patterns. Choosing mathematics in combination with physics gives the best opportunities in further education. Furthermore our constructed perspective variable seems to have a stronger relationship with gender than with SES. Boys in junior vocational education and pre-university education have access to respectively 10 and 30 extra further studies than girls. These results cannot be explained by different cognitive functioning or typical gender-bound career aspirations at the age of twelve, since in the analysis we controlled for these variables (the latter having no effect at all). Interesting is the result that the school-level covariates had no effect on educational perspectives. In other studies (Steedman, 1983; Kreft, 1987) effects are often found favouring comprehensive schools. And in Coleman's study (Coleman et al., 1984) the private schools proved to be outstanding. That the type of education has no effect is simply a result of our standardizing procedure, which produces equal means and variances for all types of education. Somewhat surprising is the differential IQ-effect, as this covariate shows significant effects for low SES but not for high SES pupils. One might hypothesize that family support explains the unexpected subject combination choices by high SES pupils, whereas the educational system might be meritocratic for low SES pupils. Though the results are not completely comparable with research concerning the effects of tracking in U.S. high schools (e.g. Alexander et al., 1978; Oakes, 1985) these also point to the possible sustaining effects of educational stratification on unequal opportunities in further education.

As for the efficiency dimension of school success, school effects were less pronounced. The clear advantage found for the private sector could be fully ascribed to selectivity processes at the intake of secondary schools. As far as private schools produced more efficient school careers, this turned out to be an effect for high SES pupils only. Also surprising is the result that a cohesive school organisation seems to matter more for high SES pupils than for low SES pupils. One explanation might be that their family may have aspirations which are too high for them, which some schools can and others cannot fulfil. Complementarily, there is less variation between secondary schools in school success for low SES pupils. This being the case, the National Educational Priority Program (OVB) might as well concentrate more on raising overall school performances, since this might be the only way to produce significantly better opportunities for low SES pupils.

# REFERENCES

Aitkin, M. & Longford, N. (1986). Statistical Modelling Issues in School Effectiveness Studies. *Journal of the Royal Statistical Society,* Series A (General) *149*, (1), 1-43

Alexander, K.L., McPartland, .M. & Cook, M.A. (1981). Using standardized test performance in school effects research, In: Kerckhoff, A.C. & Corwin, R.G. (eds.), *Research in sociology of education and socialization.* Greenwich: JAI Press.

Bidwell, C.E. & Kasarda, J.D. (1980). Conceptualizing and measuring the effects of school and schooling. *American Journal of Education. 88,* (4), 401-430

Bosker, R. & Van der Velden, R. (1985). Onderwijspositie en selectie (School success and selection). In: W.J. Nijhof & E. Warries (eds.), *De opbrengst van onderwijs en scholing* [The output of school and schooling] Lisse: Swets en Zeitlinger.

Bosker, R., Hofman, A. & Van der Velden, R. (1985). Een generatie geselecteerd. Deel 1: de loopbanen [A generation selected. Part 1: the school careers]. Groningen: RION.

Bosker, R., Van der Velden, R. & Hofman, A. (1985). Een generatie geselecteerd. Deel 3: technisch rapport scholen [A generation selected. Part 3: technical report, schools]. Groningen: RION.

Brutsaert, H. (1986). *Gelijke kansen en leerlinggerichtheid in het secundair onderwijs* [Equal opportunities and pupil-centeredness in secondary education]. Leuven: ACCO.

CBS (Netherlands Central Bureau of Statistics) (1980). *Statistiek van het VWO, HAVO en MAVO; keuze van vakken* [Statistics on pre-university education, senior and junior secondary general education]. 's-Gravenhage: Staatsuitgeverij.

Coleman, J.S., Hoffer, T. & Kilgore, S. (1984). Achievement and segregation in secondary schools. A further look at public and private schooldifferences. *Sociology of Education. 55,* 162-182.

Cremers, P. (1980). Constructie van een schaal voor bereikt niveau van voortgezet onderwijs [The construction of a scale for school success]. *Tijdschrift voor Onderwijsresearch, 5,* 80-91.

Cuttance, P. (1983). Towards a sociological account of the effects of schools on student outcomes. Montreal: AERA-paper.

Dekkers, H. (1985). Soms kiezen meisjes anders. Scholen, dekanen, vakken [Sometimes girls choose differently. Schools, schoolcounselors and subjects]. Nijmegen: ITS.

Glebbeek, A.C. (1983). Jeugdwerkloosheid en het onderwijs (Youth unemployement and education]. *Jeugd en Samenleving. 13,* (5-6).

Jöreskog, K.G. & Sörbom, D. (1984). *LISREL VI, users guide.* Uppsala: University of Uppsala

Kreft, G.G. (1987) Models and methods for the measurements of schooleffects. Amsterdam: Universiteit van Amsterdam.

Kuyper, H. & Van der Werf, M. (1987). De invloed van het gedrag van docenten op prestaties in keuze van, en attituden ten opzichte van wiskunde door meisjes in het AVO/VWO [The effects of teacher behaviour on mathematics achievement, choice of mathematics and attitudes towards mathematics]. Groningen: RION.

Longford, N. (1986). *Variance component analysis: manual.* University of Lancaster

Meijnen, G.W. (1977). Maatschappelijke achtergronden van intellectuele ontwikkeling [Social background and intellectual development]. Groningen: Rijksuniversiteit.

Meijnen, G.W. (1984). *Van zes tot twaalf* [From six to twelve]. Harlingen: Flevodruk

Meijnen, G.W. (1986). Ongelijke onderwijskansen en effectieve scholen [Unequal educational opportunities and effective schools]. In Van der Wolf, J.L. & Hox, J.J. (eds.): *Kwaliteit van onderwijs in het geding* [Questioning the quality of education]. Lisse: Swets & Zeitlinger.

Oakes, J. (1985). *Keeping track. How schools structure inequality.* New Haven and London: Yale University Press.

Raudenbush, S., & Bryk, A.S. (1986). A hierarchical model for studying school effects. *Sociology of Education, 59,* 1-17.

Roeleveld, J., Van den Eeden, P., & De Jong, U. (1985). Scholengemeenschappen met MAVO en schoolloopbanen [Comprehensive schools with MAVO departments and school careers. Enschede: ORD-paper.

Rutter, M., Maughan, B, Mortimore, P., & Ouston, J. (1979). *Fifteen thousand hours.* London: Open Books.

Steedman, J. (1983). *Examination results in selective and nonselective schools.* London: the National Children's Bureau.

Tacq, J. (1986). Van multiniveau-probleem naar multiniveau-analyse [From multi-level problems to multi-level analysis]. Amsterdam: NSAV-paper.

Tesser, P. (1986). Sociale herkomst en schoolloopbanen in het voortgezet onderwijs [The relation between social background and the school career in secondary education]. Nijmegen: ITS.

Appendix 1: The scaling of educational positions

Figure 1: The scaling of educational positions

| | | | | | |
|---|---|---|---|---|---|
| | top | | | | |
| | 12 | VWO-6 | | | |
| | 11 | VWO-5 | | | |
| | 10 | VWO-4 | HAVO-5 | | |
| | 9 | VWO-3 | HAVO-4 | | |
| Educational | 8 | VWO-2 | HAVO-3 | MAVO-4 | |
| ladder | 7 | VWO-1 | HAVO-3 | MAVO-3 | LBO-4 |
| | 6 | VWO-0 | HAVO-1 | MAVO-2 | LBO-3 |
| | 5 | | HAVO-0 | MAVO-1 | LBO-2 |
| | 4 | | | MAVO-0 | LBO-1 |
| | 3 | | | | LBO-0 |
| | bottom | | | | |

# Appendix 2: Required subject combinations in 1983-1984

Two years (HAVO and VWO) and one year (MAVO and LBO) before graduation pupils have to choose approximately 7 out of 14 subjects. Only in these 7 subjects national examinations are held. Further studies have specific prerequisites in terms of the specific subjects followed. These prerequisites differ for each type of secondary education; VWO, HAVO, MAVO and LBO. In 1983-1984 the prerequisites could be classified as follows:

1.  *University*
    Access only for students from VWO
    Number of courses (studies):                                     77
    a) no specific prerequisites:                                    23
    b) at least mathematics and physics:                             21
    c) other prerequisites:                                          26

2.  *Higher vocational education (HBO)*
    Access only for students from VWO and HAVO
    Number of courses (studies):                                    134
    I. For VWO students:
    a) no specific prerequisites:                                    95
    b) at least mathematics and physics:                             27
    c) other prerequisites:                                          12
    II. For HAVO students:
    a) no specific prerequisites:                                    83
    b) at least mathematics and physics:                             27
    c) other prerequisites:                                          24

3.  *Senior vocational education (MBO)*
    Access only for students from VWO, HAVO and MAVO and LBO
    Number of courses (studies):                                     83
    I. For VWO students:
    a) no specific prerequisites:                                    83
    II. For HAVO students:
    a) no specific prerequisites:                                    83
    III. For MAVO students:
    a) no specific prerequisites:                                    29
    b) at least mathematics, physics and one modern foreign language: 39
    c) other prerequisites:                                          15
    IV. For LBO students:
    a) no specific prerequisites:                                     1
    b) at least mathematics, physics and one modern foreign language at C-level    43
    c) other prerequisites:                                          39

# EDUCATIONAL INNOVATION OR SCHOOL EFFECTIVENESS: A DILEMMA?

Wijnand Th.J.G. Hoeben*
RION Institute for Educational Research, University of Groningen

School improvement is the confessed and expressed aim of all educational innovators and of those concerned with policy and practice of education. Theories on educational innovation, however, focus primarily on the problems of adoption, implementation and incorporation of new ideas and methods, while supposing that educational practice along those ideas will improve the schools towards greater effectiveness. School effectiveness research focusses primarily on factors that may contribute to a greater school effectiveness. Educational innovation and school effectiveness therefore seem to be different programmatic concepts for different schools of thought on school improvement. Sometimes they even seem to be concepts for different paradigms for research, policy and action in education.

Educational innovation focusses on what is new in education with the risk of underestimating the importance of traditional practices that are proven worthwhile. This influences the view of what education should be about: its goals and objectives. It influences also the ideas about factors that are important to improve schools. Efforts to persuade schools to bring new ideas into practice and efforts to research these ideas tend to focus on the processes of adoption, of implementation and of incorporation and relating them to characteristics of the innovations and their developmental processes. Theorists furthermore tend to focus on educational change with innovators as change-agents. (Fullan & Pomfret, 1977; Fullan, 1982; Leithwood & Montgomery, 1982; Loucks & Hall, 1977; Harriet & Gross, 1979; Dalin, 1978; Havelock, 1978.

The concept of school effectiveness primarily deals with students' achievement. A school's effectiveness is defined by the level of achievement of its students. Researchers focus primarily on factors that raise the level of achievement. Practitioners use descriptions of students' levels of achievement as indicators for the school's effectiveness and as a starting-point for decisions about possible school improvements. Ideally, described levels of

* With thanks to Egbert Harskamp for providing the data on which this paper is based and to Cor Suhre for assisting with the LISREL-analysis.

achievement are part of a feedback loop of a school's self-evaluation and self-improvement. If the achievement level is not satisfactory, the school should try and improve its functioning in order to reach higher levels in future. Factors that contribute to higher effectiveness as identified by researchers should be considered in a plan for school improvement. (Brookover et al., 1979; Edmonds, 1979; 1982; Purkey & Smith, 1983; Reynolds, 1982; Rutter et al., 1979; Wellish et al., 1978; Fraser et al., 1987).

Although theories on educational innovation and on school effectiveness do in fact focus on different concepts, they have a concern in common for school improvement. Therefore differences may be reconciled by regarding both sets of theories as supplementary. Theories on school effectiveness focus on bringing about high levels of students' achievement and on improving schools in such a way that they are more effective in this regard. In order to achieve this, schools frequently have to innovate themselves. Theories on educational innovation focus on how schools may innovate themselves by explaining problems and solutions during the processes of adoption, implementation and incorporation of an innovation. From the point of view of school improvement, theories on educational innovation focus on the proces of innovation, while theories on school effectiveness focus on its contents and objectives. Because differences might be explained by the primary concerns of the two sets of theories on process and product of an innovation respectively, the theories in fact may supplement each other. The hypothesis might be formulated that adoption, implementation and incorporation of an innovation improves a school in such a way that its instructional processes are more effective, thereby raising the level of students' achievement.

The hypothesis is investigated in a secondary analysis of research into the innovation of Dutch primary schools (Harskamp & Rijken, 1988). The research aimed at a description of the progress a representative sample of Dutch primary schools made in their proces of innovation towards the new "Basic School" as required by law. The school's progress had to be compared with the progress described some years earlier and the schools' progress had to be explained by internal and external influences. Elements of educational policy figured heavily as external influences. Data on students' achievement were available for half the schools, as were data on instructional processes. In a secondary analysis the three kinds of data could be linked together to provide a preliminary test of the hypothesis and to make further explorations possible.

## METHODS

There were in fact two samples. The first sample contained all schools (n=359) that had started their innovation on a voluntary basis before parliament passed the law in 1985. The second was a random sample (n=641) from all other schools. For the purposes of this secondary analysis the two samples are combined into one sample of a thousand schools of which 53% (524) responded. The resulting sample may still be called representative as is shown by a comparison between responding and nonresponding schools (Suhre, 1988). The resulting sample is 6.6% of the total population of primary schools in the Netherlands.

Progress in innovation was measured by a questionnaire asking about phases of innovation in five areas regarded to be instrumental for the purposes of the innovation. The law formulates as its purpose that education is provided such that pupils from 4 to 12 years of age will have an uninterrupted process of development and achieve the necessary cognitive, social and cultural skills. The instrumental areas of innovation are:

1. development and innovation of the school curriculum;
2. differentiation and individualisation;
3. professional development of the teaching staff;
4. not only the organisational , but also the educational, integration of kindergarden and traditional primary school;
5. broadening of the teaching content.

The items proved to be scaleable, for the five instrumental subscales as well as for the combined scale: progress in innovation.

Data on the following instructional variables were available. Instructional time was measured by the total amount of time available for teaching language and arithmetic. Implementation of the basic curriculum was measured by the proportion of the pupils that are taught the essential elements of the language curriculum, and the essential elements of the arithmetic curriculum respectively. Pupil evaluation was measured by questions about the monitoring of their achievements. The mastery level was estimated by the proportion of pupils that according to the teacher have mastery over the essential elements of the language as well as arithmatic curriculum.

Data on pupils' achievement were available from 219 of the 524 schools in the sample. The data were mean scores of the schools, based on the results of their pupils on a standardized test that was delivered by the Dutch Central Institute for Test Development (CITO). It consists of three subtests: language, arithmetic and processing of information in general. Each subtest contains sixty items. They have high internal consistency ($\alpha$=.85 to $\alpha$=.93). The content validity for the important subjects is high. The test is a good predictor for success in secondary education.

As an independent variable at the pupil level, available information on the socio-economic status of their parents was aggregated at the schoollevel as the modal socio-economic status of pupils. As an independent variable at the school level educational leadership was measured, based on the estimated frequency of twelve activities of typical educational leaders (evaluating

159

teachers, stimulating in-service training, giving suggestions and directions to teachers, etc.).

In the secondary analysis the following techniques are used: analysis of co-variance, multiple regression analysis and LISREL VI (Jöreskog & Sörbom, 1983).

The analysis of variance and covariance is used to get an initial estimate of the influence of progress in innovation in the five instrumental areas on pupil achievement after statistical correction for modal socio-economic status. The multiple regression analysis is used to compare the influences of the modal socio-economic status, of instructional variables and of progress in innovation. The LISREL-analysis is used to explore within the available data the ways in which educational innovation may influence instructional variables and pupil achievement.

# RESULTS

As a first step in the analysis the schools that progressed to the implementation or the incorporation of the innovation in the five selected areas were compared with the schools that got only as far as the phases of orientation on adoption. The mean achievement score of the two groups of schools in each of the areas was computed after statistical correction for the modal SES (Table 1).

Table 1: Mean achievement scores of schools (n=219), related to their progress in innovation on five areas (after statistical correction for the modal SES).

| areas of innovation | Phases of innovation | | correlation between progress in innovation and achievement |
| | oriëntation and adoption | implementation and incorporation | |
| --- | --- | --- | --- |
| school curriculum | 128 (n=18) | 130 (n=201) | r=.10 (p=.07) |
| professional development | 129 (n=122) | 131 (n=97) | r=.11 (p=.05) |
| differentiation | 130 (n=133) | 130 (n=86) | r=.07 (p=.14) |
| integration | 129 (n=88) | 131 (n=131) | r=.07 (p=.16) |
| broadening of content | 130 (n=161) | 129 (n=58) | r=.05 (p=.24) |

160

The differences in mean achievement scores were negligible. In an analysis of variance no differences were significant. The correlations between progress in innovation in the five areas and the achievement scores of schools controlling for a modal SES were also computed (Table 1). The correlations were low and not significant. The correlation coefficient between achievement scores of schools and their total progress in innovation was also low and not significant ($r = .04$; $p = .10$).

Inspection of correlation coefficients might help to give some insight into these negative findings. The correlation coefficients of achievement scores of schools with their progress in innovation and educational leadership are negligible (less than statistically significant). The correlation coefficients of achievement scores with three of the five instructional variables are moderate. The correlation of achievement with modal SES of pupils is relatively high (Table 2).

Table 2: Matrix of correlation coefficients ($r > .11$; $p < .05$).

| | 1 | 2 | 3 | 4 | 5 | 6 | 7 | 8 | 9 |
|---|---|---|---|---|---|---|---|---|---|
| 1. achievement scores | - | | | | | | | | |
| 2. modal SES | .45 | - | | | | | | | |
| 3. mastery level | .31 | .25 | - | | | | | | |
| 4. pupil evaluation | .18 | .06 | .20 | - | | | | | |
| 5. implementation of the arithmetic curriculum | .20 | .15 | .40 | .15 | - | | | | |
| 6. implementation of the language curriculum | .07 | .09 | .30 | .12 | .63 | - | | | |
| 7. institutional time | .06 | .01 | .06 | .01 | .04 | .10 | - | | |
| 8. progress in innovation | .04 | -.02 | -.07 | .25 | -.13 | -.15 | -.01 | - | |
| 9. educational leadership | .09 | .07 | .02 | .29 | .03 | .02 | .10 | .27 | - |

Progress in innovation is correlated only with educational leadership, pupil evaluation and negatively with implementation of the arithmetic curriculum and of the language curriculum. The finding that educational leadership in these Dutch primary schools is only correlated with their progress in innovation and with pupil evaluation and not with other instructional variables nor with the achievement scores of schools may be meaningful in discussions about school effectiveness.

Multiple regression analysis with the schools' achievement scores as dependent variable may help to give some more insight in the relative influences of the different variables. Variables were stepwise introduced in the analysis according to their contribution to the variance explained. After the schools' modal SES had been introduced in the regression model, the instructional variables explained only 7% of the total variance, while the schools' progress in innovation and their educational leadership did not contribute anything (Table 3). This analysis seems to be conclusive. In explaining schools' effectiveness the socio-economic status of their pupils has the most important influence, instruction has a modest influence, and innovation and educational leadership seem to have no influence at all. The possible consequences of these findings for theory and practice of educational innovation and of school effectiveness in the Dutch primary schools could be far-reaching.

Table 3: Proportions of variance in schools' achievement scores, successively explained by SES, instructional variables, innovation progress and educational leadership

| Step | Variable | r-Square | Change |
|------|----------|----------|--------|
| 1. | modal SES | .199 | .199 |
| 2. | mastery level | .239 | .040 |
| 3. | pupil evaluation | .253 | .015 |
| 4/5. | implementation of the curriculum | .264 | .010 |
| 6. | instructional time | .267 | .003 |
| 7. | progress in innovation | .268 | .001 |
| 8. | educational leadership | .268 | .000 |

To test the conclusiveness of these findings a linear structural equation model was developed in which possible influences of educational leadership and progress in innovation on instructional variables and the influences of these variables on achievement scores were hypothesised. After a first analysis this model was modified by adding one path of influence. The modified model has an optimal fit with the empirical data ($X^2=17.56$; P=.68; goodness of fit=.98). According to the modified version the implementation of the basic curriculum, pupil evaluation and the estimated mastery level of pupils are of crucial importance in influencing achievement scores of schools, next to the socio-economic status of their pupils. Educational leadership and the schools' progress in innovation seem to play a role in influencing the instructional variables, especially pupils' evaluation (Figure 1). The total effects of educational leadership and progress in innovation on achievement, however, remain modest compared with the total effects of instructional variables.

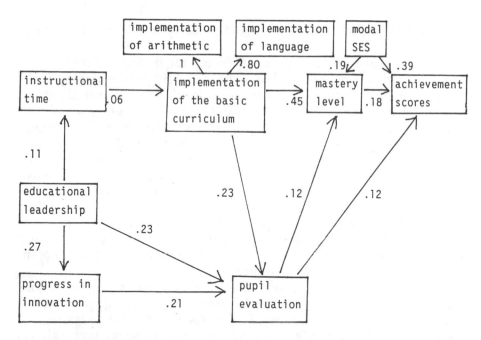

*Figure 1:The modified linear structural equation model of the influences of educational leadership, innovation and instruction on schools' achievement scores (with LISREL estimates of maximum likelihood).*

# DISCUSSION

One has to keep in mind that these are the findings of a secondary analysis of research aiming at the description and an explanation of differences in schools' progress in innovation. Achievement scores were available only of approximately half the schools in the sample. It is generally supposed that among the schools that do not use the service of the Dutch Central Institute of Test Development (CITO) schools with low achievement scores are overrepresented. No data on this issue are available, however. Furthermore, the instructional data included in the analysis are such that they could easily be obtained by a questionaire administered to headmasters. The validity of such measurements may be questioned. Multiple correlations on the five subscales of progress in innovation between responses of headmasters and of teachers in a subsample ranged between .41 and .50 (Harskamp & Rijken, 1988, 36-37). Taking the different positions of teachers and headmasters into consideration these correlations may be regarded high and as indications of the validity of headmasters' responses. Nevertheless, if the research questions of this secondary analysis had been the primary objectives of the research, the instructional variables would probably have been measured in another way.

Such cautionary remarks are not necessary for the measurement of the schools' progress in innovation. The findings that differential progress is not correlated with differences in achievement, neither in the analysis of the separate subscales nor in the analysis with the total innovation scale, should be a concern for both theorists and practitioners of innovation. The findings that the instructional variables as measured explain 7% of the variance in achievement, while progress in innovation nor educational leadership explain any variance may be regarded as anomalous for theorists on educational innovation as well as for theorists on school effectiveness. The findings should also cause practitioners to pause and think before outlining their plans for school improvement along the lines of theories of educational innovation and of school effectiveness. The findings provide a support for those theorists and practitioners who regard school improvement primarily a problem of improvement of instruction (Fraser et al., 1987).

Some anomalous findings may be explained by traditions and regulations in Dutch primary education. The first of these anomalies concerns the lack of influence of educational leadership. Dutch headmasters have no tradition of educational leadership; they are firsts among equals in the teaching staff. As a consequence, their influence on instruction and achievement may be less than the influence of colleagues in other countries. At present there are some developments that may allow Dutch headmasters in primary education to grow into positions of leadership.

Another anomalous finding concerns the influence of instructional time. As well as in the regression analysis as in the LISREL analysis, the influence of instructional time appeared to be minimal. This finding may very well be the consequence of the very detailed regulations in Dutch primary schools for the distribution of the available time among the different teaching subjects in the school curriculum. Especially for the teaching of arithmetic and language, only very slight variations are allowed. High correlations with other instructional variables and especially with achievement may therefore not be expected. Theories on the management of instructional time and of its influences on achievement, furthermore, tend to focus on time on task. Data on time on task of pupils were not available for this analysis. The hypothesis that inclusion of such data in the analysis would have enhanced the importance of instructional variables is consistent with other research (Frederick & Walberg 1980).

The only data on pupil characteristics available for this analysis were data on the socio-economic status of their parents, aggregated to school level as modal SES. Availability of data on their cognitive background and their dispositions to learn would first of all have explained much more of the variance in achievement scores of schools. Secondly, the contribution of SES in this explanation would have been lower. Thirdly, the possibility has to be faced that some of the variance at present explained by instructional variables could be explained by pupils' cognitive background and disposition to learn. This possibility, however, may not be seen as reducing the anomalous character of the present findings. In the contrary, this possibility is a further argument for the lack of influence of educational leadership and progress in innovation. It should be a concern for theorists of educational innovation and school effectiveness in their efforts to influence their theories.

The exploratary analysis of the lineair structural equation model (LISREL) has some results that may give hope to theorists of educational innovation and those of school effectiveness. The analysis proves that variables of these theories may have influence on the improvement of instruction toward higher productivity and effectiveness. In the present analysis educational leadership and progress in innovation proved to be of influence on the way schools evaluated their pupils, thereby having a small total effect on the schools' achievement. Theories of school effectiveness, instead of concentrating on contributing factors at the school level, should concentrate on the ways such factors could improve instruction thereby contributing to a higher achievement of schools. Theories on educational innovation, instead of focussing on phases of adoption, implementation and incorporation, should give more attention to influences of innovation on instruction, especially on its effectiveness. School improvement should concentrate on improving the instruction by the schools' teachers by using the available research (Fraser et al., 1987). Educational leadership and other effective factors at the school level, as well as educational innovation should be seen as a function of the improvement of instruction. There are no effective schools without effective teachers. There seems to be also no successful innovation without effective teachers.

# REFERENCES

Brookover, W., Beady, C., Flood, P., Schweitzer, J. & Wisenbaker, J. (1979). *School social systems and student achievement: Schools can make a difference.* New York: Praeger Publishers.

Dalin, P. (1978). *Limits to educational change.* London.

Edmonds, R.R. (1979). Effective schools for the urban poor. *Educational Leadership, 37,* (1), 15-24.

Edmonds, R.R. (1982). Programs of school improvement: an overview. *Educational Leadership.*

Fraser, B.J., Walberg, H.J., Welch, W.W., & Hattie, J.A. (1987). Syntheses of educational productivity research. *International Journal of Educational Research, 11,* 145-252.

Frederick, W.C., & Walberg, H.J. (1980). Learning as a function of time. *Journal of Educational Research, 73,* 183-194.

Fullan, M., & Pomfret, A. (1977). Research on curriculum and instruction implementation. *Review of educational Research, 47,* (1).

Fullan, M. (1982). *The meaning of educational change.* Teachers College Press, Columbia University, New York.

Havelock, R.G. (1969). *Planning for innovation through dissemination and utilization of knowledge*. Ann Arbor.

Herriot, R.E., & Gross, N. (eds.) (1979). *The dynamics of planned educational change*. Berkeley.

Leithwood, K.A., & Montgomery, D.J.(1982). A framework for planned educational change: application to the assessment of program implementation. *Educational Evaluation and Policy Analysis, 4*, (2).

Loucks, S.F., & Hall, G.E. (1977). Assessing and facilitating the implementation of innovations: a new approach. *Educational Technology, 17*.

Purkey, S.C., & Smith, M.S. (1983). Effective schools: a review. *The Elementary School Journal, 83*, (4).

Reynolds, D. (1983). The search for effective schools. *School Organization, 2*, (3), 215-237.

Rutter, M., Maughan, B., Mortimore, P. Ouston, J., & Smith, A. (1979). *Fifteen thousand hours: secondary schools and their effects on children*. Sommerset: Open Books.

Suhre, C. (1988). *Schools ensnared: increasing response in survey research*. Groningen: RION (unpublished)

Wellisch, J.B., MacQueen, A.H. Carriere, R.A., & Duck, G.A. (1978). School management and organization in succesful schools. *Sociology of Education, 51*, (3).

# EFFECTIVE SCHOOLS AND EQUAL OPPORTUNITIES

Mart Jan de Jong & Sjaak F.A. Braster
Erasmus University, Rotterdam

## WHEN ARE SCHOOLS MORE EFFECTIVE?

Research outcomes show all kinds of different characteristics that purportedly constitute effective schools. Purkey and Smith (1983) have shown that there is some order in this chaos. After a review of the literature they present a list of nine organization-structure variables and a set of four process variables. However, in the same year Ralph and Fennessey (1983) write that the following five factors are widely touted: strong administrative leadership, safe and orderly school climate, an emphasis on basic academic skills, high teacher expectations and a system for monitoring pupil performance. Many of these factors, but not all, are also presented in a list of twelve key factors by Mortimore et al. (1988). So, even synthetic reviews of the literature do not put an halt to the broadening of the spectre of causes of effectiveness. Fortunately, there is a lot more agreement on the general idea of effectiveness:

School X is more effective than Y, if it enhances more progress in the development of its pupils than school Y.

Every statement about the effectiveness of schools is always related to a specified aspect of human development. If people disagree on what kind of development is most important, then they will also disagree on their assessment of the quality of a school. Nevertheless, it is fair to say that the large majority of researchers have cognitive development and school achievement scores in mind when they speak of effective schools. The same is true for most of the parents.

It is not our intention to discuss and explore all kinds of problems with the conceptualization and measurement of school effectiveness, let alone to present some solutions for them. For more extensive discussions of these topics we point at the work of various scholars (Goldstein, 1984; Gray, 1981, Madaus, 1979; Reynolds, 1985). We only want to make clear that the definition given above needs to be modified, because the comparison of schools can only be done in a reliable and valid fashion if the student bodies of these schools are similar. It seems necessary to add an extra condition to our definition:

School X is more effective than school Y with *a similar group of pupils,* if it enhances more progress in the educational development of its pupils than school Y.

According to this definition it is impossible to compare the effectiveness of schools of a different type or level of education. If schools are of the same kind, but different in their balance of intake, ethnically, socio-economically or with respect to ability, we have to be very cautious with our comparisons of schools, even after controlling for some relevant variables.


# EQUALITY OF OPPORTUNITIES

Research has made abundantly clear that children from lower socio-economic strata and from various minority groups enter the educational system with lower levels of cognitive development than children coming from middle class families. At the end of their educational careers the gaps do still exist or have become even larger. Moreover, higher percentages of children from disadvantageous backgrounds are relegated to special education or drop out of school.

In the light of large differences in home background and ability the aim of equal educational attainment for everyone is unrealistic (Coleman, 1973; 1975). Therefore, most of us speak of equal opportunities when each child achieves according to its ability. We use intelligence tests as a useful proxy for innate abilities, although they are culturally biased to some degree. Nevertheless, they are valid and reliable instruments to predict the level of educational attainment that is feasable for each individual (Jensen, 1979). This is partly so, because the educational system is also culturally biased to the life style of the middle class of the dominant ethnic group.

We get nearer to the aim of equal educational opportunities when the correlation between intelligence and school achievement or educational attainment gets higher and approaches 1. At the same time the statistical relation between socio-economic status and educational attainment has to decrease. This last relationship cannot become nil as long as there is an association between social status of parents and IQ-scores of children. In the USA the average correlation found is about .35 (Jencks, 1972). In the Netherlands similar correlations have been found (Meester & De Leeuw, 1983). To get rid of this relation between socio-economic level and ability people have to be distributed at random over different layers of the system of social stratification. Of course this is purely academic. The aim of equal educational opportunities is directed at a meritocratic system of stratification and not at a system organized by a lottery.

# THE MEASUREMENT OF SCHOOL EFFECTIVENESS
## AND EDUCATIONAL EQUITY

With the necessary definitions in our rucksack we can now start to explore the relation between effectiveness and educational equity. This might be highly relevant, because many of those who are interested in the promotion of more equal educational opportunities are interested in the effective school movement, and vice versa. Some well-known studies in these field have been carried out in educational priority areas (Edmonds, 1979; Rutter et al., 1979; Mortimore et al., 1988).

The question is whether educational inequalities in a state or nation will be reduced considerably if all schools would become equally effective. Of course, it is very unlikely that this will happen. May be, it is more fruitful and realistic to ask ourselves what will happen if the group of schools that now are functioning badly, would become just as effective as schools who produce average results. Since schools in educational priority areas receive extra budgets to minimize educational inequality, it may be better to pose this question in yet another form: will the changing of nowadays ineffective schools in educational priority areas into schools with an average level of effectivity produce much more equality?

It is not the aim of this paper to present exact estimates, but to offer some empirical support for the idea that more effective schooling can only be part of the solution to educational inequity. We can use data from a study carried out by one of us. However, that study was not set up with the reason to establish precise estimates for the school system of a nation. The data were gathered to describe and explain differences in educational careers between Dutch and minority children in Rotterdam (De Jong, 1987; 1988). Nevertheless, we think that these data, gathered in the last grade of 53 elementary schools, can be of great use for our purpose. (The number of 53 schools emerged after eliminating five schools with less than 8 pupils for which an almost complete data set is available). We have data on ethnic and socio-economic background indicators. With these scores we can calculate the percentage of migrant children in the last grade of each school and its social composition. We also have scores for non-verbal intelligence and Dutch word knowledge. The last score will be used as an indicator for school achievement and a school's effectiveness. Word knowledge may not be mentioned by many schools as an aim of their language lessons, but a good understanding of Dutch, whether it is a pupil's native tongue or his/her second language, will have the utmost priority in the large majority of schools. It is clear that understanding the meaning of words and the way they are related to each other is an necessary condition for understanding any language.

To assess the quality or effectiveness of the school we averaged the word knowledge scores of its pupils. Of course we have to correct this for characteristics of its pupils. First, we assume that there is a (linear) relation between non-verbal intelligence and word knowledge. In our group of 970 pupils this correlation is .44. We assume that a school with many children with high scores on non-verbal IQ, has a group of pupils with more learning potential than a school with only a few pupils with high IQ scores. So, to 'similarize' the quality of the schools' pupils, we constructed prediction scores for each child based on the regression equation of word knowledge on non-verbal IQ.[1] By subtracting the prediction score from the observed score we create a new variable, indicating *individual educational equity* scores (IEE-scores). Schools who have many pupils that score above their predicted scores, thus, having high IEE-scores, seem to be more effective than schools with a majority of pupils scoring below the predicted score. One-way analysis of variance of the IEE-scores with schoolnumber as a factor reveals that differences between schools are statistically significant. The between-schools variance accounts for 19.9 per cent of the total variance. (Without this correction, the analysis of variance of the original word knowledge scores shows that 27.4 per cent of the variance could be accounted for by the schools).

So far, we have made no amendments for the social and ethnic background of the pupils. Cultural factors continue to have an important impact on cognitive development, even after controlling for innate ability. Parents with higher levels of education and higher job status can and do help their children better with their intellectual growth. Moreover, middle class parents have more possibilities to help their children with school assignments and other educational problems than lower class parents. At the individual level social status correlates with word knowledge: $r = .48$. The correlation between social status and non-verbal IQ is much weaker: $r = .28$. Also there are significant relations with ethnic background[2]: with word knowledge $r = -.38$ and with non-verbal IQ $r = -.27$. The correlation between ethnic background and socio-economic status is -.43. To arrive at a more valid assessment of the effectivity of schools we have calculated new prediction scores based on the regression equation of word knowledge on IQ, social status and ethnic background.[3] Again difference scores between observed and predicted scores have been calculated. These scores could be called *school effect* scores (SE-scores). Now the one-way analysis of variance shows that schools are only accountable for 11.7 % of the total variance in inequality between individuals.

# SCHOOL COMPOSITION AND SCHOOL EFFECTIVENESS

If all socially disadvantaged children attend schools that offer poor quality teaching, whereas, on the other hand, priviliged children attend schools that are very effective, this would explain a considerable amount of educational inequality. But is it true?

Indeed, it is true that working class kids do not often attend the same schools as the offspring of the upper class. It is also true that the number of so called black schools, or all-minority schools, is increasing in the Netherlands - a segregative tendency that is getting on the nerves of many politicians and educationalists (De Jong, 1989). Nonetheless, there is no reason to think that children are neatly distributed over all the schools according to their class, rank or estate. In our data set the frequency distribution of school compositions does not show a bimodal, or trimodal shape, but the shape of a normal distribution, indicating that the large majority of schools in our sample have a socially and ethnically mixed population (Table 1).

At the school level many correlations are higher than at the individual level. This is a common phenomenon for aggregated data. We find a correlation of .84 between averaged word knowledge and social mix of the school. The correlation with percentage of minority children is -.67. At first sight these strong correlations seem to indicate that schools with many lower class and minority children are particularly ineffective, and, thus, are responsible for much inequality of opportunities. But this would be a rather hasty conclusion. It is better to look at the relation between the success of schools in promoting higher school effect scores and social composition. This correlation is rather moderate: r = .35. For the percentage of migrant children we find an r of -.21. The first relationship is also reflected in the analysis of variance presented in Table 1.

Table 1: Word knowledge, individual educational equity and school effect scores by social composition

|  | word kn. | IEE | SE | n |
|---|---|---|---|---|
| lower lower class | 19.6 | -8.6 | -3.5 | 7 |
| upper lower class | 27.9 | -1.9 | 0.1 | 23 |
| lower middle class | 33.5 | 1.4 | 0.1 | 17 |
| middle class | 42.9 | 7.8 | 2.9 | 6 |
| F-ratio | 27.1 | 15.5 | 2.6 |  |
| stat. sign. | .00 | .00 | .06 |  |
| $R^2$ | .62 | .49 | .14 |  |

We conclude that at school level only 13.9 % of the variance in school effectiveness is accounted for by social composition. So, educational quality and social composition are only moderately related with each other. The statistical significance is .06, just above the five per cent level.

171

The schools can be divided into four groups of educational priority: no priority, light priority, heavy and very heavy priority. This coincides with an increasing amount of extra staff per school. Schools with many minority children are entitled to extra teaching staff. According to Dutch policy indigenous children, who do not belong to the lower social strata, are counted as 1 for the calculation of the number of teaching staff. Dutch children from lower class backgrounds are counted as 1.25. Ethnic minority children count as 1.9. So migrant children almost count for 2. The seven light priority schools in our sample have one extra teacher for one or two days a week, the 16 heavy priority schools have on average one full time extra teacher, whereas very heavy priority schools usually have one and a half or two full time teachers on top of the normal staff. Of course, level of priority is strongly related to ethnic and social composition. Going from no priority to heavy priority status they have on average 20, 52, 59 and 75 per cent working class children, and 8, 23, 37 and 60 per cent migrant children.

Table 2 shows the results of three analyses of variance by priority status: that three analyses show weaker relations than with social composition as a factor. May be, this indicates that the policy of offering extra budgets and staff has some positive effects already. Although heavy priority schools, that is schools with a majority of lower class pupils and many migrant children still show lower achievement scores on a language test, and their pupils also are less succesfull in achieving the level of word knowledge that fits their IQ, this is not related to the effectiveness of the schools. Nowadays heavy priority schools seem to be almost as effective as light or no priority schools. There is no significant relationship between priority status and school effectiveness.

Table 2. Word knowledge, individual educational equity and school effect scores by educational priority status

|  | word kn. | IEE | SE | n |
|---|---|---|---|---|
| no priority | 39.6 | -3.7 | 1.0 | 19 |
| light priority | 31.0 | 0.5 | 1.0 | 7 |
| heavy priority | 27.2 | -2.7 | -0.7 | 16 |
| very heavy priority | 22.9 | -5.8 | -1.7 | 11 |
| F-ratio | 14.9 | 9.2 | 1.2 | |
| stat. sign. | .00 | .00 | .33 | |
| R2 | .48 | .36 | .07 | |

# MORE EQUALITY BY IMPROVING EDUCATIONAL
# PRIORITY SCHOOLS?

It is far from easy to improve the quality of a school team that is not function-ing well. Because of various laws and regulations weak school leaders can-not be fired overnight, nor can good headmasters be hired on short notice. The same is true for bad and good teachers. It may even be more difficult to change the attitudes, policies and practices of failing teams into successful ones (Cuban, 1984; Rosenholtz, 1985). But let us not be too pessimistic. It must be possible to turn a few ineffective schools into excellent ones. Some schools might be improved enough to reach a normal standard of teaching, while others might not improve at all, or only a little bit. So, improving a group of schools in such a way that they become as effective as average schools seems a challenging but feasible goal.

Extra money and human effort is spend on educational priority schools. Let us assume that this would have the following success: the now ineffec-tive priority schools become as effective as the average school. What impact will this have on the inequality of educational opportunities, and which effect will this have for the children in these schools? To assess this possible impact we have selected those priority schools with SE-scores half a stan-dard deviation below the total average. Fourteen of the 27 (very) heavy priority schools in our sample fall in this category. Seven heavy priority schools have a normal rate of effectiveness, and six do a better than average job. On average the low quality priority schools score 4.5 points below the grand mean. So, if the quality of these schools is improved to an average level their mean SE-scores have to be raised by 4.5 points.

What impact will this have on inequality? The easiest way to calculate this effect is to add 4.5 points to the individual school effect score of every pupil in these 14 schools. Since the educational effect score equals the word knowledge score minus predicted word knowledge (based on a regression on IQ, social and ethnic background) we can also add 4.5 to the word knowledge score of all the 187 pupils (19.3 %) who attend these 14 schools.

After these manipulations we have analyzed our data once more. At the individual level the original correlation between word knowledge and social background is .48. After increasing the scores of 187 pupils the correlation is a little bit lower: .46. The effect on the correlations with ethnic background is very much alike: a decrease in strength from -.38 to -.36. The first impression is that inequity has decreased with only two per cent. However, we have to remind ourselves that inequality of opportunities has been defined in terms of lack of development of ability. So we calculated the difference between the word knowledge score predicted on the basis of non verbal intelligence and the observed word knowledge score. We repeated this procedure after increasing the word knowledge score of all the children in the until now very ineffective priority schools. Again statistical analyses show that the correlations before and after this procedure vary. The original correlation at the individual level between social background and realized potential for word knowledge is .40. After increasing the observed language scores of the pupils of these 14 schools with 4.5 the correlation with social background is slightly lower: .38. Now, we can safely conclude that the effect on educational opportunity is very moderate indeed.

Since the above mentioned changes get us nowhere, we got a little bit annoyed with our results. Therefore we considered some other models. To obtain much more equity we not only would have to improve the quality of ineffective schools, but also to *deteriorate* schools that are doing well, to bring the bad and good schools on the same level. This could be done by offering the good head masters and teachers 50 per cent higher salaries, if they would take on a job in an ineffective priority school. However, this model might appear to be a ridiculous zero sum game to most of us. A more serious alternative might be the model in which all ineffective priority schools become just as effective as the good functioning (that is half a s.d. above average) non priority schools. To achieve this we have to raise the individual scores in these 14 schools with 9.2. However, again the results are far from being spectacular. The correlation between word knowledge and social background shrinks from .48 to .43. The correlation with IEE-scores declines from .40 to .34. So, if a quarter of the schools in our sample, or half of the heavy priority schools are transformed to very effective ones, then the reduction of the variance in unequal educational opportunities is less than five per cent.

Several factors are responsible for this result. Firstly, only part of the lower class and minority pupils attend these 14 schools. Their peers in other schools that are not very effective still get the same kind of low quality schooling, and are unaffected by improvement measures. Secondly, also the children with a somewhat more privileged home background in these 14 schools profit from the increased quality of their education. Thirdly, the inequality of opportunities *within* schools does not seem to be affected by measures that improve the educational climate of schools as a whole. If the quality of teaching improves, then all children will profit to the same degree. Children vary in diligence, perseverance, and achievement motivation. They also vary in their attitude toward learning, school and their teacher. Even good teachers will fail to motivate all children equally. So differences within classes will remain and not all children will develop according to their ability.

174

# THE IMPACT OF IMPROVED SCHOOLS ON THEIR PUPILS

We have seen that the effects on inequality are moderate. Is this also true for the twenty per cent pupils who on average have experienced an increase in word knowledge of 4.5 or 9.2 points? An increase of 4.5 points equals a period of half a year in language development, and 9.2 almost equals a period of one year. For a large number of these pupils an increase of 4.5 can also mean the difference between the level necessary for lower vocational education (lbo) and the lowest level of non-vocational secondary education (mavo), or the difference between higher general education (havo) and universitary preparatory schools (vwo). An increase of 9.2 would mean that more pupils will attain even higher levels of education. If extra budgets for priority schools could lead to a success of this size, we think it is worth the effort.

## NOTES

1. Predicted word knowledge = -3.37 + 5.22 (NV-IQ)
2. Parent(s) born in the Netherlands or parents born in other countries.
3. Predicted word knowledge = -2.31 + 3.64 (NV-IQ) + 1.24 (SES) - 5.22 (Ethnic)

## REFERENCES

Coleman, J.S.(1973). Equality of opportunity and equality of results. *Harvard Educational Review, 43*, (1).

Coleman, J.S. (1975). What is meant by "an equal educational opportunity"? *Oxford Review of Education,*1.

Cuban, L. (1984). Transforming the Frog into a Prince. Effective Schools: Research, Policy, and Practice at the District Level. *Harvard Educational Review, 54*, (2).

Edmonds R. (1979). Effective Schools for the Urban Poor. *Educational Leadership, 37* (1), 15-24

Goldstein H. (1984). The Methodology of School Comparisons. *Oxford Review of Education, 10*, (1).

Gray, J. (1981). School Effectiveness Research: Key Issues. *Educational Research, 24*, (1).

Jencks, C. et al. (1972). *Inequality: A Reassessment of the Effect of Family and Schooling in America.* New York: Basic Books,

Jensen, A.R. (1979). *Bias in Mental Testing.* London: Methuen.

Jong, M.J. de (1987). *Herkomst, kennis en kansen.* Lisse: Swets & Zeitlinger.

Jong, M.J. de (1988). Ethnic Origin and Educational Careers in Holland. *The Netherlands Journal of Sociology, 24*, (1).

Jong, M.J. de (1989). Toenemende apartheid in het Nederlandse onderwijs. *Pedagogische Studiën, 66*, (2).

Madaus G.F. et al. (1979). The Sensitivity of Measures of School Effectiveness. *Harvard Educational Review, 49,* (2).

Meester, A. & J. de Leeuw (1983). *Intelligentie, Sociaal Milieu en de Schoolloopbaan.* Leiden: Vakgroep Datatheorie, Rijksuniversiteit Leiden.

Mortimore, P. et al. (1988). *School Matters.* Somerset: Open Books.

Purkey S.C. & M.S. Smith (1983). Effective Schools: A Review. *The Elementary School Journal, 83,* (4).

Ralph J.H. & J. Fennessey (June 1983). Science or Reform: Some Questions about the Effective Schools Model. *Phi Delta Kappan.*

Reynolds, D. (ed.) (1985). *Studying School Effectiveness.* London: Falmer.

Rosenholtz S.J. (May 1985). Effective Schools: Interpreting the Evidence. *American Journal of Education.*

Rutter, M. et al. (1979). *Fifteen Thousand Hours: Secondary schools and their effects on children.* Somerset: Open Books.

# EDUCATIONAL PRIORITY AND SCHOOL EFFECTIVENESS[1]

Paul Tesser
Institute for Applied Social Science (ITS), Nijmegen

and

Greetje van der Werf
RION, Institute for Educational Research, University of Groningen

## INTRODUCTION

In 1985 a new national educational priority program was implemented in The Netherlands, aimed at improving educational opportunities for disadvantaged children. An important part of the program consists of providing schools with extra teaching staff, proportional to the rate of children from lower income families and from families that belong to an ethnic minority group. Another part of the program consists of providing priority areas with extra facilities. Such priority areas are constituted by schools in co-operation with educational and welfare agencies. To receive extra facilities the areas have to submit a plan of activities to support schools and the other agencies in their educational priority programs.

Before the start of the national program it was determined that a comprehensive and 'hard' evaluation would take place, in order to show whether the new policy was effective or not and how it could be improved.

The central part of the evaluation is a longitudinal study of successive cohorts of children in primary schools. In that study students are tested, the implementation of the policy is measured and background and family characteristics of the students are registered. In the cohort studies data collection will take place once in two years, in about 800 schools. Later on the cohorts will be followed in secondary education.

During the period September 1987 until June 1988 we conducted a preliminary study in 200 schools in order to test the instruments and to make a

177

description of the starting situation of the schools, concerning school, teacher and student characteristics and concerning the way of using the extra facilities.

In this article we firstly will describe the evaluational model and design of the central part of the evaluation. After that the design and some results of the preliminary study will be given.[2]

# EVALUATION MODEL

In developing a comprehensive model of school effects on students' learning outcomes and educational careers we linked up with the Dutch tradition of longitudinal school career research. In this tradition much work has been done in the development of (causal) models of educational achievement based on correlational data. For evaluation purposes we included the educational priority facilities given to schools in a more general model of achievement differences. In that way we can evaluate the priority policy by estimating the model parameters. Comparison of model parameters over years allows us to estimate developmental trends in policy effects. The basic model is a model at student level in which effects of social background on school success are mediated by achievement in language and arithmetics. We extended the model with cultural resources as a mediating variable between social background and school success. Furthermore we modeled cognitive abilities (intelligence) as a separate latent variable distinct from achievement and mediating effects from social background on achievement in language and arithmetics.

This leads to the lower part of the model in Figure 1. The model is essentially longitudinal. The longitudinal character can and will be worked out further by breaking down the variables cognitive abilities and achievement over time, i.e. capabilities and achievement measured in grade 4, grade 6, grade 8 etc.

In the model presented thus far schools were not mentioned yet. Therefore we extended the model to a two stage multilevel model in which school variables are assumed to have effects on the parameters of the individual level model. As individual level models are basically regression models, school effects are effects on the intercepts and slopes of the regressions of school success on achievement, capabilities etcetera within schools.

For our model based evaluation of educational priority we have to assume a rather complex multilevel model because we can hardly imagine that material facilities given to schools have simple direct effects on within school success intercepts and regression slopes. On the grounds of the literature on school effectiveness and schooling for disadvantaged children we assume that achievement of students can be affected by effectiveness characteristics of schools and by special didactic strategies for disadvantaged children. If material and personnel facilities are to have any effect on school success it must be mediated by school effectiveness and special strategies for the disadvantaged.

A more direct effect can be imagined for group size. The situation is further complicated by the two components of the priority policy mentioned earlier : the general component and the area component. In fact the area component introduces a new level in the model. For the moment we restrict ourselves to treat it as an extra support for school effectiveness and special strategies, i.e. a contextual variable on school level.

At this point we can introduce our extended multilevel model of school success differences that incorporates effects of the priority policy. The model is depicted in Figure 1.

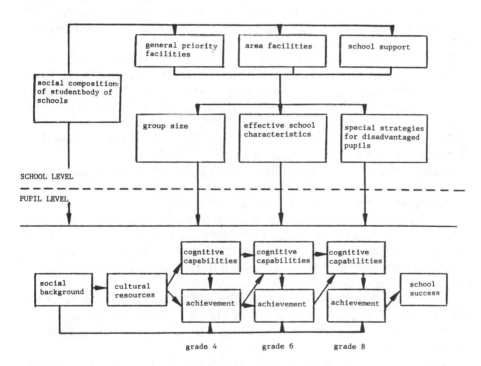

*Figure 1: Extended multilevel model for differences in school success*

The model is a cohort model. It describes the relations between variables on school level and on student level that are relevant for differences in success within year cohorts of primary school children.

The data of the preliminary study were used to explore some parts of the model. Analyses were made of the relationships between the most important variables on the school level and the variables social background and school success on the student level. The variables are described in the next section.

# VARIABLES

Schools that receive priority facilities can use these for a lot of different activities. They can try to improve education for all students, but also for the specific target groups of the priority program. In order to study the implementation of the program it is necessary to find out for what educational characteristics the facilities are used in order to improve education and whether schools participating in the program can be distinguished from each other and from schools that do not participate.

Relevant characteristics are in the first place those that have demonstrated their effect on the outcomes of all students. We deduced these characteristics from research into effective schools (e.g. Purkey & Smith,1983; d'Amico, 1982; Edmonds, 1979; Rutter, 1983; Mackenzie, 1983) and into teacher and instruction effectiveness (e.g. Walberg, 1986; Bloom, 1984; Madaus et al., 1980; Brophy & Good, 1986; Peterson & Walberg, 1979). We called these characteristics 'general effectiveness characteristics'.

In the second place relevant characteristics are those that are expected to be effective for the specific target groups of the priority program. These characteristics were deduced from strategies that were developed in different compensation programs aiming at improvement of educational success of disadvantaged children. We called them 'special strategies for disadvantaged students'. Special activities concerning children from ethnic minorities, like lessons in their own language and culture (OETC) and intercultural education, also belong to these strategies.

The general effectiveness characteristics and the special strategies for disadvantaged children are summarized in Figure 2. The variables are distinguished according to the level on which they are measured (school and classroom level).

Other school level variables in the preliminary study were: social composition of the student population of the school; general priority facilities; area facilities; school support; group size.

The student variables were : social background, indicated by students' priority weights 1.00, 1.25 or 1.90, respectively refering to middle or higher class, lower class and ethnic minority students ; school success, indicated by headmasters' recommendation for level of secondary education.

| | School level | Teacher level |
|---|---|---|
| Effective school and classroom variables | - instructional leadership<br>- central registration of learning outcomes<br>- orderly school climate<br>- high expectations<br>- stressing basic skills<br>- high aspirations | - learning time<br>- structured lessons<br>- orderly classroom<br>- minimum goals<br>- homework<br>- stressing basic skills<br>- regular evaluation<br>- appropriate content<br>- clear goals |
| Special strategies for disadvantaged children | - family activation<br>- OETC<br>- intercultural education<br>- remedial teaching<br>- parental participation | - connecting learning with home experiences<br>- thematical lessons<br>- differentiation<br>- language compensation |

*Figure 2: Summary of effectiveness variables and special strategies for disadvantaged children.*

# METHOD OF THE PRELIMINARY STUDY

The preliminary study was carried out in 202 schools. The sample consisted of two parts, a core part consisting of a 80 schools random sample of all primary schools and additional samples of schools with high proportions of lower SES children and ethnic minority children. All school and classroom variables were measured by means of written questionnaires, added with interviews. Childrens' background characteristics and their recommendations for secondary education were registered from the school administration.

# RESULTS

In the analysis of the data we wanted to identify factors on school level influencing educational effectiveness in relation to the social background of students.

In discussing educational effectiveness it is not always clear what is meant by effectiveness. The concept of effectiveness often is rather loosely defined in terms of average student outcomes or average achievement level. However, as we know very well from school career research, roughly thirty to forty percent of variance in achievement level is explained by social background. So when we look at differences between the average levels of educational achievement of different schools we have to take into account differences that are determined by individual factors like social background.

In earlier analyses effects of school variables on individual achievement were estimated by means of student level regression equations. It was concluded that after controlling for social background school factors explained hardly any variance in student outcomes (Coleman et al., 1966; Jencks, 1972).

It can be shown that when school variables are treated on the individual level important aspects of the structure of the data are neglected. To overcome the shortcomings of the individual model different solutions were proposed. The most general and most adequate approach for the analysis of this kind of data appears to be the two stages approach. In this approach individual level models are estimated within schools and the within schools parameters are treated as dependent variables in second stage between schools equations (Van den Eeden & Saris, 1984).

In the preliminary study we have data on student level about social background ( students' priority weights) and headmasters recommendation of level of secondary education.(rec-i-j). The within schools student level model for these variables is:

$$rec_{ij} = a_j + b_j Weight_{ij} + E_{ij} \quad (1)$$

In the second stage the model parameters a-j and b-j are the dependent variables. We try to explain between schools variance of these parameters by means of school factors in school level regression equations:

$$a_j = A_0 + A_1 S_j + U_j \quad (2)$$
$$b_j = B_0 + B_1 S_j + V_j \quad (3)$$

By substituting (2) and (3) in (1) the two stage equations can be rewritten in one equation containing three error terms: one between student error term, one school intercept error term and one school slope error term. This model is called the random coefficient model (De Leeuw & Kreft, 1985). In the model intercepts and slopes are divided into fixed and random parts. By establishing the variance of the random parts the relative contribution of school and student variables to the total variance of the dependent variable can be estimated.

In the random coefficient model the school specific intercepts $a_j$ can be taken as unbiased estimators for school effectiveness. The main question is to find school variables that attribute significantly to variance in the a-j intercepts. In the evaluation of the educational priority program b-j coefficients are of interest as well. The policy aims at reducing the strength of the relation between background and educational level. In the random coefficient model this relation is represented by the $b_j$ coefficients. The question is whether we can identify school variables that significantly contribute to the variance in the $b_j$ coefficients.

182

In our analysis we used the VARCL program of Longford (1988). This program estimates the coefficients and the variances of the error terms of the model presented above. We estimated the effects of the school variables one by one because some of the variables are related. In reporting the results of the analyses we distinguish four 'blocks' of school level variables: structural variables, school effectiveness characteristics, classroom and instructional characteristics and special strategies for disadvantaged students.

The analysis started with some reference models, i.e. models without explanatory variables on school level. In the first reference model only the variances of the school and pupil error terms were estimated. In the second model 'weight' was added as a control on pupil level. In the third model we allow for random variance in the slopes of recommendation on weight. The results are in Table 1.

Table 1: Between and within variance components of three reference models (absolute, Var, and proportional, Pvar)

| | Var $U_j$ | Pvar $U_j$ | Var $E_{ij}$ | Pvar $E_{ij}$ | Var $V_j$ |
|---|---|---|---|---|---|
| $Rec_{ij} = A_0 + U_j + E_{ij}$ | .049-* | 4.7 | .996 | 95.3 | |
| $Rec_{ij} = A_0 + .45*weight_{ij} + E_{ij} + U_{ij}$ | .032-* | 3.4 | .921 | 96.6 | |
| $Rec_{ij} = A_0 + .46*weight_{ij} + E_{ij} + V_j + U_j$ | .030-* | 3.2 | .908 | 96.8 | .035* |

* = significant parameter

In Table 1 it can be seen that less than five percent of variance in educational success of students at the end of primary school can be attributed to differences between schools. Differences between students within schools are much larger than differences between schools. Between schools variance is much reduced by controlling for social background. As we can see from the results of the second model the between schools variance component is reduced to 3.4 percent by adding weight to the model. More than 25 percent of the between schools variance can be attributed to social background of students if we assume equal slopes of recommendation on weight in all schools.

From the results of the third model we can see that the assumption of equal slopes is not supported by the data. Slopes of recommendation on priority weight differ significantly between schools. In some schools social background is related less strongly to recommendation than in other schools.

The results of the reference models can be used as a baseline for the evaluation of the contribution of school level variables. By introducing school level variables we expect to reduce the between schools error variance of the reference models. As mentioned before effects of school variables are investigated by estimating a series of random coefficient models with one school variable at the time.

The presentation of the results is restricted to those models in which there is in one way or another a significant contribution of the school variables (Table 2). One gets a quick impression of the relevance of a school variable by comparing the Var- U-j of a specific model with the Var U-j of the second reference model:.032.

Table 2. Parameter estimates and variance components of models with school variables

| School variables | $A_1$ | $B_0$ | $B_1$ | Var $U_j$ | Var $E_{ij}$ | Var $V_j$ |
|---|---|---|---|---|---|---|
| **Structural variables** | | | | | | |
| % working class students | -.003* | .45* | | .026* | .911 | .026* |
| % ethnic minorities | .01* | .58* | -.005* | .031* | .909 | .012* |
| % working cl.+ethnic min. | .01* | .76* | -.005* | .031* | .909 | .017* |
| General facilities | -.01* | .45* | | .028* | .907 | .037* |
| Area facilities | .33* | .52* | -.19* | .030* | .908 | .022* |
| School support | .38* | .69* | -.18* | .030* | .908 | .027* |
| Group size | -.02 | .19 | .01* | .028* | .909 | .029* |
| **School effectiveness characteristics** | | | | | | |
| High aspirations | .008* | .45* | | .025* | .907 | .035* |
| High expectations | .007* | .45* | | .024* | .908 | .036* |
| **Instructional characteristics** | | | | | | |
| Structured lessons | .003* | .46* | | .026* | .890 | .021* |
| Special strategies | no significant effects | | | | | |

All structural school variables have effects on the school intercepts of head-masters' recommendation. The proportion of working class students has the strongest effect. Regardless of individual social background, students in schools with low proportions of working class students get higher recommendations for secondary education than schools with high proportions of working class students. The effect on the slopes is not significant. There is remaining significant variance in slopes of recommendation on weight between schools. The proportion of ethnic minority students has a positive effect on advice intercepts and a negative effect on the slopes. This combination of effects shows up in most of the models with the structural school variables. It could mean that schools scoring high on these variables are more effective for ethnic minority students and less effective for middle class students. However there are indications that the social background of the middle class students in these schools is a bit lower than in the other schools and that might be an alternative approach for the results. This shows that one has to be careful with these kind of results.

Only two variables in the block of effective school variables have significant effects. High expectations and high aspirations result in higher recommendations for all students. About 25 percent of between school variance in recommendation can be attributed to expectation and aspiration differences. The effect holds if we control for proportion of working class students

Of the block of effective teacher and instruction variables only the variable structured lessons, which refers to the use of achievements tests as a diagnostic instrument, shows a significant effect. Structuring of lessons appears to be an effective variable for raising the level of students recommendation regardless of social class.

About the last block of variables, the special strategies for disadvantaged children, we can be very short. None of the variables in this block has a significant effect on any part of the model.

## CONCLUSIONS

The analyses of the data of the preliminary study of educational priority show some interesting results. On the individual level we see again the well known and firm relation between social background and educational success at the end of primary school. We showed that schools with high proportions of working class students tend to be less effective than schools with lower proportions of these students. It is not yet clear how this result could be interpreted or explained. Our study confirms the relevance of teacher expectations and aspirations and the diagnostic use of achievement tests for effective education. Students of all kinds of social backgrounds get higher recommendations of teachers who have higher expectations and aspirations of their school career possibilities. The same holds for the diagnostic use of achievement tests which might refer to a goal directed, well structured learning process with regular feedback to pupils and accommodation of learning contents to learning results.

Apart of these substantive results we have shown that the multi level approach and the use of random coefficient models for estimating effects is a fruitful tool for investigating effective school concepts.

## NOTES

1. With thanks to Lia Mulder and Marga Weide for their contribution to the research projects and especially for their assistance in analyzing the data.
2. Both studies are conducted with financial support from the National Institute for Educational Research in The Netherlands.

# REFERENCES

d'Amico, J. (1984). Using effective schools for the urban poor. *Educational Leadership, 37*, 15-24.

Bloom, B.S. (1984). The 2 Sigma problem: The search for methods of group instruction as one-to-one tutoring. *Educational Researcher, 4*, 4-16.

Brophy, J.E. & Good, T.L. (1986). Teacher behavior and student achievement. In Wittrock, M.C. (red). *Handbook of research on teaching*, (pp.328-376). New York Macmillan Publishing Company.

Coleman, J., Campbell, E., Hobson, C., McPartland, J., Mood, A., Weinfeld, F. & York, R. (1966). *Equality of educational opportunity*. Washington D.C.: U.S. Government printing Office.

Eeden, p. van den & Saris, W.E. (1984). Empirisch onderzoek naar multilevel uitspraken. *Mens en Maatschappy, 59*, 165-178.

Edmonds, R. (1979). Effective schools for the urban poor. *Educational Leadership, 37*, 15-24.

Jencks, C.S. (1966). *Inequality: a reassessment of the effect of family and schooling in America*. New York: Basic Books.

Leeuw, J. de & Kreft, I. (1985). *Random coefficient models for multilevel analysis*. Leiden.

Longford, N.T. (1988). *Variance component analysis: manual*. Princeton: Educational Testing Service.

Madaus, G.F., Airasan, P.W. & Kellaghan, T. (1980). *School effectiveness. A reassessment of the evidence*. New York.

Mackenzie, D.E. (1983). Research for school improvement: an appraisal of some recent trends. *Educational Researcher, 4*, 5-17.

Peterson, P. & Walberg, H. (1979). *Research on teaching: concepts, findings and implications*. Berkeley, CA: McCutchon.

Purkey, S.C. & Smith, M.S. (1982) Too soon to cheer? Synthesis of research on effective schools. *Educational Leadership, 40*, 64–69.

Rutter, M., Maugham, B., Mortimore, J., Austin, J. & Smith, A (1979). *Fifteen thousand hours. Secondary schools and their effects on children*. London: Open Books, Publishers Ltd.

Walberg, H. (1984) Improving the productivity of America's schools. *Educational Leadership, 41*, 19-30.

# RESULTS OF INTEGRATED EDUCATIONAL POLICY

Annemieke de Vries

RION, Institute for Educational Research, University of Groningen

## BACKGROUND AND PROBLEM

The commission for the research project, which is the subject of this paper, was given by the board of the'Educational Priority Area Lelystad' (information about the Educational Priority Program is given in the article of Tesser and van der Werf, elsewhere in this book). The board wanted to gain insight in the problem of truancy to enable measures to be taken on the level of the boards of the schools and on the level of the schools themselves. Participants in the research project were all the schools of Lelystad. The results are compared with results of similar research projects in other cities and with national results for effect variables. This shows some interesting results regarding the effectiveness of the policies of individual schools and of the boards of schools at local level.

The building of the city of Lelystad was started in 1967 after the drainage of a part of the IJsselmeer. In the beginning an overrepresentation of the middle and higher social class came to Lelystad. In a later stage many inhabitants of the city of Amsterdam, from the redeveloped quarters, settled in Lelystad. During the last few years the percentage of broken families, the percentage of persons financially dependent on the government and the percentage of people from other countries has increased strongly. Therefore Lelystad is designated as an 'Educational Priority Area'.

Presently, there are three public schools for secondary education and two protestant schools. One public school and one protestant school have two school types: LBO-MAVO; the other three schools have all four school types: LBO-MAVO-HAVO-VWO. Furthermore, three schools have an IBO. (IBO = individual vocational education; LBO = lower vocational education; MAVO = junior general secondary education; HAVO = senior general secondary education; VWO = pre-university education).

The board of both the public and the protestant schools conduct a consistent policy for their schools. The policies of both boards coincide on several essential features.

It is unique in the Netherlands that all five schools have an heterogeneous period, four schools during two years, one school during three years. Over and above this, all five schools have a profiled LBO-MAVO examination (that is: a pupil can do some subjects on the LBO level and other subjects on the MAVO level) and an advanced pupil-tutoring system. Besides all the schools try to realize the characteristics of the effective schools.Both the public and the protestant schools have structural consultation with each other.

Despite the resemblance, there are also differences in the policy of the individual schools. They are in fact, when it comes to attracting new pupils, rivals of each other. The difference of the schools is apparent in the different images which they have: more or less severe. According to their images and their school-types the schools attract a different population of pupils.

The key questions in the research project were:
(1) What is the amount, according to the pupils, of the truancy as far as duration, frequency and kind is concerned and which pupils does it concern as far as year of study and type of school is concerned?
(2) Which characteristics and factors are related to truant behaviour?
(3) Does a connection exist, on the level of the school, between characteristics, factors, measures of the schools and truant behavior?
(4) What are the differences compared with the results of other research projects?
In this paper the questions 3 and 4 occupy a central position.

## THE THEORETICAL FRAMEWORK

Some information is available from the literature about truancy and specially about early school-leavers, but this is not always consistent. One may divide the literature into literature about motives and personality traits of pupils and literature about the contribution of the school. For this paper, the contribution of the school is relevant.

There is often no clear distinction made between truancy and dropping out. Mostly it is assumed that truancy ends in dropping out. That is perhaps an explanation for the fact that the findings sometimes contradict the findings of research on truancy alone.

According to De Vries and Peetsma (1986), the literature shows that dropping out and truancy are specially connected with social class factors and with individual characteristics of pupils: pupils from underprivileged social classes, pupils who are less gifted (or think they are), pupils who attend

188

schools with an one-sided, less-gifted population of children and an one-sided, lower-social-class population. As to the climate of the schools De Vries and Peetsma find less consistent results.

According an analysis, executed by themselves, the size of a city, the type of school and the percentage of pupils from other countries are connected, independently of each other, with dropping out and with truancy. They assert that the best prediction can be obtained by a (linear) combination of the three features. They interpret the percentage of pupils from other countries as a so called 'proxy-measure' for the mean score of the social-economical and cultural background of the population of pupils of a school. They assert that all the other variables they have examined are not connected with truancy and dropping out: the size of the school, denomination, philosophy of the school, the tutoring system and the amount of say of the pupils.

De Vries asserts that schools differ in the rate of truancy and dropping out. According to De Vries it is thinkable that the differences between individual but comparable schools are in fact wholly or partly the result of the developed local configurations of which they are a part. Differences in truancy and dropping out may also be a result of this configuration. As an example he says that in the case of one school being severe the other will be less severe because there is a public for both kinds of schools.

# DESIGN

*Variables*
The following groups of variables can be derived from the previous sections:
- truant behaviour and motives for truancy (intrinsic and extrinsic)
- features of the pupils (gender, living with one parent or both parents, country of birth of the parents)
- career at school (repeating of classes in the primary school and in the secondary school)
- school culture at home and activities in the free time
- the feeling of wellbeing at school:
    . attitude to oneself in the situation of the school
    . attitude to the teachers
    . attitude to the school
    . expectations of the future, ambitions for the future
- the extent to which pupils notice the measures against truancy
- measures which pupils think will reduce the amount of truancy.
- the policy of the individual schools against truancy.

Truancy is operationalized as staying away from school for one hour or longer without permission.

## The Gathering of the Data

The variables are elaborated in a questionnaire with closed-ended questions. Only the question for effective measures was an openended question. The data concerning the policies of the schools were obtained from the school heads.

The questionnaire was filled out in January 1988, anonymously, in the roll class, by almost all of the 4000 pupils in secondary education in Lelystad. As far as the most important truancy variables is concerned, the data from all questionnaires has been processed. Afterwards, a sample of one thirty part is taken at random, for each class of each year of study. The other variables were processed only for this sample. The comparison with the results of the variables for truancy showed the sample as representative.

## Analysis of the Data

The character of the research is descriptive and exploratory. Frequencies are found for all variables. Scales are constructed for well-being at school, each with a number of items. The alpha of the complete scale is .80. Afterwards relationships are traced. The truant behaviour is considered as the dependent variable, the other variables can be considered as independent variables. Because of the limited commission of the project and the limited number of schools we have not worked out the connections between the variables, nor the relative contribution of each variable to truancy. Next, we have compared the results of each individual school and have compared the results with results of projects in other cities and with national data.

# DIFFERENCES BETWEEN THE SCHOOLS

All schools for secondary education in Lelystad have given their complete cooperation to the research project. We wish to avoid giving the schools 'labels of quality' which could have consequences for both the educational standard and the enrolments. Therefore, we have tried to keep the schools anonymous. The denomination, the types of superstructure and the size of the schools are not recorded. These variables do not appear to be clearly connected with truancy or the feeling of well-being at school, in as far as we can say something about this with information on only five schools. We have designated the schools as school A, B, C, D and E.

In Table 1 the results are recorded, for each school, with regard to some relevant variables.

190

Table 1. Results for each school with regard to several relevant variables.

|  | A | B | C | D | E |
|---|---|---|---|---|---|
| **Features of pupils** | % | % | % | % | % |
| - not living with both parents | 28 | 21 | 21 | 19 | 15 |
| - mother from another country | 20 | 20 | 22 | 14 | 18 |
| - father from another country | 22 | 24 | 24 | 15 | 18 |
| - repeating of classes in primary education | 28 | 23 | 20 | 18 | 17 |
| **Schoolculture at home** |  |  |  |  |  |
| - not a member of the library | 36 | 23 | 22 | 23 | 14 |
| - (not a member of clubs | 48 | 38 | 35 | 32 | 25) |
| **Levels of truancy** |  |  |  |  |  |
| - non truants | 68 | 66 | 66 | 60 | 54 |
| - light truants* | 22 | 30 | 26 | 32 | 41 |
| - moderate truants* | 6 | 4 | 5 | 4 | 4 |
| - persistent truants* | 5 | - | 3 | 4 | 2 |

*light      = 1 or a few hours a few times a year
*moderate = a few hours a few times in a month or a few days a few times in a year
*persistent = a few hours a few times in a week or a whole day or a few days in a week or in a month

|  | A | B | C | D | E |
|---|---|---|---|---|---|
| **Experiences of the pupils with regard to the policy of the school** | % | % | % | % | % |
| - easy to stay away unnoticed | 23 | 25 | 28 | 37 | 37 |
| - always punishment when pupils truant | 24 | 23 | 21 | 14 | 10 |
| **The feeling of well-being at school (the lower the score, the more positive the result)** |  |  |  |  |  |
| - Attitude toward oneself |  |  |  |  |  |
| . mean | 1.50 | 1.42 | 1.51 | 1.39 | 1.39 |
| . deviation | .40 | .30 | .35 | .33 | .33 |
| - Attitude toward teachers |  |  |  |  |  |
| . mean | 1.48 | 1.52 | 1.53 | 1.46 | 1.47 |
| . deviation | .33 | .30 | .35 | .33 | .30 |
| - Attitude toward to the school |  |  |  |  |  |
| . mean | 1.37 | 1.31 | 1.35 | 1.30 | 1.30 |
| . deviation | .23 | .20 | .23 | .22 | .18 |
| - All scales together |  |  |  |  |  |
| . mean | 1.46 | 1.41 | 1.46 | 1.38 | 1.38 |
| . deviation | .27 | .20 | .24 | .24 | .22 |

The individual schools differ considerably from each other with regard to the background features of the pupils. The schools B, C and specially school A score more 'unfavourably' than the schools D and E. Nevertheless the percentage of truants is lower at the first three schools than at the last two schools (also if we correct for the years five and six).

Of course, the extent of truancy, and not only its incidence, is important. School A has a somewhat higher percentage of persistent truants than the other schools; however considering the background characteristics of the pupils, the result seems to us rather positive. And school B, which also has rather 'unfavourable' background characteristics of pupils, does not have any persistent truant at all. So, in contrast to what is expected in the theoretical framework, the schools with rather 'unfavourable' background characteristics of pupils do not have more truants than the schools with more 'favourable' background characteristics of pupils.

The pupils of schools with a higher percentage of truants (D, E and F) find it easier to stay away and get less consistently punished than the pupils of the other schools (A, B and C). So the measures taken by the schools A, B and C to reduce truancy seem to be effective. Special the measures of school A, which school is the only one that uses the computer for registration of absence and which gives a monthly report to parents concerning the extent of absence of their child, seem to make it difficult to stay away.

Concerning the score on the scale 'feeling of well-being at school', the schools differ significantly from each other.

The mean score on a scale like this is often integrated as the 'school climate' of a school. The 'school climate' is the result of the interaction between the policy of a school and the background characteristics of the pupils. So it is not surprising that the schools D and E have a more positive score than the schools A and C.

Remarkable is the positive score of the pupils of school B on the scales 'attitude toward oneself' and 'attitude toward the school'. Also remarkable is that this school has no persistent truants. The pupils of school A have a remarkably positive 'attitude toward teachers'. This must be, if we consider to the scores of the other subscales, the result of the efforts of the teachers. Taking background characteristics into account, the score of school C is the most negative. At this school the pupils have very often the feeling that the teachers treat them unfair.

The conclusion from what we have said above is that efforts of individual schools can reduce the percentage of truants and can enhance the feeling of wellbeing at school.

# COMPARISON WITH RESULTS OF OTHER
# RESEARCH PROJECTS

The most recent research projects with which we can make comparisons apply to the cities of Leeuwarden (Jaspers et al.,1984), of Arnhem (Bosch,1986) and of Utrecht (Anker & De Kort, 1987). Table 2 shows the characteristics of the samples and the schools of each city and the data with regard to a number of relevant variables. A question-mark is entered where the data are unknown.

The percentage of truants is lower in Lelystad than in the other cities, and furthermore the percentage of persistent truants is also lower, despite the fact that the background characteristics of pupils of Lelystad are less favourable than those of the other cities and despite the fact that the percentage of truancy is higher in the fifth and sixth class (classes not represented in the other cities). We don't have exact data of the socio-economic status of the inhabitants of the cities but there is not a big difference between Lelystad, Arnhem and Utrecht. In Leeuwarden the socio-economic status is somewhat better.

We saw that measures of control can reduce the percentage of truants. From the answers above we cannot deduce that there is more control in the schools in Lelystad than in the schools in the other cities. Therefore, we conclude that control cannot be the explanation for the positive result for Lelystad. Comparison with the other variables also gives a positive result for Lelystad. The pupils of Lelystad have repeated less often in secondary education and are less often transferred from a higher schooltype to a lower schooltype than the pupils of the other cities. And repeating in secondary school and transfer to a lower school type are the variables which have a rather strong connection with playing truant in the other cities. In Lelystad there is no connection between these variables at all. Repeating in the primary school had no connection with playing truant in any of the cities. In Lelystad more children have repeated in primary school than in the other cities. Many pupils of Lelystad who repeated in the primary school lived in that period outside Lelystad. Furthermore the pupils of Lelystad go more often with pleasure to school than the pupils of other cities, also after correction for the school year (pupils in the higher years go with more pleasure to school than pupils of (specially) the second and the third year (our findings and Stoel, 1980). In all studies there is a connection between the attitude towards school and playing truant.

From what is noted above we can conclude that the pupils of the schools of Lelystad, although their background characteristics are less 'favourable', not only play truant less often than the pupils at the schools in the other cities, but also score more positively on variables which are often 'effect variables' in studies about effectiveness of schools.

Table 2. Characteristics of samples and schools; differences between Lelystad, Leeuwarden, Arnhem and Utrecht with regard to relevant variables.

|  | Lelystad | Leeuwarden | Arnhem | Utrecht |
|---|---|---|---|---|
| number of pupils | 1262 | 1745 | 1235 | 1172 |
| number of schools | (all) 5 | ? | 9 | 9 |
| number of multilateral | | | | |
| school groups | 5 | 2 | 0 | 2 |
| years of study | 1-6 | 1-5* | 2-4 | 1-4 |
| schooltypes | | | | |
| - IBO | yes | yes | no | yes |
| - LBO and MAVO | yes | yes | yes | yes |
| - HAVO and VWO | yes | yes | yes | ? |
| * only pupils who are of school age | | | | |
|  | % | % | % | % |
| **Background characteristics** | | | | |
| - not living with both parents | 15 | 14 | 12 | ? |
| - two parents from other | | | | |
| countries | 12 | - | 7 | ? |
| **Truancy** | | | | |
| - percentage of truants | 38 | 46 | 53 | ? |
| **Frequency of truancy** | | | | |
| - incidental | 90 | 86 | 82 | 83 |
| - monthly | 8 | 10 | 12 | 15 |
| - weekly | 2 | 4 | 5 | 3 |
| **Truancy noticed by school** | | | | |
| - always | 10 | 13 | 11 | 15 |
| **School career** | | | | |
| - repeated year(s) in the | | | | |
| primary school | 20 | 12 | 17 | ? |
| - repeated year(s) in the | | | | |
| secondary school | 10 | 17 | 20 | ? |
| - repeated year(s) in primary | | | | |
| & secondary school | 2.3 | ? | 4.5 | ? |
| - transferred to lower school | | | | |
| type | 2 | 12 | 20 | ? |
| **Opinion about school** | | | | |
| - pleasant | 49 | 45 | 41 | ? |
| - fair | 47 | 44 | 51 | ? |
| - unpleasant | 3 | 11 | 6 | ? |

To gain more insight in the validity of this assertion, we have, as far as possible, compared the effect variables with national data.


# COMPARISON WITH NATIONAL DATA

Data for comparison are available from the C.B.S. The C.B.S. follows yearly a sample of pupils who started their secondary school career in 1983: the so-called S.L.V.O. cohort. The most recent data are related to the state of affairs at September 1986, that is at the start of the fourth year. We compare the data with data of pupils of Lelystad who started in September 1987 in the fourth year. The comparison is not altogether pure because in Lelystad at the beginning of the fourth year there are also pupils who have been longer than three years at school, having repeated a class. And no pupil of the S.L.V.O.-cohort has been more than three years in secondary education. Therefore, the comparison gives more an indication about the situation in Lelystad than that exact conclusions can be drawn.

In Table 3 we show the data on several variables for the pupils of Lelystad and the pupils of the national sample.

Table 3. Differences between the pupils of Lelystad and pupils in a national sample at the start of the fourth year with regard to some relevant variables.

|  | Lelystad % | national sample % |
|---|---|---|
| repeated in secundary education | 21* | 25 |
| LBO-MAVO | 66.6 | 69.1 |
| HAVO | 25.2 | 15.1 |
| VWO | 9 | 15.6 |

* including pupils who have repeated the fourth year.


The pupils of Lelystad have less often repeated a class in secondary education, they are enrolled somewhat less often in the lower school types LBO/MAVO and they are enrolled more often in the school type which prepares for higher vocational education (the HAVO), than the pupils of the national sample. But the pupils of Lelystad are enrolled less often in the school type that prepares for the university (the VWO) than the pupils of the national sample. This is a consequence of the fact that a lot of children attend this school type outside of Lelystad. Their parents fear that the level of education in Lelystad is rather low because of the heterogeneous classes.

According to the inspector, the results of examinations in Lelystad don't deviate from the results for the educational area to which Lelystad belongs; he finds that for Lelystad a positive result, in view of the background characteristics. The results of examinations in Lelystad deviate positively from the results in the big cities.

On basis of what is noted above, we think that the conclusion is justified that the level of secondary education in Lelystad is certainly not negative compared with the national level, allowing for the background characteristics of the pupils of Lelystad.

# COMMENTARY

### The Differences between the Schools

Allowing for the assumptions from the literature about the connection between background characteristics and truancy, we find unexpected results when we compare the results of the individual schools.

Individual schools, in this case schools with relatively many pupils from an 'unfavourable' background situation, have succeeded in influencing positively the level of truancy of their pupils. It is possible that schools which expect on the grounds of the characteristics of their pupils a rather high rate of truancy take special measures. These measures can give them a head start on the schools with less pupils with 'unfavourable' characteristics.

A clear and fair policy with regard to the pupils seems to be very important. At the school where the pupils have a rather low feeling of wellbeing at school the pupils feel themselves much more often unfairly treated than at the other schools.

### Explanation of the Positive Results for Lelystad

Besides an indication of positive results for individual schools, there is also an indication of positive results at local level.

As said before, the boards of both the public and the protestant schools have a consistent policy for all schools. We think that the integrated policy can be the explanation for the positive results. We discuss below the characteristics of this integrated policy once more briefly in relation to their effects.

### a. The heterogeneous period (at four schools during two years, at one school during three years)

In the other projects the researchers found that truancy has a strong connection with repeating a class in the secondary education and with transfer from a higher to a lower schooltype.

During the heterogeneous period pupils don't often repeat a class because they can work on their own level. Because after the heterogeneous period pupils come into a schooltype suited to them, they also repeat a class less often in the higher years in comparison with the pupils of the categorial schools and they don't get transferred downwards so often.

## b. A profiled LBO-MAVO examination
This profiled LBO-MAVO examination leads to a strong decline in repeating a class and in transferring downwards for the pupils in the rather high-risk group, the LBO/MAVO pupils.

## c. The pupil tutoring system
The pupil tutoring system aims for an optimal school career for each pupil and, as a condition for it, a personal feeling of well-being at school. An important part of the support during the school career is the attention for the school choice during the heterogeneous period. By way of special projects the pupil becomes acquainted with his own possibilities and interests and with the possibilities in school and career. The feeling of well-being is pursued via counselling for personal and school problems and of conflicts between pupils and with teachers.

The explanation is no more than an hypothesis. It would be very interesting to test this hypothesis in a research project in the only other city in the Netherlands where all schools have an integrated eductional policy: Almere.

In the Netherlands one often hears the statement: 'educational innovation stands or falls with the devotion of the teachers'. Much is achieved in Lelystad and this is due mainly to the efforts of the teachers who have developed and executed all the innovations.

# REFERENCES

Ankers, A. & Kort, G. de (1987). *Uit de school geklapt. Een onderzoek naar spijbelen en schoolverlaten in Utrecht.* Utrecht: Afdeling onderzoek ROVU, gemeente.
Bernard, Y. (1986). Amsterdamse jongeren in het voortgezet onderwijs: hun beleving van school en vrije tijd. In: R. Grob et al., *'Eigenwijs in onderwijs: Beleving, verzuim en verlaten van school'.* OOMO-reeks. Nijmegen.
Bosch, P.A.M. (1986). *Met het oog op Stiemen. Een onderzoek naar schoolverzuim en voortijdig onderwijsverlaten in Arnhem.* Arnhem: Afdeling Onderzoek en Statistiek.
CBS (1987). *Schoolloopbaan en herkomst van leerlingen bij het voortgezet onderwijs: cohort 1982, SLVO, peildatum september 1986.* CBS-mededelingen, no. 7871.
Jaspers, J. et al., (1984). *Van school gaan: verslag van een onderzoek in Leeuwarden naar de problematiek rondom het voortijdig schoolverlaten in het voortgezet onderwijs. Deelverslag 1.* Leeuwarden.
Ministerie van Onderwijs en Wetenschappen (1986). *'Schoolverzuim, brief van de staatssecretaris van Onderwijs en Wetenschappen'.* Tweede Kamer. 's-Gravenhage.

Stoel, W.G.R. (1980). *De relatie tussen de grootte van scholen voor voortgezet onderwijs en het welbevinden van leerlingen. Resultaten van een empirisch onderzoek in de Nederlandse onderwijssituatie.* Haren: RION.

Vonk, G.J.M. (1986). *Voortijdig schoolverlaten in de gemeente Groningen.* Haren: RION.

Vries, G.C. de (1987). Verzuim uitval en de bijdrage van de school. *'Pedagogische Studiën', 12,* (2), 94-104.

Vries, A.M. de & Bosveld, H.E.P. (1988). *Vruchten van een geïntegreerd onderwijsbeleid. Een onderzoek naar spijbelen in Lelystad.* Lelystad.

Vries, G.C. de & Peetsma, Th. (1986). *Voortijdig schoolverlaten in het voortgezet onderwijs.* Amsterdam: SCO.

# GENERALIZIBILITY OF INSTRUCTIONAL AND SCHOOL EFFECTIVENESS INDICATORS ACROSS NATIONS; PRELIMINARY RESULTS OF A SECONDARY ANALYSIS OF THE IEA*) SECOND MATHEMATICS STUDY

Jaap Scheerens, Henk C.R. Nanninga & W.J. Hans Pelgrum
Department of Education, University of Twente, Enschede

## INTRODUCTION

Despite research in various disciplines (psychology, sociology, economics) there is as yet no established causal model of school effectiveness (see e.g. Hanushek, 1986). Although there is a growing consensus regarding a set of potential predictors of school-outcomes, critics still have every reason to question the consistency, stability and applicability of this set of indicators (cf. Ralph & Fennessey, 1983; Kyle, 1985).

The best-known formulation of effectiveness predictors is the so-called 5-factor model of school effectiveness, first formulated by Edmonds (1979):
- strong educational leadership;
- emphasis on basic skills achievement;
- safe and orderly climate;
- high expectations of pupils' achievement;
- frequent evaluation of pupils' progress.

Other major school effectiveness studies (Rutter et al., 1979; Brookover et al., 1979; Madaus et al., 1979, and Mortimore et al., 1988) have yielded more elaborate sets of predictors, though generally in line with the "five-factor model". Scheerens and Stoel (1988) propose a multi-level conceptual model of school effectiveness, in which school level variables are seen as supportive conditions for instructional measures at the classroom level that have

---

*) IEA = International Association for the Educational Achievement

been found to be associated with high achievement. An important, recently started, line of research on school effectiveness, looks at the generalizibility of school effectiveness predictors across contexts. "Context" can be defined either as type of school (Firestone & Herriott, 1982; Stoel & Scheerens, 1988) or as student-body composition (Wimpelberg, Teddlie & Springfield, 1987). These studies show there is reason to believe that the set of significant effectiveness predictors will vary across contexts. However, there is also evidence that certain classroom and school factors are valuable effectiveness predictors in several contexts, for example structured teaching and time on task (cf. Kyle, 1985).

This paper discusses the results of a study aimed at exploring the generalizibility versus context-specifity of school and instructional effectiveness predictors, across nations.

In a secondary analysis, data from the IEA second mathematics study*) were used to compare degrees to which schools achieved different results in different countries, and the consistency in school level and class level variables that could explain these differences between schools.

The fact that we carried out a secondary analysis implies that we had to take for granted certain limitations of the available data with respect to our research aim. These were: predictor variables that from the literature appear important could only be partially covered, and the fact that in about half of the countries only one class per school was investigated, so that school effects could not be distinguished from class effects.


*General Description of the Original Study and its Resulting Data Base*
The Second International Mathematics Study (hereafter referred to as SIMS) was conducted in the following countries: Belgium (Flemish and French), Canada (Ontario and British Columbia), England, Finland, France, Hong Kong, Hungary, Israel, Japan, Luxembourg, The Netherlands, New Zealand, Nigeria, Scotland, Swaziland, Thailand, Sweden and the USA. In this study a multi-level approach was used to investigate students' achievement in mathematics, and its determinants, at the level of the second grade of secondary education.

The study contained a cross-sectional and longitudinal part. The cross-sectional part involved the collection of data at one point in time (near the end of the school year), whereas the longitudinal part consisted of collecting pre- and post-test data at the beginning and end of the school year. Data were collected about student achievement in mathematics, with a multiple choice test of 154 items, common to the tests used in the cross-sectional and longitu-

---

*) The data were made available on tape by the International Coordinating Centre for that study, in Wellington, New Zealand.

200

dinal part of the study, distributed across subtests called Arithmetic, Algebra, Geometry, Statistics and Measurement. A multiple matrix sampling design was used to collect the test data of students. This consisted in giving each student a core booklet of 40 items and one out of four rotated forms (containing 34 or 35 items for respectively the cross-sectional and longitudinal part of the study). Furthermore, additional data were collected at the level of students, teachers and schools. All data were collected by means of questionnaires and/or paper and pencil tests. The documentation accompanying the tapes contains a description of the variables for which data were collected at each level.

Table 1 contains an overview of numbers of the various units (students, teachers, schools and classes per school) for those countries included in the analyses presented in this paper, as well as some descriptive statistics on the outcome variable.

Table 1: Number of students, teachers, schools and classes per school for selected countries, means*) and standard deviations on mathematics achievement

| Country | Students | Teachers | Schools | Classes per school | Mean | stand dev. |
|---|---|---|---|---|---|---|
| 15 Belgium (Fl.) | 3282 | 150 | 150 | 1 | 53.36 | 26.50 |
| 16 Belgium (Fr.) | 1558 | 83 | 82 | 1 | 53.23 | 19.88 |
| 22 Canada (Br. Col.) | 2228 | 87 | 87 | 1 | 52.07 | 20.66 |
| 25 Canada (Ontario) | 4597 | 170 | 106 | >1 | 47.26 | 20.62 |
| 39 Finland | 4484 | 206 | 98 | >1 | 43.60 | 19.52 |
| 40 France | 8230 | 338 | 174 | >1 | 48.83 | 18.98 |
| 43 Hong Kong | 5548 | 130 | 125 | >1 | 48.43 | 19.69 |
| 44 Hungary | 1754 | 70 | 70 | 1 | 58.65 | 20.67 |
| 50 Israel | 2540 | 93 | 68 | >1 | 44.10 | 22.56 |
| 54 Japan | 8091 | 212 | 212 | 1 | 61.58 | 18.56 |
| 59 Luxembourg | 2106 | 107 | 42 | >1 | 36.63 | 15.61 |
| 62 Netherlands | 5500 | 236 | 236 | 1 | 54.96 | 21.66 |
| 63 New Zealand | 5252 | 193 | 100 | >1 | 43.77 | 21.16 |
| 72 Scotland | 853 | 274 | 58 | >1 | 50.90 | 22.67 |
| 76 Sweden | 3571 | 186 | 97 | >1 | 36.53 | 16.48 |
| 79 Thailand | 3806 | 98 | 98 | 1 | 42.56 | 17.77 |
| 81 USA | 6792 | 277 | 157 | >1 | 44.71 | 21.63 |
| Total | 70192 | 2910 | 1960 | | | |

*) Means were computed without applying sampling weights.

We shall now describe which variables were selected from the data bases for investigating the research problem.

### Variables

The dependent variables of the IEA second mathematics study were multiple choice tests in arithmetic, algebra, geometry, statistics and measurement. In all secondary analyses, we used the total score across these sub-tests. Total scores for each student were calculated by calculating the percentage of items administered to a particular student, that was correct. Although this might introduce some error variance due to the difference in difficulty between rotated forms, for the purpose of our analyses this effect is assumed not to be important.

First of all we selected a sub-set of available predictor variables, categorized as school variables, class variables, teacher variables and pupil variables, that had some correspondence to relevant school effectiveness predictors, as appears in the literature. Since this sub-set was still as many as 73 variables, we used a further reduction procedure. Working from the correlation matrix of all independent variables and the dependent variable, where student and class scores were aggregated up to the school level, we used the following selection criteria:
- the independent variable had to correlate .10 or more with the dependent variable in at least 5 countries;
- any particular independent variable should not correlate over .20 with any other independent variable;
- the total number of missing cases should not be higher than 30% in more than three countries.

Where predictor variables failed on any one of these criteria, but were seen, considering the literature, as particularly relevant these variables were included in the analysis. These variables were: number of meetings of mathematics teachers (smeet), estimate by teachers of number of pupils belonging to the top in mathematics (ttop), degree of urbanization of the school area (sarea) and the use of teacher-made tests (townst).

Using these selection criteria we arrived at the following list of 15 predictor variables:

*pupil characteristics*
- father's occupation (yffocci)
- father's education (yfeduc)

*teacher characteristics*
- experience as a mathematics teacher (in years - texpmth)
- time spent on keeping order (in minutes per week - tordert)
- time spent on teaching (in minutes per week - tlisst)

*opportunity to learn*
- items of test covered in tuition (totl)

*expectations*
- pupil's expectation of the number of years he/she will follow formal education (ymoreed)
- estimate by teacher of the number of pupils who belong to the top in mathematics (ttop)

*instructional characteristics*
- total time (hours) spent on homework (yahwkt)
- the use of published tests (tpubst)
- the use of teacher made tests (towntst)

*school characteristics*
- the number of women teachers in mathematics (ssommf)
- the number of men teachers that teach only mathematics (sallmm)
- the number of meetings of mathematics teachers (smeet)

*contextual characteristics*
- degree of urbanization of the school area (saera)
- class size (klgrt)


*Analyses*
Apart from providing some basic descriptive statistics on the data set, our analyses aimed to answer two questions:

(1) do the between-schools variances differ between countries?
(2) which school and instructional characteristics are stable predictors of achievement across countries?

Variance component analysis, using the VARCL-computing programme (cf. Aitkin & Longford, 1986) - was carried out to estimate between-school variances per country and to disentangle school and class effects, for those countries where data on more than one classroom per school were available. This type of analysis was also used to obtain estimates of the effect of specific school and classroom variables in terms of proportions of explained variance (in answer to question b, stated above).
  Variance component analysis was chosen because it belongs to a class of techniques (along with Raudenbush & Bryk's HLM procedure, Raudenbush & Bryk, 1986) that is most efficient for analyzing multi-level data (cf. Aitkin & Longford, 1986). By allowing for the coefficients for slopes and intercepts to be considered as random effects, this technique also offers possibilities for testing interesting substantive hypotheses about the equality of education in a particular school (cf. Brandsma & Knuver, 1988) - when slopes are treated as outcomes.

The formulation of the model with random intercepts and random slopes is as follows:

$$y_{ij} = (\alpha + \alpha_j) + (\beta + \beta j)x_{ij} + \delta z_j + e_{ij}$$

where:

$y_{ij}$ = dependent variable (score of pupil i in school j)
$\alpha$ = intercept
$\alpha_j$ = random part of intercept
$\beta, \delta$ = regression coefficients
$\beta_j$ = random part of the regression coefficient
$x_{ij}$ = pupil score on co-variate
$z_j$ = score on school or classroom level variable
$e_{ij}$ = individual error term

Analysis of more or less restricted versions of this model makes it possible to partition the total variance into school (and/or classroom) and pupil components; to examine the "fit" of the model when specific sets of school (or class) level variables are added; to investigate (under the assumption of random effects) the significance of variances in slopes and intercepts among units, and, finally, to determine the effect-size of sets of predictor variables defined at the school and/or classroom level and individual predictor variables in terms of percentage of variance explained. Further details on the use of this particular technique for multi-level analysis are provided in the references stated above.

# RESULTS

## School and Class Effects

One problem in using the SIMS data set for secondary analyses with respect to school effectiveness is the confounding of school and class effects. We can only separate school and class effects when data are available on more than one classroom per school. This is the case for 10 of the 17 countries (see Table 1). So far we have analysed the data for five countries, USA, Sweden, France, New Zealand and the Netherlands.

By investigating the so-called "null-model" (excluding all predictor variables), variance component analysis by means of the VARCL programme yields intra-class correlations as a measure of the proportion of total variance explained by schools and classrooms respectively. The results for the four countries are presented in Table 2.

Table 2: Estimates of the variance explained by schools and classes expressed in terms of the intra-class correlation coefficient for four countries; assuming schools are sampled at random within countries and classroom are sampled at random within schools; the coefficients shown between brackets are the intra-class correlation coefficients after controlling for fathers' occupation (yfocci)

| Country | School variance component | Classroom variance component |
|---|---|---|
| USA | .10 (.09) | .46 (.44) |
| New Zealand | .01 (.004) | .45 (.42) |
| France | .06 (.05) | .17 (.15) |
| Sweden | .00 (.00) | .45 (.43) |

The results summarized in Table 2 give an impression of (a) the degree to which classrooms differ within schools and (b) the degree to which schools still differ in average achievement, when the between-class effect has been accounted for. The very low values of the school variance component for New Zealand and Sweden signifies that in these countries it does not make much difference which school pupils attend, but that it matters more in which classroom pupils are placed. If this were the general pattern in school effectiveness studies, one would be tempted to give up the idea of "school effectiveness" and instead turn to questions of classroom or teacher effectiveness. In our data set, however, the size of class effects may well be inflated due to streaming.

Table 2 also gives an impression of the heterogeneity in contrast to the homogeneity of national school systems. The USA data indicate that in this country there is both heterogeneity at the classroom and the school level. The figures for France, on the other hand, show relatively little variance either between classrooms or between schools (this finding corroborates Pelgrum's results, Pelgrum, 1988).

### Effects of Specific School and Class Variables
To examine the effects of specific school and class variables we used the VARCL programme to estimate the association (in terms of a standardized regression coefficient) of each predictor variable with mathematics achievement, when father's occupation is controlled for. The results are shown in Table 3. Coefficients that exceed two standard errors of sampling are significant.

Predictor variables that show the strongest and most consistent association with mathematics achievement are educational expectations expressed by pupils (ymoreed) and by teachers (ttop), and opportunity to learn (totl).

We further divided the total set of predictor variables into a sub-set containing all variables defined at the school level, a sub-set containing all variables defined at the class level and computed the amount of variance in

Table 3: Effect of separate predictor variables in terms of standardized regression coefficients; standard errors of sampling are shown between brackets; coefficients > 2 standard errors are significant

| pred. var. | country USA | N.Zld | France | Sweden | Neth. |
|---|---|---|---|---|---|
| yfocci | .04 (.01) | .08 (.01) | .08 (.01) | .05 (.02) | .01 (.01) |
| ymoreed | .13 (.01) | .16 (.01) | .21 (.01) | .14 (.01) | .12 (.01) |
| yahwkt | -.001 (.01) | .02 (.01) | .002 (.01) | .03 (.01) | -.02 (.01) |
| texpmth | .05 (.03) | .09 (.03) | .05 (.02) | -.03 (.04) | .11 (.03) |
| tordert | -.12 (.03) | -.15 (.03) | -.06 (.02) | -.03 (.04) | .02 (.03) |
| tlisst | .003 (.03) | .06 (.03) | -.01 (.02) | .07 (.04) | .07 (.03) |
| ttopp | .31 (.03) | .32 (.03) | .13 (.02) | .27 (.04) | .09 (.03) |
| tpubtst | -.04 (.04) | -.03 (.03) | .01 (.02) | .04 (.04) | -.05 (.03) |
| towntst | .01 (.04) | -.05 (.03) | -.02 (.02) | .02 (.04) | -.01 (.03) |
| totl | .25 (.03) | .08 (.03) | -.02 (.02) | .11 (.04) | .33 (.03) |
| saera | -.04 (.04) | .004 (.03) | -.02 (.03) | .004 (.04) | -.07 (.03) |
| ssommf | .004 (.04) | -.03 (.04) | -.01 (.03) | -.07 (.04) | -.05 (.03) |
| sallmm | -.002 (.04) | .02 (.03) | .02 (.03) | .01 (.04) | .23 (.04) |
| smeet | .01 (.04) | .01 (.03) | -.01 (.03) | .02 (.04) | .03 (.03) |
| klgrt | -.001 (.01) | .03 (.01) | .02 (.01) | .03) (.01) | .03 (.01) |

pupils' achievement that was explained by these two sets of variables in each country, after controlling for all predictor variables defined at the student level. The results are shown in Table 4.

The results in Table 4 indicate how little variance the school variables explain, when classroom variables have been taken into account.

Finally, we examined how well selected sets of predictor variables explained between-class and between-school variances respectively, when father's occupation was controlled for. For each country those predictor variables were selected that were significantly associated with achievement (see the results in Table 3). The results are summarized in Table 5.

Table 4: Percentage of pupil variance explained by all school, resp. classroom variables, that is those variables that were measured at the school or classroom level respectively

| | % of variance explained by all school variables in model | % of variance explained by all classroom variables in model |
|---|---|---|
| USA | 2% | 26% |
| New Zealand | 0.2% | 30% |
| France | 0% | 8% |
| Sweden | 0% | 23% |

Table 5: Effects of selected sub-sets of predictor variables in terms of explained between-class and explained between-school variance.

|  | % of between-classroom variance explained by selected variables | % of between-school variance explained by selected variables |
|---|---|---|
| USA | 57% | 11% |
| New Zealand | 69% | 0% |
| France | 47% | 19% |
| Sweden | 51% | 0% |
| Netherlands*) | - | 65% |

*) Since for the Netherlands' data on only one class per school was available, there was no way to separate classroom and school variance components.

The results in Table 5 indicate that the selected sets of predictor variables operate at the class level to a larger degree than at the school level; this should come as no surprise since most predictor variables are defined at the classroom level rather than at the school level.

# DISCUSSION

The results of this secondary analysis suggest that a small number of school/class characteristics show a consistently positive association with mathematics achievement. These factors are: positive expectations of pupils' achievement (the variables ymoreed with an average association of .15 with achievement and ttop, average association of .22) and opportunity to learn (totl average .15)*).

Other variables that, in the literature on school and instructional effectiveness, have repeatedly shown positive associations with achievement such as frequent evaluation (here represented in the variables tpubst and towntst), teachers' experience (texpmth) and indicators of "time on task" (texplm) were found to have weak and/or inconsistent effects.

The educational significance of the positive results might be challenged on conceptual and statistical grounds. One could argue that associations of variables such as "positive expectations" and "opportunity to learn" with achievement, are something of a tautology. In the worst case, opportunity to learn could reflect the purposeful training of test items. "High expectations" - it has been said before (Ralph & Fennessey, 1983) - might just as well be

---

*) averages are based on the coefficients in Table 3.

seen as the effects of high achievement rather than one of its causes. Statistical objections to the effects that were found in this study are that the effects are small and that background factors of pupils such as social economical status and intelligence were not sufficiently accounted for. As to the first type of criticism, we should like to point out that correlations of about .10, however low in an absolute sense, may still represent educationally meaningful effects (cf. Bosker & Scheerens, 1989). We cannot counter the objection of insufficient control of student background variables: this is one of the limits imposed by the fact that we had to depend on an existing data base. The one variable we used, "father's occupation", is a proxy-variable for social economical status; as appeared from the analysis, it did not explain much variance in achievement (average association of .05, over 5 countries, see Table 3).

The results further show many differences between countries as far as average achievement and between-school variance is concerned (Tables 1 and 2). Differences in the between-school variances can be interpreted as consequences of more integrated and centralized, as compared with more differentiated and decentralized, national educational systems. In those cases where the available data allowed us to disentangle school and classroom variance, we found that generally more variance is explained by classes than by schools. Moreover, we discerned specific patterns of classroom and school variances, where one country had both a sizable between-school variance and a large between-classroom variance (the USA), other countries showed almost no between-school variance but large between-classroom variances (Sweden, New Zealand) and finally France showed a pattern of low between-school variance and relatively low between-class variance (see Table 2).

A final conclusion concerns the relative importance of "independent" variables defined either at the school or classroom level. The question whether indicators (i.e. predictors) of school effectiveness are genuine school characteristics, or aggregated classroom characteristics, has repeatedly been posed in the literature on school and classroom effectiveness. Our data support the position that the case for "effective classrooms" is stronger than that for "effective schools". First, because we found that in all countries where this was analyzed, the between-class variance was much larger than the between-school variance and secondly, because the independent variables defined at the school level explained far less variance than the independent variables defined at the classroom level (see the results in Table 5). However, we cannot be really definite on this last conclusion since important school level variables, such as "educational leadership" and "school policy" were not included in the data set, and classroom effects may well be inflated due to streaming.

# REFERENCES

Aitkin, M. & Longford, N. (1986). Statistical Modelling Issues in School Effectiveness Studies. *The Journal of the Royal Statistical Society*, Series A (General), *149*, Part 1, 1-43.

Bosker, R.J. & Scheerens, J. (1989). *Criterion definition, effect size and stability, three fundamental questions in school effectiveness research.*. This volume, pp. 241-252.

Brandsma, H.P. & Knuver, A.W.M. (1988). De invloed van school- en klaskenmerken op rekenprestaties in het onderwijs. In J. Scheerens en J. Verhoeven, *Schoolorganisatie, beleid en onderwijskwaliteit*. Lisse: Swets & Zeitlinger.

Brookover et al. (1979). School social systems and student achievement: schools can make a difference. New York: Praeger.

Edmonds, R. (1979). Some schools work and more and more can. *Social Policy, 9*, 28-32.

Firestone, W.A., & Herriott, R.E. (1982). Prescriptions for effective elementary schools don't fit secondary schools. *Educational Administration Quarterly, 18*, (2), 39-59.

Hanushek, E.A. (1986). The economics of schooling: production and efficiency in public schools. *Journal of Economic Literature, 24*, 1141-1177.

Kyle, R.M.J. (1985). *Reaching for excellence. An effective schools sourcebook*. Washington: US Government Printing Office.

Madaus, G.F., Kellaghan, T., Rakow, E.A., & King, D. (1979). The sensitivity of measures of school effectiveness. *Harvard Educational Review, 49*, 207-230.

Mortimore, P., Sammons, P., Stoll, L., Lewis, D., & Ecob, R. (1988). *The junior school project; technical appendices*. London: ILEA, Research and Statistics Branch.

Pelgrum, W.J. (1988). Mathematics in Middle Schools in Western European Countries. *International Journal for Educational Research, 12* (5), 523-532.

Ralph, J.H., & Fennessey, J. (1983). Science or reform: some questions about the effective schools model. *Phi Delta Kappan*, p. 689-695.

Raudenbush, S.W., & Bryk, A.S. (1986). A hierarchical model for studying school effects. *Sociology of Education, 59*, 1-17.

Rutter, M., Maughan, B., Mortimore, B., Ouston, J., & Smith, A. (1979). *Fifteen thousand hours: secondary schools and their effects on children*. Cambridge Mass.: Harvard University Press.

Scheerens, J. & Stoel, W.G.R. (1988). *Development of theories on school-effectiveness*. Paper presented at the AERA convention. New Orleans.

Scheerens, J, Nanninga, H.C.R. & Pelgrum, W.J. Generalizibility of instructional and school effectiveness indicators across nations. To be published in the *International Journal of Educational Research, 14*.

Stoel, W.G.R., & Scheerens, J. (1988). *The stability of school effects across contexts and nations*. Paper presented at the AERA convention. New Orleans.

Wimpelberg, R.V., Teddlie, C., & Springfield, S. (1987). *Sensitivity to context: the past and future of effective schools research*. Washington: AERA paper.

# TEACHER AND SUPERVISOR ASSESSMENT OF PRINCIPAL LEADERSHIP AND ACADEMIC ACHIEVEMENT

Richard L. Andrews
University of Washington, Seattle

## PERSPECTIVE

The school principalship has been the subject of hundreds of studies over the past thirty years. The central role of the principal has been viewed, variously, as building manager, administrator, politician, change agent, boundary spanner, and instructional leader. Principal attributes and hypothesized correlates selected for investigation are in large part derived from value stances concerning the relative importance assigned these several roles (Glasman, 1984). During the last decade, value stances have tended to center on the principal as instructional leader, accountable for the academic achievement of students. Taken collectively, the "effective schools" body of studies (e.g., Lezotte & Passalacqua, 1978; Frederiksen & Edmonds, 1979; Edmonds, 1979; Brookover et al., 1979, Lazarus & Canner, 1980; Brookover & Lezotte, 1977; Lipham, 1981) tends to reflect the view of Sweeney (1982): "The direct responsibility for improving instruction and learning rests in the hands of the school principal." Most studies of this type tend to examine those schools in which achievement levels are high for all students or where achievement differences between subpopulations of students are minimal, in attempts to isolate commonalities among in-school variables. This basic approach has been criticized for its emphasis on outlier schools (Glasman, 1984; Purkey & Smith, 1982; Mackenzie, 1983).

More recently, the emergence of career ladder plans, teacher centers, and the recommendations of the Carnegie Commission on "lead teachers" suggest a diminuation of the principal's role as instructional leader. Discussion of these efforts reflect a political orientation and a concern for authority and power, with either teachers or principals seen as appropriate leaders. For the most part, such discussion has not been informed by considerations of achievement and other school outcome measures. At the same time, one aspect of organizational authority has remained inviolate: proponents of either teacher or principal leadership have been content to let responsibility for evaluation of principals remain with the supervisors of principals. Again, however, legitimation of top-down evaluation has been based on traditional hierarchical structure rather than on considerations of outcome measures.

The research described here was undertaken to investigate the relationship between two independent variables (teacher perceptions of the principal as instructional leader, supervisor perceptions of the principal) and the dependent variable of average gain scores of students in 61 of 67 elementary schools in a large urban school district, with scores disaggregated by student ethnicity and student free-lunch status as an SES surrogate measure. As such, the study assumes the value stance of Sweeney (1982), but moves beyond the limits of the "outlier" school approach; the study further examines the efficacy of supervisor evaluation of principals as instructor leaders on the basis of outcomes, thus moving beyond the limits of political authority discussions.

## OBJECTIVE

The purpose of this research was (1) to determine the relationship between teacher and supervisor perceptions of the principal as an instructional leader, and two-year CAT Total Reading and Total Mathematics average gain scores disaggregated by student ethnicity and free-lunch status (a surrogate for SES); (2) to determine the relationship between perceptions of the principal and eleven other characteristics of schools; and (3) to determine the relationship between the eleven other characteristics and disaggregated two-year gain scores, controlling for perceptions of the principal.

## METHOD AND DATA SOURCES

Teachers, principals, supervisors, students, and parents in a large urban school district participated in a two-year study of the relationships between twelve organizational characteristics of schools and student academic achievement. Participation was district-wide, involving all of the district's 67 elementary schools. Numerous questionnaires pertaining to the study were administered over the two-year period; only those instruments pertinent to that aspect of the study reported here are discussed below. In this study, the school was the unit of analysis, using the average scores of teachers, supervisors, students, and parents for each of the study variables.

### Teacher Perceptions of the Principal as an Instructional Leader

Data were obtained from teachers through administration of the Staff Assessment Questionnaire (SAQ). The SAQ includes 176 Likert-type items pertaining to nine characteristics of schools as developed by the project team. Completed SAQs were received from 2,303 teachers (74%). Nineteen of the items pertain to perceptions of principal leadership, with respondents assessing the principal as instructional source, resource provider, communicator, and extent to which the principal is a "visible presence." Based on responses from 2,145 teachers, the Strong Leader factor yielded a Cronbach Alpha of .93. For the principal leadership variable, test-retest reliability based on a three-week interval with an N of 30 schools was .89; one-year interval with 63 principals was estimated at .73.

### Administrator Perceptions of the Principal

The Supervisor Questionnaire was administered to all five supervisors of elementary principals. Supervisors were asked to rate each of the principals they supervised, using the SAQ rating range from 0 as low to 100 as high, and to provide an estimate of how the staffs in the respective schools would rate their principals using the SAQ range.

### Parent Perceptions

The school level analysis of four parent variables (Early Identification, Positive Learning Climate, Communication, Involvement) was based on 58 Likert-type items on the Parent Questionnaire, with responses from 8,547 parents.

### Student Academic Achievement

The analysis reported here is based on two-year average gain scores on Total Reading and Total Mathematics on the California Achievement Test (CAT) of a sample of 4,508 grade-3 to grade-6 students in 61 elementary schools; students in the sample attended the same school over a three-year period and were administered the CAT during the each spring of that same period. Of the 4,508 students, 2,547 (57.1%) were White; 878 (19.4%) were Black; 780 (17.3%) were Asian; the remaining 276 students (6.2%) were members of Hispanic, Native American, or other ethnic groups. No analysis of the scores of this latter group was completed due to insufficient numbers of students in each school.

### Data Analysis

Analyses of variance were conducted, using leadership of the principal as a classification variable and CAT Total Reading and Total Mathematics average NCE gain scores per year as the dependent variable. Three principal leadership groups were created for the analysis, using each school's average of staff or supervisor assessment ratings of the principal: (1) Strong Leaders (at least one standard deviation [sd] above the mean score of all elementary principals), (2) Average Leaders (between one sd above and one sd below the mean), and (3) Weak Leaders (at least one sd below the mean). Additional analyses were conducted to determine the relationships between the principal leadership variable and other school variables, and to determine the relationships between the other variables and disaggregated gain scores, controlling for perceptions of the principal.

Inspection of the data suggested that there was little difference in mean scores for each of the groups of schools when comparing schools by student perceptions. This seems to be true whether schools were grouped by supervisor perceptions or teacher perceptions of the principals as instructional leaders. However, when schools were examined for staff perceptions of their schools, some obvious trends in the data are present.

For example, while the mean scores for the different groups of schools appear similar when schools were grouped by supervisor ratings, they exhibit a considerable range when grouped by teacher ratings. Further, there was greater within variation in each of the three groups when grouped using supervisor ratings than when using teacher ratings. For example, for the variable Learning Climate, when schools were grouped by supervisors' ratings, the mean scores for the three groups of schools were 76.50, 77.37, and 78.38, respectively. When grouped by teacher ratings, the mean scores were 88.99, 81.19 and 57.16. The standard deviations were similar for the three groups based on teacher ratings (5.01, 6.70 and 8.44); however, there were wide variations in the standard deviations when grouped by supervisor ratings (25.45, 18.02, and 5.50, respectively).

Such a clear pattern, however, was not evident in the data from parent perceptions about the schools. Variations between groups of schools tend to be greater when they are grouped using supervisor ratings than when using teacher ratings of the school principals. On the other hand, the variation within groups as revealed by the standard deviations is quite similar.

Mean scores and standard deviations among the groups of schools when compared on student academic achievement (see Table 1) reveal wide variations similar to the staff perceptions of their working conditions. Average yearly gain scores in math range from a high of 4.73 and 4.54 for Free Lunch and Black students in schools where teachers perceive their principals to be strong insructional leaders. The lowest yearly gain scores in math (-2.31 and -1.71) were observed for Black students in schools in which principals were perceived as weak by teachers and in which principals were perceived as weak instructional leaders by their supervisors.

The results of data analyses using analysis of variance on student, staff, and parent perceptions of their schools are presented in Table 2.

As can be seen in Table 2, there were no signficant differences found for student or staff variables when the schools were grouped by supervisor ratings of school principals. However, significant differences were found for

214

Table 1: Mean Scores and Standard Deviations for Reading and Math Achievement by Leadership Groups Created When Using Supervisor and Teacher Ratings of Elementary School Principals

| Variables | | Supervisor Ratings | | | Teacher Ratings | | |
|---|---|---|---|---|---|---|---|
| | | Strong (n=ll) | Ave. (n-39) | Weak (n=11) | Strong (n=11) | Ave. (n=39) | Weak (n-11) |
| Student Achievement (Average Annual Gain Scores using NCE) | | | | | | | |
| Total | X̄ | 2.13 | 1.68 | 2.41 | 2.77 | 1.89 | .89 |
| Reading | Sd | 2.50 | 3.40 | 2.65 | 2.57 | 2.66 | 1.86 |
| By Ethnic Group | | | | | | | |
| White | X̄ | 1.74 | .97 | 1.63 | 1.61 | 1.06 | .95 |
| | Sd | 2.60 | 1.93 | 1.93 | 1.63 | 1.98 | 2.33 |
| Black | X̄ | 1.87 | 1.26 | 1.66 | 4.54 | 1.08 | .01 |
| | Sd | 3.62 | 4.17 | 2.80 | 4.85 | 3.49 | 3.16 |
| By SES | | | | | | | |
| Non-Free | X̄ | 1.41 | 1.03 | 2.56 | 1.22 | 1.31 | 1.02 |
| Lunch | Sd | 2.45 | 2.01 | 2.70 | 1.55 | 2.18 | 2.40 |
| Free | X̄ | 3.19 | 1.79 | 2.16 | 4.73 | 1.98 | .28 |
| Lunch | Sd | 4.91 | 3.53 | 3.03 | 3.76 | 3.79 | 1.94 |

three of the four parent variables. Just the opposite was found when the schools were grouped by teacher ratings of the instructional leadership of the school principals. Group mean scores for one of the four student variables were significantly different, group mean scores for all eight of the staff variables were significantly different; however, there were no signficant differences found for any of the parent variables. In each case, where differences were found, these differences were positively related to the extent to which the teachers perceived their principal to be a strong instructional leader.

Presented in Table 3 are the results of the analyses of variance using supervisor ratings and teacher ratings as the independent variable and NCE average annual gain scores as the dependent variable.

As can be seen in Table 3, when the schools were grouped using supervisor ratings, there were no significant differences in average annual gain scores among the three groups of schools. However, when the schools were grouped by teacher ratings of the principals as instructional leaders, the average gain scores were significantly different among the three groups for 5 of the 10 analyses. In each case where significant differences were found, they were positively related to teacher ratings of principal performance as an instructional leader.

Table 2: Mean Squares, df, F-ratios, and Level of Significance When School Variables were Compared for Elementary Schools Grouped by Either Supervisor or Teacher Ratings of Principal Leadership

| Variables | Supervisor Ratings | | | | Teacher Ratings | | | |
|---|---|---|---|---|---|---|---|---|
| | MS | df | F | Sig. | MS | df | F | Sig. |
| **Students** | | | | | | | | |
| High Expectations | .0956 | 60 | .226 | ns | .039 | 61 | .098 | ns |
| Learning Climate | .364 | 60 | 1.37 | ns | .689 | 61 | 2.468 | ns |
| Sex Equity | .749 | 61 | .397 | ns | .055 | 61 | .103 | ns |
| Multi-Cult. Educ. | .015 | 60 | .116 | ns | 39.086 | 61 | 4.35 | .02 |
| **Staff** | | | | | | | | |
| Dedicated Staff | 11.818 | 61 | .086 | ns | 902.596 | 61 | 8.370 | .001 |
| Freq. Monitoring | .145 | 60 | .004 | ns | 316.611 | 61 | 17.922 | .001 |
| High Expectations | 6.708 | 60 | .110 | ns | 521.526 | 61 | 7.959 | .001 |
| Early I.D. Learn. | 4.329 | 61 | .635 | ns | 60.032 | 61 | 9.244 | .001 |
| Learning Climate | 6.794 | 61 | .019 | ns | 3682.873 | 61 | 16.894 | .001 |
| Curr. Continuity | 5.393 | 60 | .316 | ns | 57.196 | 61 | 7.798 | .04 |
| Multi-Cult Educ. | 2.55 | 60 | .000 | ns | 425.207 | 63 | 9.158 | .001 |
| Clear Goals | 13.254 | 61 | 1.204 | ns | 59.049 | 62 | 6.240 | .001 |
| Sex Equity | 1.996 | 60 | .007 | ns | 10.385 | 63 | 10.571 | .001 |
| **Parents** | | | | | | | | |
| Learn. Climate | 16.658 | 60 | 3.506 | .05 | 13.254 | 63 | 2.479 | ns |
| Early I.D.Learn. | .454 | 60 | .001 | ns | .426 | 63 | 1.232 | ns |
| Communication | 10.735 | 61 | 4.635 | .01 | .645 | 63 | .248 | ns |
| Parent Part. | 30.51 | 61 | 6.573 | .01 | 16.364 | 63 | .361 | ns |

## RESULTS

When leader groups were created using teacher assessment, students in Strong Leader schools had significantly greater NCE gain scores in both Total Reading ($p < .017$) and Total Mathematics ($p < .035$) than did students in schools rated by teachers as having Average or Weak Leaders. The direction of gain scores, while somewhat inconsistent for White and Non-Free-Lunch students in Average or Weak Leader schools, were consistently highest for Strong Leader schools. The order of gain scores for Black and free-lunch students was consistent across groups, from highest for Strong Leader schools to lowest for Weak Leader schools. The greatest differences were found for Free-Lunch students in reading ($p < .003$), and for both Black ($p < .009$) and Free-Lunch ($p < .005$) students in mathematics. Non-significant differences in gain scores among all subpopulations of students were obtained when considered in terms of either supervisor perceptions of principals or supervisor predictions of teacher's perceptions of principals.

Table 3: Mean Squares, df, F-ratios, and Level of Significance of Student Achievement Using Average Annual NCE Gain Scores over a Two-Year Period of Time when Schools were Grouped by Either Supervisor or Teacher Ratings of Principal Leadership

| Variables | Supervisor Ratings | | | | Teacher Ratings | | | |
|---|---|---|---|---|---|---|---|---|
| | MS | df | F | Sig. | MS | df | F | Sig. |
| TOTAL READING | 2.0 | 61 | .193 | ns | 12.344 | 61 | 1.259 | ns |
| By Ethnicity | | | | | | | | |
| White | 3.178 | 61 | 1.386 | ns | 1.602 | 61 | .389 | ns |
| Black | 1.802 | 61 | .113 | ns | 72.763 | 61 | 5.414 | .01 |
| By SES | | | | | | | | |
| Non-Free Lunch | 6.417 | 61 | 1.393 | ns | .496 | 61 | .012 | ns |
| Free Lunch | 8.233 | 61 | .592 | ns | 66.090 | 61 | 5.647 | .01 |
| | | | | | | | | |
| TOTAL MATH | 2.39 | 61 | .233 | ns | 31.900 | 61 | 3.546 | .05 |
| By Ethnicity | | | | | | | | |
| White | 7.644 | 61 | .920 | ns | 7.880 | 61 | .975 | ns |
| Black | 10.738 | 61 | .727 | ns | 114.933 | 61 | 5.751 | .005 |
| By SES | | | | | | | | |
| Non-Free Lunch | 2.456 | 61 | .167 | ns | 12.208 | 61 | 1.412 | ns |
| Free Lunch | 13.845 | 61 | 1.562 | ns | 81.011 | 61 | 6.874 | .002 |

Further analyses indicated that when principals were grouped by teacher ratings (1) all of the staff variables with the exception of Clear Goals, were significantly related to the Principal Leadership variables; (2) there were no significant differences among the three groups of schools in terms of parent variables; (3) first-year principals were equally likely to be perceived as either "strong" or "weak"; and (4) perceptions of the principal were not significantly related to ethnicity, gender, or years of experience of the principal. When principals were grouped by supervisor ratings, there were non-significant differences in terms of student outcomes and staff variables, but significant differences in terms of parents' perceptions.

The findings suggest that teacher perceptions of the principal as an instructional leader are critical to the reading and mathematics achievement of students, particularly among historically low-achieving students, as contrasted with the findings of non-significance of supervisor perceptions of principals as instructor leaders. In addition, the findings suggest that staff ratings of the principal are also related to other in-school variables, while supervisor ratings are not related to in-school variables; however, supervisor ratings were related to parental perceptions of the schools. These findings support our previously reported findings (see Andrews, Soder, & Jacoby, 1986; Andrews & Soder, 1987) concerning the relationship between academic achievement of students and principal leadership when the leadership of the principal is viewed from the perspective of teachers.

# IMPLICATIONS

The findings of this research suggest that supervisors of principals and teachers in those principals' schools use different data in arriving at decisions concerning the instructional leadership of school principals. Teachers seem to formulate their views of the school principal from what is happening to them personally and to other teachers in the school, and the impact of the school on students. On the other hand, supervisors seem to arrive at their conclusions concerning the instructional leadership behavior of principals from environmental effects (e.g., parental perceptions). Clearly, these findings suggest that the role of the school principal is complex and demanding. Conclusions about the effectiveness of school principals will depend on the data sources we use to generate information during the evaluation process. Smith and Andrews (1987) argue that the performance of school principals should be based on both the processes that principals use as they go about their day-to-day activities and on the outcomes we expect from our schools. These findings support such a view. Teacher perceptions as a data source are important for assessing the processes that principals use and have important implications for outcomes as well. However, there is more to the role of the school principal than just instructional leadership activities. The functions include community relations, building management, and district relations. The perceptions of teachers seem to generate little weight into these variables. The broader frame of reference of the supervisor seems to be a more valuable source of information for these other variables.

These findings suggest that both supervisor's perceptions and teachers' perceptions are valuable sources of information when considering the total role of the school principal and when performance is considered from both the processes that principals engage in as well as student outcomes.

# REFERENCES

Andrews, R. L., & R. Soder. (March 1987). Principal Leadership and Student Achievement. *Educational Leadership.*

Andrews, R. L., R. Soder, & D. Jacoby. (April 1986). *Principal Roles, Other In-School Variables, and Academic Achievement by Ethnicity and SES.* Paper presented at the meeting of the American Educational Research Association, San Francisco, CA.

Brookover, W. B., & W. L. Lezotte. (1977). *Changes in School Characteristics Coincident with Changes in Student Achievement.* East Lansing, MI: Institute for Research on Teaching, College of Education, Michigan State University.

Brookover, W. B., Beady, C., Flood, P., Schweitzer, J. & Wisenbaker, J. (1979). *School Social Systems and Student Achievement: schools can make a difference.* New York: Praeger.

Edmonds, R. R. (1979). Effective Schools for the Urban Poor. *Educational Leadership, 37,* (1) 15-24.

Frederiksen, J. R., & R. R. Edmonds. (1979). *Identification of Instructionally Effective and Ineffective Schools.* Paper presented at the Annual Meeting of the American Educational Research Association, San Francisco.

Glasman, N. S. (1984). Student Achievement and the School Principal. *Educational Evaluation and Policy Analysis 6,* (3), 283-296.

Lezotte, L., & J. Passalacqua. (1978). Individual School Buildings: Accounting for Differences in Measured Pupil Performance. *Urban Education, 13,* 283-293.

Lipham, J. M. (1981). *Effective Principal, Effective School.* Reston, VA.: National Association of Secondary School Principals.

Mackenzie, D. E. (1983). Research for School Improvement: An Appraisal of Some Recent Trends. *Educational Research, 12,* (4), 5-16.

Purkey, S. C., & M. S. Smith. (1982). Too Soon to Cheer? Synthesis of Research on Effective Schools. *Educational Leadership, 39,* 74-69.

Smith, W. F., & R. L. Andrews. (1987). Clinically Supervision for Principals. *Educational Leadership, 45,* (1), 34-38

Sweeney, J. (1982). Research Synthesis on Effective School Leadership. *Educational Leadership, 39,* 346-352.

# CLASS HETEROGENEITY, TEACHER AND PUPIL TIME-EXPENDITURE AND READING ACHIEVEMENT IN SCHOOLS FOR SPECIAL EDUCATION IN THE NETHERLANDS

Berend Schonewille
Free University, Amsterdam

## CLASSROOM COMPOSITION AND THE EDUCATIONAL PROCESS

Can teachers in homogeneous classes be more effective in their instruction and in enhancing student-achievement than teachers in heterogeneous classes? According to Slavin (1987), the large tradition of research, caused by this question has resulted in a widespread agreement, that grouping students according to their ability resulting in more or less homogeneous classes, which are instructed in all subjects has little or no effect in enhancing student achievement. When ability grouping is reduced to one or two subjects, however, and instruction for the remaining subjects takes place in not-ability-grouped (heterogeneous) settings, (homogeneous) ability grouping may increase student achievement (Slavin, 1987). So there are indications that classroom composition – in terms of class-heterogeneity – influences the output of the process of education.

This paper is a report of an investigation for the field of Special Education into the effects of class heterogeneity on teacher behavior (several time for instruction measures as well as measures of procedural and behavior management time), pupil behavior (several time-on-task measures) and pupilachievement (achievement-gain-scores on a reading test).

Aim of the study is to find those teacherbehaviors (in terms of time expenditure) that are positively related to high achievement-gain-scores and to answer the question if those behaviors are influenced by class composition.

## RESEARCH-QUESTIONS

Teacher and pupil time expenditure patterns have been used as operationalisations of the educational process. This approach dates back to the ideas of Carroll (1963), Bloom (1974) and the Beginning Teacher Evaluation Study (Fisher, Filby, Marliave, & Berliner, 1978). The use of time-on-task in educational research has been widespread and has been reviewed in many articles (e.g. Frederick & Walberg, 1980; Smyth, 1981 and more recently by Veenman, Lem, Voeten, Winkelmolen & Lassche, 1986).

Influence of class composition can thus be translated in the general question of difference between homogeneous and heterogeneous classes together with the following specific questions of (1) teacher and pupil time expenditure patterns; (2) the relationship between teacher and pupil time expenditure patterns on the one hand and pupil achievement on the other hand; (3) individual teacher time spent to high and low achieving (on a pretest) pupils; (4) the relationship between individual teacher attention and pupil achevement. The last question can be stated in another way, can percentage of individual-attention-time be regarded as an effective teacher behavior?

## DESIGN AND INSTRUMENTATION

The investigation has been carried out in 20 classes (318 pupils, 8-11 years of age) of schools for Special Educaton for primary learning disabled children in the Netherlands. At the beginning and the end of schoolyear 1986/87 a reading achievement test was administered for each pupil. During 10 reading lessons each teacher and 6 pupils (chosen using stratified random sampling with 3 reading levels per class) were observed separately but synchronically by two observers each using a micro-computer. Using 10-second-intervals 3 teacher-scores and 4 pupil scores (2 pupil-behavior-scores and 2 scores concerning teacher-behavior toward this particular pupil) per interval were recorded. A total of more than 32000 intervals were observed. Teacher-behavior-scores concerned position in the classroom (8 categories), focus of attention (8 cat.) and kind of behavior (13 cat.). Pupil-behavior-scores concerned setting (8 cat.), on-/off-task behavior (7 cat.), level of teacher-attention (6 cat.) and kind of teacher-attention (8 cat.).

The standard deviation of all reading-scores (pre-test) in a class served as a measure of heterogeneity of reading achievement. Standard deviation-scores ranged between classes from 9.3 to 22.3. Heterogeneity effect analyses consisted of comparisons of teacher- and pupil-time expenditure measures in the 10 relatively homogeneous and the 10 relatively heterogeneous classes.

## TEACHER AND PUPIL TIME EXPENDITURE IN HOMOGENEOUS AND HETEROGEOUS CLASSES

According to Thompson et al. (1982) teacher behavior was divided into three main categories: academic behavior, immediately directed to the task (the subject of reading); procedural behavior, task preparation behavior; management behavior, directed to managing pupil distractions, pupil off-task behavior etc. Main and subcategories as well as the different percentages of time spend to these (sub)categories of behavior have been listed in Table 1 for the teachers in general and according to their relative heterogeneity.

## Teacher Behavior

In general the teachers in this investigation appear to spend 56.6% of their time to academic behavior, for the most part consisting of listening behavior (40.0%). 22.9% of the time was spent on all kinds of procedural behavior, such as composing subgroups of children, telling subgroups what today's tasks are etc. Management took up to 12.4% of the time: monitoring, motivating behavior and pupil-behavior management. Heterogeneity analysis is possible by comparing the time patterns, shown in the 2nd and 3rd column. Two of the (academic) kinds of behavior appear to be significantly different on a t-test : listening behavior occurred much less in homogeneous classes while giving instructions occurred much more (p <= .05).

When compared with research in regular elementary schools done by Veenman et al. (1987), substantial differences appear on the level of the main categories of academic and procedural behavior. The teachers in this study

Table 1: Teacher time expenditure (in percentages) : in general and within homogeneous and heterogeneous classes.

| | In general | Homog. classes | Heterog. classes | Veenman et al.(1987) Single-age classes | Multiage classes |
|---|---|---|---|---|---|
| N | 20 | 10 | 10 | | |
| ACADEMIC | 56.6 | 53.4 | 59.8 | 69 | 78 |
| Listens | 40.0 | 33.5 | 46.6 | | |
| Asks question | 3.2 | 4.4 | 2.0 | | |
| Gives answer | 0.4 | 0.4 | 0.4 | | |
| Gives instructions | 7.6 | 10.2 | 4.9 | | |
| Aks to repeat | 1.3 | 1.2 | 1.5 | | |
| Corrects pupil | 4.1 | 3.7 | 4.4 | | |
| PROCEDURAL | 22.9 | 24.7 | 21.1 | 12 | 9 |
| Asks to read or stop | 1.5 | 1.1 | 2.0 | | |
| Procedural(general) | 21.4 | 23.6 | 19.1 | | |
| MANAGEMENT | 12.4 | 11.2 | 13.6 | 11 | 8 |
| Monitoring | 5.7 | 4.5 | 6.8 | | |
| Classroom-management | 5.5 | 5.6 | 5.3 | | |
| Motivating behavior | 1.2 | 1.1 | 1.5 | | |
| OTHER BEHAVIOR | 8.1 | 10.7 | 5.5 | 8 | 5 |

223

appear to be less involved in academic and more in procedural activities. However, it is too early to conclude from this that teachers in this study are less efficient in their use of time, because there is no knowledge of what can be regarded as a normal pattern of time expenditure in schools for primary learning-disabled children. One might expect a different kind of pattern because all kinds of behavior and learning problems do accumulate in schools for primary learning disabled children.

## Pupil Behavior

Pupil behavior was also divided into three main categories: on-task, procedural and off-task behavior. Table 2 shows for the 126 observed pupils what their behavior was like. During 64.1% of their time pupils were on-task; during 13.3% of the time they were involved in procedural activities and 22.6% of their time was scored as off-task or other behavior. Comparison of the behavior patterns of the 64 homogeneously grouped pupils with the 62 heterogenously grouped pupils showed two significant differences on the level of main categories and four significant differences on the subcategory level (using t-test; p<.05;significant differences underlined). Homogeneously grouped pupils show less on-task behavior and more procedural behavior. During more of their time they were asking and waiting for help and engaged in other procedural activities; furthermore, they show more disturbing off-task behavior (although absolute percentages are very low in this case as with asking and waiting for help, which diminishes the relevance of the differences).

Table 2: Pupil time expenditure (in percentages) : in general and in homogeneous and heterogeneous classes.

| | In general | Homogen. classes | Heterog. classes | Veenman et al.(1987) Single-age classes | Multiage classes |
|---|---|---|---|---|---|
| N | 126 | 64 | 62 | | |
| ON-TASK | | | | | |
| Is working | 64.1 | 61.2 | 67.1 | 78 | 72 |
| PROCEDURAL | 13.3 | 15.4 | 11.0 | 12 | 14 |
| Asks for help | 0.4 | 0.6 | 0.2 | | |
| Waits for help | 0.9 | 1.6 | 0.2 | | |
| Procedural(other) | 12.0 | 13.2 | 10.6 | | |
| OFF-TASK | 22.6 | 23.4 | 21.9 | 10 | 14 |
| Silent off-task | 12.9 | 12.7 | 13.1 | | |
| Disturbing off-task | 0.4 | 0.7 | 0.2 | | |
| Other behavior | 9.3 | 10.0 | 8.6 | | |

When compared with the data from the study by Veenman et al. (1987) substantial differences appear on the level of the main categories of on-task and off-task behavior : pupils in this study being less on-task and more off-task. As was the case with teacher behavior, definite conclusions cannot be drawn until more research on this topic has been carried out.

## Is Teacher and Pupil Time Expenditure Related to Achievement Gain?

The data in Table 1 describing teacher behavior are class level data. Reading achievement gain was measured by taking the difference between the before and after scores on the reading test. Thus, reading achievement gain (individual level data) had to be aggregated to a class level achievement score (by computing the mean class achievement) in order to be able to relate teacher time and reading achievement gain. Although Shavelson, Webb and Burstein (1986) present objections against the use of class level means in teacher effectiveness research, because it may hide important information about the within class variability in student performance, carrying out this kind of analysis in this paper seems justified by the fact that these class level data will be completed by individual level data presented in the next two paragraphs. Of course, the problem of different level data does not show up when relating pupil time measures to pupil gain scores.

Table 3 shows two kinds of correlations: teacher time with class level achievement and pupil time with individual achievement. The difference becomes clear when one takes into account the different N's for the two types of correlations. Only one out of nine reported correlations between teacher behavior and mean class achievement gain reaches the .05 significance level. It is the (negative) correlation of -.40 between time spent on academic behavior by the teachers in general and the mean class gain scores : higher percentages of time spent on academic kinds of behavior vary with lower mean class gain scores. This is contrary to what one might expect on the basis of the following two hypotheses: (1) that the quality of instruction (Bloom) is improved with more academic teacher time; (2) that with improved quality of instruction mean class gain scores will rise (other things being equal). More detailed research will be necessary although a part of the explanation of this unexpected outcome of the class level analysis is given by the results of the additional analysis, which follow.

The correlations between pupil time measures and individual reading achievement gain are somewhat different. Again, only the significant (3 out of 9) correlations will be discussed. Two of them are in accordance with the expectations : for homogeneously as well as heterogeneously grouped pupils there is a (negative) correlation of -.25 between off-task time and achievement gain scores (the more off-task a pupil is, the lower the achievement gain will be). This needs no further explanation. The third significant correlation, however, cannot be as easily understood : the (negative) correlation of -.24 between on-task behavior and achievement gain scores for the heterogeneously grouped pupils. For these pupils higher percentages of on-task time go together with lower gain scores. Additional analyses, which took into consideration mean class reading level and individual reading level (pre-test), showed higher levels of on-task behavior, but lower levels of achievement gain for the higher level pupils, their impact however being higher because of a slight overrepresentation of high level pupils in the sample.

In general, the data presented in Table 3 only partly support Doyle (1977) that measures of student classroom behavior are positively related to learning outcomes.

Table 3: Teacher and pupil-time expenditure as related to reading-achievement-gain-scores.

|  | In general | Homogen. classes | Heterog. classes |
|---|---|---|---|
| N(classes) | 20 | 10 | 10 |
| AxOc | -.40* | -.47 | -.31 |
| PxOc | .30 | .04 | .47 |
| MxOc | .14 | .33 | -.00 |
| N(pupils) | 118 | 58 | 59 |
| OnxOi | -.11 | .11 | -.24* |
| PxOi | .14 | .20 | .01 |
| OffxOi | .03 | -.25* | -.25* |

*:p<.05

| | |
|---|---|
| A:academic teacher-behavior | On:On-task-behavior(pupil) |
| P:procedural teacher-behavior | P:Procedural behavior(pupil) |
| M:management behavior teacher | Off:Off-task behavior (pupil) |
| Oc: class level output measure | Oi : Individual level output measure |

## Individual Attention in Homogeneous and Heterogeneous Classes

According to Van der Leij (1985) the intensity level of teacher behavior from the point of view of the pupil is an important aspect, especially in Special Education. Underlying hypothesis of this investigation is that the more intensive the level of teacher behavior is, the more and the better the pupil will learn. It was further assumed, that teacher behavior is most intensive when directed to the individual pupil.

Intensity level was measured as a pupil characteristic (the third pupil observation score), which made it possible to compute for each pupil the percentage of his or her time that the teacher paid attention to him or her. Table 4 shows the mean percentages of individual attention time separately for high and low achievers, according to their class size (small classes: 15 or less pupils) and heterogeneity. High achievers are those pupils with pre-test reading scores within the upper third of their own class distribution, while low achievers had scores within the lower third of the class distribution. High and low is, thus, referring to the relative reading level of the pupil within the classroom and not to the absolute reading level (data for pupils with a middle position will be left out of discussion here). In general, low achievers get individual teacher attention during 10.1% of their time and high achievers only during 6.2% of their time. Low achievers get more individual teacher attention than high achievers - levels of class size and class heterogeneity held constant - but these differences do in no case reach the .05 significance level on a t-test. The only found significant (p<.05) difference in mean percentage of individual teacher attention was for high achieving pupils in large-sized classes : heterogeneously grouped pupils do get more than twice the attention given to the homogeneously grouped pupils. To analyse these differences in more detail a variance analysis was carried out with class heterogeneity and relative reading level within class as factors using class size as a covariate. Class size was taken as covariate because it could be expected to be of great importance in teacher time sharing decisions. The results of this variance analysis are shown in Table 5. Class size does indeed contribute significantly in explaining the variance in individual teacher attention : in small classes (up to 15 pupils) low achievers score 11.2% individual attention time and high achievers 7.3%, while in large classes (16 or more

Table 4: Individual teacher attention in percentage of pupil-time and correlated to individual reading achievement, in general and according to class size and heterogeneity.

|  | In general | Small sized | | Large sized | |
|---|---|---|---|---|---|
|  |  | Homogen classes | Heterog classes | Homogen classes | Heterog classes |
| Low achievers |  |  |  |  |  |
| N (pupils) | 42 | 14 | 10 | 8 | 10 |
| Ai | 10.1 | 9.7 | 13.2 | 8.6 | 8.6 |
| AixOi |  | -.3935 | -.1830 | -.0185 | -.1522 |
| N |  | 12 | 9 | 8 | 10 |
| Sign. of r |  | .103 | .319 | .483 | .337 |
| High achievers |  |  |  |  |  |
| N (pupils) | 43 | 13 | 10 | 8 | 12 |
| Ai | 6.2 | 6.5 | 8.2 | 3.0 | 6.4 |
| AixOi |  | -.0047 | .7168* | -.3345 | -.2409 |
| N |  | 12 | 9 | 8 | 12 |
| Sign. of r |  | .494 | .015 | .209 | .225 |

Ai : pupil level percentage of individual teacher attention time;

Oi : individual level output measure.

Table 5: Results of covariance analysis of individual teacher teacher attention for high and low achievers in homogeneous and heterogeneous classes, using class size as the covariate.

| Source of variance | Sum of squares | Df | Mean square | F | Sign. of F |
|---|---|---|---|---|---|
| Covariates | | | | | |
| Class size | 258.330 | 1 | 258.330 | 6.689 | .012 |
| Main-effects | 452.206 | 2 | 226.103 | 5.854 | .004 |
| Relative reading level | 317.690 | 1 | 317.690 | 8.226 | .005 |
| Class-heterogeneity | 147.770 | 1 | 147.770 | 3.826 | .054 |
| 2-way interactions | 1.911 | 1 | 1.911 | .049 | .825 |
| Level x Heterogeneity | 1.911 | 1 | 1.911 | .049 | .825 |
| Explained | 645.831 | 4 | 161.485 | 4.181 | .004 |
| Residual | 3089.648 | 80 | 38.621 | | |
| Total | 3735.478 | 84 | | | |

pupils) low achievers score 8.6% and high achievers only 5.1% individual attention time. Relative reading level within class and class heterogeneity taken together as main effects do also contribute significantly, but the relative reading level within class does contribute more than does class heterogeneity. There is no interaction between relative reading level within class and class heterogeneity. The total model explains significantly the variance in individual teacher attention.

The conclusion that can be drawn from this analysis is that class size on its own does significantly explain variance in individual teacher attention, and that, with class size held constant, class heterogeneity and relative reading level within class taken together explain significantly the variance in individual teacher attention but the relative contribution of class heterogeneity in this explanation is smaller than the relative contribution of the relative position within class.

### Is Individual Attention Time Related to Achievement?
In general, the correlation between percentage of individual teacher attention and individual achievement gain is negative and low but not significant (r= −.015; N=118; p=.438). Table 4 shows that the correlations for low and high achievers according to class size and heterogeneity do match the above stated general correlation. The only exception is the significant correlation for heterogeneously grouped high achievers in small sized classes. This correlation is strong (.72) and at the same time positive. This means that higher levels of individual teacher attention go together with higher achievement gain scores for these pupils, who already are high-achievers.

In general, however, these data do not support the hypothesis that individual teacher attention is an effective kind of teacher behavior.

# CONCLUSIONS

In this paper data have been presented concerning the use of time by teachers and pupils during reading lessons in Special Education schools for primary learning disabled children. Comparison of time expenditure patterns have been made with data from a study focused on regular elementary education. It was argued, however, that data from time studies in regular elementary education can be regarded as a frame of reference, but can not be used as a norm for time expenditure data from research in Special Education. Nevertheless, the underlying research showed less academic and more procedural time on the part of the teachers and less on-task and more off-task time on the part of the pupils. There were some differences in use of time between teachers and pupils in homogeneous and heterogeneous classes. A class level correlational analysis revealed an unexpected negative correlation between academic teacher behavior and reading achievement. On-task behavior by heterogeneously grouped pupils proved to be – also unexpected – negatively related to reading achievement.

An important feature of the underlying investigation was that teacher behavior has been gathered at the individual pupil level. Percentages of individual teacher attention were shown to be different for low and high achievers. Variance analysis showed significant differences in individual teacher attention due to class size, pupil reading level within class and class heterogeneity. In general there was no correlation between individual teacher attention and individual reading achievement gain. Only for the high achieving heterogenously grouped pupils in small sized classes a strong positive correlation could be traced.

Though no strong evidence has been found in the above presented data for individual teacher attention to be an effective type of teacher behavior this investigation has shown the possibility of looking for effective kinds of behavior on the level where teaching and learning meet each other, i.e. the level of the pupil. This might be an interesting development in teacher effectiveness research which as was mentioned earlier has been criticised for leaning too heavily on the aggregation approach. As such it might be helpfull for heterogeneity research which tries to find those conditions on the level of classroom composition that might favor or disfavor teaching effectivity.

# REFERENCES

Bloom, B.S. (1974). Time and learning. *American Psychologist, 2*, 682-688.

Carroll, J.B. (1963). A model for school-learning. *Teachers College Record, 63*, 723-732.

Dahllof, U.S. (1971). *Ability-grouping, content validity and curriculum.* New York: Teachers College Press.

Doyle, W. (1977). Paradigms for research on teacher-effectiveness. In: L.S.Shulman (ed.) *Review of Research in Education.* Vol. 5, 1977.

Evertson, C.M., Sanford, J.P., & Emmer, E.T. (1981). Effects of class-heterogeneity in Junior-High-School. *American Educational Research Journal, 18*, 219-232.

Fredrick, W.C., & Walberg, H.J. (1980). Learning as a function of time. *Journal of Educational Research, 73*, 183-194.

Kulik, C.C. & Kulik, J.C. (1982). Effects of ability-grouping on secondary school students: a meta-analysis of findings. *American Educational Research Journal, 19* (3), 415-428).

Leij, A. van der, (red.) (1985). *Zorgverbreding, bijdragen uit speciaal onderwijs aan basisonderwijs.* Nijkerk: Intro. [Contributions to mainstream education by Special Education].

Schonewille, B. (1985). *Heterogeneity as a research factor in educational research.* Amsterdam, Free University (internal report).

Shavelson, R.J., Webb, N.M. & Burstein, L. (1986). Masurement of teaching. In Mervin C. Wittrock (ed.) *Handbook of research on teaching.* New York: MacMillan Pucl. Comp.

Slavin, R.E. (1987). Ability-grouping and student achievement in elementary-schools: a best-evidence synthesis. *Review of Eductional Research, 57,* (3), 293-336.

Smyth, W.J. (1981). Research on classroom-management: studies of pupil engaged learning time. *Journal of Education for Teaching, 7*, 127-148.

Veenman, S., Voeten, M., & Lem, P. (1987). Classroom-time and achievement in mixed-age classes. *Educational Studies, 13,* (1).

# THE EFFECT OF ASPIRATION LEVELS SET BY TEACHERS FOR THEIR PUPILS ON LEARNING ACHIEVEMENT

Anna A. van der Hoeven-van Doornum
Institute for Applied Social Sciences, Nijmegen

Marinus J.M. Voeten
Department of Educational Sciences, Nijmegen

and

Paul Jungbluth
Institute for Applied Social Sciences, Nijmegen

## INTRODUCTION

The idea that aspiration levels influence learning achievement comes from the theories of self-fulfilling prophecy and teacher expectations. In our study we were interested in two questions:

– What are the bases of aspiration levels?
– What are the effects of aspiration levels on learning achievement?

Self-fulfilling prophecies are the effects of teacher expectations. We must distinguish between effects of self-fulfilling prophecy in manipulated experiments and in natural situations as the classroom. Our investigation bears upon real classrooms, so-called ecological situations. We interviewed teachers at the beginning of grade 8 - that is the last year of the primary school on their own pupils. Teacher expectations are mainly based on the perceived learning performance and the social background of the pupil. In the natural situation teachers expect that their present judgments and beliefs of the learning ability of their pupils will be confirmed in the future. Teacher expectations also indicate how teachers perceive the possibility of the pupil to benefit from instruction. The effect of these expectations is called the sustaining expectation effect. The expectations of the teachers will be reinforced and sustained in the future.

We supposed that the sustained effect of teacher judgments on learning achievement is mediated by aspiration levels teachers set for their pupils. When we speak of aspiration levels we generally do not consider the specific learning contents of reading or mathematics the pupil has to master. Aspiration levels are general goals the teacher wishes to attain with the pupil. We make a distinction between two kinds of aspiration levels: cognitive goals as 'high demands for this pupil and emphasis on reading and mathematics and the level for secondary education the teacher anticipates for the pupil at the beginning of grade 8.

It was our hypothesis that high aspiration levels have a mediating role in influencing learning achievement. To test this hypothesis we specified a model for aspiration levels and teacher expectations (Figure 1).

## DATA COLLECTION

The study was carried out with 11- and 12 year old pupils in grade 8 of 53 schools for primary education in the eastern and southern part of The Netherlands. The study included several questionnaires about contextual and individual variables such as school climate and instruction. An extensive questionnaire about aspiration levels is filled out by the teacher for each individual pupil. In addition, there were achievement tests and an intelligence test for the pupils. Information about the socio-economic status was directly collected from the parents. The variables we used in the study are:

Test scores:
  Test score on a reading test at the beginning of grade 8;
  Test score on a mathematics test at the beginning of grade 8;
  Standardized test score on reading and mathematics tests at the end of grade 8.
IQ scores:
  VIF: Verbal Intelligence Factor, mean score on three verbal intelligence tests, such as reasoning and verbal comprehensing;
  PIF: Non-verbal Intelligence Factor, mean score of three spatial reasoning tests, such as perceptual speed and pattern meanings.
Socio-economic Status:
  Father's occupation, score with a range of 39-77, mean=50.
Teacher expectations at the beginning of grade 8:
  Educational level achieved by the parents (low, middle, high);
  Educational support of the pupil by the parents;
  Learning ability;
Aspiration levels:
  Cognitive goals;
  Anticipated secondary education.
Recommended type of school for secondary education at the end of grade 8.

232

Table 1: Descriptives of IQ scores, test scores, recommendation for secondary education and socio-economic status of pupils in grade 8 (N=701).

|  | variable | mean | sd | range | min-max |
|---|---|---|---|---|---|
| begin grade 8 | IQ | 12.87 | 2.49 | 1-20 | 3-18 |
|  | PIF: non-verbal IQ | 13.05 | 3.03 | 1-20 | 2-19 |
|  | VIF: verbal IQ | 12.73 | 2.67 | 1-20 | 5-20 |
| begin grade 8 | mathematics test | 11.39 | 5.36 | 1-24 | 1-24 |
| begin grade 8 | reading test | 11.81 | 3.43 | 1-24 | 2-21 |
| end grade 8 | Standardized test (math. & reading) | 534.43 | 10.79 | 500-550 | 501-550 |
| end grade 8 | recommendation secondary education | 22.95 | 10.20 | 10-40 | 10-40 |
|  | socio-economic status | 50.14 | 10.04 | 39-77 | 39-77 |

Table 2 presents the descriptives and internal consistency (Cronbach's alpha) of teacher expectations and aspiration levels. The scales are groups of items, constructed with factor analysis, with a range of 1 (low) to 5 (high). The variable 'educational level achieved by the parents' has a range of 1 to 3 (low, middle and high) and the variable 'anticipated type of secondary education' has a range of 10 (vocational education) to 40 (pre-university education).

Table 2: Descriptives and internal consistency (Cronbach' alpha) of teacher expectations and aspiration levels.

|  | variable | N items | int. consist. | mean | sd |
|---|---|---|---|---|---|
| begin grade 8 | educational level | 1 |  | 1.79 | .81 |
|  | educational support | 5 | .88 | 3.80 | .76 |
|  | learning ability | 5 | .91 | 3.46 | .86 |
|  | cognitive goals | 9 | .86 | 3.61 | .71 |
|  | anticipated type of secondary education | 1 |  | 22.82 | 9.70 |

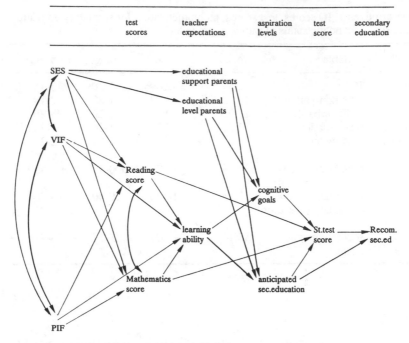

|              | test<br>scores | teacher<br>expectations | aspiration<br>levels | test<br>score | secondary<br>education |
|--------------|----------------|-------------------------|----------------------|---------------|------------------------|

*Figure 1: Model for aspiration levels and learning achievement*


# DUTCH EDUCATIONAL SYSTEM

The Dutch secondary school system is divided into four types (Figure 2). Students are allocated by selection. The selection is mainly based on the recommendation of the principal of the primary school and on scores on achievements tests. Both, the parents and the secondary school value the recommendation of the primary school's principal.

| age 4-12 year | | 13- | 14- | 15- | 16- | 17- | 18- year |
|---------------|---------------------|-----|-----|-----|-----|-----|----------|
| primary education | secondary education | grade | | | | | |
| | vocational training | 1 | 2 | 3 | 4 | | |
| | junior secondary school | 1 | 2 | 3 | 4 | | |
| | senior secondary school | 1 | 2 | 3 | 4 | 5 | |
| | pre-university education | 1 | 2 | 3 | 4 | 5 | 6 |

*Figure 2: Overview of the Dutch educational system*


234

# RESULTS

To answer the first question we used the Lisrel procedure to test the model. Figure 3 shows the result of our analysis. The model we started with did not fit the data. We modified the model to improve the fit. The result is a chi-square of 30.46 with 19 degrees of freedom, probability =.046 and Adjusted Goodness of Fit .971. The anticipated type of secondary education appeared to be the best explained variable of the model. Table 3 presents the direct and total effects of the exogenous and endogenous variables on the cognitive goals and the anticipated type of secondary education. The verbal intelligence and the judgment of the teacher of the learning ablity have the strongest effects on the aspiration levels.

Comparing the result of the present model with our original model, we can still conclude that aspiration levels are explained by teacher expectations. However, the relationships we can detect with Lisrel are somewhat different from our original asssumptions: some are missing. In addtion, we can identify a number of direct relationships, which we did not expect to be there: Socio-economic status, the verbal intelligence factor VIF and the Test scores influence directly the aspiration levels.

Table 3: Direct and total effects of SES, non-verbal and verbal intelligence, and teacher expectations on cognitive goals and the anticipated type of secondary education.

|  | direct effect | | total effect | |
|---|---|---|---|---|
|  | cognitive goals | antic. sec. education | cognitive goals | antic. sec. education |
| SES | - | .13 | .04 | .24 |
| PIF | - | - | .16 | .20 |
| VIF | .09 | .09 | .45 | .48 |
| Math. score | - | .18 | .12 | .31 |
| Read. score | .16 | .13 | .30 | .25 |
| Ed. support parents | .17 | - | .17 | - |
| Ed. level parents | - | .13 | - | .13 |
| Learning ability | .49 | .47 | .49 | .47 |

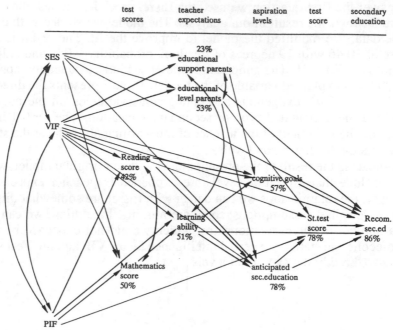

| test<br>scores | teacher<br>expectations | aspiration<br>levels | test<br>score | secondary<br>education |
|---|---|---|---|---|

*Figure 3: Model for aspiration levels, grade 8 (N=701)*

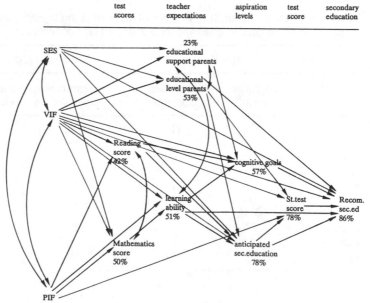

| test<br>scores | teacher<br>expectations | aspiration<br>levels | test<br>score | secondary<br>education |
|---|---|---|---|---|

*Figure 4: Model for aspiration levels and learning achievement, grade 8 (N=701)*

236

To answer the second question, we added to the model the test scores obtained at the end of the year and also the recommendation for the secondary school (Figure 4). As a result the model looks more complicated. All variables in the model have a direct or indirect effect on test scores and recommendation at the end of the year, see Table 4. The verbal intelligence is directly related to all the dependent variables in the model. Note that variables related to socio-economic status do influence the anticpated type of secondary school at the beginning of the school year as well as the recommendation at the end of the school year.

With respect to our assumptions, we found relationships between the aspiration levels and test scores as well as the recommendations. These effects are rather small, except the relationship between the anticipated type of secondary education and recommendation.

We can illustrate the practical implications of the effect of anticipated schooltypes on recommendations as follows: We divided the pupils on their learning achievements at the beginning of the year in five groups from low achievers to high achievers. For every group of achievers we looked at the anticipated and the recommended type of secondary education. In every group we see the same pattern (Table 5 and Figure 5). Note that, although the pupils belong to the same achievement group they get different recommendations according to the anticipated type of school. Here is shown how higher aspiration levels lead to higher types of secondary education.

Table 4:  Direct and total effects on the standardized test score and recommendation at the end of grade 8. (*=not significant)

|  | direct effect | | total effect | |
|---|---|---|---|---|
|  | St.test score | Recommend. | St.test | Recommend. score |
| SES | - | .06 | .13 | .27 |
| PIF | .09 | - | .23 | .19 |
| VIF | .25 | .05 | .59 | .50 |
| Math. score | .31 | .02 | .39 | .30 |
| Read. score | .05* | .02* | .14 | .21 |
| Ed. support parents | - | .004* | .02 | .004 |
| Ed. level parents | .06 | .04 | .09 | .14 |
| Learning ability | - | .06 | .16 | .37 |
| Cognitive goals | .12 | -.04 | .12 | -.03 |
| Antic. sec. ed. | .21 | .66 | .21 | .70 |
| St. test score |  | .16 |  | .16 |

237

Table 5: Recommended type of school for secondary education at the end of the term compared with anticipated secondary education for five groups from low to high achievers at the beginning of the term.

| | learning achievement at the beginning of the year | | | | |
|---|---|---|---|---|---|
| | low | modest | mean | high | very high |
| recommended second. education at the end of the year | anticipated secondary education | | | | |
| vocational | vocational | vocational | vocational | vocational | - |
| junior | junior | junior | junior | junior | - |
| senior | - | senior | senior | senior | senior |
| pre-univ. | - | - | - | - | pre-univer. |

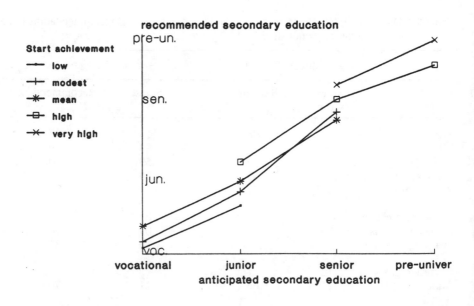

Figure 5: Recommended secondary education compared with anticipated sec. education

238

# CONCLUSIONS

It was our aim to better define the factors that determine the aspiration levels that teachers set for pupils and to investigate the effect of aspiration levels on learning achievement. We may conclude that with regard to aspiration levels, the type of secondary education the teacher anticipates at the beginning of the term, is the best explained variable. We have seen that the verbal intelligence has the strongest influence on this variable. This goes via the judgment of learning ability. In addition, the test scores on mathematics and reading and the socio-economic status have considerable direct or indirect contributions. We can also see that the anticipated secondary education at the beginning of the term is the best predictor of recommendations at the end of the term. It is our conclusion that the anticipated type of secondary education is a better predictor for recommendation than the testscores during the year. In this study we have shown that students may enter higher or lower levels of secondary education depending on the aspiration levels set for them. In that sense aspiration levels work out as a form of teacher effectiveness.

# CRITERION-DEFINITION, EFFECT SIZE AND STABILITY, THREE FUNDAMENTAL QUESTIONS IN SCHOOL EFFECTIVENESS RESEARCH

Roel J. Bosker*
RION, Institute for Educational Research, University of Groningen

and

Jaap Scheerens
University of Twente, Enschede

## INTRODUCTION

Three points of criticism concerning the validity of the current empirical school effectiveness models are that effects are insignificantly small, that the effect criterion (mostly achievement) is not well chosen and that school effects are unstable. In this paper these issues are reconsidered.

## CRITERION DEFINITION

The major challenges to the choice of a particular effectiveness criterion are critical questions concerning the ultimateness, fairness, validity and economy of the actual output measures.

We assume that school effectiveness is to be primarily concerned with output, and therefore should not dwell upon views of organizational effectiveness in which input- and process-characteristics are also seen as effectiveness criteria (cf. Cameron & Whetten, 1983). From these points of view our basic perspective on school effectiveness is that of productivity (see also Scheerens & Stoel, 1988).

---

*) Order of authors was determined alphabetically.

# ACHIEVEMENT OR ATTAINMENT MEASURES

The predominant criterion in school-effectiveness studies from various disciplinary origins is achievement. Attainment measures depend on formal "levels" in the school-careers of pupils. Roughly speaking educational attainment scores express the level that individuals or groups of pupils have reached after a certain number of years of schooling. Examples of discrete attainment levels are the end of the primary school period and the end of the secondary school period. Particularly when an educational system consists of many school types, to which societal value is attributed in various degrees, attainment scales can become quite differentiated (see e.g. Bosker & Van der Velden, 1989).

When discussing the option of either choosing attainment measures or achievement measures, various underlying dimensions for this choice can be discerned. First of all the choice may depend on different connotations of effectiveness (e.g. maximalization of output vs. enhancing "quality"). Secondly, preferences concerning "band width" vs. specifity of output measures could determine the choice, i.e. the question whether an overall output measure or a more narrowly defined performance indicator is to be preferred. Thirdly, the question of the predominance of a more practical vs. a scientific interest in establishing effectiveness may lie at the background of this choice. Attainment measures are close to the economic notion of effectiveness as maximalization of output, where output is measured as the amount of products that results from a particular production process. In education "pupils that pass their exams" can be seen as the products of the process of schooling. Achievement, on the other hand, fits better in an interpretation of effectiveness in terms of "quality". Achievement tests as effectiveness criteria capitalize on more fine-grained quality-differences of the units of output.

Attainment measures are cruder output measures than achievement tests, but at the same time they usually imply a broader coverage of the whole spectrum of educational objectives. The passing of a final examination (attainment indicator) depends on achievement in many subjects, whereas achievement tests in school effectiveness studies are often limited to arithmetic and language tests.

School-effectiveness is both a subject of scientific inquiry and an "applied" field of interest in educational policy and management. When issues of consumer demands, monitoring of schools and accountability are at stake one cannot do without attainment indicators. In the case of inquiry into determinants of school-effectiveness, i.e. input-output, or input-process-output studies, researchers will want output indicators that differentiate more strongly between qualities of the "units of output" and prefer achievement tests.

In summary, it is our contention that attainment measures are called for when purely economic and "applied" perspectives of effectiveness predominate or in case one wishes to explore, in the tradition of sociology of education, the contribution of schools to a person's status attainment. Achievement measures are more likely to be chosen when "quality of education" is at stake and when a more psychological interest in cognitive development (or an educational interest in schools as organizations) has the upper hand.

Finally, it should be mentioned that the choice between attainment or achievement can be avoided in two ways: a) by using both and b) in the case of a decision oriented use of achievement tests (as when performance standards in the form of cutting scores on tests determine further career options).

### Intermediate and "Ultimate" Effectiveness Measures

Are attainment or achievement measures obtained at the end of a particular period of schooling to be considered as the ultimate productivity measures or would only more long term "civil effects" of schooling, such as employment or job level reached by graduates, qualify as such? Or, moving into the other direction on the scale of ultimateness of effectiveness measures, could we use "intermediate" effects like attendance and drop-out rates as substitute effectiveness criteria? (e.g. Rutter et al., 1979).

In our opinion searching for ultimate school effects is like looking for the holy grail, since one can go on and on in stating even more ultimate effects. The most likely, be it arbitrary, points in the school careers of pupils to measure school effects are indeed when a particular period of schooling is terminated and transition to a higher school-type or into the labour-market takes place. "Post-school" effect measures could be seen as important in macro-level applications of educational indicators for purposes of monitoring national school-systems. Also, post-school effect-measures could be seen as important criteria to gain insight into the predictive validity of effect measures at the end of the period of schooling. Attendance and drop-out rates are better treated as process-measures in school-effectiveness studies, because they generally function as "means" rather than as desired "ends" of schooling.

### General versus Curriculum Specific Achievement Tests

When the decision is taken to use achievement rather than attainment output data, there is a further option in the choice of the type of test. Madaus et al. (1979) have provided arguments in favour of curriculum-specific tests and against the use of general achievement tests (like the Scholastic Aptitude Test). One of their arguments is that larger school (or class-) effects are demonstrated when curriculum specific tests (exams in their case) are used. Before offering a few lines of thinking in determining the choice of output measure along this particular dimension, we would like to state that "general vs. curriculum specific" achievement measures should be seen as a continuum with many discrete scale-points rather than a dichotomous choice between two extremes.

Varying from curriculum specific to "general aptitude" measures we could discern the following types of measures:
- trained test items;
- content specific measures;
- Rasch-scales of narrow content areas;
- subject specific tests;
- general scholastic aptitude tests;
- intelligence tests.

A general guideline to choose from these alternatives would be to use the more specific measures up to the degree that the application purpose is closer to the micro situation of classroom-instruction. A line of thinking which perhaps offers a more fundamental solution to this problem of choice, within the content of school effectiveness research, would be to choose the type of outcome measure that has the greatest predictive validity with respect to the more ultimate educational effects. To give an example: when measuring achievement at the end of a specific stream of vocational education, we might prefer content-specific measures, assuming a close connection between the curriculum and skills that are required in the job-situation. We may note here, however, that this latter kind of criterion choice further depends on the theory one holds about the relationship between education and the labour market. Departing from a credentials or screening theory certification, itself would be the best criterion for school effectiveness, whereas achievement is more connected to the human capital philosophy.

### Controlling for Confoundedness of Effect-measures
So far we have assumed that the measures on attainment or achievement scales can indeed be interpreted unequivocally as criteria of school-effectiveness. This is not so. One source of confoundedness of these output measures that is well-known is the initial or even innate ability of pupils. In school-effectiveness studies it should be attempted to separate the contribution of innate characteristics of pupils from the "net"-effect of school characteristics. Although this source of confounding the interpretation of output measures is well-known, critical reviewers of effective schools research have noted that in many cases control for innate characteristics of pupils is inadequate (Purkey & Smith, 1983).

A second source of possibly biased interpretations of school-effects are selective policy-measures at the school-level. Examples are: lenient versus a strict policy in letting pupils pass from one grade to the next, a more or less conservative policy in allowing students in secondary education to go in for their final examination, a more or less reluctant attitude when it is to be decided to send pupils to special schools (primary education) or to "lower" categories of secondary education (when a country has a differentiated secondary education system).

244

This type of "selectivity bias" is usually accounted for when "economic" measures of school output, measured at the school level, are used, for instance number of graduates divided by the total number of pupils in the cohort that entered the school as many years back as the normal duration of the school-period. Usually in individual level measures of attainment selectivity will also be accounted for, because drop-outs will still receive a score on the attainment scale. When individual level achievement data are used as the effect-criterion this type of selectivity-bias is usually neglected, however. The consequence of this practice is that the corresponding estimation of school-effects might well be confounded and corresponding policy- or managerial decisions consequently unfair. The general solution to this problem would be to obtain some kind of measure of the selectivity-policy of schools and use this information as an additional independent variable (defined at the school-level) to separate its effect from the other independent variables that stand for the more genuine determinants of school-effectiveness. Statistical techniques to model attrition-bias may help in solving the problem of separating selectivity effects from the influence of other independent variables (see e.g. Hausman & Wise, 1979).

## EFFECT SIZE

First and foremost it should be realized that what we call school effects are comparative rather than absolute measures; we do not compare the effects of schooling to no schooling at all but we compare variations in schooling, since we are bound to what actually happens in educational practice.
Comparative school effects are usually expressed in two ways: an overall effect of schools in terms of the between school variance relative to the total variance in pupil achievement; a specific effect of a particular school characteristic either expressed as a proportion of the between school variance accounted for or as the proportion of variance in individual achievement that is accounted for by the specific school characteristic.

### Effect-size as a Function of the Choice of Dependent and Independent Variables and the Unit of Analysis
Effect-size depends, up to a degree, on the choice of the *dependent* variable. As is to be expected specific characteristics of instructional processes (particularly content covered) will show up more clearly when curriculum specific tests rather than general scholastic aptitude tests are used as the dependent variable. This phenomenon was empirically demonstrated by Madaus et al. (1979). Effect-sizes are also relatively higher when subject-matter areas are tested that depend more exclusively on schooling and instruction; so, effects in arithmetic and mathematics are usually somewhat higher than

245

effects in a subject like (native) language, which is also learned at home. There is further empirical evidence (cf. Mortimore et al., 1988) that measures of progress in achievement (i.e. when a covariance analysis design is used with previous achievement as the covariate) show larger effects than measuring achievement at only one point in time.

As was already implied in the above, *independent* variables that are closer to the output measures - like content covered and "time on task" will most likely explain more variance than school variables (like leadership-styles and variations in organizational structure) that are further removed from the instructional process. As Rutter (1983) points out the strength of association between school characteristics and achievement will be depressed because of the smaller variance in the former characteristics. If we could manage to measure curricular characteristics like opportunity to learn at the level of individual pupils we might even expect larger effect-sizes.

## Empirical Estimates of the Size of School-effects
A method to gain insight into the strengths of relationships between school measures and output data would be to average effect-sizes found in a number of studies. We have made a modest effort to do so by looking at 12 Dutch effectiveness studies.

We examined the average between school variance. Only in 6 studies (out of 12) was the between school variance computed. The average percentage of the total variance accounted for by the factor "school" is 12. This estimate is in line with the findings in major Anglo-Saxon studies, like, for instance, Coleman, 1967 (ca. 9%) and Mortimore, 1988 (11%). It should be noted that effects on various types of dependent variables were all thrown in one hat, which is of course a bit of a rough procedure. Because of the different statistics that were used, we did not attempt to synthesize effects of individual school variables.

This rudimentary attempt at research-synthesis leaves us with the impression that - unless perhaps one could get access to the primary data of studies - it is at present very difficult to quantitatively summarize the results of school effectiveness studies. Research synthesis would strongly benefit from a more complete and standardized manner of reporting school effects. In the subsequent section we will turn to the issue of alternative ways of expressing school effects.

## Towards More Insightful Ways of Expressing School Effects
The most common way of expressing school effects is to report the between school variance, i.e. the proportion of total variance that is accounted for by schools. Next, in subsequent analyses, one could establish the contribution of specific school variables to the between school variance (see e.g. Madaus et al., 1979).

Yet, expressing effects in terms of "proportions of variance accounted for" still leaves many questions open about the "meaning" of effects.

A further step towards better interpretable effect standards would be to try and express effects in terms of intervals on the scale of the output variable. In experimental or quasi-experimental studies the difference between means of experimental conditions are useful points of reference for such intervals (cf. Cahan, Davis & Cohen, 1987), for instance, by expressing the interval between the experimental and control group mean in terms of the number/ fraction of standard deviations. One could thus adapt – be it arbitrary – conventions like: "an effect of 0.3 standard deviations or greater is indicative of a meaningful difference". Since school-effectiveness studies are non-experimental, schools could only be grouped on an ad hoc basis in, for instance, the highest scoring 20%, the "middle 60" and the lowest scoring 20%. Though this procedure would inevitably imply exploiting chance, it might still be adopted to make the results of school-effectiveness studies amenable to the interpretation of effect-sizes according to established conventions. Purkey and Smith (1983, p. 428) conclude in their review of the school effectiveness literature that, when comparing the bottom 20% of low-scoring schools with the top 20% of high-scoring schools, the difference in average achievement for sixth grade pupils is about two thirds of a standard deviation.

The, in our opinion, most insightful way of expressing school effects would be to combine the contrasting of "successful" and "unsuccessful schools" with the attachement of some kind of societal value to score-levels on the output variable. Some examples are: to indicate the increased chance of pupils who have visited an elementary school with a certain favorable characteristic (e.g. emphasis on cognitive objectives) of being referred to a higher type of secondary education, to express attainment measures in monetary values (Stoel, 1984), and to express differences in successful and unsuccessful schools in terms of IQ-points, or other scores that are geared to age norms - so that effects can be expressed in average gain in, for instance, "reading age" (Rutter, 1983; Mortimore, 1988). These applications show that though school effects might be moderate or low in terms of percentage of variance accounted for, they may still have quite significant societal consequences. For instance, Rosenthal and Rubin (1982), investigated effect-sizes for cases where the criterion variable is measured as the "success" or "failure" rate. They show that only 10% of variance accounted for, implies a point-biserial correlation of the dichotomous treatment variable with the criterion variable of .32 and a difference in success rate from 34% to 66%. In this case the success rate might express the reduction in illness rate, or, in the context of education, the percentage of exam passes. And, to give a final example, the effect size of 2/3 of a standard deviation reported by Purkey and Smith would mean roughly one full grade level of achievement, in other words, the average pupil in the 20% highest scoring school would be roughly 1 school-year ahead of the average pupil in the 20% lowest scoring school.

We are painfully aware of the fact that we have not given numerical answers to the question "how large should a school effect be to be called significant". We will make so bold as to give an impression: when 15% of the variance in the individual level output variable is explained by the factor school – after relevant background characteristics of pupils have been controlled – school characteristics that explain 2 or 3% of the individual level variance are probably meaningful.

# STABILITY OF EFFECTS

## *Introduction*
Our position that stability is a vital issue in school effectiveness research is based on the contention that it is a necessary condition for further theory development. The assumption of consistency in achievement and/or attainment is rather crucial in more than one way. Since we might expect that organizational characteristics of schools are more or less stable over time, we must know if the rank order of schools on output remains the same no matter when we measure the effect. If schools affect achievement in another way, each year, and organizational features remain more or less the same, the resulting "overall" correlation between the school characteristics and the output index must be near zero. Another aspect of stability over time is the possible existence of grade-specific effects. If school effects vary across grades this would mean – especially in primary education – that these effects are in fact teacher effects.

## *Empirical Evidence*

### *Stability over time*
The most fundamental requirement for a school effectiveness theory is the psychometric test-retest conceptualization of reliability: is the correlation of two independent measures with the same instrument of a latent trait high enough, i.e. is a school effective irrespective of the year in which effectiveness is measured. Research on this topic is pointing towards the direction of stable school effects across years. Rutter et al. (1979) were the first to present results in this area. Their research shows that examination results and delinquency-rates are stable across years (associations - rank-correlations - of near .80). Yet, on the basis of Rutter's findings we cannot be sure whether stability was just a function of the balance of intake or could indeed be attributed to certain organizational or curricular school characteristics.

The correlation over years of properly assessed (secondary-) school effects, that is to say assessed in a multi-level framework, amounts to approximately .80 resp. .60 in the U.K. (Willms, 1987; Goldstein, 1987) and to approximately .70 – when analyzing seperate school types (De Jong & Roeleveld, 1988) – to .96 "overall" in the Netherlands (Bosker et al., 1988). Research in elementary schools (grade one to four) in the USA gives results ranging from .34 to .66 (Mandeville, 1987), though these figures might be somewhat deflated because of the inadequacy of the statistical models used. Mandeville does not seperate sample variance from true parameter variance. In not doing so, the stability is underestimated since measurement "noise", that sometimes amounts to near 80% of the observed between year variance, confounds the effects (see Willms & Raudenbush, 1988).

From a theoretical point of view stability across grades is a more interesting question. Only little is known about this topic. Mandeville and Anderson report correlations across grades near .10 (grade 1 to 4 in elementary schools) when using mathematics and language effects. Their explanation for this inconsistency of school effects across grades is plausible. In using curriculum specific tests, some variation may occur as a function of the degree to which the specific subject is taught to the pupils. In a provisional analysis - only cross-sectional data were used - of a large Dutch sample of primary schools (earlier research reported by Brandsma & Knuver, 1988) we find an intra-school-correlation between grades for arithmetic of .64 and for language of .49. Bosker et al. (1988) found rank-correlations ranging from .40 to .80 between grades in Dutch secondary education, but these figures may be somewhat inflated because of the dependency in the observations (the same pupils are tested in these grades, and the criterion variable is cumulative over years). Rutter reports rank-correlations across grades for pupil misbehaviour ranging from .23 to .65. His figures for school attendance are more encouraging (near .80).

These results suggest that teacher effectiveness may be a more probable cause of differences between schools than characteristics defined at the school level. This conclusion may be corrobarated when we look at the differences between classes within grades.

When using the data reported by Ecob for the UK (in Mortimore et al., 1988, p. 130. columns 1 and 2) we find intra-grade-correlations for stability that only partly contradict our proposition. (See Table 1).

Table 1: Stability across classes within grades

|             | grade 2 | grade 3 |
|-------------|---------|---------|
| reading     | .63     | .93     |
| mathematics | .46     | .65     |

## Implications

Let us first summarize the presented research on stability of school effects. (Table 2).

Table 2: Range of stability estimates for school effects

|  | primary | secondary |
|---|---|---|
| across years | .35-.65 | .70-.95 |
| across grades | .10-.65 | .25-.90 |

The presented figures in Table 2 mostly correlations. So even when in some cases the correlations are .60 or more, we should realize that an important part of the variance is not accounted for. We feel that the theoretical implications are quite interesting. As for the grade specific effect we might refer to the Mandeville & Anderson hypothesis of school and grade specific curricula and also to the teacher effectiveness hypotheses (i.e. that not the school but individual teachers are to be seen as the primary locus of effectiveness). Considering this type of instability it could be argued that school effectiveness had better be assessed at the end of a particular period of schooling, since in this case if at least incorporates the cumulative - and not the individual - effects of teachers.

Contingency theory points to another cause of instability of effects, since organizations, being adaptive to external circumstances, might be instable themselves.

Finally Goldstein (1987) gives an interesting explanation of the variance not accounted for by schools. He found that in assessing school and year effects, without adjusting for intake differences, the between year component decreases to 5% of the school and year variance. Besides, only the intake differences seem to vary across years and across schools, which leads him to the conclusion 'that the schools may tend to compensate for yearly intake differences in achievement in order to produce only small year-to-year differences in the overall examination results' (p. 59/60).


# CONCLUSIONS

Our general conclusion is that the choice of an effect criterion strongly depends on the effectiveness perspective and the theory one wishes to corroborate. It seems necessary to specify more criterion-specific effectiveness theories as a necessary prerequisite to overall effectiveness models (i.e. a stable set of predictor variables for various criteria).

Our most important remark concerning the effect size is, that even small effects may be relevant, if only because the effects should be multiplied by the number of pupils benefiting from outstanding schools. The best way to make effects more insightful might be to translate them to their societal impetus by means of, for instance, cutting scores.

With respect to the stability issue our main conclusion is that school effects do exist even though they may vary across grades, classes, and time. A final remark is, that school effectiveness theories have led to a shift in focus from pupils to schools as the central unit of interest. Despite this shift research designs concentrate on the pupil. It is our contention that more refined designs are needed at the school level together with the sophisticated designs we usually employ when investigating variation between pupils. Next to the longitudinal designs for pupils, a repeated measurement design at the school level would surely help us to better locate the sources of variations in outcomes. Apart from more refined research designs school effectiveness research is badly in need of theory development in order to stimulate inquiry into the questions "why what works in education".

# REFERENCES

Aitkin, M. & Longford, N. (1986). Statistical Modelling Issues in School Effectiveness Studies. *Journal of the Royal Statistical Society, Series A (General), 149,* (1), 1-43.

Anderson, L.W. & Mandeville, G.K. (1986). *Towards a solution of problems inherent in the identification of effective schools.* AERA-paper. San Francisco.

Bosker, R.J., Guldemond, H., Hofman, R.H. & Hofman, W.H.A. (1988). *Kwaliteit in het voortgezet onderwijs.* Groningen: RION.

Bosker, R.J., Guldemond, H., Hofman, R.H. & Hofman, W.H.A. (1989). De stabiliteit van schoolkwaliteit. In: J. Scheerens & J.C. Verhoeven (Eds.), *Schoolorganisatie, beleid en onderwijskwaliteit.* Lisse: Swets & Zeitlinger.

Bosker, R.J. & Velden, R.K.W. van der (1989). Schooleffecten en rendementen. In: J. van Damme & Dronkers (Eds.), *Jongeren in school en beroep.* Lisse: Swets & Zeitlinger.

Brandsma, H.P. & Knuver, J.W.M. (1988). Organisatorische verschillen tussen basisscholen en hun effect op leerlingprestaties. *Tijdschrift voor Onderwijsresearch, 13,* (4), 201-212.

Cahan, S., Davis, D. & Cohen, N. (1987). The definitional interpretation of effects in decision oriented evaluation studies. *International Journal of Educational Research, 11,* 91-104.

Cameron, K.S. & Whetten, D.A. (1983). *Organizational effectiveness: a comparison of multiple models.* New York: Academic Press.

Cuttance, P. (1987). *Modelling variation in the effectiveness of schooling.* Edinburgh: CES.

Doddema-Winsemius, H. & Hofstee, W.K.B. (1987). Enkele controversiële onderwijsdoelstellingen in de context van evaluatie. *Pedagogische Studiën, 64,* (5), 192-201.

Goldstein, H. (1987). *Multilevel models in educational and social research.* London: Charles Griffin & Co.

251

Gray, J., Jesson, D. & Jones, B. (1986). The research for a fairer way of comparing schools examination results. *Research papers in Education, 1*, (2).

Hausman, J.A. & Wise, D.A. (1979). Attrition bias in experimental and panel data: the Gary Income Maintenance Experiment. *Econometrica, 47*, 455-473.

Jong, U. de & Roeleveld, J. (1988). *Openbaar en bijzonder onderwijs: een constant verschil?* NSAV-paper. Antwerpen.

Knuver, A. (1987). *Schoolkenmerken en leerlingfunctioneren; een replicatie-onderzoek.* Groningen: Rijksuniversiteit.

Linden, W.J. van der (1987). *Het zwalkend niveau van ons onderwijs.* Diës-rede, Universiteit Twente.

Mandeville, G.K. & Anderson, L.W. (1986). *A study of the stability of school effectiveness measures across grades and subject areas.* AERA-paper. San Francisco.

Mandeville, G.K. (1987). *The stability of school effectiveness indices across years.* NCME-paper. Washington.

Madaus, G.F., Kellaghan, T., Rakow, E.A. & King, D. (1979). The sensitivity of measures of school effectiveness. *Harvard Educational Review, 49*, 207-230.

Mortimore, P., Sammons, P., Stoll, L., Lewis, D. & Ecob, R. (1988). *The junior school project; technical appendices.* London: ILEA, Research and Statistics Branch.

Purkey, S.C. & Smith, M.S. (1983). Effective schools: a review. *The Elementary School Journal, 83*, 427-452.

Raudenbush, S.W. (1988). *The analysis of longitudinal multilevel data.* Paper for the seminar on policy applications of multilevel analysis. Washington.

Raudenbush, S. & Bryk, A.S. (1986). A hierarchical model for studying school effects. *Sociology of Education, 59*, 1-17.

Rosenthal, R. & Rubin, D.B. (1982). A simple, general purpose display of magnitude of experimental effect. *Journal of Educational Psychology, 74*, 166-169.

Rowan, B., Bossart, S.T. & Dwyer, D.C. (1983). Research on effective schools. A cautionary note. *Educational Researcher,* april, 24-31.

Rutter, M., Maughan, B., Mortimore, P. & Ouston, J. (1979). *Fifteen Thousand Hours. Secondary schools and their effects on children.* Somerset: Open Books Publishing Ltd.

Rutter, M. (1983). School effects on pupil progress. Research findings and policy implications. *Child Development, 54*, 1-29.

Scheerens, J. & Stoel, W.G.R. (1988). *Theory development on school effectiveness.* AERA-paper. New Orleans.

Stoel, W.G.R. (1984). Vergroting klassen tast kwaliteit voortgezet onderwijs aan. *Didaktief,* january.

Stoel, W.G.R. (1986). *Schoolkenmerken en het gedrag van leerlingen en docenten in het voortgezet onderwijs.* Groningen: RION. (internal publication)

Willms, J.D. (1987). Differences between Scottish Education Authorities in their Examination Attainment. *Oxford Review of Education, 13*, (2), 211-232.

Willms, J.D. & Raudenbush, S.W. (1988). *Estimating the stability of school effects with a longitudinal, hierarchical linear model.* AERA-paper. New Orleans.

# FACTORS AFFECTING STABLE
# CONTINUATION OF OUTCOMES
# OF SCHOOL IMPROVEMENT PROJECTS

Joseph Bashi and Zehava Sass
The Van Leer Jerusalem Institute
Hebrew University of Jerusalem

Sustaining the outcomes of an intervention project is considered by Van Velzen et al. (1985) to be the weakest link in the process of change in schools. One of the reasons mentioned, in regard to this weakness, is the fact that the movement for increasing effectiveness in schools is still in its infancy, and thus not enough data has accumulated to enable the generation of valid and widely applicable conclusions.

On the theoretical level, one strives to identify those components the presence or absence of which will increase the likelihood of sustaining the outcomes of a school intervention project.

On the practical level, the question is of vital importance to the policymaker, for the likelihood of sustaining outcomes is a major criterion in his/her consideration of whether to adopt a given project.

The absence of sufficient knowledge of the necessary conditions for sustaining achieved outcomes burdens policymakers in their task of improving educational systems.

The study sponsored by the Rand Corporation in the mid-1970's (Berman & McLaughlin, 1977), investigated projects which sustained their outcomes with varying degrees of success or failure. Though the time range for judging the relative success of sustaining outcomes was short, a number of generalizations and strategies were offered to explain the findings.

The Rand Study, as well as other sources, offers numerous proposed strategies for school improvement. Yet but few of these strategies relates explicitly and unequivocally to those components which, according to speculation, supposition, or findings, ought to affect the continuation of project outcomes.

Berman and McLaughlin (1977) distributed questionnaires to officials who had been involved in the projects – district superintendents, inspectors, principals, and teachers – in an attempt to identify the elements that had had the greatest influence on sustaining changes. Cobert (1983) interviewed

253

teachers one year after the conclusion of the experiment. He asked them how they and their colleagues had changed, and to what extent these changes had sustained. Huberman and Miles (1984) investigated stability in the utilization of the new program, the precentage of those using it, and the extent of its institutionalization and incorporation into the normal structure and processes of the school.

We can identify three clusters of variables which can either facilitate or impede the sustenance of the outcomes:
(1) In-school factors, relating to the structure of the school.
(2) Contextual factors, relating to out-of-school variables.
(3) Factors relating to the intervention process itself.

Each of these three categories of factors deserves a separate discussion. However, it will suffice here to present a brief discussion of the connection between the first two categories and the probability of sustaining project outcomes; thereafter we will concentrate our discussion principally on the third category of factors, namely those relating to the intervention process.

### 1. In-School Factors Relating to the Structure of the School:
On a simplicity-complexity continuum, schools tend to simplify their actions to such an extent that they lose their efficacy. The teaching-learning situation is complex. Teachers tend to simplify the situation and act on a level of minimal complexity. It is more convenient to emphasize the subject-matter curriculum and demand uniformity of pupil tasks, than to take into consideration the specific skills and interests of each individual pupil.

### 2. Contextual Factors:
In this category of factors we include those out-of-school variables which either directly or indirectly affect the functioning of schools. These include administrative supervision and the reinforcement of specific work patterns relayed by the administration to the school staff; community expectations of the school; the degree of school independence in determining teaching curricula; criteria for evaluating school outputs; etc.

If a given school undergoes a change process which does not take these environmental factors into consideration, effective school activities will remain isolated and limited, in the absence of appropriate sources of reinforcement. This, in turn, can inversely affect the likelihood of sustaining project outcomes.

### 3. Factors Relating to the Intervention Process itself:
This category of factors is of central importance for sustaining project outcomes. These factors, in contrast to the former two catagories, can be relatively easily manipulated. The innovator can thus attempt to influence them at the planning stage and in the course of the project itself.

Furthermore, the literature on school effectiveness virtually ignores the effect of proposed strategies on post-innovation outcome sustenance. We strongly believe that educational innovators must consider this relationship during the projects themselves, in order to help guarantee sustained outcomes after the projects have been terminated. Relating to the element of sustenance affects decisions regarding which topics will be treated, and regarding the proper course of action to be taken in dealing with these topics.

In what follows we shall present some of the theoretical assumptions we adopted while planning and implementing the school intervention project that we conducted in 1984-1987. The project itself, along with its results, will be described later. We shall emphasize two factors:

– The degree to which the variables that were addressed are central or peripheral to the school culture, and the influence of their centrality on the preservation of change;
– Locating the optimum point between the effort invested by teachers and the effectiveness of their work, as an important basis for sustaining the effect.

*Selection of the School Elements Addressed by the Intervention Project:*
The processes of cultural change in the context of intercultural encounter may provide a helpful conceptual framework and contribute to a better understanding of the processes involved in changing schools and making them more effective. This framework will allow us to understand the process and indicate factors that accelerate or retard it, including factors that have a bearing on the preservation of the effect achieved by the intervention program.

A full development of a conceptual framework borrowed from processes of cultural transition is beyond the scope of this article. Here we shall relate only to those dimensions that are relevent to the processes of sustaining the changes that stem from the intervention project.

To use the terms of the proposed conceptual framework, we have here an encounter between a target culture (the school) and the culture of the agent of change (the donator culture).

A school is an organic system of interwoven components that unite to form a particular cultural pattern – the school culture.

Like every culture, the school culture, too, has its own pattern. It also has a core composed of the more central elements of the school culture. Around this core congregate the elements of lesser importance, and these are in turn surrounded by peripheral elements whose significance and influence on the pattern is relatively slight.

The school culture can be described, in the illuminating geometrical terms of Kurt Levin, as a circle, its center being the core of the culture, while elements are distributed in space outward from the center, such that the importance of the elements progressively decreases with increasing distance from the center.

Processes of change are intended to influence the pattern of the school culture. Processes that do not affect the central elements of the pattern do not arouse resistance to absorbing them, and clearly will not produce major changes in the pattern. Such changes, if not absorbed and assimilated by the pattern, will not be preserved; even if they are, they cannot be pointed out and treated as a significant change that has occurred in the school culture.

The process of change is relatively more difficult as the proposed cultural changes impinge more closely on the core of the culture or affect its elements; the intensity of the resistance is a function of the proximity of the targeted elements to the core of the culture.

Projects that seek to modify peripheral variables will not arouse resistance; the process will be characterized as a pleasant experience with which both sides are satisfied. A process of change that aims at significant modification of elements close to the core of the culture, or within the core, will arouse much more serious resistance than that which can be anticipated for changes in peripheral elements. The resistance originates in the inertial unwillingness of the pattern to change and waive its existence as such.

Recognition of the fact that significant change is a painful process points to an attempt to effect changes in central variables that are close to the core of the school culture. At the same time, it should be remembered that the payoff for the pain and unrelenting resistance is a higher probability of preserving precisely those changes in elements close to the core of the culture that have been modified. Such a change is more significant for the pattern of the culture, and, it may be assumed, will also be better preserved.

For example, we assume that one core element in any school culture is the concept of time.

An intervention program that takes upon itself to modify the concept of time and aspires to differential learning time for different students will arouse resistance, because it impinges upon the core of the culture or upon elements that are very close to it.

"Learning for mastery" is an approach that differentiates the learning period of different students with the goal of bringing them to mastery of certain skills.

This change requires a different pattern of student-teacher interaction. The teacher's roles are altered. Early diagnosis and constant follow-up of the achievements of each student become central elements of the instruction and learning situation.

Obviously, modifying a curriculum or various units within standard subject-matter, is easier than the concept just described and poses a simpler challenge to the teacher, since habits of instruction, the pattern of interaction with the students, norms for evaluating the learning output, as well as other elements, do not have to change. It may be expected that such changes will be accepted more readily and with less resistance. Yet they can be expected to effect no significant change in the pattern of the school culture. By contrast, dealing with problems of discipline, various norms of assessment, patterns of instruction, and the like, impinge much more directly on teachers' work habits and the pattern of work in the school.

### *The Optimum Point between the Effort Invested by Teachers and their Effectiveness:*

The schematic diagram below is intended to illustrate the desirable optimum point between the effort invested by teachers and their effectiveness. The graph assumes a positive correlation between effort and effectiveness. (This function is not necessarily linear; the graph is linear for illustrative purposes only.)

Let us assume that a school, at the beginning of a process of change, is located at point A, where both teacher effort and effectiveness are relatively low. At this point, in order to achieve a greater level of effectiveness, teachers must expend greater effort – in order to arrive at point B, for example.

In general, project effectiveness is measured by the location of point B: a "successful" project is one for which the point B is located higher on the graph. While striving for greater effectiveness (point B') however, one must realize that teachers are not capable of maintaining high and stable levels of effort over long periods of time; over time they are likely to "slide" down the graph and approach the initial point of both low effectiveness and minimal effort.

Innovators must build components into the change process itself that can help teachers reach a higher level of effectiveness while expending the mini-

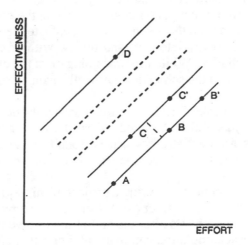

*Figure 1: A linear representation of teacher effort effectiveness relationships*

mum effort possible, in order to increase the probability that the results will be sustained over time. That is, innovators must realize that the endeavor to raise point B to point B' or point C to point C' may produce "results" that are just effects of the experiment itself, doomed to fade away after termination of the project.

The proper strategy for innovators builds elements of stability and continuity into the pattern of intervention. This strategy is likely to produce smaller, but more stable, effects.

Such a strategy was adopted in the project we conducted in the elementary schools of two Israeli towns in 1984-1987. The goal of the project was to improve the educational results of nine elementary schools in these towns. The project was executed in all the elementary schools in these towns, which included public schools of both secular and religious orientation.

The project covered some 2500 pupils from kindergarten through grade six, as well as around 140 teachers. In one of the towns, 47% of the pupils were defined as socio-economically disadvantaged; for the second town, the corresponding figure was 65% (the national average of disadvantaged elementary school pupils is 21%).

In each school, all the teachers and students, as well as the other functionaries connected with the school, were involved in the project. The principal was treated as the central and dominant figure in the school. Each principal received ongoing personal guidance and also participated in a special course for school principals designed as part of the project.

This primary goal of this school intervention, with its holistic approach, was to enhance student scholastic achievement, while simultaneously improving the schools and making them more effective in many other respects.

A diagnostic approach was adopted for the project; the central theme was to establish a continuum of defined and gradual goals; teachers, working with each student individually, could advance along the continuum with that student. From time to time the teacher would evaluate the student's achievements by means of appropriate tests and review with him or her the points that required remediation. While this was going on at the class level, the goal was to effect changes at the school level as well, changes on both levels being often closely interrelated.

At the end of the project's three-year course scholastic achievements had risen significantly, as will be detailed below. Details of the underlying assumptions and operational strategy can be found in our article: "Coherent Strategy Components of an Outcome-Based school Improvement Project" (in press).

One of the central concerns, during a project of this sort aimed at modifying schools, is to sustain the effect and suffer as small a retreat as possible in the functioning of the schools after the end of the intervention project.

The element of accumulation can make an important contribution to sustaining outcomes. One of the identifying marks of weak schools is that ideas,

258

materials, and habits that would lead to the desirable routines are not accumulated and preserved. The reasons for this failure are linked to how the school operates and the rapid turnover of staff. Thus the accumulation of materials, habits, and norms that could withstand the turnover of teachers is a very important element in sustaining outcomes.

A "resource room" was set up in each of the schools where the project described above was conducted. Here materials prepared by teams of teachers or by individual teachers were accumulated and preserved. This accumulation facilitated the teachers' work in the classroom. Recycling of the existing materials gradually made it easier for the teaching staff.

Parallel to establishing resource rooms and accruing materials in them was the need to ensure that there be someone to stock the resource rooms and someone to teach teachers new to the schools to use them. To this end we made a relatively large investment in a relatively small number of teachers, thereby creating a core group of teachers who had mastered the various aspects of school culture as it became more effective and would be able to transmit this body of knowledge to their colleagues.

The accumulation of varied study materials in the resource rooms, along with the creation of appropriate and convenient conditions for using these materials, are what shifted the school graphs upward.

Thus, in the project described above we implemented the findings of Berman and McLaughlin in the 1977 Rand study which revealed the insignificance of educational method on sustaining outcomes, and the need for change in the various elements of the school, and the importance of defining clear project goals and giving practical training to teachers while providing maximum assistance regarding problems that arise in transition to the new work method.

At the same time, we added what we believe to be a crucial element - increasing effectiveness while working for maximum economy of the energy expenditure on the part of teachers who are undergoing the processes of change.

In conclusion, when the intervention project succeeds in inculcating its proposed work methods into the core of the school culture, or close to it, and at the same time provides tools to enable teachers to adhere to those methods in a manageable fashion, the probability of sustaining the effect is increased, if for no other reason that it is a new source of the professional satisfaction of which teachers have so great a need.

In the foregoing we have presented and grounded assumptions about ways to increase the likelihood of sustaining the effect of school intervention projects. These include a recommendation that projects address more central elements in the school culture, and that an effort be made to decrease, to the extent possible, the energy that teachers must expend in order to continue to apply the new method. As was noted above, one of the central goals of our project was to enhance student scholastic achievement. For this reason, the project was accompanied by ongoing assessments. Because of our desire to confirm hypotheses with respect to sustaining outcomes, we decided to follow up the results for a period of two years following project termination. At the present time, one year after the end of the project, criterion-referenced tests and norm-referenced tests have been administered in the schools that participated in the project.

### Results of Minimum Competency Basic Skills Tests

Figure 2 presents the percentage of failures on the minimum competency basic skills tests in arithmetic and reading comprehension given in the schools at three points in time: after the first year of the project, at the end of the project, and after the first follow-up year.

As can be seen, there was a significant decline in the percentage of failures during the last two years of the project, and an additional significant decline

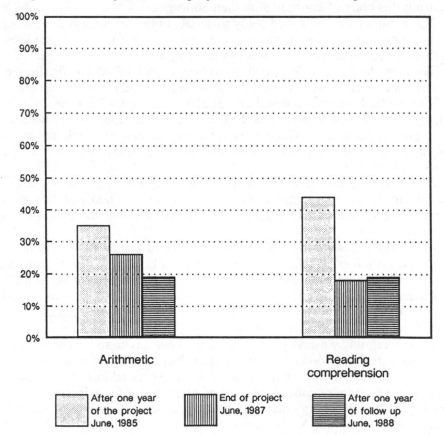

*Figure 2: Comparison of percentage of failures in the schools at three points in time*

260

in the percentage of failures in arithmetic during the follow-up year. For reading comprehension the percentage of failures remained stable during the first follow-up year.

From the relevant literature we learn about a threshold percentage of failures that is extremely difficult to surpass. For the tests in question this threshold seems to be somewhere between 10% and 20%. At the end of the project, most of the classes had reached this figure in reading comprehension tests, though not in arithmetic. During the follow-up year, the results on the reading-comprehension test remained the same, while the percentage of those failing the arithmetic test decreased to a level comparable to that for the reading-comprehension test.

### Results of Norm-referenced Tests

Table 1 compares the mean scores for the standardized tests administered in June 1987, at the end of the project, and for those administered in June 1988, at the end of the first follow-up year. A comparison to the national averages is also included.

Table 1: Mean scores on the norm-referenced tests - at end of project, one year later, and the national average

|  | Nat. Average | Project, 6/87 | Project, 6/88 |
|---|---|---|---|
| Reading comp., grade 3 | 65 | 61 | 61 |
| Reading comp., grade 4 | 63 | 61 | 63 |
| Reading comp., grade 5 | 66 | 66 | 67 |
| Arithmetic, grade 2 | 73 | 75 | 77 |
| Arithmetic, grade 3 | 67 | 66 | 70 |
| Arithmetic, grade 5 | 63 | 65 | 68 |

Comparison of the mean scores at the end of the follow-up year with those at the end of the project shows that in no case did the results deteriorate. In one case – reading comprehension for third grade – there was stability, while all the other results evinced a rise in the mean scores, ranging from one to four percent. That is, it can be said that the results remained stable during the first year after the project, with even a slight tendency to improve.

It is interesting that at the end of the first follow-up year the mean scores on all the tests, with one exception, are equal or superior to the national averages, despite the disadvantaged background of students at the schools involved.

We examined the percentage of students who exceed the national mean. Table 2 presents these percentages at project termination and one year later.

Table 2: Percentage of students scoring above national average

|  | End of project | End of follow-up year |
|---|---|---|
| Reading comp., grade 3 | 44% | 49% |
| Reading comp., grade 4 | 49% | 55% |
| Reading comp., grade 5 | 53% | 56% |
| Arithmetic, grade 2 | 61% | 67% |
| Arithmetic, grade 3 | 52% | 68% |
| Arithmetic, grade 5 | 59% | 65% |

From this table we see that on both tests and at all grade levels there was an increase in the percentage of students who scored above the national average.

The results indicate that the schools continued to work in the spirit of the project, giving differential attention to students at different levels. This can be seen from the fact that there was simultaneously a decline in the percentage of failure (evidence of continued effective attention to the weaker students) and a significant increase in the number of students scoring above the national average (evidence of continued effective attention to the stronger students).

With the results of the first follow-up year in hand, we can conclude that, at least at this juncture, the project's underlying assumptions have been vindicated.


# DISCUSSION

This article proposes three clusters of factors that influence the preservation of the results of intervention projects. Special emphasis was placed on factors connected to the pattern of the intervention itself.

Two dimensions for understanding the factors that influence maintenance of outcomes were proposed: the extent to which elements targeted for change are central or penpheral to school culture, and the need to diminish the effort required to achieve a given degree of effectiveness so that the required energy expenditure will be reasonable and plausible over the long term.

Intervention programs that ignore these two dimensions decrease the likelihood that their effect will be sustained. Maintaining outcomes requires much further exploration and investigation. We know very little about the elements that accelerate or retard such maintenance. We do not know which elements are included in each of the clusters discussed above, nor are there any long-term follow-up studies that could elucidate many theoretical and practical questions.

It may well be that one of the reasons for the lack of adequate follow-up studies is the fact that follow-up after an intervention project cannot be a passive enterprise; the agent of change views the follow-up as an institutionalization phase. The interaction between the agent of change and the school continues. The demarcation between the intervention phase and the institutionalization phase is not clear-cut. The two stages co-exist at a certain point in the life of the project, as was described above. By the same token, the boundary between the termination date of the project and the first follow-up period is poorly defined; many elements of activities conducted during the two periods overlap, or are similar.

Comprehensive follow-up studies that would trace the preservation of the effects of school intervention projects could answer both theoretical and practical questions. The theoretical question relate to the elements of the efficiency programs that make a significant contribution to sustaining the outcomes after the termination of the project.

In the practical realm, such comprehensive studies could provide policy makers with data on which to base their decisions. The question of sustaining effects is of prime importance for the policy maker who is trying to learn from an experiment and decide whetherd pr to the elements of the efficiency programs that make a significant contribution to sustaining the outcomes after the termination of the project.

In the practical realm, such comprehensive studies could provide policy makers with data on which to base their decisions. The question of sustaining effects is of prime importance for the policy maker who is trying to learn from an experiment and decide whether when all other conditions are equal. That is, if policy makers do not encourage dissemination of the work methods proven to be effective in an experimental project they diminish the likelihood that the results will be sustained, all other conditions being equal; but if they do decide to disseminate the model, they increase that probability.

# REFERENCES

Bashi, J. and Sass, Z. (in press) *Coherent Strategy Components of an Outcome-Based School Improvement Project.*

Berman, P., McLaughlin, M.W. et al. (1977). *Factors Affecting Implementation and Continuation*, Rand Corporation, Vol. VII, R-1589/7-HEW.

Cobert, H.D. (1983). *School Context and the Continuation of Innovative Practices*, Presented at the AERA, March 1983.

Huberman, M. and Miles, M. (1984). *Innovation Up Close* Andover. Mass. Plenum Press.

Miles, M.B., Ekholm, M., and Vandenberghe R. (1987). *Lasting School Improvement: Exploring the Process of Institutionalization*, Leuven: Acco.

Van Velzen, W.G. Miles, M.B. Ekholm, M., Hameyer, V. and Robin, D. (1985). *Making School Improvement Work: A Conceptual Guide to Practice*, Leuven/Amersfoort: Acco.

# TOWARDS A MORE COMPREHENSIVE CONCEPTUALIZATION OF SCHOOL EFFECTIVENESS

Jaap Scheerens
University of Twente, Enschede

and

Bert P.M. Creemers
RION, Institute for Educational Research, University of Groningen

## INTRODUCTION

School effectiveness research has its roots in quantitative sociological input-output studies and economic research on educational production functions (Coleman et al., 1966; Hanushek, 1979). The second wave of school effectiveness research emphasized "process" rather than "input" correlates of school output and employed (in general) more in-depth investigation of relatively small samples of schools (Edmonds, 1979; Brookover et al., 1979; Rutter et al., 1979). The main outcomes of this period of school effectiveness research - sometimes characterized as the five-factor model of school effectiveness - still dominate practical thinking on school effectiveness: many school improvement projects have tried to implement the five-factor model, with varying degrees of success (e.g. Miller et al., 1985).

Apart from these two research traditions which are usually labelled as "school effectiveness" research, we should mention a large body of research which comes under the heading of "instructional effectiveness" (see Brophy & Good, 1986, for a comprehensive review). This body of research, directed at the classroom level as opposed to that of the school, has developed independently from the school effectiveness research traditions. Recently, however, we see a blending of approaches. In research syntheses on "educational productivity", both input and process variables at the school and the classroom level are incorporated (Walberg, 1984; Fraser, 1987) and in recent effectiveness studies school- and classroom level variables are combined in multi-level models of educational achievement (Mortimore et al., 1988; Brandsma & Knuver, 1988).

265

The field of school effectiveness research is plagued by many methodological and technical research problems (c.f. Ralph & Fenessey, 1983; Bosker & Scheerens, 1989). Apart from these problems, which involve seeking an appropriate way of conducting this kind of empirical research, there is very little theory on school effectiveness. Despite a growing consensus on "what works in education", there are relatively few theoretical explanations available regarding to the question "why things work in education". In addition to integrating school- and instructional level variables in empirical research we feel that conceptual models are needed which can serve as frameworks for hypothetical explanations of relationships between various levels of analysis of educational systems.

In this paper we attempt to contribute to the development of such models by means of a critique of the state of the art of conceptualizing school effectiveness (i.e. the so-called five-factor model), by examining the overall structure of a multi-level school effectiveness model and by further specifying some of the basic substantive ingredients of this model, most notably instructional variables and organizational and contextual conditions. To illustrate some of the points we wish to make, we give an overview of school effectiveness studies in the Netherlands, and compare the outcomes to the results of major Anglo-Saxon effectiveness studies.

## CONCEPTUAL CRITIQUE OF THE "5-FACTOR" MODEL

Five school characteristics are repeatedly mentioned in the literature as malleable correlates of educational achievement. These are:
- strong educational leadership
- high expectations of student achievement
- emphasis on basic skills
- a safe and orderly climate
- frequent evaluation of pupils' progress

The causal status of the "5-factor" model is correlational. This means that although the 5-factors are usually seen as "causes" of student achievement, in a strict methodological sense no such strong statements concerning causal ordering are warranted. We shall not here go into further methodological criticism of the research basis on which the 5-factor model rests: for this we refer to the reviews cited earlier, in particular Ralph & Fennessey, 1983. But, given the correlational status of the model, some questions about the model must be raised, also at the conceptual level.

First of all, the question of whether the factors are causes rather than effects of high achievement is particularly hard to ignore for the "high expectation of student outcomes"-factor. It is quite plausible that feedback from satisfying student results at an earlier stage leads to high expectations for the future. Perhaps the expectations-achievement correlation can best be seen as a genuine reciprocal relationship (which is hard to demonstrate using causal analysis).

Secondly, there is a hint of tautology in emphasis on basic skills (as a determinant) and exclusively measuring basic skills as the dependent variable. If we were to measure outcomes in the affective domain, instead of achievement, goal consensus on basic skills would be a less likely cause of the measured dependent variable. The basic factor here seems to be goal-measurement disparity. This variable, we believe, could better have been used as a control variable or covariate, rather than as a causal factor which distinguishes effective from non-effective schools.

In the third place, the question should be raised whether the five factors are really independent factors. This question could be answered by examining the correlations between the factors. But even at face value, we might wonder whether "frequent evaluation" and "orderly climate" could not better be seen as aspects of strong instructional leadership, than as independent causes. A fourth question, which is somewhat related to the former, concerns the locus of the factors. Sometimes they are seen as all being aspects of school leadership (e.g. Sweeney, 1982), whereas in other cases they are seen as aspects of school climate. Not all the factors are exclusively defined at the school-level; progress-monitoring and evaluation should perhaps even be primarily taken as a variable at the teacher or classroom level.

What remains of the five-factor model, after considering these critical conceptual questions, is firstly a general idea of what is and what is not essential and secondly, a feeling that we need more refined effectiveness models. We believe that elements like a high achievement orientation, shared by teachers and management, and both structural and cultural conditions for closely monitored learning, are the core elements of the effective-schools model and that the methodological critique concerning the disparty (or closeness) of educational objectives and effectiveness measures points to a third condition: access to knowledge or "opportunity to learn".

More refined models of school-effectiveness have been developed by Glasman & Biniaminov, 1981; Murphy et al., 1982; Clauset & Gaynor, 1982; Squires, Huitt & Segars, 1983; Schmuck, 1980; Blom, Brandsma & Stoel, 1985; Ellett & Walberg, 1979; Duckworth, 1983.

Usually, these models contain at least two levels at which effectiveness indicators are defined, namely the school level and the classroom level. They also take background characteristics of pupils (aptitudes, socio-economic status) into account as control variables (individual student level). Some of these models contain a third "context" level at which effectiveness indicators are defined (Schmuck, 1980; Blom, Brandsma & Stoel, 1985). Finally, it is worth noting that several models are non-recursive (i.e. contain reciprocal relationships).

# SOME PERSPECTIVES FROM ORGANIZATIONAL THEORY

To a large extent, empirical school effectiveness research has developed outside the field of educational administration. So, for instance, within the divisional structure of the American Educational Research Association, the Special Interest Group on effective schools belongs to the evaluation division and not to the educational administration division. In the Netherlands as well, school effectiveness researchers operate outside the professional network of researchers of educational administration. Despite some clear exceptions (e.g. Firestone & Wilson, 1987; Hoy & Ferguson, 1985) this institutional separation, in our opinion, has led to an underscoring of the relevance of some perspectives from organizational theory to questions of school effectiveness. Two of these perspectives are: contingency theory and alternative views on organizational effectiveness.

## Contingency-theory

The research basis of the 5-factor model of school-effectiveness consists largely of studies of urban primary schools with a low SES-student population conducted in the United States and England. The claims of the "effective schools movement" that imply a more general applicability of the five-factor model seem rather strong, given this relatively narrow empirical basis. The idea of a universally valid set of effectiveness indicators is at odds with a perspective in organizational theory, known as contingency theory, or "the situational approach" (Thompson, 1967; Mintzberg, 1979). Contingency theory can be seen as a reaction against earlier organizational theories that emphasized particular ideal-type organizations, e.g. based on the ideas of scientific management or the human relations approach.

The basic idea of contingency theory is the dependency of the effectiveness of organization structures on situational or contextual conditions, such as the complexity of the environment, the nature of the core technology and factors like age and size of the organization. Organizational structures should "fit" these contextual conditions. It should be noted that the contingency-perspective does not make the life of researchers of organizational phenomena any easier. For one thing, contingency-factors are not seen as independent external causes, but as conditions that can be partly controlled by the organization. Thus, reciprocal relationships appear when we consider empirically verifying hypotheses of organizational functioning. Yet another complicating aspect of contextual determinacy is the possibility that different contingency factors "pull" the organization in different directions. Moreover, contingency hypotheses require very complicated research designs, because empirical verification of the fit of contextual and structural variables are only one step, after which it still remains to be shown whether a "fitting arrangement" does indeed lead to effectiveness (see Kickert, 1979).

The generalizability vs. the situational dependency of the five factor model of school-effectiveness is an important issue for future research in this area. Several authors report findings that support the contingency of effectiveness indicators on factors like the distinctions between primary vs. secondary schools (Firestone & Herriott, 1982), high vs. low SES student body composition (Teddlie et al., 1987) and vocational vs. general secondary education (Stoel, 1986). As a further illustration of contextual determinacy of school-effectiveness indicators we would like to point to a specific type of contextual dimension of schools, namely the surrounding national educational systems. In Table 1 we present a general overview of school-effectiveness research in the Netherlands.

Table 1 shows that school-effectiveness research in the Netherlands is still in its infancy: there are relatively few studies, all conducted during the last three to four years. The dependent variables which were used in these studies were either achievement test data, examination results, educational attainment measures or, in two cases, affective measures like pupils' attitude towards school. The independent variables were mostly measured by means of questionnaires and interviews. Simple correlations, regression analysis and ANOVA were the most frequently used analyses. The general appearance of

Table 1: Overview of Dutch effectiveness studies

| Indicator \ author | general measure of school-climate | educational leadership | orderly climate | basic skills | high expectations | frequent evaluation | private/public distinction | direct instruction | achievement orientation |
|---|---|---|---|---|---|---|---|---|---|
| Meijnen, 1985 | | | | | | | | + | |
| Marwijk-Kooy, 1985* | + | | + | | + | + | + | | |
| Hoeven van Doornum, Jungbluth, 1987 | | | | | | | + | | |
| Stoel, 1986* | | | + | | | + | | | |
| Bosker, Hofman, 1987 | | | | | | | | | + |
| Brandsma, Stoel, 1987* | | + | | | | + | | | |
| Vermeulen, 1987 | | | + | | | | | | |
| Tesser, 1985* | | | | | | | | | |
| Van der Wolf, 1985 | | | | | | | | + | |
| Brandsma, Knuver, 1988 | | | | | | | + | | |
| Van der Werf, Tesser, 1989 | | | | | + | + | | | + |
| De Jong, 1988 | | | | | | | | | + |

* secondary schools; unmarked: primary schools; + means significant positive relationship with effectiveness indicator

this overview does not offer much support for the 5-factor model of school-effectiveness, although individual studies show positive results for individual factors like strong leadership, orderly climate and frequent evaluation. So, the main findings from Anglo-Saxon effectiveness studies ar hardly replicated within the educational context of the Netherlands. This is also illustrated by Vermeulen's (1987) study, which was a close replication of an American study, conducted by Schweitzer (1984). Whereas Schweitzer found high correlations (.58 up to .79) between all five effectiveness factors and achievement, Vermeulen found only one significant correlation.

It could be argued that the studies are too few and too disverified to warrant more definite conclusions. Moreover, individual studies have been criticized for lack of reliability of the measurement of the independent variables and for not using the proper techniques of analysis (e.g. Creemers, 1987). However, such findings provoke questions about the contextual mechanisms (i.e. characteristics of the Dutch educational system) which could explain these findings.

Three tentative explanations are that a) Dutch schools lack a tradition of educational testing and school-based evaluation, and accordingly this variable would explain little variance, b) achievement orientation does not generally rank high in the teaching philosophy of Dutch schools, and c) "leadership", and particularly educational leadership is a phenomenon that is somewhat at odds with the predominant view of Dutch school leaders as "first among their equals" (i.e. teachers).

# ALTERNATIVE VIEWS OF ORGANIZATIONAL EFFECTIVENESS

The way effectiveness is defined in the main stream of school effectiveness research conforms to the notion of organizational productivity and its theoretical background of economic rationality. The productivity view of effectiveness sees output of the organization's primary process as the criterion to judge goal attainment and emphasizes the search for organizational characteristics that maximize output. When the constraint of "least costs" is added to the maximization of output, effectiveness is transformed into the even more demanding notion of efficiency.

In organizational theory productivity is sometimes thought of as one among several criteria of effectiveness (Cameron & Whetten, 1983, Faermann & Quinn, 1985). Adaptability to the environment, commitment of individual members to the organization, continuity and regularity in the functioning of the organizations and responsiveness to external constituents are put forward as alternative effectiveness criteria. We do not share the

opinion that these alternative effectiveness criteria are equivalid and independent. Instead, we feel that the above mentioned criteria should be ordered
according to a means-end distinction, with "production of an organization's
primary output" as the ultimate criterion (see Figure 1).

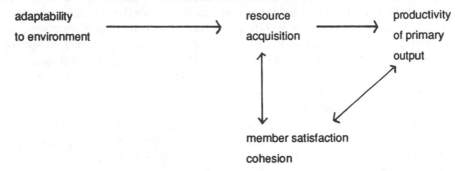

*Figure 1: Means-to-end relationships of organizational effeciveness criteria*

Incidentally, the arrows in Figure 1 should not be seen as linear relationships.
It is very conceivable that overinvestment in one of the supportive criteria
would be counterproductive to the ultimate criterion of maximizing output.
For instance a school could "lose itself" in doctoring the interpersonal relations among the staff to a degree where the actual work would suffer, or a
school could invest so heavily in resource acquisition that too little time and
energy would be left for an achievement-oriented policy. A final remark on
the configuration of effectiveness criteria depicted in Figure 1 is that it is
quite amenable to be used from the perspective of contingency-theory as
described in the previous section. In a period when a school's external environment induces all kinds of new demands, it is quite understandable that a
lot of energy should be spent on input characteristics like the redesign of
curricula, the acquisition of new teaching materials etc. Faermann & Quinn
(1985) relate changing emphasis on the alternative effectiveness criteria to
an organization's life cycle.

School-effectiveness research could benefit from the broader scope of
conceptions of organizational effectiveness by using the "supportive criteria" as sources of inspiration to explain the mechanism by which the factors
at the "independent" side of the productivity equation affect primary output.
For instance, goal consensus and cohesion among the teaching staff could be
the basis for factors like "emphasis on basic skills" and achievement orientation. Likewise, a certain degree of formal structure (even in the professional
bureaucracy) could be seen as a prerequisite for the orderly climate of effective schools.

# EFFECTIVENESS AT THE CLASSROOM LEVEL

In the section on the five-factor model of school effectiveness we drew attention to the fact that some of the school characteristics that are thought to be associated with student achievement can also be defined at the classroom level (emphasis on basic skills, frequent monitoring of pupils' progress, an orderly atmosphere and high expectations of pupils' achievement). When we conceive of a conceptual model of school effectiveness as a causal model of student achievement, it is quite obvious that we need to include explanatory variables defined at the classroom level. In fact it is to be expected that these variables explain more variance in student achievement since they are physically closer to the behavior and dispositions that are central in our measures of student achievement (empirical evidence confirming this expectation is presented by Fraser et al. (1987) and Scheerens et al. (1989)). In considering causal models of student achievement the first category of variables that must be taken into account are student background variables, such as intellectual capacity and home-evironment. Although these variables explain the major part of the variance in student achievement they cannot easily be influenced by education - at least not in the short run. This means that this category of variables will mainly be used as a control factor in models of school effectiveness: i.e. a factor that has to be taken into account in order to facilitate interpretation of other - malleable - factors.

Another category of variables important to learning which can be influenced at least partly by education consists of factors related to motivation. Micro-theories (i.e. theories defined at the classroom level) on student achievement start with an ideal-type notion of how learning takes place. Models which have received empirical support include those developed by Carroll (1963), Harnischfeger & Wiley (1976), Cooley & Leinhardt (1975); Bloom's (1976) concept of learning for mastery is based on this latter theory.

Meta-analytical studies (Kulik & Kulik, 1989; Walberg, 1984) show that mastery-based instructional systems are very effective. Essential to these instructional systems is that, given students' behaviour on entrance, careful evaluation and diagnosis of the weaknesses and strengths of students can lead to the achievement of predetermined objectives. A common component in the model of Carroll, Cooley and Leinhardt and Bloom is the quantity of instruction, also described as the opportunity to learn. With respect to the quality of instruction, the instructional systems emphasize different aspects, such as clarity of instruction (Carroll), structuring knowledge (Cooley and Leinhardt) and evaluation and feedback (including reinforcement and correctives) (Bloom). When we look at the "media of instruction" such as teacher activities, classroom organization, curriculum methods and textbooks, we can conclude that those directed to the above-mentioned factors, contribute to the students' learning. Brophy and Good (1986) emphasize that achievement is related to the quality of instruction provided by the teacher:

272

time allocation, classroom management, opportunity to learn, etc. Providing information, structuring, clarity and some redundancy and sequencing are important factors contributing to student's achievement. A specific behaviour which is confirmed by the meta-analysis of Fraser (in press) is *wait* time: the pause between question and answer. Also guidance for work and home-assignment contribute to higher achievement, as these activities provide practice and application opportunities and so enlarge opportunity to learn. Doyle (1986), Kounin (1970), Gump (1967) and Good & Brophy (1986) emphasize that the management of classrooms should aim for an orderly and quiet atmosphere to increase students' opportunity to learn.

This brief excursion into the literature on classroom effectiveness indicates a rough similarity between school-level and classroom-level correlates of student achievement, most notably with respect to factors like evaluation and feedback, a clear achievement oriented mission, and order as a prerequisite to the quantity of instruction. In the final section we shall use this similarity to sketch a model that integrates school and classroom-level correlates of achievement.

# A COMPREHENSIVE MODEL OF SCHOOL EFFECTIVENESS

The conceptual structure that lies at the background of all that has been said in the previous sections is a multi-level model containing a school, a classroom and an individual level within a school context, see Figure 2.

We realize that the conceptual mapping of school effectiveness undertaken so far, does not answer the question *why* certain organizational characteristics correlate positively with achievement. On the basis of our review in the previous section we expect that we can derive a point of departure in learning and instructional theories, for which empirical evidence exists. The conceptual map, summarized in Figure 2, does provide a framework for indicating critical relationships that are in need of further explanation, e.g. by relating the already available empirical findings and new empirical hypotheses to more general principles or theories.

We believe that the critical organizational relationships in the school effectiveness model indicated in Figure 2 are the relationships between levels, specifically between the school and the classroom level, the classroom level and the individual level and between contextual conditions and organizational characteristics. The most straightforward way of thinking about these cross-level relationships is through the idea that higher levels should provide facilitative conditions for the central processes at lower level. This line of thinking calls for an inside-out analysis, which in this case means that our starting point for hypothesizing supportive conditions located at higher levels must be the principles of learning at the individual level.

273

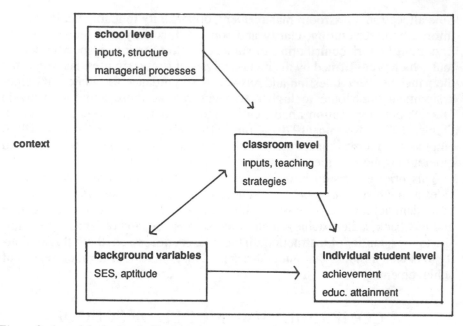

*Figure 2: A model of school effectiveness*

First of all, we know that social-economic status and aptitudes of students are important for explaining educational results. Next, we have to look at the principles of effective instruction. From research syntheses of instructional effectiveness and research on teaching (Walberg, 1984; Fraser et al., 1987) we conclude that the important conditions of effective teaching include direct instruction (i.e. a conglomerate of factors such as the use of reinforcement, highly-structured learning tasks, frequent monitoring of student progress), time-on-task (including homework assignments) and opportunity to learn (i.e. closeness of achievement measurement and content covered). Fraser concludes that the amount of instruction, enhanced by using the school days more effectively or by increasing homework, especially leads to improvement in students' outcomes. In his analyses successful methods of instruction that lead to greater achievement are: mastery-learning, (with emphasis on reinforcement and feedback) cooperative learning, personalized and adaptive instruction, advance organizers, national science curricula, high teacher expectations, longer wait time and good questioning techniques.

At the next level up, we should look for managerial, structural and cultural conditions conducive to effective instruction. An important managerial condition is the provision of evaluative facilities throughout the school, regulations for frequent assessment of student progress, tracking systems, computerized test-service systems, absenteeism registration, procedures for school-

274

based review and teacher assessment. We could summarize this managerial principle by referring to "the evaluative potential of the school organization" (Scheerens, 1987), which is firmly rooted in control theory, cybernetics, and rational management theory. We believe that, as far as schools are concerned, an evaluation-centered, or retro-active style of management has certain advantages over a pro-active, planning-centered approach (cf. Borich & Jemelka, 1982).

The concept of 'goal coordination' from control theory must be seen as an important managerial factor in establishing cohesion between school members as far as the aims and major means of effective instruction are concerned.

At the cultural dimension of organizational functioning we might expect that a general orientation towards achievement, shared by school leaders and teaching personnel, would be conducive to effective teaching.

At the next level, we need to explore contextual conditions favorable to effective school management and organization. Here contingency theory can be used as the general line of thinking. For example, we should expect schools to invest relatively more energy in adaptation to the environment, and, more specifically, resource acquisition, when the environment is less certain and stable.

# CONCLUSION

In this article we have tried to use organizational and instructional theories more explicitly in the analysis and interpretation of research findings on school effectiveness. Further conceptual development is necessary.

Our conceptual analysis suggests that we concentrate hypothesis construction and empirical research on cross-level relationships within a multi-level framework of school effectiveness.

In that respect the available knowledge on instructional effectiveness should be our starting point, whereupon relationships between factors at the school- and classroom-level should be examined from the point of view that higher level factors function as facilitative conditions to lower level factors. Finally, we have drawn attention to the importance of contextual conditions for the explanation of school effectiveness. We feel that international studies, where national contexts of school effectiveness can be compared, are quite important in this respect.

It is our contention that school effectiveness should as yet be seen as primarily a programme for research and theory-development - and that we should be very cautious in making recommendations for educational practice based on our present knowledge.

# REFERENCES

Blom, M.J.T., H. Brandsma & W.G.R. Stoel (1985). Effectieve scholen in het basisonderwijs. Groningen: RION.

Bloom, B.S. (1976). *Human characteristics and school learning*. New York: McGraw Hill.

Borich, G.D. & R.P. Jemelka, *Programs & Systems*. New York: Academic Press.

Bosker, R.J. & W.H.A. Hofman (1987). Dimensies van schoolkwaliteit. In: Scheerens, J. & Stoel, W.G.R. (eds.) *Effectiviteit van onderwijsorganisaties*. Lisse: Swets & Zeitlinger.

Bosker, R.J. & J. Scheerens (1989). Criterion definition, effect size and stability. Three fundamental problems in school effectiveness research. This volume, pp. 211-252.

Bossert, S.T. (1988). School effects. In: N.J. Boyan (ed.) *Handbook of research on educational administration*. New York: Longman Inc.

Brandsma, H.P. & Knuver, A.W.M. (1988). Organisatorische verschillen tussen basisscholen en hun effect op leerprestaties. *Tijdschrift voor Onderwijsresearch, 13*, 201-212.

Brookover, W.C., Brady, C., Flood, P. et al. (1979). *School systems and student achievement - schools can make a difference*. New York: Praeger Publishers.

Brophy, J.E. & T.L. Good (1986). Teacher behavior and student achievement. In: Merlin C. Wittrock (ed.). *Handbook of research on teaching*, (3rd ed.). New York: MacMillan Publ. Comp.

Cameron, K.S. & D.A. Whetten (1983). *Organizational effectiveness. A comparison of multiple models*. New York: Academic Press.

Carroll, J.B. (1963): A model of schoollearning. *Teachers College Record, 64*, 723-733.

Clauset, K.H. & A.K. Gaynor (1982). A systems perspective on effective schools. *Educational Leadership, 40* (3), 54-59.

Coleman, J.S. et al. (1966). *Equality of educational opportunity*. Washington D.C.: U.S. Government Printing Office.

Cooley, W.W. & G. Leinhardt (1975). *The application of a model for investigating classroom processes*. Pittsburgh: University of Pittsburgh, Learning Research and Development Center.

Creemers, B.P.M. (1987). Bijdragen tot effectiviteit van scholen: discussie. In: Scheerens, J. & Stoel, W.G.R. (eds.) *Effectiviteit van onderwijsorganisaties*. Lisse: Swets & Zeitlinger.

Doyle, W. (1986). Classroom organization and management. In: Merlin C. Wittrock (ed.). *Handbook of research on teaching*, (3rd ed.). New York: MacMillan Publ. Comp.

Duckworth, K. (1983). *Specifying determinants of teacher and principal work*. Eugene, OR: Center for Educational Policy and Management, University of Oregon.

Ellett, C.D. & H.J. Walberg (1979). Principal competency, environment and outcomes. In: H.J. Walberg (ed.) *Educational environment and effects*, (pp. 140-167). Berkeley: McCutchan.

Faerman, S.R. & R.E. Quinn (1985). Effectiveness: the perspective from organizational theory. *The Review of Higher Education, 9*, 83-100.

Firestone, W.A. & Herriott, R.E. (1982). Prescriptions for effective elementary schools don't fit secondary schools. *Educational Leadership, 40*, 51-53.

Fraser, B.J. (ed.) (1987). Synthesis of educational productivity research. Special Issue of the *International Journal of Educational Research, 11*, (2).

Fuller, B., K. Wood, T. Rappoport & S.M. Dornbush (1983). The organizational context of individual efficacy. *Review of Educational Research, 51* (4), 509-539.

Glasman, N.S. & I. Biniaminov (1981). Input-output analyses of schools. *Review of Educational Research, 51,* 509-539.

Good, T.L. & J.E. Brophy (1986). School effects. In: Merlin C. Wittrock (ed.). *Handbook of research on teaching,* (3rd ed.). New York: MacMillan Publ. Comp.

Goodman, P.S., Aitkin, R.S. & Schoorman, F.D. (1983). On the demise of organisationzal effectiveness. In: Cameron, K.S. & Whetten, D.A. *Organizational effectiveness. A comparison of multiple models.* New York: Academic Press.

Grift, W. van der (1987). Zelfpercepties van onderwijskundig leiderschap en gemiddelde leerlingprestaties. In: Scheerens, J. & Stoel, W.G.R. (eds.) *Effectiviteit van onderwijsorganisaties.* Lisse: Swets & Zeitlinger.

Gump, P.V. (1967). *The classroom behavior setting: Its nature and relation to student behavior* (Final report). Washington D.C.: U.S. Office of Education, Bureau of Research (Eric Document Reproduction Service No. ED 015 515).

Hanushek, E.A. (1979. Conceptual and empirical issues in the estimation of educational production functions. *Journal of Human Resources, 14,* 351-388.

Harnischfeger, A. & D.E. Wiley (1976). The teaching-learning process in elementary schools: a synoptic view. *Curriculum Inquiry, 6,* 5-43.

Hoeven, A.A. van der & P. Jungbluth (1987). De bijdrage van schoolkenmerken aan schooleffectiviteit. In: Scheerens, J. & Stoel, W.G.R. (eds.) *Effectiviteit van onderwijsorganisaties.* Lisse: Swets & Zeitlinger.

Hoy, W.K. & Ferguson, J. (1985). A theoretical framework and exploration of organizational effectiveness of schools. *Educational Administration Quarterly, 21,* 117-134.

Kickert, W.J.M. (1979). *Organization of decision-making;* a systems-theoretical approach. Amsterdam: North-Holland Publishing Company.

Kounin, J. (1970). *Discipline and groupmanagement in classrooms.* New York: Holt, Rinehart & Winston.

Kulik, J.A. & C.L.C. Kulik (1988). *Meta-analysis in educational research.* Ann Arbor, MI: University of Michigan, Center for Research on Learning and Teaching.

Marwijk-Kooij - Von Baumhauer, L. (1984). *Scholen verschillen.* Groningen: Wolters-Noordhoff.

Meijnen, G.W. (1984). *Van zes tot twaalf. Een longitudinaal onderzoek naar de milieu- en schooleffecten van loopbaan in het lager onderwijs.* Harlingen: Flevodruk.

Miller, S.K., Cohen, S.R. & Sayre, K.A. (1985). Significant achievement gains using the effective schools model. *Educational Leadership, 43,* 38-43.

Mintzberg, H. (1979). *The structuring of organizations.* Englewood Cliffs: Prentice Hall.

Mortimore, P. et al. (1988). *School matters. The junior years.* Somerset: Open Books Publishing Ltd.

Murphy, J.F., M. Weil, P. Hallinger & A. Mitman (1982). Academic Press: translating high expectations into school policies and classroom practices. *Educational Leadership, 40* (3), 22-26.

Niskanen, W. (1971). *Bureaucracy and representative government,* Chicago; Aldine-Etherton.

Pfeffer, J. & G.R. Salancick (1978). *The external control of organizations.* New York: Harper & Row.

Pitner, N.J. (1988). The study of administrator effects and effectiveness. In: N.J. Boyan (ed.) *Handbook of Research on educational and effectiveness.* New York: Longman Inc.

Purkey, S.C. & M.S. Smith (1983). Effective schools: a review. *The Elementary School Journal, 83,* 427-452.

Ralph, J.H. & J. Fenessey (1983). Science or reform: some questions about the effective schools model. *Phi Delta Kappan,* 869-695.

Rutter, M. et al. (1979). *Fifteen thousand hours: secondary schools and their effects on children.* Cambridge, Mass.: Harvard University Press.

Rutter, M. (1983). School effects on pupil progress: research findings and policy implications. *Child Development, 54,* 1-29.

Scheerens, J. (1987). *Het evaluerend vermogen van onderwijsorganisaties.* Universiteit Twente, oratie.

Scheerens, J., Nanninga, H.C.R. & W.J. Pelgrum (1989). Generalizibility of instructional and school effectiveness indicators across nations. To be published in: Creemers, B.P.M. & Scheerens, J. (eds.) *Developments in school effectiveness research.* Special issue of the International Journal of Educational Research, vol. 13.

Schmuck, R.A. (1980). The schoolorganization. In: Mc.Millan, J.H. *The social psychology of school learning.* New York: Academic Press.

Schweitzer, J.H. (1984). *Characteristics of effective schools.* AERA-paper. Houston.

Squires, D.A., W.G. Hewitt & J.K. Segars (1983). *Effective schools and classrooms. A research based perspective.* Alexandria (Virginia), Association for Supervision and Curriculum Development.

Stoel, W.G.R. (1986). *Schoolkenmerken en het gedrag van leerlingen en docenten in het voortgezet onderwijs.* Groningen: RION.

Sweeney, J. (1982). Research synthesis on effective school leadership. *Educational Leadership, 39,* 346-352.

Teddlie, C., S. Stringfield & R. Wimpelberg (1987). *Contextual differences in effective schooling in Louisiana.* AERA-paper, Washington.

Tesser, C.J. (1986). *Sociale herkomst en schoolloopbaan in het voortgezet onderwijs.* Nijmegen: ITS.

Thompson, J.D. (1967). *Organizations in action.* New York: McGraw Hill.

Vermeulen, C.J. (1987). De effectiviteit van onderwijs bij zeventien Rotterdamse stimuleringsscholen. *Pedagogische Studiën, 64,* 49-58.

Walberg, H.J. (1984). Improving the productivity of American schools. *Educational Leadership, 41,* 19-27.

Wolf, J.C. van der (1984). *Schooluitval; een empirisch onderzoek naar de samenhang tussen schoolinterne factoren en schooluitval in het regulier onderwijs.* Lisse: Swets & Zeitlinger.

278

# SCHOOL
# IMPROVEMENT
# REPORTS

# THE FIRST THREE PHASES OF THE LOUISIANA SCHOOL EFFECTIVENESS STUDY

Sam Stringfield
Northwest Regional Educational Laboratory, Denver

and

Charles Teddlie
Louisiana State University, New Orleans

In the U.S.A., the 1980's have seen few rigorous, large-scale, school effectiveness studies. Many U.S. reviews (e.g. Purkey & Smith, 1983; Cuban, 1983; & Good & Brophy, 1986) regarded the field as possessing, at most, two large scale, reasonably high quality studies, (e.g., Brookover et al., 1979; and Rutter et al., 1979). The research base upon which the effective schools movement in the U.S. was built has been thin.

The Louisiana School Effectiveness Study (LSES) possessed the advantage of following the 1970's school effectiveness studies, and of occurring after the publication of many criticisms of that work. We were able to incorporate several suggestions made by critics, and to address concerns of our own.

This article is divided into five sections: notes on Louisiana and the organization of Louisiana's schools; a brief history of LSES; major findings of the study; models for the long-term development of effective and ineffective schools; and possible directions for future school effectiveness research.

## AN INTRODUCTORY NOTE REGARDING LOUISIANA AND LOUISIANA'S EDUCATION SYSTEM

Louisiana is located in the southern U.S.A. The Mississippi river empties into the gulf south of New Orleans, Louisiana's largest city. The state is rich in oil and natural gas, and the state's economy has risen and fallen with the price of oil.

Louisiana is not regarded as a leader in American education. Though considerable gains have been made in the last 20 years, the state ranks among the highest in the nation in adult illiteracy, student drop-out rate, and teen pregnancy. The state's college bound high school seniors score somewhat below the national average on the ACT, a national achievement test measuring academic readiness for college. Of Louisiana's approximately 4.5 million residents, roughly 950,000 are currently attending school in kindergarten through high school.

The public schools of Louisiana are governed by 67 local school boards. These locally elected boards exercise broad powers to appoint local superintendents, principals and staff, build buildings, choose curricula, and generally operate the districts' schools. As a practical matter, most schools operate in a condition of moderate autonomy. The degree of school autonomy varies from district to district, and principal to principal. This is a typical arrangement in the U.S.

# A BRIEF HISTORY OF LSES

The LSES was begun in response to a legislative mandate. The study was conceptualized as a long term examination of issues related to school level achievement among Louisiana's elementary school children. Three phases of the study have been completed.

The pilot study (LSES-I), testing instruments and methods, was conducted during the 1981-1982 school year (Teddlie, Falkowski & Falk, 1982.) For Phase II of LSES, a stratified random sample of 76 elementary schools were chosen from 12 districts, representing urban, suburban, and rural areas of northern, central and southern Louisiana. Phase II data were gathered during the winter and spring of 1983.

### LSES-II Data Sets Included:
*Student level achievement,* using a nationally standardized, norm-referenced achievement test. *A Student questionnaire of School Climate* was administered to the same third grade sample of over 5400 students. As was the case with the teacher and principal questionnaires, the student questionnaire involved a modification of the Brookover et al. (1979) instruments, together with measures of self concept and locus of control.

*The 250 third grade teachers* in the study completed *school climate, self concept* and *locus of control* questionnaires during the hours that the research team gathered student data.

The *76 principals* completed their parallel *questionnaires* at the same time, or, in rare cases, mailed in their responses.

*Secondary data* regarding students' parents' Socio Economic Status (SES) and additional school characteristics information were gathered during separate visits to school districts.

The data allowed for comparisons among highly effective, typical, and ineffective schools, and for large scale factor analytic and path analytic (e.g. Scott & Teddlie, 1987) statistical examinations of the data. (For a more complete description of research methods, and copies of the full questionnaires, see Teddlie et al., 1984).

The third phase of LSES was designed as a more detailed analysis of a smaller number of schools. It nested elements of a teacher effectiveness study within a school effectiveness design. A total of 16 schools, eight locally matched outlier pairs, were studied. The selection process involved examination of two consecutive years of state Basic Skills Test data on all third graders in 13 districts. The districts included the 12 in Phase II and one additional, large city system. Pairs were chosen through a seven step process (see Stringfield, Teddlie, & Suarez, 1985) which included schools' two year outlier status within districts (in rural areas, contiguous districts were analyzed together).

Data gathering included all of the instruments used in LSES-II, with the exception of the substitution of the research version of the *3-R's Test,* for a previous test. In addition, low inference classroom observational data were gathered using the Classroom Snapshot (CS) from the Stallings Observation System (Stallings & Kaskowitz, 1974.) High inference classroom data were gathered using a system developed for LSES-III. The categories were derived from an extensive review of research on teaching, and included the major teacher behavioral categories listed by Rosenshine (1983) among other variables. Additional high inference systems were developed for gathering school-wide on-site data.


# MAJOR FINDINGS FROM LSES-I,-II, AND -III

The purpose of this section is to briefly describe eight areas of conclusions drawn to date. More detailed discussions of the results of the studies can be found in the papers and articles in the reference list.


### Significant Between-student Variance at the Schoollevel
Several critics have argued that the amount of student level variance in achievement which is logically at the school level is trivial. In LSES, a nested analysis of variance (students nested within teachers within schools) was undertaken to determine the percentage of *school level* variance explained in third grade scores on a norm referenced achievement test. The analysis indicated that 75% of the variance was indeed between students within classes. An additional 12% was between teachers within schools, and the final 13% was between schools (Stringfield & Teddlie, 1987).

Thirteen percent of student level variance, which is statistically and educationally significant. At issue is not whether there is significant variance among schools, but can that variance be attributed to readily alterable variables. In the first three phases of LSES, the answer has been "yes."

### Generalizability of School Effectiveness Findings to Various Parts of the U.S.
No major school-effectiveness study had been conducted in the American South. That such a study was conducted in a stratified random sample of 76 schools in Louisiana, and that the results have several first-level similarities to Brookover et al.'s (1979) Michigan results, argues for the generalizability of the findings, carefully analyzed.

On the issue of international generalizability, the authors are less certain. We have read excellent school effectiveness and school studies from London (e.g. Rutter et al., 1979; Mortimore & Sammons, 1987) and the Netherlands (e.g. deCaluwe et al., 1987a, 1987b), and our impression is that our U.S. findings are largely harmonious with these.

### Stability of Outcome, Process, and Relational Measures
Ralph and Fennessey (1983), and Rowan, Bossert and Dwyer (1983) have argued that measured effects are not stable, and as such, any correlation between process measures and outcome measures may not be worthy of consideration. Three potential points of instability are implicit. They are: stability of outcome measures, stability of process measures, and the stability of the relationships between them. In LSES, data has been gathered relevant to each.

*A) Stability of aggregated outcome measures.* Rowan and Denk (1982) found that the percentage of schools which remained high outliers on the California Assessment Profile over three years was only slightly greater than chance. (A similar result was found by Brophy (1972) when looking at three years of teacher level data.)

Any school, however exemplary, is unlikely to score in the top few percentages on an outcome measure several years in a row. A more reasonable criterion might be several conservative years above (or below) the mean of schools in a given geographic area and within a specified economic span, including one or more years well above (or below) the mean. This was the criterion used in LSES-III, and it produced a clear set of outliers.

A second, reason for instability in achievement test scores in some studies may be the instability of testing practices. The conditions of testing in most U.S. schools fall below those considered necessary for optimal data gathering. Varying test administration conditions and procedures could be expected to produce instability in aggregated achievement test scores. The

LSES research team augmented locally gathered achievement data with highly controlled, experimenter administered testing.

*B. Stability of process measures.* The questionnaires used in LSES I, II and III were virtually identical. These questionnaires produced virtually identical school level factor pattern results at each study phase. Moreover, the first order principal, teacher and student factors generated in all phases, and especially in the 76 school Phase II, were very similar to the first order factors generated by Brookover et. al., (1979). Factor patterns which are stable across time within one study, and across locations and studies, would appear to meet reasonable criteria for stability.

*C. Stability of the relationships among processes and outcomes.* Finally, the test of stability of "school effects" should not be consistent aggregated scores across years, it should be scores which reflect school realities across years. If for two years a school is providing highly effective (or ineffective) instruction at one or more grades, but in year three experiences major disruptions, the proof of school effectiveness research variables would be predictable directional change in outcome measures.

In LSES-III we observed such predictable change in individual schools processes and outcomes (Stringfield & Teddlie, 1985). In studying matched outlier pairs, we observed four schools which had been negative outliers, and which were undergoing significant changes. As we gathered process data in those schools, fall and spring, we were able to correctly predict improvement in their test scores. The four schools ceased to be negative outliers. We found stable outcomes in stable contexts, variations in outcomes in predictable directions in unstable contexts. Such findings are available only to researchers melding psychometrics with in-school, in-classroom data gathering.

*The Role of "Readily Alterable" School Climate Variables*
Several researchers have argued that the between-school variance that exists is largely a function of variables beyond the control of schools. Brookover et al. (1979) found that many "school climate" variables were themselves correlated with SES. The extent of multicolinearity was such that 72.5% of between school achievement variance could be accounted for by "school climate" variables when climate variables were entered first into a stepwise multiple regression, and 4.1% when climate variables were entered after SES.

In LSES-II we loaded the SES and climate factors into a second-order factor analysis. Our first interest in this analysis was that several of the "School climate" variables were themselves rather highly correlated with SES. Most noteworthy of these were factors involving Teachers and Principals expectations for students' long term achievement.

Other second order factors loaded on non-SES, more alterable second-order factors. Most notable among these were S.O.F.-3 (largely Student perception of positive academic climate and Principals sense of school efficacy), S.O.F. -4 (family commitment to education and *student* sense of long term educational achievement), and S.O.F.-5 (absence of a negative school climate).

There are two implications of this finding. The first is that many concepts which appear similar on printed questionnaires and on first order factor analyses (e.g. principal, teacher, and student educational expectation factors) appear to be educationally separate. Data from LSES-II indicate that teachers' and principals' educational expectations for their students are highly correlated with SES. Students' educational expectations, by contrast, were not correlated with their SES. In LSES-II it was STUDENT sense of current and future academic accomplishment, and STUDENT sense of academic futility which added the greatest non-SES variance to the prediction equation.

Second, when the above five second order factors were entered into a prediction equation, both individually and as more or less easily alterable groups, the more readily alterable variables proved the better predictors of current level of achievement. In LSES, schools made a difference.

### Contextual Variables Leading to Effectiveness

Both Stallings and Kaskowitz (1974) and Brophy and Evertson (1976, 1978) found differing sets of teacher behaviors to be predictive of high achievement gain in middle versus lower SES contexts. School effectiveness researchers and practitioners have occasionally behaved as though there was one best prescription for effective schooling. LSES is the largest study in the U.S. examining characteristics of effectiveness in differing contexts.

A paper detailing finding from this phase of the LSES analyses is contained elsewhere in the current volume (Teddlie et al., 1989). To date our contextual analyses have focused on one obvious variable – SES. We believe that a host of additional contextual variables await researchers (ex. innercity-suburban-rural; public, private; principal, teaching staff; building architecture-instructional design).

### Connections between Teacher- and School-effectiveness Variables

Good and Brophy (1986) have noted the lack of connections between teacher-effectiveness and school-effectiveness research. Whatever the effects of schools, they are generated through teachers and curriculum. The teacher effectiveness research base is broader, and involves a greater variety of high quality correlational and *experimental* studies. To the extent that links between the two fields can be strongly made, the school effectiveness research base will be strengthened. In LSES-III we gathered extensive classroom observational data in 16 schools over a complete school year. Significantly more interactive instruction and higher percentages of student time on task, and more direct instruction were occurring in the "effective" schools (Teddlie, Stringfield, & Kirby, 1989).

## Leadership

Effective schools have instructionally focused leaders. This area was simple in that principal's quantitatively measured opinions of their school's effectiveness tended to predict students, residualized achievement. However, beyond gross measures, teasing out the differentiating variables required considerable qualitative analysis. Extended interviews were undertaken in 12 outlying cases, and additional differences were found only through careful qualitative analyses. Principals in *ineffective* schools tended to define their role in a limited, often passive, bureaucratic manner. Principals in highly *effective* schools appeared to be "cultural managers" who saw multiple goals for education and who saw the process of goal achievement as ambiguous and personalistic. They became involved in classroom processes, stayed close to children, and displayed a "bias for action" (Wimpelberg, 1986).

We visited more than one effective or improving school in which the actual instructional leader was not the principal, but a faculty member or informal leadership team. However, we are not aware of an effective school in which the principal did not at least facilitate the instructional functioning of the school.


## Internally Initiated School Improvement

Four of the negative outlier schools in LSES-III were undergoing self-initiated school improvement efforts during the study. These changes fell along two dimensions which we labeled "technical" and "programmatic" (Stringfield, Teddlie, Desselle & Suarez, 1986). Along the programmatic dimension lay efforts to alter the processes of the school. These fell along a continuum. At the most basic, they dealt with turning chaos into order. A midpoint was concerned with efforts to increase time available for instruction. At one school, and to a lesser extent at a second, a final point along this continuum was represented by efforts to make maximal, creative use of school time.

By "technical" improvement efforts we refer to schools which defined their need to change in terms of a single outcome measure, aggregated test scores. They focused their efforts on that measure exclusively. It is possible to raise test scores without changing a school's over all curricula or instruction. If, for example, a state-wide test is administered at the third grade and not the fifth, the strongest fifth grade teacher can be re-assigned to the third grade, and her fifth grade teaching duties can be assumed by the weakest third grade teacher. Such a change will not effect over-all school effectiveness, but it may well raise scores at the point of measurement. We observed such an occurrence.

Similarly, a variety of "test taking skills" can be taught. We observed teachers instructing students for hours in the filling in of circles and the choosing among options "a" through "d". This was time taken during regular lessons, and hence was taken away from potential teaching of academic content.

These findings were in contrast to most previous studies of school change (ex. Huberman and Miles, 1984) in several respects. Prior studies involved the use of externally developed programs. The four improving schools we observed used external programs only marginally or, more often, not at all. In LSES-III the improvement efforts were not imposed by the local districts, but were derived from an internal, often principal lead, drive to improve. The projects were atheoretical and research-free: they consisted largely of common sense, usually judiciously applied. Huberman and Miles found that change bearing innovations "lived or died" by the amount and quality of technical assistance received. The LSES improving schools neither sought nor received external assistance, their changes lived or died by dent of their own creativity, will and work. The changes were not elegant, yet they brought the school closer to the principal's and teachers' goals.

## THE PROCESS(ES) OF SCHOOL CHANGE

The first three phases of LSES have focused largely on the development of static models. LSES and a variety of other studies have taken long strides toward workable, contextual models of effective schools. While the models are incomplete, they are much advanced from 10 years ago. They nest students within classes within schools. They cross reference curricula, instruction and staff development activities. A literature is developing on the role of the central office and school board in setting an agenda and providing resources for schooling.

We are less confident regarding models for change. While we are impressed with the work of such excellent researchers of change as Berman and McLaughlin (1977), Fullan (1982), and Huberman and Miles (1984), we are concerned that virtually the entire study of change has taken place within the context of planned, often mandated programmatic shifts. We believe that the great majority of schools become more or less effective, independent of such programs.

These naturally occurring processes take years. De Caluwe, Marx and Petri (1987a, 1987b), working in the Netherlands, have proposed that ten years is not an unreasonable unit of time for discussing the meaningful institutionalization of school innovation. Americans are not accustomed to studies of such duration, however needed.

The LSES relationships with some schools span nearly six years. In the next section we reach a little beyond our quantifiable research, and try to describe how ordinary schools become more or less effective. We believe the processes of becoming more or less effective have some parallels, but that one is not the mirror image of the other. We believe that either process must be measured in units of several years.

### The Process of Becoming a Highly Effective School:

*Step 1)*
An "instructional leader" or leadership group, ideally though not necessarily including the principal, emerges or arrives. This person/group has a vision for what the school and its students could become. It involves higher levels of learning and a more generally "humanistic" set of processes than current realities would seem to justify. They are prepared to work very long hours for years to achieve their vision.

*Step 2)*
The school chooses new teachers and aides with great care. They tend to look for "spark" or "energy" and are often unconcerned with years of teaching experience or advanced degrees.

*Step 3)*
The instructional leader(s) conduct an accurate instructional audit of the school. This audit has an implicit hierarchy. That process involves a set of steps that must be followed in order, and resembles the following:

a. Is the school a safe place?
b. Is the school a healthy and orderly place?
c. Are the students achieving "the basics"?
   The focus is not on drudgery, but on achieving skills that will prepare children for the world of work and for love of life-long learning.
d. What is the current status of the text book series and supplemental readers (within and across grades)? The "teaching"and homework? Curriculum, and instruction? If, when thought of from the perspective of a perhaps slightly below average student, the lessons over a pattern of years don't follow logically (e.g. different teachers use different texts) then a move is begun to standardize a text series.
e. Is the school providing additional, enriching, stimulating activities for its students? Is the school involving the larger community in ways that are good for the students and for the community?

*Step 4)*
Effective principals become increasingly active in targeting career development for some, occasionally all staff. This targeting is largely based on their frequent in-class observations.

*Step 5)*
The level of principal awareness of research on teacher effectiveness varied in LSES from moderate to non-existent. But principals of effective schools exercised the common sense notion that hard work leads to success. Regardless of the words used to describe the desired state, all expected to see students on task when they visited classrooms.

Teachers who do not meet reasonable instructional standards were put on probation, provided assistance, then either exhibited improvement, transferred to another school/district, or were fired.

*Step 6)*
Most effective principals developed a minimum daily homework expectation.

*Step 7)*
Special programs were thoughtfully coordinated with the regular program. Staff used each other's practical specialties. Teachers were encouraged, sometimes required, to visit each other's classes.

Effective instructional leader(s) were not satisfied. They wanted more for their students. Growth almost for its own sake seemed to be part of the schools' goals.

### The Process of Becoming an Ineffective School:

Like effectiveness, ineffectiveness takes time.

*Step 1)*
The "ideal" principal for the development of an ineffective school, would not care about students or teachers. She became a principal in order to get out of the classroom. It was possible that this person already had been a principal at another school, the situation became sufficiently unappealing to the staff (or more likely, the parents), that the superintendent moved the principal to a different, probably smaller and probably lower-SES school.

*Step 2)*
The principal envisioned the job responsibilities as bureaucratic. The principal did not visit the classes, and judged teachers in terms of how little trouble emanated from their classrooms. They avoided activities which had the potential to "stir up trouble." Unfortunately, that precluded instructional leadership.

Step 3)
The principal accepted all prospective teachers were sent to them. When

290

interviewed, these principals reported having no voice in staff hiring. In LSES-II and -III, the greatest variance in principals' self-reported perceptions of control over hiring was not between districts but within. Two principals from a single district would often give significantly differing accounts of the degree of latitude the district allowed them in hiring. This was an excellent predictor of school effectiveness, especially in low-SES contexts. Principals at ineffective schools almost never fired or forced the transfer of one of their staff.

*Step 4)*
Given that other, especially effective, principals within the district were visiting classes, taking an active interest in curriculum and instruction, and trying to get ineffective teachers out of their schools; and given that it was easier to get a teacher to accept a voluntary transfer than to go through the uncertain process of firing a teacher, in all moderate to large districts, there was an annual floating of ineffective teachers from school to school. Bridges (1986) refers to this process as "the dance of the lemons." Highly effective principals did not accept their share of these less effective teachers, so that over time a disproportionate share of them came to work at the ineffective principal's schools. Ineffective teachers tended to like "teaching" for ineffective principals, because they were left alone in their room to do as they please.

*Step 5)*
Working with an increasingly ineffective staff proved discouraging to the more effective members of the professional staff who, over time, requested transfers or dropped out of education.

*Step 6)*
Over time, the school developed a reputation as an unpleasant place in which to work. Such a reputation could develop particularly rapidly if the building served an economically disadvantaged neighborhood. Competent teachers within the system then actively resisted transferring to the school.

*Step 7)*
The remaining staff developed an elaborate set of rationalizations for their behavior and for the school's performance. "Nobody could teach these kids." "People at the district office don't know anything about the real world of teaching here." All of which served to justify doing no meaningful instruction. The principal reinforced the above by writing "good" evaluations of all the teachers.

This process, particularly when occurring within a context of parents feeling alienated from the larger society is self-perpetrating. In all but highly effec-

291

tive school *districts*, the presence of such ineffective schools serves a valuable function. The central office staff are spared the effort and risks of dealing with incompetent teachers and principals, their unions, lawyers, and the courts.

Finally, the process of becoming and remaining ineffective is relatively "School Improvement Program" proof. In the absence of a strong, within school support system, any one-to-three year school improvement effort will eventually disappear, along with whatever benefits it may have temporarily brought.

# POSSIBLE DIRECTIONS FOR ADDITIONAL RESEARCH

There are four types of large scale studies needed today in the school effectiveness field. First, there is a need for additional correlational and causal modeling studies of the Brookover et al. and Teddlie et al. type. Considerable refinements in method, measurement, analysis, and results await sufficient funding.

The second need is for studies of self-directed school improvement efforts. It is our impression that this type effort is a) significantly different from, and b) much more common than externally developed school improvement packages.

The greatest need in school effectiveness research is for a several well controlled change studies. These studies should mix observations of students, teachers, and principals behaviors, with analyses of school rules, mores and cultures, staff development, curricula, other variables, and a variety of outcome measures.

Finally, there is a need for long term study of the relationship between school effectiveness and socioeconomic status. During any single year, the SES of a community remains a powerful predictor of aggregated student achievement. Yet there are indications that, over longer time spans, the ability of the schools to affect student achievement becomes a predictor of aggregated rise in the socioeconomic status of a neighborhood, city or state. In informal discussions of "school effectiveness" with city planners, geographers, real estate brokers, and school district testing department personnel, we have repeatedly been informed that the central bread winner for a middle class family determines the city and state in which the family will reside. However, these social observers consistently report that mothers choose specific houses and neighborhoods. It is the reputation of the schools, more than any other factor beyond cost, that determines the neighborhood of choice. In our increasingly mobile society, reputation is often a matter of test scores. Thus, aggregated test scores tend to create a self-fulfilling prophesy. When scores are high, the school, and hence the neighborhood, attracts affluent, well educated young couples. Studying this two way street would require a longitudinal melding of the skills of geographers and educators.

# REFERENCES

Berman, P. & McLaughlin, M. (1977). *Federal programs supporting educational change. Vol. 7. Factors affecting implementation and continuation.* Santa Monica, CA: Rand Corporation.

Bridges, E. (1986). *The Incompetent Teacher.* Philadelphia: Falmer.

Brookover, W., Beady, C., Flood, P., Schweitzer, J., & Wisenbaker, J. (1979). *Schools, social systems, and student achievement: Schools can make a difference.* New York: Praeger

Brophy, Jere E. (1973). Stability of teacher effectiveness. *American Educational Research Journal. 10,* 245-252.

Brophy, J., & Evertson, C. (1976). *Learning from Teaching: A Developmental perspective.* Boston: Alyson and Bacon.

Brophy, J., & Evertson, C. (1978). Context variables in teaching. *Educational Psychologist, 12,* 312-316.

Coleman, J., Campbell, E., Hobson, C., McPartland, J., Movd, A., Weinfield, F., & York, R. (1966). *Equality of educational opportunity.* Washington, D.C., U.S. Government Printing Office.

Cuban, L. (1983). Effective Schools: A friendly but cautionary vote. *Phi Delta Kappan, 65,* 695-696.

deCaluwe, L., Marx, E., & Petri, M. (1987a). *School Development: Models and Change.* Technical report. International School Improvement Project, Leuven, Belgium: ACCO.

deCaluwe, L., Marx, E., & Petri, M. (1987b). *Quality of Education: Summary of an advice to the Minister of Education in the Netherlands.* Zeist, Netherlands: Advisory Council for Secondary Education.

Fullan, M. (1982). *The Meaning of educational change.* New York: Teachers College Press.

Hallinger, P., & Murphy, J. (1986). The social context of effective schools. *American Journal of Education, 94,* 328-355.

Huberman, A., & Miles, M. (1984). *Innovation Up Close.* New York: Plenum.

Mortimore, P. & Sammons, P. (1987). New evidence on effective elementary schools. *Educational Leadership, 45,* (1), 4-8.

Purkey, S., & Smith, M. (1983). Effective Schools: A review. *Elementary School Journal, 83,* 427-452.

Ralph, J., & Fennessey, J. (1983). Science or reform: Some questions about the effective schools model. *Phi Delta Kappan, 64,* 689-694.

Rosenshine, B. (1983). Teaching functions in instructional programs. *Elementary School Journal, 83,* 335-351.

Rowan B., & Denk, C.E. (1982). *Modeling the academic performance of schools using longitudinal data: As analysis of school effectiveness measures and school and principal effects on school level achievement.* San Francisco: Far West Lab.

Rutter, M., Mauhan, B., Mortimore, P., Ouston, J., & Smith, A. (1979). *Fifteen Thousand Hours.* Cambridge, MA: Harvard.

Scott, C. & Teddlie, C. (1987.) *Students', Teachers', and Principals' Academic Expectations and Attributed Responsibility as Predictors of Student Achievement: A Causal Modeling Approach.* Paper presented at the American Educational Research Association, Washington, D.C.

Stallings, J. & Kaskowitz, D. (1974). *Follow Through Classroom Observation Evaluation 1972-1973.* (SRI Project URU-7370). Stanford, CA: Stanford Research Institute.

Stringfield, S., Teddlie, C., & Suarrez, S (1985). Classroom interaction in effective and ineffective schools: Preliminary results from Phase III of the Louisiana School Effectiveness Study. *Journal of Classroom Interaction, 20, 2,* 31-37.

Stringfield, S., & Teddlie, C. (1987). *School climate and socio-economic factors as predictors of student achievement in elementary schools.* Unpublished manuscript, University of New Orleans.

Stringfield, S., & Teddlie, C. (October, 1988). A time to summarize: Six years and three phases of the Louisiana School Effectiveness Study. *Educational Leadership, 46,* (1), 43-49.

Teddlie, C., Falkowski, C., Stringfield, S., Desselle, S., & Garvue, R. (1984). *The Louisiana School Effectiveness Study:* Phase II 1982-1984. Baton Rouge, LA: The Louisiana State Department of Education.

Teddlie, C., & Stringfield, S. (1985). A differential analysis of effectiveness in middle and lower Socioeconomic Status Schools. *Journal of Classroom Interaction, 20,* (2), 38-44.

Teddlie, C., Stringfield, S., & Desselle, S. (1985). Methods, history, selected findings and recommendations from the Louisiana School Effectiveness Study. *Journal of Classroom Interaction, 20,* (2), 22-30.

Teddlie, C., Stringfield, S., Wimpelberg, R., & Kirby, P. (1989). Contextual differences in models of effective schools. This volume, pp. 117-130.

Wimpelberg, R. (1986). *Bureaucratic and cultural images in the management of more and less effective schools.* Paper presented at the American Educational Research Association. San Francisco.

294

# EQUITY SCHOOLS AND EQUITY DISTRICTS

Janet Chrispeels and Sally Pollack
San Diego County Office of Education

## INTRODUCTION

In 1984, the San Diego County Office of Education initiated an effective schools process to help schools translate the effective schools research into practice. The process consisted of conducting needs assessments based on school effectiveness correlates, disaggregated test data analysis from the California Assessment Program, classroom time-on-task analysis, and archival data collection. Over one hundred schools scattered throughout the 43 school districts in the county have participated to varying degrees in the program. Most of these schools were found to be non-equity schools, i.e., did not have equitable achievement scores across all economic sub-groups of the school's population. As a result of the assessments, many of the schools have undertaken an improvement process to enhance student outcomes, especially student achievement as measured by standardized tests.

In a recent study on equity schools (Pollack, Chrispeels, & Watson 1987), the San Diego County Office of Education examined the differences found in ten elementary schools that participated in the effective schools process. Four of the schools achieved a significant measure of equity, three remained non-equity schools, and three had made some gains. The study revealed important organizational, instructional, and cultural differences between the equity and nonequity schools. Interviews with principals in the study revealed that many were supported in their improvement efforts by district office activities. Because of this input and recent research on the role of district support in school improvement, the district offices in the six districts represented by these ten schools were examined in order to describe what activities they were engaged in that supported or inhibited the achievement of equity. The purpose of this study is to report these activities.

To effect change and improve schools so they become effective for all students, several researchers have cited the importance of district and site leadership (Berman & McLaughlin, 1978; Leithwood & Montgomery, 1982; Leithwood & Fullan, 1986) and examined the district leadership roles in the improvement process (Bridges, 1983; Herriott & Muse, 1972; Cuban, 1984; Murphy, Hallinger & Peterson, 1986). The findings of Murphy, Hallinger, and Peterson (1986) indicated that patterns of district administrative control in effective districts differed from patterns found in other districts. They described the "pressure" or administrative control of principals in effective districts and found the controls to direct site level activity and administrative behavior. In their study they examined nine control functions: selection, socialization, supervision, evaluation, rewards and sanctions, goals, resource allocation, behavior control, and technological specifications. The first five they labeled "direct functions," the remaining four were labeled "indirect functions." Direct functions are designed to "influence the behavior and activities of principals." Indirect functions are "designed to constrain and form organizational structures, policies and practices that influence the principal by controlling work conditions, processes or task arrangements" (Murphy, Hallinger, & Peterson, 1986, p. 2). Both functions influence student outcomes because they have an effect on the environment (organization, instruction, and culture) in which students learn. One important finding of their study was that technological core issues were given more attention than had previously been assumed.

LaRocque and Coleman (1987) found that district approaches to implementing change differ in effective districts. They examined leadership and commitment to change in school districts and outlined approaches that encouraged and supported staff commitment to change efforts at the school site. They found these approaches applied "pressure" for change, but that only the developmental approach produced the long term growth in district effectiveness or student achievement. They described the district "developmental" approach as creating a commitment to change by setting precise expectations based on a common vision, paying attention through frequent discussion, careful monitoring of school activity, and providing continuing support through district and school-based inservice and on-site assistance.

Joyce, Hersh, and McKibbin (1983) emphasized the importance of shared decision-making in the institutionalizing of change, and that those being affected by the change must be actively involved in collaborative problem-solving and decision-making regarding the implementation of change. LaRocque and Coleman (1987) in their study of effective districts and Pollack, Chrispeels and Watson (1987) in their study of equity schools found that shared decision-making was a key to gaining a commitment to change and that pressure for change became more peer or self-imposed than authority imposed. All of the studies found that adaptation by the person responsible for change encouraged institutionalization of the change.

# THEORETICAL FRAMEWORK

Two research questions guided this study. First, how were administrative control functions used in districts to encourage and support staff commitment to change at the school site? Second, was there a parallel between practices used by districts and schools to effect organizational, instructional and climate changes in order for all students to achieve? The practices identified in the prior study on equity schools (Pollack, Chrispeels, & Watson, 1987) will be described and compared with the present study on equity districts.

For the purpose of this study, we used the following three categories as the framework to group effective school variables and direct and indirect control functions (Murphy, Hallinger & Peterson, 1986): organizational policies and practices, instructional policies and practices, and district climate/culture practices. These categories allowed for the integration of the findings from the earlier study of equity schools (Pollack, Chrispeels, & Watson, 1987), the "developmental" approach discussed by LaRocque and Coleman (1987), and the functions of control discussed by Murphy, Hallinger, and Peterson (1986). They provided the framework for examining and analyzing the data collected in this study

*1. Organizational policies and practices.* The following variables described the instructional leadership, policies and decision-making practices that guided the activities of the district office and the school site:
- The role of the superintendent, school board, district office management, and principal in leading the change effort
- Problem-solving mechanisms and shared decision-making
- The mission, goals and objectives of the district and individual schools, and their communication and distribution (indirect control function)
- Principal and staff inservice and socialization (direct control function)
- District and site budget allocations and use of resources to support school improvement (indirect control function)
- Selection, supervision and evaluation of principals (direct control function), and principal supervision and evaluation of school staff.

*2. Instructional policies and practices.* The following variables described the district and site's curriculum and instructional activities:
- Curriculum and instructional issues including curriculum development and alignment, and textbook adoption (indirect control function)
- Testing and use of test scores
- Support services for special needs

*3. Culture and climate practices.* The following variables described the culture of the district and school sites that supported school improvement.

297

- Acculturation of new principals and teachers
- Communication
- Reward and recognition policies (direct control function)
- High expectations

# METHODOLOGY

The methods used by this study included definition of equity, identification of the target schools and districts, instrumentation, and data analysis.

## Definition of Equity

Crucial to this and the previous study (Pollack, Chrispeels & Watson, 1987) was the definition of equity. The test data used in both studies were the test results from the California Assessment Program (CAP). The report of test results from the CAP presents both aggregated and disaggregated student achievement data and, therefore, greatly facilitates the application of an equity criteria. The equity schools and districts were determined by applying the following three criteria which are consonant with the concept of school effectiveness:

1. The overall performance of the students was above the comparison score band for the third or sixth grade on the California Assessment Program (CAP).
2. The students from the lowest socio-economic subgroup were outperforming similar students in the state in two or more subject areas.
3. The number of students scoring in the bottom quartile had decreased from the previous year in two or more subject areas.

## Sample Selection

The six districts selected for study contained the ten equity and non-equity schools identified in the previous study on equity schools (Pollack, Chrispeels & Watson, 1987) and represented a broad cross-section of the 43 school districts in the county. In applying the equity criteria, four districts met the equity criteria completely, and the other two districts met criteria two and three even though their scores overall were not above the comparison band.

## Instrumentation

An interview schedule was developed to assess district administrators' perceptions of their efforts to encourage and support change. A 57-item questionnaire was sent to all principals in the six districts and was given to each district administrator to complete after the interview. A survey (the San Diego County Office of Education's Effective Schools Questionnaire) and an interview had been administered to school staff in the equity schools study.

*Data Analysis*
Data from each of the principal and district administrator interviews were coded and summarized according to the major themes of the interview. Items from the questionnaire were grouped according to the three categories outlined in the section on Theoretical Framework: organizational, instructional, and culture/climate policies and practices, and the administrative control functions pertaining to each category. This data base allowed for triangulation of responses and complemented the work of Murphy, Hallinger and Peterson by addressing the need for corroborative data from the school site on district practices.

# RESULTS

## *Organizational Policies and Practices*
Organizational policies and practices described the instructional leadership, policies, and decision-making practices that guided the activities of the district and school site in the change process. The practices included direct administrative control functions of collaborative problem-solving and decision making, staff development, and selection, supervision and evaluation of principals and the indirect control functions of goal setting and resource allocation. Clear distinctions were found between equity schools and districts and nonequity schools and districts in the following organizational policies and practices.

## *Instructional Leadership*
The teacher responses in the equity schools study indicated that principals in equity schools exhibited instructional leadership by being available, accessible and highly visible; by coordinating instructional programs; by observing classrooms and giving feedback, and by making instructional issues the focus of staff meetings. Schools in which the principals did not fully engage in these practices, did not improve.

Similar patterns of instructional leadership were demonstrated by the superintendent and other district administrators in the equity districts. In the four equity districts the superintendents were perceived as extremely involved in goal setting, regularly visiting the schools, monitoring the improvement process, directing curriculum alignment, addressing curriculum issues (the technological core in Murphy, Hallinger & Peterson's terms) and gaining school board support for the improvement efforts.

## *Collaborative Problem Solving and Decision Making*
Schools that moved from nonequity to equity established curriculum committees and created other structures that facilitated collaboration and shared decision-making. In the interviews, the district administrators confirmed the

299

importance of collaborative decision making in achieving school improvement at the school site. Collaborative problem-solving and decision-making, however, was not a practice that distinguished between equity and nonequity districts.

## School and District Mission and Goals

Equity schools used test data and survey results to identify their instructional goals and objectives. In the equity schools both interview and survey data indicated a greater consistency and agreement regarding the schools' instructional mission .

At the district level, all six districts had a mission statement and all principals were aware of the districts' missions. The principals felt that the missions were aligned with the goals and objectives of the district, and that they had a moderate to significant impact on activities at the school site.

## Staff Development for Teachers and Principals

In equity schools, test scores were used to plan staff development and to allocate resources to address identified academic needs. Staff development made a difference when it was based on this needs assessment and was focused and not fragmented, as it often was in nonequity schools. Staff development of teachers was perceived by principals and district office personnel in all six districts as a major function of the district office and as an important reason for the effectiveness of certain schools.

At the district level, all six districts recognized the importance of ongoing staff development for both teachers and principals and used it as an important direct control function to drive the improvement process. The primary difference between equity and non-equity districts was the length of time a district level staff development program had been in place.

## Resource Allocation

All principals were constrained in the amount of discretionary funds and resource personnel that they had; however, in the equity schools, the resources were targeted more effectively to address identified needs. At the district level, the indirect control of resource allocation cited by Murphy et al.(1986) was consistent with the findings of this study. Resource allocation had an indirect but significant impact on school activities and on principal and district office perceptions of control of district goals and staff development activities in both equity and nonequity districts.

## Selection, Supervision and Evaluation of Principals

There was no clear pattern in the districts of selecting principals. One equity district hired exclusively from the outside; another hired primarily internally. This lack of a consistent pattern was similar to the findings of Murphy, Hallinger and Peterson (1986). The superintendents felt they had clear selec-

300

tion criteria that were tied to district goals and, in general, other administrative staff in the districts shared this perception. In principal selection, all of the districts looked for instructional and curriculum strengths, and the ability to give a model lesson and provide feedback. This focus on instructional skill and the technical core and the thoroughness of the selection process supported the findings of Murphy, Hallinger and Peterson (1986).

Supervision of principals came in the form of site visits. Superintendents in the six districts in this study reported that they visited schools frequently and that the visits had an impact on instruction and supervision of principals. However, principals in five of the districts were divided in their perception of the number of visits by the superintendent and other district office staff and on the impact of the visits.

The significant role that principals played in the improvement process was reflected in the importance that superintendents and other district staff placed on the evaluation of principals. Ninety-five percent of the principals responding to the questionnaire knew what the evaluation criteria were and the overwhelming majority stated that the criteria were consistently applied and had some impact. In the equity districts, achievement of the district goals was the focus of a principal's performance evaluation, and implementation of district and site goals was monitored on an ongoing basis

### Instructional Policies and Practices
Instructional policies and practices included curriculum and instructional issues, such as curriculum development and alignment, testing and use of test scores, and support services for special need students. In Murphy, Hallinger, and Peterson's study (1986) curriculum and instructional issues were designated "technological core" issues and were considered indirect administrative control functions.

### Curriculum and Instructional Issues
The state curriculum frameworks, testing and textbook adoption impact every area of instructional policy and practice and provide an impetus for curriculum change at both district and site levels. Murphy et al. (1986) also had studied California schools and had noted that the procedures for textbook selection exerted indirect administrative control. Three of the equity districts in the study had developed an ongoing program of curriculum development and alignment: one of the districts for the past ten years and the other two for the past three years. The one equity district with the longest involvement in curriculum development and alignment had critical objectives in place in all curriculum areas and had a process for continually revising them to reflect the state's higher standards and expectancies. The remaining three districts only recently had initiated processes of curriculum development and alignment that matched the state's guidelines.

301

## Testing and Use of Test Scores

The primary difference between equity and nonequity schools in the area of instructional change was the use of test scores to identify areas of need and to specify objectives in those need areas. Non-equity schools either did not use test scores to modify and focus curriculum and instruction or they did not use them consistently or the staff was not sure how they were used. Nonequity schools also tended to be more disapproving of the use of test scores.

In three of the equity districts with an ongoing process for developing curriculum and aligning curriculum to the testing program, tests were used as a basis for modifying the instructional program. In districts without an ongoing process of curriculum development and alignment, test score results were only occasionally used to modify instruction. District office personnel in all districts noted that use of test scores in the district often depended on the principal's emphasis in this area.

## Support Services for Special Needs

In both equity and nonequity schools the needs of the low-achiever were addressed. Many pull-out programs and resource people assisted these students. However, in the equity schools, there was greater emphasis on changes in classroom strategies for the low-achieving students, particularly in the use of manipulatives, hands-on and interactive strategies (e.g., cooperative learning). Nonequity schools, on the other hand, tended to rely more on resource people to assist low achieving students and rarely made schoolwide changes in classroom instructional practices.

In all districts surveyed, principals cited policies that existed to promote assistance for students who did not meet district academic and behavioral objectives. The interviews revealed that administrators in all six districts were developing and searching for strategies that would be effective with students with special needs. Administrators in the four equity districts specifically mentioned that the district was moving away from pull-out programs to assist students with special needs and towards strategies and programs within the regular classroom. This practice paralleled the approach found in the equity schools. The four equity districts had also developed school site teams that identified and provided classroom and other assistance to high risk students.

## Culture and Climate

Literature on effective companies is replete with examples of the importance of culture (Deal & Kennedy, 1985; Peters & Waterman, 1985). LaRocque and Coleman (1987) in their study found that the more effective districts had a culture that exhibited a nurturing and developmental approach toward schools. In this paper, several culture and climate issues were examined: the acculturation of new teachers and principals, communication and relations between school and district office personnel, rewards and recognition for students, teachers and principals, and high expectations.

*Acculturation*

Acculturation of new principals and teachers was an important issue for two reasons. First, many schools, especially in Southern California, are hiring significant numbers of new teachers to meet growing student enrollments and to replace retiring staff members. Second, if a district or school is attempting to bring about change, it is important that new employees are quickly oriented to the change process and the goals of the district and school. Interviews and questionnaire answers revealed that districts were aware of the need, but not all districts had a systematic process of orientation.

In the equity schools, communication and acculturation for new teachers was primarily accomplished through the efforts of many staff members. There was often a sense of "family" in the equity schools. In both equity and nonequity schools the principal played a part in acculturation of new staff, but in nonequity schools, the responsibility for acculturation seemed to be more for "others" to do, e.g., principal, resource people, formal orientations.

At the district level, there was no clear pattern differentiating equity and non-equity districts regarding the acculturation of new principals. All districts held regular principals' meetings that served to inform both new and established principals of district policies.

*Communication*

In the equity schools an identifiable process of solving problems and communication existed, usually involving frequent grade-level or team meetings. In equity schools, staff meetings more frequently focused on instructional concerns rather than on operational issues. Most equity schools had curriculum committees in which every member of the staff participated and felt important or honored to be a part of this curriculum improvement process. Ad hoc committees were also formed to address particular concerns like discipline policy. In the nonequity schools there was a narrow communication system in which not all staff members were informed or participated in decision-making. There were far fewer committees, and they met less frequently.

Communication and problem-solving processes between principals and district office staff were not significant in distinguishing between the equity and non-equity districts. However, it is important to note, at the time of this study, the two non-equity districts were involved in labor disputes with their teachers union indicating the lack of a good problem-solving system with their teachers.

## Rewards and Recognition

A system of rewards was one of the direct control functions examined by Murphy, Hallinger and Peterson (1986) in their study of effective districts. Schoolwide rewards for students' academic growth and progress and recognition of teachers for their exemplary teaching practices were features of equity schools found by Pollack, Chrispeels, and Watson (1987).

In both the equity and nonequity schools there were recognition and rewards for teachers and students. In equity schools, however, there was an emphasis on both schoolwide and classroom recognition. In the nonequity schools recognition occurred primarily at the classroom level. In the nonequity schools, principals tended to reward teachers for extra efforts, such as helping with a school event; whereas principals in the equity schools more frequently recognized teachers for exceptional instructional practices as well as extra efforts.

At the district level, recognition of teachers or principals did not prove to be a distinguishing characteristic. All six districts in this study used the mentor teacher program as one way of recognizing the district's outstanding teachers. In terms of their own recognition and rewards, a majority of the principals responded that they received only limited recognition. The limited amount of recognition and rewards for principals and its importance as a control function was similar to the findings of Murphy, Hallinger and Peterson (1986).


## High Expectations

Schools that had moved from nonequity to equity status made dramatic, postive changes in their expectations for student achievement. The staff at these schools made a concerted effort to raise expectations and did so either through involvement in special training programs, implementation of higher curriculum standards, improved classroom practices for low achievers, or increased efforts to recognize students for academic and behavioral accomplishments.The equity districts recognized that focusing on the students in greatest need was crucial to becoming an effective district.

A key variable that distinguished an equity from a non-equity school was whether or not students from all economic or ethnic groups were represented in gifted and talented programs. Three of the four equity districts reported there was moderate representation of all groups in these programs.

Another dimension of high expectations was the number of students who were expected to achieve the district's set of critical objectives. Three of the four equity district superintendents consistently expressed in the interviews high expectations for achievement, as did administrators in one of the improving districts. The superintendent of one of the equity districts said the key is "to believe all kids can learn and focus on them."

# SUMMARY AND CONCLUSIONS

The following summary addresses the research questions of administrative control functions at the district level and the parallel practices used by equity schools and districts.

## 1. The Extent of Control and Centrality of the Superintendent

All of the six districts exerted control of principal behavior and site level activity. Selection, supervision and evaluation of principals and socialization of principals through inservice and training were direct control functions that guided principals in school improvement efforts. Indirectly the districts exerted control or influence on the direction of school improvement through goal setting, resource allocation, curriculum and instructional development, and test data analysis.

The equity districts in this study supported LaRocque and Coleman's (1987) description of a developmental approach to change, in that 1) the district created a commitment to change by setting precise expectations based on a common vision, 2) the district paid attention to the implementation of change through frequent discussion and monitoring, and 3) the district provided continuing support through staff development and on site assistance. The area of "frequent discussion" was more evident in the districts that had been involved in curriculum development and training for a greater period of time. The "frequent discussion" had produced a greater unanimity of vision, commonality of effective implementation strategies, and validation of success.

## 2. Focus of Control

Similar to the findings of Murphy et al. (1986) once the district's goals were determined, the focus of control seemed to be on the technological core. Part of the explanation for this focus was that the State Department of Education is also paying attention to these issues. The state's actions, especially in the area of developing curriculum frameworks, textbook adoptions, and testing, are strongly influencing how districts focus their time and energy.

## 3. Variety of Control Functions

While we also found a variety of both indirect and direct control functions in use, we began to see some control functions emerging as more significant than others. Setting clear goals and direction, allocating resources, selecting good principals and providing them with training and support, focusing on instruction and curriculum, and providing staff development seemed to be the most significant control functions. Rewards, on-site monitoring or supervision through site visits, and behavior control appeared to be less significant in driving the improvement process at the school site. Additional research needs to be done to see whether or not this emerging hierarchy of control functions can be substantiated.

## 4. Pervasiveness and Interlocking Control Functions

This study substantiated the findings of Murphy, Hallinger and Peterson (1986) that control functions were pervasive, affecting "input, throughput, and output phases of school operations" (p. 33). The goals (input) set by the district were driving much of the work of the principals. Principal evaluations (output) were tied to the accomplishment of district goals. The formation of these goals in most cases was shaped in part by student outcomes (output), thus closely linking input and output. However, most of the district administrators' attention was focused on the throughput, i.e. the curriculum and instructional issues, staff development, supervision of principals, and test data analysis. It was clear that the throughput phase is seen as the vehicle for reaching the goals and thus achieving the desired outputs.

An important finding from this study was that there were equity schools in each of the six districts, but in no district did all schools meet the equity criteria. However, in the schools that had achieved equity, their practices and polices paralleled those found in the equity districts. Parallel practices were found in the areas of leadership, organization and instruction, and to a lesser degree in culture and climate.

Parallel leadership practices included the following:
- Setting expectations based on a common vision
- Articulating goals and objectives
- Being proactive and highly visible
- Focusing on curriculum and instruction
- Modeling and monitoring change
- Providing support through staff development and coaching

The following parallel organizational policies and practices were found in the equity schools and equity districts:
- Academic focus
- Goals and objectives shaped organizational activities
- Instructional leadership
- Shared curriculum decision making
- Staff development

Common instructional policies and practices were the following:
- Focus on curriculum and instructional improvement
- Testing and use of test results
- Support services for students with special needs

In the area of culture and climate, few parallel practices were identified. The only characteristic that the equity schools and equity districts shared was high expectations for student achievement. In the equity schools, communication, rewards and recognition, acculturation of new teachers, and a climate of collegiality and collaboration proved to be essential. These aspects of culture did not emerge as significant at the district level.

These two studies of equity schools and equity districts illustrated the complexity of the improvement process and the multiplicity of players from the classroom teachers to the state department of education. The studies emphasized the synergistic nature of the improvement process and the dependency of each level of schooling on each other to reach improvement goals. The state department provided the focus through curriculum frameworks, textbooks and testing. The district provided direction and support. However, it is the efforts of the individual school in operationalizing the goals and objectives through site planning, collaboration and implementation of these objectives that enabled the school to become effective for all students.

# REFERENCES

Berman, P., & McLaughlin, M. W. (1978). *Federal programs supporting educational change, Vol. III, Implementing and sustaining innovation*. Santa Monica, CA: Rand Corporation.

Bridges, E. (1983). Research on school administrators: The state of the art, 1967-1980. *Educational Administration Quarterly, 18,* 12-33.

Cuban, L. (1984). Transforming the frog into a prince: Effective schools research, policy, and practice at the district level. *Harvard Educational Review, 54,* 129-151.

Deal, T. E., & Kennedy, A. A. (1982). *Corporate cultures*. Reading, MA: Addison-Wesley.

Herriot, R. D., & Muse, D. N. (1972). Methodological issues in the school study of school effects. In F. N. Kerlinger (Ed.), *Review of Research in Education*. Ithaca, IL: F. E. Peacock.

Joyce, B. R., Hersh, R. H., & McKibbon, M. (1983). *The structure of school improvement*. New York: Longman.

La Rocque, R., & Coleman, P. (1987). *Leadership and commitment to change in school districts*. AERA-paper. Washington, D.C.

Leithwood, K., & Fuller, M. (1984). Fostering long-term growth in school system effectiveness. *Canadian Administrator, 24,* 6-13.

Leithwood, K., & Montgomery, D. (1982). The role of the elementary school principal in program improvement. *Review of Educational Research, 52* (82), 309-334.

Murphy, J., Hallinger, P., & Peterson, K. (1986). The administrative control of principals in effective school districts: The supervision and evaluation functions. *Urban Review, 18* (3), 149-175.

Peters, T. J., & Waterman, R. H. Jr. (1982). *In search of excellence*. New York: Harper & Row.

Pollack, S., Chrispeels, J., & Watson, D. (1987). *A description of factors and implementation strategies used by schools in becoming effective for all students*. AERA-paper. Washington, D. C.

# PUTTING EFFECTIVE SCHOOLS RESEARCH TO WORK: THE PROCESS OF CHANGE AND THE ROLE OF THE PRINCIPAL

Jerry D. Bamburg and Richard L. Andrews
University of Washington, Seattle

The research on effective schools (Edmonds, 1979; Brookover, 1981; Brookover et al., 1979; Andrews & Bamburg, 1988; Andrews, Soder, & Jacoby, 1986) has identified a set of characteristics, the presence of which is related to academic achievement of students. This research suggests that the strong leadership of the principal is the greatest prediction of student achievement, and strongly influences the likelihood of change (Andrews, Soder, & Jacoby, 19867; Andrews & Soder, 1987). The literature on change, however, indicates that most principals do not play instructional leadership roles in their schools (Fullan & Pomfret, 1977; Fullan, 1982; Leithwood & Montgomery, 1981; Fullan, 1988; Bamburg & Andrews, 1988). The reality is that many principals have difficulty initiating, implementing, and institutionalizing the change process in their schools. Many of them fail to understand that the change process itself is an innovation, and that to manage it successfully, the principal must understand the complexity of the change process—something for which the principal has little preparation.

In *The Meaning of Educational Change* Fullan (1982, p. 4) characterizes the difficulty of improving education as one of confusing "change" and "progress." He states, "One of the most fundamental problems in education today is that people do not have a clear, coherent sense of *meaning* about what educational change is for, what it is, and how it proceeds." "It is necessary to contend with both the *what* of change and the *how* of change. Meaning must be accomplished in relation to both these aspects." Sirotnik (1987), extends Fullan's argument and suggests that before it is possible to determine the what and how of change, a school must engage in a process of critical inquiry that is framed by the following questions:

- What are we doing?
- How did it come to be that way?
- Whose interests are (and are not) being served by the way things are?
- What information and knowledge do we have (or need to get) that bear upon the issue?
- Is this the way we want things to be?
- What are we going to do about all this?

Much has been written about the role of the principal as a change agent (Brookover et al., 1979; Berman & McLaughlin, 1978; Leithwood et al., 1978; Downey et al., 1975; Fullan, 1982, 1988); however, confusion exists about what they should do. Despite the fact that the principal views his or her role as implying leadership, when resistance to recommendations or ideas for change are encountered, principals often respond in one of two ways—they "assert authority or withdraw from the fray" (Sarason, 1982, p. 160).

Thus, part of the problem has been the lack of a clear definition of the meaning of instructional leadership. The more promising of the work on the principal as instructional leader has used the perceptions of teachers. The perception of teachers of the principal's instructional leadership activity and behavior (Andrews, Soder, & Jacoby, 1986; Andrews & Soder, 1987; Smith & Andrews, in press; Andrews & Bamburg, 1988) is both a strong predictor of incremental growth in student achievement and teachers' perceptions of the quality of their workplace. This work, based on three years of study of 100 schools and the responses of 5,000 teachers, has identified four components that contribute to staff perceptions of the principal as an instructional leader (Andrews, Soder, & Jacoby, 1986). They are: (1) resource provider, (2) instructional resource, (3) communicator, and (4) visible presence. These components serve as a basis for clarifying the kinds of activities that principals should engage in as they seek to initiate, implement, and institutionalize changes.

# DATA SOURCES

This study was initiated during the spring of 1986 in a rural school district of 1800 students (K-12) in the state of Washington. The sample consisted of four schools that have been given fictitious names. We have chosen to call them Wee Care Elementary School (K-2), Round House Intermediate Elementary School (3-5), Endeavor Middle School (6-8), and Stampede High School (9-12). The district's student population was culturally diverse (20% Native American, 5% Hispanic, 75% White) and approximately 25 percent of the students qualified for the federal free and reduced-price lunch program. Each school's principal remained the same during the study, and the staff of each school changed very little during the study.

310

To obtain an understanding of the change effort in each of these schools, multiple data sources were utilized. Quantitative data were gathered from administration of a staff assessment questionnaire (SAQ) developed collaboratively by the public schools and project reseachers (see Andrews & Soder, 1985a, 1985b; Andrews, Soder, & Houston, 1985). This questionnaire assesses staff perceptions on nine effective school characteristics (strong leadership, staff dedication, high expectations for student achievement, frequent monitoring of student progress, early identification of students' learning needs, positive learning climate, curriculum continuity, multicultural education, and sex equity. Individual characteristic subscale test-retest reliability estimates over a period of one year range from .65 to .91. The validity of the measures have been estimated using regression analysis to predict incremental growth in academic achievement (p < .001) (Andrews, Soder, Jacoby, 1986). This questionnaire was administered to the staff of each school during the spring of 1986 and 1988.

An analysis of each principal on the Strong Leadership characteristic was conducted utilizing staff perceptions of the principal as a (1) resource provider, (2) instructional resource, (3) communicator and (4) visible presence (see Table 1). Scores for each principal were determined by combining the percentage of staff members who Strongly Agree and Agree on each item for each year of data collection (1986 and 1988), and comparing the scores.

Qualitative data were collected using a variety of exhibits provided by the school district during a series of site visits conducted over six months, during which the principal and selected staff members in each school were interviewed, using an open-ended interview format.

## RESULTS

The four schools began with four quite different profiles and ended, after three years, with quite divergent profiles. Wee Care Elementary started high and remained consistent over the measurement period. Round House Elementary started the lowest of the four schools, but made progress in a positive direction in rather large increments. On the other hand, Endeavor Middle School started nearly as high as Wee Care Elementary, but declined during the study. Stampede High School's profile was similar to Round House Elementary. It made steady progress in a positive direction on most characteristics.

There was little change in the overall rating of the principal at Wee Care on instructional leadership over the duration of the study. However, there were some shifts in staff perception on individual items. These shifts were usually in a negative direction and occurred in the activities involved in being an important resource (-17 points), giving frequent feedback (-18 points) and making frequent classroom observations (-37 points). Round

House Elementary showed growth in a positive direction. In the judgment of teachers, the amount of improvement was relatively universal across all categories, with the exception of visibility in classrooms, where there was little growth. The magnitude of change in Endeavor Middle School was similar to Round House Elementary, only in the opposite direction. Further, the change was negative on all items. Stampede High School started low and made progress in a positive direction. Inspection of individual items shows a fairly consistent change in a positive direction.

# DISCUSSION

When considering the process of change it is useful to think of it as composed of three stages—initiation, implementation, and institutionalization (Giaquinta, 1973; Berman & McLaughlin, 1976; Herriott & Gross, 1979). The dimensions of instructional leadership (resource provider, instructional resource, communicator, and visible presence) utilized in this study provide a framework for considering the role of the principal. By integrating these two paradigms one can analyze the results of this study and explore the relationship between the change process and the role of the principal.

Table 1: Strong Principal Characteristics.

*Resource Provider*
1.1 My principal promotes staff development activities for the faculty.
1.2 My principal is knowledgeable about instructional resources.
1.3 My principal mobilizes support to help achieve academic goals.
1.4 My principal is an important instructional resource in our school.

*Instructional Resource*
2.1 My principal encourages the use of different instructional strategies.
2.2 Teachers in my school turn to the principal with instructional concerns or problems.
2.3 My principal's evaluation of my performance helps me to improve my teaching.
2.4 My principal assists faculty in interpreting test results.

*Communicator*
3.1 Discussions with my principal result in improved instructional practice.
3.2 My principal leads formal discussions concerning instruction and student achievement.
3.3 My principal uses clearly communicated criteria for evaluating my performance.
3.4 My principal provides a clear vision of what our school is about.
3.5 My principal communicates clearly to me regarding instructional matters.
3.6 My principal provides frequent feedback regarding my classroom performance.

*Visible Presence*
4.1 My principal makes frequent classroom visitations.
4.2 My principal is accessible to discuss matters dealing with instruction.
4.3 My principal is a "visible presence" in our building to both staff and students.
4.4 My principal is an active participant in staff development.

# INITIATION

When the efforts of the principal to initiate change are considered, utilizing the dimensions of instructional leadership, it appears that a principal must be able to promote effective communication between the principal and the staff in order to effectively initiate the change process.

## Wee Care

The principal of Wee Care Elementary was perceived in 1986 as being an effective communicator and, the percentage of staff members who continued to Strongly Agree/Agree in 1988 changed very little. This is significant because the school was destroyed by fire in December 1987 and classes were held in a variety of sites during the ramainder of the year.

## Round House

The communication scores for Round House were very low in 1986 and had moved strongly upward by 1988. The change in the staff's perceptions of the principal appears driven by his increased recogntion of the need to communicate effectively in order to initiate change successfully. All items showed positive growth, and five items show improvements that ranged from +19 percent to +48 percent. The improvement in staff perceptions of this principal's ability to effectively communicate with his staff was substantial.

## Endeavor

The staff's perception of the principal as an effective communicator declined substantially from 1986 to 1988. The directionality on every item of the communicator subscale was negative. The smallest decline was -19 percent and the largest -47 percent. Interviews with the staff at Endeavor indicate that staff members' trust of the principal also declined significantly.

## Stampede

Overall staff members' perceptions of the principal as a Strong Leader at Stampede gradually improved between 1986 and 1988, and their perceptions of his ability to communicate effectively also improved substantially. Every item changed in a positive direction. Comments recorded during interviews in 1988 confirmed that the principal was perceived as much more effective than he was in 1986.

The results on the communication component parallel each school's success in initiating the change process as measured by interviews and archival records. The ability of the principal to create a sense of openness and trust through effective communication were important components of their ability to initiate a change process successfully.

# IMPLEMENTATION

The relationship between implementation and the subscales of communicator, visible presence, resource provider, and instructional resource are more complicated. That complexity is due to (1) the interaction between the staff and the principal, and (2) conditions that existed within each individual school at the time that the change process was initiated. The results appear to support the contention that the successful implementation of change is greatly dependent upon the principal's ability to secure the necessary resources to implement change (i.e., resource provider) and the ability to lead the way (i.e., visible presence).

### Wee Care
Because of the fire that destroyed Wee Care, the principal was unable to be a visible presence in 1988 to the same degree that she had been previously. The decline in the staff's perception of the principal as a visible presence reflects this, and was the largest of any of the four components. The decline in the staff's perception of the principal as a resource provider is not large across all four items that compose that scale.

Interview comments about Wee Care's success in implementing their school improvement plan indicate that the fire's negative impact on the principal's ability to be the visible presence was substantial.

### Round House
At Round House, staff perceptions of the principal as a resource provider and visible presence indicate that his greatest area of improvement was being a resource provider. For the four items that make up that subscale, the percentage of the staff that marked Strongly Agree/Agree increased +28 percent, +40 percent, +50 percent, and +43 percent, respectively.

The amount of change on the items that make up the visible presence subscale were inconsistent. While all items show an increase the percentage of staff who marked Strongly Agree/Agree fluctuated a great deal, suggesting that he was more effective at some things than others. Thus, staff members' perceptions of the principal's ability to secure the resources needed to implement their school improvement plan were exceptionally high. Their perceptions of him as a visible presence were less so.

### Endeavor
At Endeavor Middle School, the decline in staff members' perceptions of the principal as a resource provider and visible presence were powerful indicators of their discontent. On individual items that compose the subscale of resource provider, the percentage of staff members that marked Strongly Agree/Agree declined between -12 and -34 percent between 1986 and 1988.

314

Even more sizable were the declines that occurred on visible presence, where the percentage of staff members who marked Strongly Agree/Agree declined -19 percent, -22 percent, -25 percent, and -41 percent, respectively. These results were confirmed by the information collected in interviews and provide strong evidence why Endeavor has been unable to successfully implement a school improvement plan.

## *Stampede*

As a resource provider, the principal of Stampede was not perceived by the staff as having improved very much between 1986 and 1988. A positive change was registered for each item on the resource provider scale, but none of the changes were remarkable for their size.

The changes recorded on the dimension of visible presence are larger than those for resource provider. The staff's view of the principal at Stampede High between 1986 and 1988 improved from +12 percent to an increase of +23 percent, depending upon the item. These results correspond to that obtained from interviews with the staff. Staff members indicated that the principal has made slow, steady progress during the past two years in improving his skills as an instructional leader in these areas and that Stampede's success in implementing a school improvement plan has paralleled that progress.

# INSTITUTIONALIZATION

If increases in student academic achievement can be taken as a surrogate measure reflecting the successful institutionalization of change, then the schools in this study have not institutionalized change and are not instructionally effective. This finding is also consistent with the staff's perception in each school of the principal as an instructional resource.

## *Wee Care*

At Wee Care, the scores for the principal as an instructional resource show a slight decline for three of four items between 1986 and 1988.

## *Round House*

At Round House the change in staff perceptions of the principal as an instructional resource are much more positive than at Wee Care, but even with the increases, the percentage of staff members who Strongly Agree/Agree in 1988 is lower at Round House on three of four items.

## *Endeavor*

The principal at Endeavor Middle School was perceived by her staff as having declined on every item related to being an instructional resource between 1986 and 1988.

*Stampede*
In 1988 the staff of Stampede High School has a substantially different view of the principal than it did in 1986. Of the four items listed on the instructional resource dimension, the increase in the percentage of staff members who Strongly Agree/Agree was positive on three with +17 percent, +19 percent, and +16 percent. The one item where a decline was noted was on item 2.3, where the percentage of staff members who Agree/Agree declined -3 percent. None of the principals in any of the four schools included in this study are perceived being strong instructional leaders by their staff.

# IMPLICATIONS

In *Creating Effective Schools* (Brookover et al., 1982), the authors state that "There is little consensus on the exact nature of the behaviors involved in the strong leadership role. Therefore, it is difficult to specify at this time what principal role behaviors or personal styles will be effective in every school." The principal's problem is compounded if one considers those behaviors needed to successfully initiate, implement, and institutionalize change. In *What's Worth Fighting For in the Principalship* (Fullan, 1988), the author describes the complexity of this problem when he states, "Insult having been added to injury, principals now face a double innovation, for implementing the implementation plan is an innovation."

The findings of this study provide a framework for thinking about the skills principals need and the behaviors that principals need to exhibit to be successful initiating, implementing, and institutionalizing change. The principal, once viewed as the "gatekeeper," is now responsible for being an "instructional leader." The components of resource provider, instructional resource, communicator, and visible presence identify specific areas that principals should be cognizant of as they seek to become instructional leaders.

In addition, an understanding of the relationship between critical inquiry and the initiation, implementation, and institutionalization of change is fundamental. If efforts to initiate, implement, and institutionalize change are to be successful, the principal needs to develop the knowledge and skills needed to further a process of critical inquiry. It is only when the principal can create conditions that enable the staff to engage in a dialogue that brings them to ask:
- What are we doing now?
- How did it come to be that way?
- Whose interests are (and are not) being served by the way things are?
- What information and knowledge do we have (or need to get) that bear upon the issues?
- Is this the way we want things to be?

- What are we going to do about all this?
that there will be any likelihood that schools will change to any significant degree. This study illustrates that (1) we cannot assume that principals know what it means to be an instructional leader, or (2) that they know intuitively how to successfully engage in activities that will result in the successful initiation, implementation, and institutionalization of change in schools.

The implications for administrator preservice and inservice programs are significant. The research regarding organizational change and the role of principals as instructional leaders is becoming increasingly well defined. What has not occurred is an increase in their skill to translate that research into daily practice.

Lest we despair, it should be noted that there are principals who clearly demonstrate that they understand how organizations function and that they possess the skills and abilities needed to be instructional leaders and transform knowledge into practice. Their ability to initiate, implement, and institutionalize the change process is so powerful that, in their schools, it becomes "the way we do business around here."

Colleges and universities must begin identifying these outstanding individuals and link them with prospective and practicing administrators in ongoing "mentor" relationships. Such relationships could provide prospective and practicing administrators with a much needed link between theory and practice that can result in developing instructionally effective schools that address the needs of all students.

As principals seek to become instructional leaders and implement and institutionalize changes that will result in the development of instructionally effective schools, Michael Fullan suggests an appropri-ate starting point. "The starting point for what's worth fighting for is not system change, not change in others around us, but change in ourselves." Unfortunately, the evidence indicates that they cannot make those changes without help.

# REFERENCES

Andrews, R.L. & R. Soder. (1985a). The Search for Equity and Excellence: University/ School District Collaboration on Effective Schools. Paper presented at the Annual Meeting of the AERA, Chicago, April.

Andrews, R.L. & R.Soder. (1985b). University/District Collaboration on Effective Schools. *National Forum of Education Administration and Supervision Journal 2*, 33-48.

Andrews, R.L., R. Soder, & A. Houston. (1985). The Search for Excellence and Equity: Seattle Effective Schools Project. *The Effective School Report 3*, (1), 6-7.

Andrews, R.L., R. Soder, & J. Bamburg. *Teacher and Supervisor Assessment of Principal Leadership and Academic Achievement.* Paper presented at the 1989 ICSE Conference.

Andrews, R.L., R. Soder, & D. Jacoby. (1986). *Principal Roles, Other In-School Variabales, and Academic Achievement by Ethnicity and SES.* Paper presented at the American Educational Research Association, April.

Bamburg, J. & R. L. Andrews. (1988). *Implementing Change in Secondary Schools Using Effective Schools Research.* Paper presented at the American Educational Research Association.

Berman, P. & M. W. McLaughlin. (1975). *Federal Programs Supporting Educational Change, vol. 3: The Process of Change, Appendix B: Innovations in Reading.* Santa Monica, CA: Rand Corporation.

Berman, P. & M. McLaughlin. (1976). Implementation of Educational Innovation. *Educational Forum 40,* (3), 347-370.

Brookover, W. (1981). *Effective Secondary Schools.* Philadelphia: Research for Better Schools.

Brookover, W., Beady, C., Flood, P., Schweitzer, J. & Wisenbaker, J. (1979). *School Social Systems and Student Achievement:* Schools can make a difference. New York: Praeger.

Brookover, W. et al. (1982). *Creating Effective Schools: An In-Service Program for Enhancing School Learning Climate and Achievement.* Holmes Beach, FL: Learning Publications.

Downey, L. & Associates. (1975). *The Social Studies in Alberta-1975.* Edmonton, Alberta: L. Downey Research Associates.

Fullan, M. (1982). *The Meaning of Educational Change.* New York: Teachers College Press.

Fullan, M. (1988). *What's Worth Fighting for in the Principalship.* Toronto, Ontario: Ontario Public School teachers Federation.

Fullan, M., & A. Pomfret. (1977). Research on Curriculum and Instruction Implementation. *Review of Educational Research 47,* (2), (Winter): 335-397.

Giaquinta, J. (1973). The Process of Organizational Change in Schools. In *Review of Research in Education,* edited by F. N. Kerlinger (pp. 178-208). Itasca, IL.: F. E. Peacock Publishers.

Herriott, R.E., & Neal Gross, (eds.). (1979). *The Dynamics of Planned Change.* Berkeley, CA: McCutchan.

Leithwood, K. et al. (1978). *An Empirical Investigation of Teachers' Curriculum Decision Making process and Strategies Used by Curriculum Managers to Influence such Decision Making.* Unpublished report, Ontario Institute for Studies in Education.

Leithwood, K. & D. Montgomery. (1982). The Role of the Elementary Principal in Program Improvement: A Review. *Review of Educational Research 52,* 309-339.

Sarason, Seymour B. (1982). *The Culture of the School and the Problem of Change.* (2nd ed.) Boston, MA: Allyn and Bacon.

Sirotnik, K. (July 1987). *The School as the Center of Change.* Occasional Paper, 5, Center for Educational Renewal, College of Education, University of Washington.

# DEVELOPING INSTRUCTIONAL LEADERSHIP TEAMS IN HIGH SCHOOLS[1]

Philip Hallinger[2]
Vanderbilt University, Nashville

A highlight of the 1988 National Principals' Center Conversation occurred during a skit in which principals and staff developers representing over 100 principals' centers shared in a roast of the mythical "principal as instructional leader". The educational leadership literature exhorts principals to aspire to instructional leadership, leaving guilt and shame for those who would not or cannot reach this lofty goal.[3] It has, however, become clear to many that the current system for training and developing principals, the political context of school districts, and the nature of the job role conspire against principals who would assume the role of instructional leader (Cuban, 1988; Murphy et al., 1987). The spontaneous bursts of laughter, exhalations of relief, and knowing nods during the performance of the skit reflected tacit recognition of this reality, even among an audience highly committed to the development of school leadership.

It is not my intention to turn on our mythical hero. Instead, I would like to suggest some ways in which secondary school principals can exercise instructional leadership while remaining among the cast of mortals. The concept presented here involves the systematic development of an instructional leadership team to carry out the critical functions of curriculum and instructional coordination and supervision. I will describe:

(1) the rationale for exercising instructional leadership through teams in high schools;

(2) a framework of instructional leadership functions which can be used to organize the work of the team;

(3) a process for clarifying and allocating the roles of members of the instructional leadership team;

(4) a method for assessing the status of instructional leadership in the school;

(5) an approach to developing the instructional leadership skills of team members.

# THE RATIONALE FOR INSTRUCTIONAL LEADERSHIP TEAMS

Since the onset of the effective schools and school improvement literature in the late 1970s, considerable evidence has accumulated pointing to the pivotal role played by elementary school principals. Findings from these studies of effective elementary school leadership have subsequently been used as the basis for training programs developed for *all* principals. However, organizational differences between elementary and secondary schools have led some to question whether these findings hold true in secondary schools (Firestone & Herriott, 1982). Thus, even if high school principals accept instructional leadership as a key role, they are left without clear models of how effective instructional leadership is exercised in secondary schools.

High school principals who would exercise strong instructional leadership confront many of the obstacles faced by elementary school principals, and more. Educators have long assumed that principals have the tools to provide instructional leadership because they were once teachers themselves. Unfortunately, preparation as a teacher does not ensure that a principal is capable of helping teachers improve classroom instruction or coordinating curriculum. In high schools this is compounded by the fact that the principal typically supervises a large number of teachers with a wide variety of subject matter specializations. It is particularly difficult for secondary principals to schedule the uninterrupted blocks of time necessary for coordinating curriculum, observing lessons, and conferencing with teachers. Thus, secondary principals are forced to delegate more of their instructional leadership functions than is the case in elementary schools.

The complex organizational structure of high schools places additional constraints on the principal who would emulate the elementary school instructional leader. Because the high school principal must delegate many leadership functions, there is less direct contact with teachers, students, and parents. The less frequent interaction reduces the principal's opportunities to personally communicate key values. In addition, high schools generally serve broader, more diverse constituencies who may hold varying expectations of the principal, and of the school itself. In combination with the reduced contact, this makes it more difficult for a single leader to shape, communicate, and reinforce a vision of what the school can become.

Consequently, few high school principals will find themselves placed in a school setting that requires their particular brand of knowledge and skill, and which provides the necessary resource support for them to be *the instructional leader*. If this is the case, how can the high school principal exercise strong instructional leadership?

The few researchers who have explored instructional leadership in high schools find that the principal shares this role with others, taking the lead in specific areas, and delegating other functions. For example Hord, Hall and Stiegelbauer (1983) found that successful implementation of innovations in high schools is best accomplished by principals who work closely with a "consigliere". The "consigliere" is a staff member who handles many of the formal and informal routine tasks necessary for project implementation. The work of Little and Bird (1984; Bird & Little, 1985) further supports the notion that secondary school principals exercise instructional leadership through the delegation of responsibilities, and by working closely with teams of administrators, supervisors and teachers.

In support of these findings, current discussions of school reform have focused attention on the potential benefits of teacher involvement in instructional decisions both at the classrooms and school levels (Carnegie Forum 1986; Hallinger & Richardson, in press). Although the empirical evidence is still thin, it seems reasonable to accept the premise that curricular and instructional decisions which structure involvement among those who must implement the decisions (i.e., staff) will be stronger ones. This is particularly relevant at the secondary level where the organization's size and complexity distance the principal from intimate knowledge of specific instructional issues and subject matter.

Thus, a case can be made for decentralizing instructional leadership in high schools. The implication is that high school principals can exercise strong instructional leadership by systematically utilizing administrators and teachers to assist in the coordination and monitoring of curriculum and instruction. Of course, this is not really new information.

Most high school principals would respond: "but, I already utilize a team approach to school management." While it is true that all high school principals delegate some responsibility for instructional supervision and curricular coordination, research and experience suggest that the instructional leadership function in many high schools is exercised in a fragmented and inconsistent manner. Those to whom instructional leadership has been delegated are often unclear as to the exact nature and extent of their tasks, authority and responsibilities. In addition, many subordinates have not developed the skills to effectively carry out their responsibilities.

Thus, delegation often results in uneven and inconsistent performance of the instructional leadership role, exactly what principals have been admonished to avoid. Upon recognition of this situation, the principal may try to provide *strong instructional leadership* by reducing delegation, centralizing the role and becoming the *strong instructional leader*. And so the circle is complete.

I have tried to suggest that what perpetuates this vicious circle is not the personal inadequacy of the high school principal, but the inadequate development of the instructional leadership capacity of the school. Principals who delegate instructional leadership functions must clarify role expectations and provide the necessary training and support to ensure that subordinates have the skills necessary to perform the tasks. A major impediment to effective delegation is the absence of an agreed upon language for discussing the elements of the instructional leadership role. Thus, the first step in forging an effective team is to develop a common definition of instructional leadership.

## DEFINING INSTRUCTIONAL LEADERSHIP

Instructional leadership is comprised of three dimensions: 1) defining the school mission, 2) managing the instructional program, and 3) promoting the school learning climate. Each dimension contains several more narrowly conceived job functions. For example, the dimension defining a school mission consists of two instructional leadership functions, framing school goals and communicating school goals. In turn, each job function includes a variety of representative principal practices and behaviors (see Hallinger & Murphy, 1985, 1987; Hallinger et al. 1983) This framework of instructional leadership is displayed in Figure 1. A brief definition of each dimension of this framework is provided below.

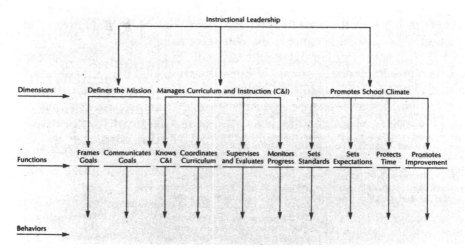

*Figure 1: Instructional Leadership Framework*

322

## Defining the School Mission

Instructional leaders have a clear vision of what the school is trying to accomplish and become. Defining the school mission entails leading the staff in the development of a mission and communicating this mission to the entire school community. The mission should reflect the primary value orientation of the school. The following slogans encapsulize the value orientations of somewhat longer school mission statements: "together we can"; "all children can learn"; "... school, a fun place, a learning place".

The school mission, when put into practice, should evoke a sense of shared purpose among staff, students, and community. This common commitment unites all the school's activities. School goals evolve from the mission, specifying the more specific areas of school-wide focus. The development of a few annual, school-wide goals delineates responsibility, promotes accountability, and provides a unifying framework for instructional improvement.

## Managing the Instructional Program

Instructional leaders work closely with staff in areas specifically related to the evaluation, development, and monitoring of curriculum and instruction. Traditionally, instructional management has been defined as instructional supervision and evaluation. Research on effective schools indicates, however, that instructional leaders should pay equal, if not greater, attention to two other related functions: coordinating the curriculum and monitoring student progress. Instructional leaders coordinate curriculum by ensuring that students receive appropriate instruction in areas identified by the school, district, and state. Monitoring student progress both within individual classrooms and across grades is an equally potent, though underemphasized, area of instructional leadership activity.

## Promoting a Positive Climate

School learning climate refers to the norms and attitudes of the staff and students that influence learning in the school. Instructional leaders shape the learning climate through both direct and indirect activities. The key functions within this dimension include:

- maintaining high visibility in order to communicate priorities and model expectations;
- creating a reward system that reinforces academic achievement and productive effort;
- establishing clear, explicit standards for students and staff that embody the school's expectations of students;
- protecting instructional time from interruptions and promoting the effective use of instructional time in classrooms;
- selecting, supporting participating in high-quality staff development programs consistent with the school's annual program goals.

A coordinated program and a moderate level of consistency in the standards and expectations communicated throughout the school support teacher effectiveness and foster student growth.

This framework incorporates the major instructional leadership responsibilities that must be carried out in order to promote the ability of teachers to effectively instruct students across the many departments in a high school. A principal can use this framework with members of an instructional leadership team to allocate and clarify areas of individual and collective responsibility, assess the leadership needs of the school, and to focus staff development efforts. In the next section I discuss the allocation and clarification of instructional leadership functions among team members.

## ALLOCATION OF ROLES AMONG AN INSTRUCTIONAL LEADERSHIP TEAM

A major problem faced by principals who delegate instructional leadership tasks is the lack of clear areas of responsibility. The framework described above can be used to address this problem. The functional nature of the framework facilitates discussion and communication of role expectations in terms of specific practices. Principals can allocate task responsibilities to assistant principals, department chairs, supervisors and teachers according to the various leadership functions.

Instructional leadership teams can be organized in different configurations based upon the needs of the school, and the skills and roles of existing personnel. A principal in a small high school may choose to form one instructional leadership team comprised of assistant principals and department chairpersons. Alternatively, the principal in a larger high school school with a complex array of programs may wish to coordinate instructional leadership functions through a central leadership team and delegate specific areas of responsibility to sub-units. In the latter case, general meetings might be held with the full team to discuss issues of curricular coordination or monitoring student progress, but a sub-unit might meet to discuss teacher evaluation results.

The organization of the instructional leadership team is also related to the allocation of responsibilities. From the principal's perspective, there are three ways in which instructional leadership responsibilities can be allocated. First, the team can be *collectively responsible* for all or part of an instructional leadership function. For example, a principal may determine that all members of the team share the common task of communicating school goals. Functional responsibilities shared by all members are delineated in terms of general policies and more specific practices. Second, individual members of the team can assume responsibility for selected functions. For example, de-

Table 1: Sample Allocation of Instructional Leadership Functions[5]

*Instructional Leadership Team #1*
  Members: Principal, Assistant Principal, Student Activities Coordinator, Director of
    Counseling Services, Media Specialist, Dept. Leaders
  Functions: Framing School Goals, Coordinating Curriculum, Developing Academic
    Standards, Promoting Professional Development, Monitoring Student Perform-
    ance

*Instructional Leadership Team #2*
  Members: Principal, Assistant Principal
  Functions: Supervising and Evaluating Instruction

*Principal*
  Functions: Communicting School Goals, Protecting Instructional Time, Providing In-
    centives for Students and Teachers, Promoting Professional Development

*Assistant Principal*
  Functions: Protecting Instructional Time

partment chairpersons may be responsible for instructional supervision or curriculum coordination for their departments. Third, the principal may maintain full authority over a specific function. Thus, a principal might choose or be required by policy to personally evaluate non- tenured teachers.

The particular manner in which instructional leadership functions are allocated will vary from school to school. In this model the principal's greatest challenges as instructional leader are finding the proper balance of delegation and control, and developing the capacity of team members to carry out their roles. For illustrative purposes, an example of how one high school organizes and allocates responsibilities is shown below in Table 1.

# ASSESSING INSTRUCTIONAL LEADERSHIP

After the team has been organized and roles have been clarified, the principal must ensure that members have the necessary skills to perform their roles successfully. Unfortunately, assistant principals, department chairpersons, and other supervisors seldom receive the type of training and development needed to meet the high expectations currently held for instructional leaders. In order to systematically develop the instructional leadership capacity of the school, it is useful for the principal to obtain a reading of the degree to which the various functions are currently being performed. This instructional leadership profile can then be used to determine priorities for intervention and provide a baseline for the evaluation of professional improvement efforts.

The instructional leadership framework described earlier was used to develop an instrument that assesses the instructional leadership of an individual principal or of an instructional leadership team (Hallinger & Murphy, 1985, 1987). The *Principal Instructional Management Rating Scale (PIMRS)*[4] defines each of the job functions displayed in Figure 1 in terms of specific practices and behaviors. The instrument contains 50 statements of specific instructional leadership behaviors. The practices that make up each job function in the *PIMRS* do not represent the full range of behaviors necessary to provide instructional leadership; rather, each job function contains a representative sample of critical behaviors. Respondents indicate the degree to which they perceive the specific practice to have been performed over the prior school year (e.g., the extent to which "needs assessment or other methods have been used to secure staff input on the development of school goals"). Answers are displayed on a five-point Likert scale ranging from "Almost Never" (1) to "Almost Always" (5).

The *PIMRS* can be administered as a self-assessment instrument to the principal and members of an instructional leadership team. If desired, supervisors and teachers can also be asked to complete the instrument in order to provide contrasting perspectives on the school's instructional leadership. Ideally this is done after responsibilities have been allocated among team members.

The *PIMRS* is scored by calculating the mean for each job function. A higher score on a function suggests more active instructional leadership in

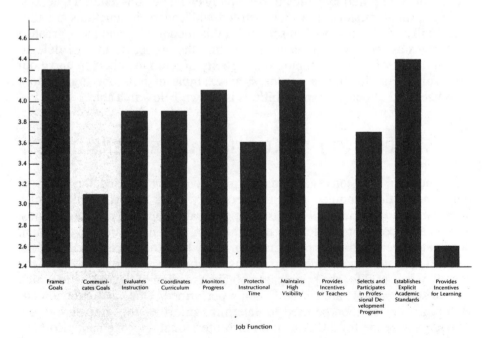

*Figure 2: Sample Profile from the Principal Instructional Management Rating Scale.*

that area. Higher ratings across the various job functions are interpreted as more active instructional leadership. It should be emphasized that *PIMRS* ratings measure perceptions of *leadership activity*, not *quality* of instructional leadership. The ratings are compiled into a profile that can assist in diagnosing areas of need and determining areas for practical intervention and professional improvement. A sample instructional leadership profile is displayed in Figure Two.

# DEVELOPING THE INSTRUCTIONAL LEADERSHIP TEAM

Initially, the instructional leadership profile is used to diagnose the instructional leadership needs across the school. For example, the profile may indicate great strength in the areas of *framing goals* and *communicating goals,* but relative weakness in the areas of *curricular coordination* and *providing incentives for learning.* This would suggest areas for collective attention among members of the instructional leadership team. The principal may wish to collect additional information, formally or informally, to validate these perceptions.

After task responsibilities have been allocated and members of the team are confident the leadership profile is accurate, the principal can take a coordinated approach to team development. On functions where task responsibility is collectively shared (e.g., communicating school goals), the team determines specific steps all members can take to strengthen schoolwide leadership on this function. This may entail development of new school policies or practices, closer attention to the implementation of current policy, or whatever the team feels is appropriate to address the need.

On functions where task responsibility is primarily delegated (e.g., curriculum coordination and instructional supervision to assistant principals and department chairpersons) an individualized plan is developed. For example, when instructional leadership profiles are analyzed by department, the principal may find that certain chairpersons require assistance and support, while others do not. Or, the profile may suggest the need for skill refinement in instructional supervision among all chairpersons. The principal may then choose to provide the training directly, or arrange for staff development through other channels. In either case, the principal assumes the leadership role of staff developer, working collaboratively to improve the effectiveness of the school's instructional leadership team.

In one instance, a high school principal, using this approach, identified supervision and evaluation as an area in which he and his staff needed to develop additional expertise. This was also consistent with a broader schoolwide goal of improving the classroom instruction of teachers. He scheduled monthly professional development sessions for his instructional leadership team in which they worked together developing their instructional supervision skills. Eventually, team members took responsibility for making monthly presentations on effective instructional practices at faculty meetings, an unanticipated outcome of their own professional development activities.

The effectiveness of the team's interventions in school policy and practice and the impact of leadership development efforts provided to team members can be assessed by the principal. The *PIMRS* profile provides the baseline data for such evaluations. Annual or bi-annual administration of the *PIMRS* or a similar scale can be used to profile the team's progress and assess its development. Performance feedback to the team collectively as well as to individual members is critical to the effective functioning and development of the group.

# CONCLUSION

This model of leadership appraisal and development starts from the premise that the high school principal's instructional leadership role differs from the centralized leadership role portrayed in the literature on effective elementary schools. In the real world of secondary schools, principals assume direct responsibility for selected instructional leadership functions, but must delegate partial or full responsibility for other functions to subordinates. This results in diffusion, rather than centralization, of the instructional leadership role in the school. From this perspective, the high school principal's instructional leadership role is appropriately viewed as a "leader of leaders".[6]

*In no way does this conclusion diminish the high school principal's responsibility for exercising instructional leadership.* I believe that instructional leadership is just as critical to the development of quality high schools as elementary schools. The approach presented here, however, shifts the high school principal's attention to those areas where it will have the most impact. For the most part, this entails the systematic development of a leadership team that has the capacity to provide coordination in a large, complex organization. The principal is the initiator and leader of the team and remains responsible for its performance.

This approach to instructional leadership in high schools releases the principal from the double bind created from the unattainable expectations fostered by research on effective elementary schools and the constraining characteristics of high schools as large, complex, political organizations. It is unlikely that the mythical version of the *principal as instructional leader* will find a home in many high schools. It is, however, possible for high school principals to become effective instructional leaders by developing the leadership capacity of staff. The model presented here represents one potentially powerful method of applying research on effective instructional leadership to the secondary level when implemented in an organized, thoughtful manner.

## NOTES

1. This work has benefitted from the ideas and support of Professors Larry Cuban and Edwin Bridges of Stanford University and Joseph Murphy of Vanderbilt University.
2. Philip Hallinger is Associate Professor of Educational Leadership and Director of the Center for Advanced Study of Educational Leadership, in Peabody College of Vanderbilt University.
3. The notion that the research on effective schools engenders unnecessary guilt among secondary principals was suggested by Dr. Anthony Ciaglia, principal of the Peekskill Middle School, Peekskill, NY.
4. The *PIMRS* is a copyrighted instrument. Researchers and practitioners interested in using the *Principal Instructional Management Rating Scale* should contact Dr. Philip Hallinger, Director, Center for Advanced Study of Educational Leadership, Peabody College, Vanderbilt University, Nashville, TN 37203; (615) 343-7092.
5. Table 1 describes the Instructional Leadership Team Organization at North Myrtle Beach High School in North Myrtle Beach, South Carolina. It was developed by the principal, Harriet Blanton, and her staff.
6. See Larry Cuban's book, *The managerial imperative and the practice of leadership in schools* (1988) for an insightful examination of pressures that limit the practice of school leadership and discussion of other conceptions of the school leader's role.

## REFERENCES

Bird, T. & Little, J.W. (1985). *Instructional leadership in eight secondary schools: Final report*. Boulder, CO: Center for Action Research.

Carnegie Forum on Education and the Economy. (1986). *A nation prepared: Teachers for the 21st century*. New York: Carnegie Corporation.

Cuban, L. (1988). *The managerial imperative and the practice of leadership in schools*. Albany, NY: SUNY Press.

Firestone, W. & Herriott, R. (1982). Prescriptions for effective elementary schools don't fit secondary schools. *Educational Leadership, 40,* 51-53.

Hallinger, P., and Murphy, J. (1985, November). Assessing the instructional leadership behavior of principals. *The Elementary School Journal 86,* (2), 217-248.

Hallinger, P., & Murphy, J. (1987, September). Assessing and developing principal instructional leadership. *Educational Leadership,* 55-62.

Hallinger, P., Murphy, J., Weil, M., Mesa, P., & Mitman, A. (1983, May). School effectiveness: Identifying the specific practices and behaviors for principals. *NASSP Bulletin 67,* 463, 83-91.

Hallinger, P. & Richardson, D. (In press). Models of shared leadership: Evolving structures and processes. *The Urban Review.*

Hord, S., Hall, G., & Stiegelbauer, S. (1983). *Principals don't do it alone: The role of the consigliere*. Paper presented at the annual meeting of the American Educational Research Association, Montreal.

Little, J.W. & Bird, T. (1984). *Is there instructional leadership in high schools?* Paper presented at the annual meeting of the American Educational Research Association, New Orleans.

Murphy, J., Hallinger, P., Lotto, L., & Miller, S. (1987, December). Barriers to implementing the instructional leadership role ofthe principal. *The Canadian Administrator, 27,* (3), 1-9.

# DEVELOPMENT OF EFFECTIVE SCHOOLS: A PROCESS FOR AN EFFECTIVE SCHOOL MODEL

Rufus Young, Jr
St. Louis Public Schools, St. Louis

## INTRODUCTION

The purpose of this paper is to present the organization and replication process of the St. Louis SHAL[1]/Effective School Program and show how school effectiveness positively influences student academic achievement.

While attending the 1979 Conference of the National Alliance of Black School Educators, I became aware of Ronald Edmonds and his work, "The Search for Effective Schools Project." Through this research, Edmonds had identified effective schools which teach basic skills to the children of minorities and the poor as effectively and successfully as children of the middle class were being taught.

Several years prior to 1979, Christopher Jencks and his now famous *Inequality* study had put forth just the opposite notion. From the Jencks' study, school people were let "off the hook" for being responsible for providing successful outcomes for children from less than middle class home backgrounds. Jencks' research strongly suggested that the learning outcomes of schools were more than equally influenced by family background. That is, children from poor and/or minority homes could not expect the schooling experience to significantly change their adulthood plight from that of their parents. Ronald Edmonds' research findings unequivocally rejected this notion. He and his colleague, Lawrence Lezotte, asked the question: "Are there schools that are institutionally effective for poor children?" The answer came back *yes*. These schools, however, have common bonds that have come to be known as the *Effective School Correlates*.

### Strong Administrative Leadership
Effective school research indicates that school principals assume the role of the instructional leader and play an integral part in decisions made as they relate the instructional program.

### High Expectations
A large body of research establishes that some teachers have differential expectations for students, and these expectations result in differential treatment and differential outcomes among students. A cyclical process is set in motion often referred to as the "self-fulfilling prophecy." High expectations in the effective schools permeate the entire school setting and are conveyed through particular behaviors of the principal and teachers. Teachers not only believe that all children can learn; but they believe that they can teach them.

### Positive School Climate
The school climate in effective schools is characterized as being safe, orderly, and conducive to learning. The climate affects how students feel and learn. In an effective school, there is evidence of pride, a sense of community, and a sense of spirit.

### Total School Instructional Emphasis
In an effective school, the instructional focus is broad and pervasive, understood by all personnel, and is facilitated by the decision-making of the principal and teachers, emanating from a uniform district-wide curriculum. The instructional focus addresses the accountability of staff for student outcomes.

### Ongoing Assessment
In a major effort to ensure minimum mastery of all skills by all students, results of regular assessment of pupil progress identify skills that have been learned and skills that are to be learned. The results of these assessments provide direction for the classroom instructional programs. Periodic check points are established in which the principal and staff review the progress and revise the programs to meet the instructional objectives.


# PROJECT SHAL REPLICATION MODEL

Following an introduction to the Edmonds' research, a request for program assistance was conveyed to The Danforth Foundation[2] Vice President, John Ervin. After a series of conversations with Dr. Ervin, a proposal for the implementation of an educational intervention project involving a cluster of schools was submitted. The funding was granted, and Project SHAL was organized.

Over a seven year period, 117 schools have been systematically brought into the program using the replication model. Presently, there are six tiers of schools based on the time of initiation of schools into the program, beginning with Project SHAL which comprised Tiers I, II, and III.

The St. Louis/SHAL Effective School Program developed around the Ronald Edmonds Effective School Correlates has two goals: 1) to develop a school improvement model that not only improves academic achievement but can be replicated; and 2) to increase the average student achievement to the national norm while significantly reducing the number of students in the lower quartiles.

The school staffs would learn the philosophy, tenets and practices of effective schools and institute school programs in keeping with the five correlates. Through participation in Project SHAL, the minds and hearts of the school staffs would be changed. No longer could school improvement be dependent upon the acquisition of new personnel, materials, or pre-packaged programs. The staffs would have to rethink, design and redesign existing services as they learned the research and research implications of effective schools. Project SHAL, where every child can — WILL — learn, translated the practices of effective schools, eroding traditional beliefs and eradicating failed educational methods to come upon different ways of believing and educating those students whose failures had been previously accepted.

## Program Structures

### Executive Council
The Project SHAL Executive Council consisted of the principals, the Project Coordinator ( responsible for carrying out the Project administrative tasks such as engaging speakers, setting time schedules, arranging meetings, etc.), the manager of the Management Academy (an inservice for administrators), The Danforth Foundation Vice President, and the Area Superintendent (responsible for the 33 schools that would become ultimately involved in the project.) Sometimes, however, membership of this group was expanded to include others who had some particular role at a given time. The Executive Council functioned as the initial planning group for the Project.

It was quickly recognized that in order for the Project to make the intended impact on school staffs and to involve all school staffs in reviewing, studying, and internalizing effective school research findings, more individuals would need to be involved in the total planning of the Project. As a result, the Project SHAL Administrative Council was formed.

### Administrative Council
The governing body of the Project, the Administrative Council, had the responsibility to plan the various activities to be conducted within the Pro-

ject. The membership of the Administrative Council included the Executive Council members and an additional fifteen members (representatives of teachers, classified personnel, parents from the four schools, Area Office administrators, and a Board of Education representative.) The Administrative Council met monthly and had as its main purpose to make ongoing plans for the Project while monitoring all of the activities of the Project.

*Task Force Groups*
Even with the Executive Council and Administrative Council structures, there remained a need to develop an organization that could help process the effective school information and place it in the framework of school strategies, programs, and outcomes. For this purpose, five Task Force Groups (one to represent each of the effective school correlates) were organized.

The Task Force Groups, with technical assistants from local colleges and universities, had the responsibility to provide leadership to:
1) Develop a complete, clear definition of each of the correlate areas;
2) Outline what needed to be done to provide an adequate basis for effective work in each correlate area;
3) Determine potential resources for work in each correlate area;
4) Pilot some possible implementation strategies in each of the four schools;
5) Design and conduct staff training activities; and,
6) Design and administer the Project Assessment Instrument.

Four of the Task Force Groups were chaired by principals, and the fifth group, Basic Skills, was chaired by the Project Supervisor.
   Each Task Force Group was made up of teachers and staff members from each school.

The groups were divided into committees. The six basic committees were:
1) Correlate-definition
2) Correlate-information
3) Correlate-resources
4) Correlate-strategies
5) Strategy implementation
6) Correlate/strategy staff training/orientation

The groups met twice each month for four months for three hours each meeting.

The Task Force Group sessions were generally divided into three parts:
1) Information giving and sharing
2) Committee reports
3) Presentations of strategies for possible implementation

As a result of the Task Force Groups and their structure and design, approximately 80% of all Project SHAL participants were directly involved in making major decisions about the Project and it programs.

The organizational structure, developed as a part of the institution of Project SHAL, provided opportunities for leadership for the Project participants. The organizational structures made it possible for the information and knowledge about effective schools to be received on a first-hand basis by more than three-fourths of the participants. Through the organizational structures, participants were involved in the design and development of their own orientation to effective school research, the Project assessment, program design and implementation.

### Project SHAL: An Effective School Implementation/Replication Model Process

Project SHAL is a four-stage model – orientation, program design, implementation and institutionalization. These stages are not discrete, nor do they take place in isolation, but are orchestrated as a part of the total process. However, in order to make the operation of Project SHAL vivid and easy to follow, the four stages of the model are discussed separately.

The replication model process is a four-level design consisting of three levels of development:
a) Awareness or interest (Characterized by mobilization, knowledge and persuasion)
b) Evaluation or trial (characterized by implementation and decision making)
c) Adoption or adaptation (characterized by incorporation and conformation)

There are four levels of activity in the process:
a) Recognition and orientation
b) Exploration and design
c) Implementation (trial, pilot, application)
d) Institutionalization and Renewal (advocacy)

The five effective school correlates serve as the program elements.
a) Administrative Leadership
b) School Climate
c) High Expectations
d) Focus on Instructional Program
e) Ongoing Assessment

The Project SHAL replication model at each stage is applied across the effective school correlates.

# RECOGNITION AND ORIENTATION

During the Orientation Stage, strong commitment from the district administrative units are developed. Task forces are organized by correlate, and trained. Baseline data for school programs are calculated and analyzed.

The emphasis is on the training of school people who are committed to the belief that every child can learn. To meet the training needs of the school staff, several types of orientation activities are conducted.

(1) Total Project Staff Inservice Meetings
(2) Executive Committee/Administrative Council Discussions
(3) School Meetings/In-School Meetings
(4) Visitations to other school districts
(5) Publication of a project newsletter
(6) Task Force meetings
)7) Technical Assistants working with schools

This stage of the model is further characterized by awareness, interest, mobilization, knowledge, commitment and assessment.


# EXPLORATION - PLANNING AND PROGRAM DESIGN

The Planning and Program Design Stage conducted across the five correlates provides opportunity for the total project participants to work together to plan and design programs by grade and school groups. Many of the staff training activities are ongoing and, in some instances, summer institutes and other two or three day conferences are conducted.


### Administrative Leadership
The principal establishes building goals and sets norms; remakes schedules to support large blocks of learning and common planning time. The principal fosters open communication, decision making, and problem solving channels to refocus efforts on instruction.


### School Climate
The school staff analyzes and makes plans to improve identified problem areas. Committees are formed to plan strategies. Factors such as discipline, rules, and building organization affecting instruction are examined and made consistent with effective school outcomes. A safe and orderly environment is the responsibility of everybody.

### High Expectations
Standards are set for group achievement. Emphasis is placed on positive expectations. A significant group of teachers become believers in the positive relationship between achievement and teacher expectations.

### Instructional Focus
Teachers agree on skills to be taught and some common goals to be attained. Ongoing workshops are conducted to introduce successful basic skills approaches such as, time on task, direct instruction, mastery learning, and learning styles. The staff begins to design spiral curriculum.

### Regular and Continuous Assessment
Standards are set for passing and failing. Grading standards are determined. Homework policy is established.

In summary, this stage is characterized by exploration, design, problem solving, analysis, setting standards and norms, decision making, team building, and program development.

## IMPLEMENTATION (TRIAL/PILOT) APPLICATION

The Implementation Stage is an organized and structured opportunity for the school staffs to put into place the school programs which address the five effective school correlates. This stage is characterized by total involvement of all staff members. School staffs conduct programs which focus on the five effective school correlates. All school policies, procedures and program supports are implemented.

### Administrative Leadership
The principal is consumed with carrying out a program which supports the five effective school correlates. The principal is highly visible, schedules instructional supervision sessions and staff development. The principal strives to achieve norms; knows the school, pupils, parents, staff and neighborhood.

### School Climate
Respect and courtesy permeate the building. A sense of community and pride is felt and exhibited through informal gatherings. Staff members feel that they are a part of the school — and are responsible for all students and classroom discipline. Students know the rules and the school's code of conduct which is enforced fairly and consistently.

### High Expectations
Success is seen as attainable by everyone. There are increased numbers of

students receiving honors for academics, good citizenship, and attendance. The principal and teachers conduct ongoing discussions relative to the school goals and objectives and their high expectations for student achievement.

### Commitment to Teaching Basic Skills
Teachers and students engage in planned learning activities. There are planned instruction-oriented staff meetings. Mathematics and reading instruction focus on mastery learning. Alternative approaches to teaching difficult to learn students are instituted. Students are grouped and regrouped for instructional purposes. The number of Chapter I pull-out programs are reduced.

### Regular and Continuous Assessment
Specific measures for monitoring student achievement and behavior are used to make decisions about school improvement and student placement and promotion.

# IMPLEMENTATION STAGE/STAFF DEVELOPMENT

A major focus of the implementation stage is continued staff development, supported by program monitoring. The staff develop ment activities relate directly to Effective School Research, Effective School Correlates, teacher behaviors, and general meth ods and strategies for the improvement of student achievement.

### Effective School Research
*Effective School Research:* A comprehensive review of contemporary research by educators such as, Ronald Edmonds, Benjamin Bloom, Wilbur Brookover, James Comer, Lawrence Lezotte, et al, is presented. This information serves as the common knowledge base for all participants.
*Effective School Correlates:* A study of the behaviors, tenets, and practices encompassed by each of the five effective school correlates.

### Learning Related to Mastery Teaching
*Teaching for Mastery:* A training session in which the staff is presented a conceptual framework for mastery learning. This framework was based on the premise that all children can learn and included the effective teaching behaviors identified in the effective school literature.

### Maximizing Staff Potential
*Power Management:* A leadership training component in which principal and staff identify their personality and leadership styles and the impact each has on the other.

*Participatory Planning and Decision Making Model:* A model for involving small groups or the total staff in decision making at the school.

*Team-Building:* A training session in which emphasis is placed on building the staff into a collegial, cooperative unit inclusive of all staff members in some function in the effective school process. Leaders are trained to identify strengths and weaknesses of the staff as well as their own potential for positive influence in bringing about change.

### Instruction

*Teacher Expectations and Student Achievement (TESA):* Teachers are trained to use fifteen identified teacher behaviors that positively impact student learning. The training process includes research presentation, role play, classroom practice, and peer feedback.

*Reading for Mastery:* A training session designed to assist teachers in recognizing that students must be taught at their level of success before they can be further challenged. Teachers are trained in diagnosing the reading levels of students, dividing them into skill level groups across the school, and then teaching them to read via a language approach as opposed to an isolated skills approach.

*Missouri Math Effectiveness Program:* A research-based teaching model for mathematics developed by Dr. Thomas Good. This model incorporates tenets of time-on-task and direct instruction.

*Clinical Supervision:* A supervisory model based upon positive, non-punitive interactions between the principal and teachers. The principal provides instructional supervision through collaborative interactions with teachers.

### Instructional Strategies

*Direct Instruction:* A session for teachers to strengthen their role as the person in charge of instruction. Active teaching techniques are presented and practiced.

*Time-On-Task:* A training session for teachers in management methods that focuses on reducing the amount of time spent on non-instructional tasks, i.e., attendance, collection of lunch money, etc. which increase time-on-task and increase academic achievement.

*Test Taking Strategies:* A training sessions in which teachers are oriented to test-taking strategies that can be taught to students.

## INSTITUTIONALIZATION AND RENEWAL

During this stage, school staffs institutionalize school effectiveness programs. This stage is characterized by schools with well-defined goals; where teachers, administrators, parents, and community are involved in structured programs and activities which espouse the five effective school correlates.

## Administrative Leadership

The principal coordinates instructional programs; emphasizes student achievement; sets broad school-wide goals and objectives; transmits well-defined set of goals to the faculty, parents and community; plays a dominant role in the decisions about the selection of instructional strategies and program planning. The principal evaluates and carefully monitors the instructional process and sets standards of performance for teachers and staff.

## School Climate

The discipline code is strictly enforced. The school is orderly without being rigid, quiet without being oppressive, and the atmosphere is conducive to the business of teaching and learning. The principal aggressively seeks and obtains political, parental and financial support.

## High Expectations

The staff believes all children can learn to master basic skills objectives. Teachers expect all students to gain one year or more on standardized tests. Instructional programs are instituted which support student academic expectations (tutors, remedial, enhanced parental involvement, learning teams.)

## Commitment to Teaching Basic Skills

The principal requires that instructional objectives guide the school's programs. The majority of staff articulate commitment to basic skills mastery for all children. Total effective school support programs are in place. Staff continuously seeks programs and activities to enhance learning of all children. Staff development is the focus of all faculty meetings. The principal is the instructional leader. The five effective school correlates are visible through programs. Achievement is emphasized.

## Regular and Continuous Assessment

Standardized tests are used to measure academic achievement along with teacher-made tests and periodic reviews of school-wide objectives are made.

# EVALUATION OF MODEL

The replication model has been reviewed twice – in 1984, involving 13 schools and in 1982, involving the four original pilot schools. However, in 1985, the model was field-tested in nineteen schools. Some general findings are listed below (Achilles and Young, 1979):

(1) The Replication Model provides an accurate and useful implementation guide.

(2) The longer the model is implemented, the better the students achieve based on standardized tests.

(3) Three years is probably the minimum time of implementation before positive results can be recognized.

(4) School size seems to influence results, with small schools having more positive results.

(5) The principal's energy and vision are extremely important to the success of program implementation, especially at the outset. However, as the program gets going, emphasis shifts from the principal to the teachers and staff.

(6) Many of the indicators at the Institutionalization and Renewal phases are initiated at earlier stages of the model.

## STUDENT ACHIEVEMENT OUTCOMES

The *Interim Evaluation Report - Project SHAL,* compiled in 1982, noted that "preliminary statistical analyses show that, even in its short time of operation, Project SHAL has recorded outstanding successes ... The SHAL schools have scored impressive gains in moving pupils from low to high quartiles in reading and math. It is safe to report that SHAL schools are making outstanding progress toward achieving the goal of getting pupils at or above national norms on the California Achievement Tests for reading and math. The second goal of SHAL, a replication model, has been achieved. All indications point to SHAL as a winner."

The implementation of the SHAL Replication Model and the improvement of student achievement have marked the continued success of the St. Louis Effective Schools Program.

The achievement results (see Chart 1) from 1981 - 1987 show the increase of elementary grades scoring at and above the national norm. In the three Tier I elementary schools, 20% of the grades were at or above the national norm in 1981. In 1987, 93% of the grades were at or above the national norm. In the seven Tier II elementary schools, 13% of the grades were at or above the national norm in 1981. In 1987, 92% of the grades were at or above national norm.

The two Tier III elementary schools had no grades at or above national norm in 1982, but in 1987, 83% of the grades were at or above national norm. The twenty-nine Tier IV elementary schools increased from 20% of the grades at or above national norm in 1984 to 73% of the grades in 1987. The twenty-four Tier V elementary schools increased from 51% of the grades at or above national norm in 1985 to 87% in 1987.

The academic success of students at the middle schools (see Chart 2) is similar. The four Tier I and II middle schools had no grades at or above national norm in 1981. However, in 1987, all grades in these four schools were at or above national norm. The one Tier III middle school had no grades above the national norm in 1982; in 1987, all grades were at or above the national norm. The nine Tier IV middle schools had 18% above the national norm in 1984; and in 1987, the percent of grades scoring above the national norm have increased to 81%. The ten Tier V middle schools have shown an increase in the percentage of grades scoring at or above the national norm from 86% to 97%.

In 1981, only 14% of the students in the Tier I middle school passed the State mandated eighth grade competency test. In 1987, 95% of the students passed all parts.

### Proficiency Ladder

In 1986, a Proficiency Ladder was developed to describe the levels of student outcomes.

*Effective School.* An effective school has high expectations for all students and ensures that there is no difference in the proportion of students from the various socio-economic levels scoring above the 50th percentile in the basic skills; with 50% or more of the students scoring at or above national norm and a maximum of 10% scoring in the lowest quartile.

*Excellent School.* An excellent school has high expectations for all students and ensures that there is no difference in the proportion of students from the various socio-economic levels scoring above the 50th percentile in the basic skills. The standards of excellence are met for student achievement when 90% score at or above the 50th percentile in math, 85% score at or above the 50th percentile in language; and, 80% score at or above the 50th percentile in reading; with a maximum of 7% scoring in the lowest quartile.

*Exemplary School.* An exemplary school has fully operationalized the five effective school correlates. The exemplary school ensures that there is no difference in the proportion of students from the various socio-economic levels scoring above the 50th percentile in the basic skills. The standards for excellence are met for student achievement when 90% score at or above the 50th percentile in math; 85% score at or above the 50th percentile in language; and, 80% score at or above the 50the percentile in reading; with 0-3% scoring in the lowest quartile and 90% of the students demonstrate mastery of 90% of the local Criterion Referenced Test (CRT) objectives.


# NOTES

1. The acronym SHAL represents the first letters of the name of the four schools in the original project - Stowe Middle, Hempstead Elementary, Arlington Elementary, and Laclede Elementary.

2. The Danforth Foundation, established in 1972, is a national educational philanthropic organization dedicated to enhancing the humane dimensions of life. Activities of the Foundation traditionally have emphasized the theme of improving the quality of teaching and learning.

Chart 1

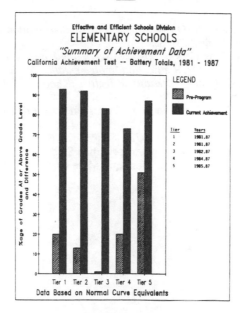

**Chart 1**

Chart 2

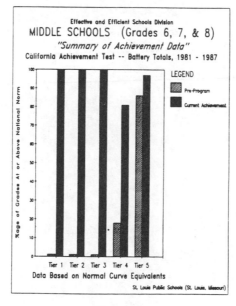

**Chart 2**

343

# REFERENCES

Achilles, Ch. & Young, R. Jr. (1984). *Successful Implementation of Effective Schools.* Unpublished Mass., Project SHAL.

Achilles, Ch. & Young, R. Jr. (1985). *Effective Schooling Implementation Takes Time, But Results Grow: Project SHAL Replication/Implementation Model.* Field Test.

Brookover, W.B., et al. (1982). *Creating Effective Schools.* Holmes Beach, Florida: Learning Publications, Inc.

Edmonds, R.R. (1979). Effective Schools for the Urban Poor. *Educational Leadership, 37,* 15-24.

Edmonds, R.R. & J.R. Frederiksen. (1978). *Search for Effective Schools,* Unpublished Manuscript, Harvard University Center for Urban Studies.

Edmonds, R.R. (1979). Some Schools Work and More Can. *Social Policy, 9,* 28-32.

# EFFECTIVE SCHOOLS AND EFFECTIVE LOCAL SCHOOL SYSTEMS

Walter Ackerman, Hanoch Flum, David Gordon and Malka
Gorodetsky
Ben Gurion University of the Negev, Beer Shera

## INTRODUCTION

Research on effective schools has tended to see the individual school as the relevant unit of analysis. Despite the benefits of this approach, it may not be desirable in all circumstances. The school-focused perspective encourages us to view local education system as *aggregates* of individual schools rather than as a group of schools which form a *system*. Such a reductive stance may lead to our overlooking much of importance in understanding local education systems, and in trying to help improve their effectiveness. The move from school aggregates to system may require us to conceptualize educational effectiveness in a significantly different way.

Individual schools exist first and foremost for their students. As a result a school's effectiveness has usually been defined in terms of its efficiency in helping students learn, its holding power and the degree to which discipline problems are minimal. School systems do not exist for students alone. They also exist for the cities and towns in which they are situated, cities and towns which grow and decay, exemplify social harmony or exist as foci of social tension and chaos. It is not self-evident that the defining properties of effective educational *systems* are the same as those of individual schools.

The outcome variables of an effective local system relate to the entire population (and even people outside the local area.) They are external to the schools themselves. They are also very general and abstract, perhaps more influenced by communication networks and mass media than by the specifics (e.g., achievements scores) linked to specific schools. The process variables associated with effective schools (e.g., strong leadership focussed on promoting learning, efficient monitoring of student progress, and accountability ethos, etc. (Clark, Lotto & Astuto, 1984) may not be the same as those which characterize effective school systems.

345

In this paper we question whether and to what extent the classic findings about effective individual schools are relevant when we are interested in the effectiveness of an entire local education system. This general question entails the discussion of three more specific questions:
- what are the defining characteristics of effectiveness of a local system?
- are these defining characteristics related to the defining characteristics of individual schools?
- are the process variables which characterize effective school systems similar to those that characterize individual effective schools?

Our interest in the topic arises from of our involvement in a major intervention project in the entire education system of a town called Rotem. We have committed ourselves to being accountable to improving the effectiveness of the entire Rotem education system.

### The Rotem Education System

Rotem has a population of approximately 30,000. It has 10 elementary schools, three junior high schools and two high schools. In Israeli jargon Rotem is called a *development town,* which means: (1) it was founded to help absorb the wave of immigration of North African and Asian Jews in the 1950's and to meet security needs;
(2) ethnic composition has remained largely the same over the years; (3) it is situated in an outlying area.

Education in development towns is considered to be of a much lower standard than that in towns and cities in the country's center. However, until about 10 years ago, the image of Rotem's educational system was surprisingly high. It was considered to be an innovative and interesting system which produced educational leaders who afterwards made their mark on the national level or in local systems in the center of the country. Its most famous feature was that the first open schools (à la Britain in the 1960's) in Israel were established in Rotem.

About 10 years ago the educational system's image began to deteriorate. This was not the result of a publicized sudden drop in student achievement scores. There were three main reasons for the change. First, the general images of the town had changed as increasing mobility of its population resulted in quite high negative immigration figures. Second, and a related point, teacher turnover was very high (although it must be stressed that it had always been quite high); authorities found it difficult to replace certified teachers who had left. In certain disciplines there was a severe shortage of teachers. Third, one of the junior high schools had a history of serious internal conflict and instability over a number of years. As approximately 30%-40% of the town's student population had studied or would study in this school, this clearly had a negative impact on the image of the entire education system.

346

We were approached to undertake an extensive evaluation and intervention project in the entire Rotem education system. Our proposed intervention strategy was based on the assumption that the aims of an educational intervention must not be pre-set, but rather should flow from the results of a preliminary evaluation of the system, both with regards to its outputs (student achievement, etc.) and its *processes*. Even though our proposal was very open-ended, we had made some decisions even before beginning the evaluation stage:

(1) We were committed to encouraging increased interaction between various components of the system.
(2) We were committed to building a local organization which would continue and maintain the changes we assumed would be initiated during our four-year stay.
(3) We were particularly interested in examining and, if necessary, improving the articulation between schools and local industry.
(4) We assumed that much of our work would be concerned with improving the effectiveness (in the classic sense) of individual schools, particularly with regards to an hypothesized lack of an accountability ethos.

We began our project with a prolonged series of meetings of principals and teacher staffs of all the schools, and also with local educational authorities, parent committees, teacher union representatives, etc. Through these meetings we learned a great deal about local expectations from our project. First of all, we discovered that the local educational leadership was mainly interested in the outcomes evaluation which they felt would supply them with information they lacked about the system. In other words, as previously mentioned, the image of the town's education system at this point is not based on solid figures concerning student achievement!

Teachers reactions stressed two points above and beyond the expected skepticism and wariness.

(a) Why evaluate the schools? The problems are somewhere else - "they" are to blame, "they" being the local town council or the Israeli Ministry of Education or "the town". There is too much politics or too little financial or moral support or whatever.
(b) There is no point in trying to improve the system unless we come to grips with the problem of teacher turnover. All other problems pale in comparison.

These reactions indicated that the lack of an accountability ethos was probably a serious syndrome of the entire system. They also suggested that dealing with the Rotem system would probably require us to relate to many variables and outcomes different from those normally discussed in relation to individual school effectiveness (e.g., the centrality of the system's image). These

347

reactions triggered the concerns of this paper. Our experiences in Rotem do *not* constitute *proof* that effectiveness at the system and school levels is different; they only hint at the importance of the issue. We have not yet completed the evaluatory phase of our project, so we cannot report any "findings" in the classic sense. The questions we will be discussing are of a conceptual and theoretical nature, which at best can be *illustrated* by field experiences. Still we suggest that it will be helpful to keep our sketch of the Rotem project in mind in relating to our theoretical discussion of the issues involved.

### What are the Defining Characteristics of Effectiveness at the Local Level?

We will not define the effectiveness of a local education system in terms of the quality of education it provides its student population, although this is obviously a central aspect of local educational effectiveness. In terms of our paper a local education system is effective if it helps promote the positive growth of the local town or city and also if it is successful in enlisting support for itself and for the educational enterprise itself. (Meyer 1977)

Perhaps the most central characteristic of an effective system is its *positive image* as active and dynamic. Such an image creates expectations and these, by themselves can amplify the effectiveness of the system (through a mechanism similar to the "Pygmalion in the classroom" effect which has been identified at the individual student level) (Rosenthal & Jacobson, 1968). The system's image functions both as *process* and outcome. Here we must distinguish between expectations within the system and expectations held by people outside. We assume that the former lead to the *maintenance* of the image. The image itself contributes to morale and is a source for behavior which maintains the image.

With regards to expectations held by people outside to the system, the image seems to be strongly related to at least two other variables:

(a) the extent to which the system is seen as interesting and innovative and has at least some schools that are in some way "special". Innovativeness itself is an important component of a positive image; but variability and "specialness" are usually linked to the ability of the system to cater to the *special needs of specific populations*. This latter property is an important component of effectiveness in its own right; it is also extremely important for the system's image. A system known to be effective in dealing with retarded or delinquent children is *sadly*, not going to have a positive image for the general public. In the public's eye the special populations of particular importance are the gifted, creative, artistic students. It is essential for a system's image that the system is seen as offering good solutions for the education of these students.

(b) the extent to which the system is seen as a *harmonic* one, i.e., one that does not exacerbate social tensions. If a system's image is associated with things like bussing, parental protests over attempts to promote, say, social integration, then the system will be seen as a problematic one even if student grades are high.

The image of an education system also influences the degree of confidence it inspires, particularly for entrepreneurs and investors from the area and outside. The latter are interested in the quality of the local "educational products" as this is reflected in the potential of the local population to work productively in, say, new industrial ventures. This potential will be reflected in the skills they have learned in various educational frameworks and in their approach to work in general. Thus an important component of an effective local education system will be its attractiveness for investors.

It follows almost immediately from the foregoing, and in particular from our definition of local effectiveness, that a further important outcome variable is a *town's holding power*. There will be minimal out-immigration from a town with an effective educational system (in particular to neighboring towns without change of work place).

In addition an effective local education system serves not only the young but also is a focus for *cultural activities for all members of the community*. It encourages *parent involvement* in the schools and promotes *life long learning*. The system addresses the needs of adults who need to upgrade certain skills or learn new technologies because of changes in the world of work and in society in general.

In summary, the characteristics of an effective local education system that seem to us to be of particular importance are:

I. *The defining characteristics*
(1) helping to promote city growth;
(2) success in enlisting local support for itself and education in general

II. *The characteristics which follow from the defining characteristics*
(1) the system's image
(2) the existence of "special" innovative educational institutions
(3) the ability of the system to cater for the special needs of specific populations
(4) the contribution of the system to promoting and maintaining social harmony
(5) attractiveness for investors
(6) the system's holding power
(7) the extent to which the system is a focus for cultural activities for the entire community

(8) the degree to which the system encourages parent involvement
(9) the degree to which the system provides opportunities for lifelong learning

*Are The Characteristics of an Effective Local Educational System*
*Related to the Defining Characteristics of Individual Effective Schools?*
In this section we discuss some of the defining characteristics of effective local educational systems. We will examine the relationship between these and some of the defining characteristics of individual effective schools.

(a) *Achievement Scores in the Schools and the Local System's Image*
Do high achievement scores in the schools lead to a positive image, and is this image created only if there are high scores in all the schools? It is reasonable to assume that the answer to the first question is positive. Information on satisfactory achievement is passed on by parents and functionaries to the entire population; this helps create a positive image for the entire system. However we suggest that a positive image will also be created if *one or two schools* attain highly impressive scores. In such cases the effective schools become the dominant feature of the system in public consciousness. Student achievement can influence a system's image through two different mechanisms – reasonable achievement in all schools or exceptional achievement in one or two. These two mechanisms lead to two very different intervention strategies in the local system.

In choosing whether to concentrate efforts in one or two schools or to work with all the schools, one must also consider the fact that the relationship between achievement scores and image is not linear. The image of a local system will change more and more dramatically as the achievement scores in some of the schools improve more and more. Thus an intervention program oriented to changing the system's image will probably prefer to concentrate on inducing noticeably significant change in one or two schools.

It should be stressed however that the relationship between image and achievement is not a very strong one. As we saw in Rotem, the system's image changed for the worse despite the absence of objective findings on a drop in achievement. In fact we discovered that the scores in reading comprehension in the low status junior high school are the same or better than those in the other two junior highs! As indicated above, a system's image is related to the extent to which the system (1) is seen as interesting and innovative with special schools catering to special populations; (2) is seen as promoting and maintaining social harmony. A further variable strongly related to system image is the extent to which the *processes* (not outcomes) are conceived as interesting, of high quality etc. The public is likely to view the system as good because it believes the *teachers* are good (whatever that means) rather than because it knows that student achievement is high.

In addition, despite the cynicism of the idea, the presence of a few ineffective schools might heighten the image of the effective ones. Continued comparison highlights the competence of the effective schools. This might be particularly relevant as regards the town's holding power. Perhaps a town "needs" a few high status schools with good reputations *and others with low status and reputation* in order to remain attractive for its middle class population.

### (b) *School Achievement and Attracting Investors*

Conceiving school effectiveness in terms of achievement scores emphasizes the dominance of the traditional school disciplines. On the other hand, investors often require manpower characterized by creativity, divergent thinking, integrative ability and other skills not measured by the usual achievement tests in schools. A school system which can boast of its effective schools in the traditional sense may not necessarily appear attractive to investors. The latter will need to be convinced that the system's schools (or other educational frameworks and activities) have other outcome characteristics, more relevant to their needs.

### (c) *School Drop-Out and Local System Out-Migration*

A high drop-out rate is one of the characteristics of ineffective schools. Dropping out emphasizes the school's impotency in dealing with its more problematic students. We believe that this ineffectiveness at the local school level does not necessarily lead to out-migration, especially if the system provides various educational options for different populations. A single school need not necessarily deal with the problem of dropouts. Treatment by the system may be sufficient and may even lead to the attraction of students from outside the system.

### (d) *Effective Schools and The Enlisting of Local Support for Education*

Here we relate to school effectiveness in general. Clearly, if parents have the feeling that even one of the schools (elementary, junior and senior high) that their children attended was ineffective, this will have a negative effect on their belief in and support of the local system. A positive experience in even only one of the schools their children attended will probably be sufficient to reinforce their belief in *the importance of education in general.* One positive experience is probably sufficient for people to conclude that education *can be of a high standard*, and that it is worthwhile to support efforts for the improvement of educational standards. This is precisely what we meant by local support for *education itself.*

The above examples emphasize the difference between effectiveness at the school and local system levels. Once again we see that the local education system is not simply an aggregate of schools, but is rather a new entity whose output variables do not derive directly from those of the school. If this is so, perhaps the two levels are more closely linked with regards to their process variables.

351

*Are the Process Variables Which Characterize Effective Systems Similar
to Those That Characterize Individual Effective Schools?*

Effective schools are different from less successful institutions because of
certain attitudinal and behavioral patterns held in common by their teachers
and administrators. Taken together these ways of thinking and working make
up the ethos of the school (Rutter 1979) and contribute to the creation of its
climate (Anderson 1982). Even though research indicates that it is the combination of factors rather than any one of them singly which influences outcomes, we will here address ourselves to several discrete process variables
for the purposes of our discussion:

(a)  strong leadership;
(b)  emphasis on systematic monitoring of student progress;
(c)  the existence of an accountability ethos;
(d)  teamwork and cooperation between teachers.

It is generally agreed that the leadership style of the principal is an important
component of the move toward greater effectiveness. Principals who have a
definite point of view – an educational vision you like – which they actively
and consistently promote appear to be a necessary if not altogether sufficient
condition; their style may be characterized as democratic-authoritarian. This
type of leadership can permit individual teachers to develop their own strategies for the achievement of clearly enunciated goals; indeed autonomy in the
classroom is another important element in the profile of the effective school.
Acceptance of and identification with the "vision" of the principal need not
limit the creativity of the teacher in the day to day work with children.

At first glance we have good reason to believe that in order for an entire
system to be effective, its director should function in a manner similar to that
of the principal just described. This is particularly so in the case of highly
centralized systems; the director of the system is to the principal of the
individual schools as the principal is to the teachers. Looking at the relationship between the director and the principal in this way, however, seems to us
to undermine the effectiveness of the latter.

The roles of both the director and the principal are the same in certain
important respects. Both are expected to bring some clearly defined idea of
education to their work. The relation of the director to the principal, however, must be different from that of the principal to the teacher. While the
principal can require of teachers that they identify with his/her point of view,
that demand does not deny autonomy in the territory of the classroom.

This is not to say that teachers are not entitled to their own point of view
regarding the educational process. It is rather to suggest that working within
the conceptual framework developed by the principal need not adversely
affect the creativity of the teacher. By contrast, the director who insists that
principals adopt his/her point of view, limit their independence in significant

352

measure. Permitting the principal to develop an individual strategy for the achievement of the director's goals falls short of satisfying the defined necessity of the effective principal to develop and promote his/her own point of view.

The foregoing suggests that in order to be effective a system must encourage and permit diversity among its individual schools (Metz, 1986). The role of the director is to inspire each of the principal's to work at his/her idea of what his/her school might be and to provide the support and resources required for the attainment of particular goals. This approach, important when we consider the relationship between schools and the quality of life in the community they serve, also permits parents and pupils a range of choice from among a variety of educational options. Thus the relationship between the director and the principals seems to suggest that a different leadership style is needed at the two levels. Effective schools need strong leaders, effective local systems need encouraging and supportive facilitators.

What we have suggested here raises questions regarding two additional characteristics of effective schools – monitoring and accountability – when raised to the level of an entire system. If each school is encouraged to develop a direction determined by its principal, where is the locus of monitoring and what is its nature? At what point, for instance, does a system wide testing program and the demand for certain levels of achievement hamper the individual school in pursuit of its own goals? May not monitoring devised and conducted by a central office adversely affect the uniqueness of individual schools? Diversity does not, of course, reduce the accountability of each school; nor does it suggest that the system as a whole remain unaccountable. It does, however, lead us to ask as to the meaning of the accountability of a system characterized by variability among schools.

Our work in Rotem thus far has confronted us with yet another difficulty in applying a single school process variable to a system as a whole. Teamwork and a high level of cooperation between teachers has often been cited (Rutter 1979) as a factor important to the effectiveness of a school. In attempting to apply this principle to a group of schools, suggesting that their teachers work together on some matter of importance to all of them, we encountered resistance from the principal of the weakest school. We learned that the acknowledged deficiencies of the school and its reputation had created a sense of inferiority which made it difficult for its teachers to work together with the teachers of the stronger schools. It may be that teamwork among teachers from schools of different quality does not have the same positive effect as cooperation between teachers of varying levels of competence in the same schools (Goodlad 1975).

# CONCLUSION

Does our discussion lead to the conclusion that findings on effective schools are of no use when we are concerned with interventions at the local system level? Not quite. As noted in the introduction, school systems do not exist *only* for students but *also* for the cities in which they are situated. However they also *do* cater to those students! For their sakes, at the very least, we cannot ignore ineffectiveness at the school level and must incorporate individual school improvement strategies in our general intervention strategy for the local system. Our discussion must be seen as a caveat about concentrating *all* our efforts on improving individual school effectiveness, and also provides us with a tentative checklist of systemic properties which might be useful in planning system-wide interventions. At present what is lacking is a similar checklist of process variables related to effectiveness at the system level (i.e., process variables which are not simply parallels to the classic process variables identified at the school level). We hope that when we complete our work in Rotem, we will be able to propose such a checklist.

# REFERENCES

Anderson, C.S. (1982). The Search for School Climate: A Review of the Research. *Review of Educational Research, 52,* (3), 368-420.

Clark, D.L., Lotto, L.S., & Astuto, T.A. (1984). Effective schools and school improvement: A comparative analysis of two lines of inquiry, *Educational Administration Quarterly, 20,* (3), 41-68.

Goodlad, J.I. (1975). *The dynamics of educational change.* New York: McGraw-Hill.

Metz, H.M. (1986). *Different by design.* New York: Routledge and Kegan Paul.

Meyer, J.W. (1977). The effects of education as an institution, *American Journal of Sociology 83,* (1), 55-77.

Rosenthal, R. & Jacobson, L.F. (1968). *Pygmalion in the Classroom.* New York: Holt Rinehart and Winston.

Rutter, M. et al. (1979). *Fifteen Thousand Hours.* Cambridge, MA: Harvard University Press.

Sarason, S.B. (1982).*The culture of the school and the problem of change.* Boston: Allyn and Bacon.

# THE ROLE OF SCHOOL COUNCILS IN SCHOOL EFFECTIVENESS: A VICTORIAN PERSPECTIVE

Tony Townsend
School of Education, Chisholm Institute of Technology,
Frankston

## EFFECTIVE SCHOOLS AND THE AUSTRALIAN VIEWPOINT

It would be true to say that the school effectiveness movement and the school effectiveness research has not met with universal support in Australia. A common form of the definition of effective schools that has emanated from the United States is the one provided by Gerald Rosander, Superintendent of Schools in San Diego County.

> Effective schools are those in which all students master basic skills, seek academic excellence in all subjects, and demonstrate achievement through systematic testing. As a result of improved academic achievement, students in effective schools display improved behavior and attendance. (1984)

In Australia the emphasis on standardised achievement tests as being the single key element of an "effective" school has been met with various levels of skepticism. There are a number of Australian researchers that clearly indicate their concern that a concentration on effectiveness means a diminution of concern about other equally relevent educational issues,
such as equality, participation and social justice. Angus (1987) argues that simplistic notions of "effectiveness" and "school improvement" lead to a series of activities which are "socially conservative and educationally regressive". Ashenden (1987) argues that performance indicators which can be used as the arbitrary determinants of school effectiveness diminish issues of social justice within schools, and the Victorian State Board of Education (1986) cautions:

That defining outcomes as achievement on standardised tests may induce schools to begin a major re-allocation of resources into basic skill areas at the cost of other areas of curriculum.
(1986, p.12)

Of course effectiveness as the major focus of school operations is not seen as being universally accepted even in the United States. Perhaps Mario Fantini identifies the rightful place of "effectiveness" best of all when he defines "excellence" as:

$$\text{Excellence} = \begin{array}{lll} \text{Quality} & + \text{ Equality} & + \\ \text{Effectiveness} & + \text{ Efficiency} & + \text{ Participation} \end{array}$$

(1986, p.44)

In many respects the definition quoted above represents the aspirations of those within the Victorian system of education over the past fifteen or so years. At different points along the way, the history of education in Victoria clearly shows how legislation, the establishment of support service units and the work of various groups within the Victorian educational community have continued to press towards the establishment of a framework of "excellence" within which schools could work. A short look at some of these aspects will demonstrate the progression.

## SCHOOL BASED DECISION MAKING IN VICTORIA

Parent participation in school decision making in the state of Victoria has almost come a full circle since the first school was established in Collins Street, Melbourne by the Scots Church in 1836. From that date until the Education Act of 1872, when the State School system became free, compulsory, secular and centralised, local communities had a say in what was to be taught and who was to teach it. For the next century parents were quite actively discouraged from having any say in their child's education. From 1973 after publication of the influential Karmel Report, named after the Chairman of the Australian Schools Commission that was commissioned to write the report by the Federal Government, the issues of equality of educational achievement, devolution of responsibility, diversity of educational organisation and community involvement in school decision-making were first canvassed on a National level. Finally, after eighteen months of negotiations between the Victorian Government, Education Department officials, parent groups such as VICSSO and the Victorian Parents Federation and teacher unions, the 1975 School Councils amendment to the 1958 Education Act was passed.

356

School Councils with common powers were at that time established in all State Schools in Victoria. The powers and duties included the usual range of duties relating to grounds maintenance, generating public interest in the school and ensuring that teachers had accommodation, but two major new responsibilities emerged. The new council, in addition to those duties listed above, would:

(a) advise the Principal and staff of the school as to the general educational policy of that school.

(b) ensure that all moneys coming into the school are expended for proper purposes.

After further consideration of the issues involved and a change of Government in 1982, the first of these was changed in 1984 to read:

(a) To determine the general educational policy of the school within the guidelines issued by the Minister.

(The 1984 School Council Amendment to the 1958 Education Act)

The other responsibilities remained as they were in 1975. Of course this turned the entire decision-making process upside down. However, since the education of the children at the local state school had clearly now become a partnership responsibility between parents and teachers, it was fitting that the membership of the Council reflected this. Parents and teachers had roughly the same number of members on the new councils with the opportunity student representation in secondary schools and for members of the local community to be co-opted onto the Council. As the system began to function those involved at the school level discovered that, in fact, the school, rather than anyone in it, had far more control over the curriculum than it ever had before, and that as a school there was a prospect for more local development than had ever been the case previously.

Of six Ministerial Papers on Decision Making in Victorian Government Schools, perhaps the most important of these for school effectiveness was Paper Two, The School Improvement Plan. The Plan aimed to provide the assistance schools needed to adopt collaborative processes that would enable the school to reflect on "their total practice" and to "improve the learning experiences of all students". By the start of 1987 more than half of Victorian Government Schools had joined the School Improvement Plan and a Ministry survey at the end of 1986 showed that over 90% of the schools involved had been happy with the progress that the school had made under the plan. It is anticipated that by the end of 1988 nearly ninety percent of Victorian Government Schools will have joined the plan.

357

A further development that began in the post-primary schools and eventually became normal practice in most of the larger primary schools as well, was the exercise of the option for School Councils to be involved in the selection process for Principals of their school. This new development was a logical extension of the local control of policy. Previously, without some input into the selection of the person who will put that policy into practice, giving School Councils the power to determine policy was a hollow gift indeed.

## CHANGING ATTITUDES: RESPONSES TO CHANGING ROLES

Over the past ten years a number of studies have been conducted that have determined local school responses to what the role of the school should be and the role parents should play in the determination of what happens in the school. A number of studies have tried to identify the key functions of the school and there appears to be only a general degree of unanimity between parents and teachers as to the major directions that the school should be taking. In three such studies the major directions of school achievement were identified as being academic or intellectual pursuits, personal and emotional development and social, moral and citizenship skills. Bartollotta and Finn (1980) indicated that parents and Dunmall (1980) both parents and teachers gave intellectual development top priority and personal development second priority. Cotter (1981) found that although parents and teachers disagreed about the order of importance, with teachers placing academic pursuits as top priority while parents placed social and moral development and personal development as having higher priority than academic pursuits, both groups placed the three mentioned as the top three priorities in a list of six.

However other studies indicate that intellectual development as expressed by literacy and numeracy should not be seen to be the sole indicator of a school's success. Downer and Maunder (1982) found that only twenty two per cent of parents from a rural towntown and thirty seven per cent of the parents from the local farming community agreed with the statement that "primary schools should only be judged by their success in teaching students reading, writing and arithmetic." (1982) A second study by

Jefferson (1980) found that thirty five percent of parents, thirty five percent of students, but only five percent of teachers felt "we should judge the success of the school by the performance of its students in English and Mathematics." A Gallup Poll of over 2000 people across the country in 1985 indicated that fifty six percent of the respondents felt that the main purpose of education was to equip young people to be good citizens and thirty seven percent of therepondents indicated that the major purpose was to equip young people for the workforce. ("The Herald", June 4 1985).

Finally, the study conducted by a group of Graduate students at Chisholm Institute of Technology (Aglinskas, Donohue, Finch, Graham, Petrie and Norman, 1988) has found that the statement "an effective school largely concentrates on basic skills" rated seventh of fifteen statements, behind dedicated and qualified staff, a safe and orderly environment, early identification of children at risk, good leadership, home school relations and a positive school climate.

These studies clearly indicate that there is no unanimity within Victoria for the proposal that schools should be directed solely towards academic areas of learning and, in fact, there is almost a clear statement of the opposite view, that other areas such as personal development and good citizenship are the directions that the community wishes education to go.

The studies seem to indicate that different communities will consider different aspects of the total curriculum as being more important than others. The School Council legislation enables local communities to respond to these emphases but at the same time ensures that certain local needs do not ignore the need for the maintenance of certain core elements of the curriculum which are determined as the minimum necessary by Government.

A second set of studies indicates a gradual acceptance of parent and school council involvement in various aspects of school based decision making.

These studies looked at the attitude of various groups within the school community to parents being involved in various levels of decision making within schools. The interesting point about this collection of studies is the changing attitudes of principals and school councillors towards the roles that have gradually moved from a centralised to a local decision making process.

Hawkesworth (1980) and McAlpine (1981) found that all principals and the majority of school councillors felt that parents should be involved in budget preparations, financial decisions and responsible for the control of grounds and facilities. Critchley (1982) on the other hand found that only fifty five percent of urban parents as compared to seventy eight percent of rural parents wanted to be involved in budgetary decisions.

These three studies show that principals and school councillors, who had been involved in decisions about finance and the management of buildings and grounds since 1975 were far more accepting of these responsibilities than the general parent group.

McAlpine (1981) and Downer and Maunder (1980) found that school councillors and parents felt that they should be responsible for giving advice on school policy. Skidmore (1982) found that teachers who felt that parents should hardly ever be involved in planning and curriculum activities in the school in 1980 felt that they should be when asked again in 1982. Hawkesworth (1980) , Phillips (1981) and McAlpine (1981) found that a minority of Principals were happy with school council or parent input into curriculum planning but that none of them were prepared to accept total control of the curriculum by school council. However the same studies indicated that in the schools surveyed more than half of the principals indicated that there was parental involvement in curriculum decision making. Critchley (1982) found that a majority of parents felt that they should be involved in curriculum development.

Once again these surveys show that there is a gradual acceptance of parents being involved in policy development and the curriculum process as time has gone on. Since 1975 many school councils established education sub-committees as part of their decision making structure, and the value of parents and teachers working together on these committees, together with the introduction of parents being used as teaching aides in the classroom has broken down many of the attitudinal barriers that prevented parent participation.

Hawkesworth (1980) and McAlpine (1981) found that only a small minority of principals indicated some willingness in school councillors or parents having a say in the selection of school staff and Phillips (1981), Downer and Maunder (1982) and Critchley (1982) found that only a minority of parents and school councillors wanted to be involved.

However Aglinskas et al (1988 ) found that more than eighty per cent of principals, school councillors and parents agreed with the school council being involved in the selection of senior staff. In the same study only fifty seven percent of teachers were in agreement with the school council being involved in the selection of senior staff. This change seems to have largely come about with the practice of school councils having a role in Principal selection and the realisation by the people involved that power to determine the general educational policy of the school would only be successful if school councils also had an input into the senior personnel who would have responsibility for putting that policy into practice. It is interesting to note, however, that the teachers who were not on school councils have not really changed their opinion much at all.

Whereas the Gallup Poll referred to earlier ("The Herald, June 4 1985) found that more than fifty percent of the people surveyed felt that the teaching programme to equip the students for either their becoming good citizens or for the workforce was inadequate, Aglinskas et al (1988) indicated that a vast majority of principals, school councillors, staff and parents accepted that their school was effective, or if not fully effective, then effective in some ways.

In the Aglinskas et al (1988) study the majority of respondents identified parents, teachers and students working cohesively together as being the most acceptable definition of an effective school with a safe and happy environment closely following. The more academically oriented possibilities such as a concentration on basic skills, promoting and achieving learning and growth and total potential development were less well supported, but were nevertheless ranked 4th, 5th and equal 6th respectively. This seems to indicate a general acceptance that issues other than academic achievement are seen to be important by members of local school communities, and that this has implications for any movement towards the development of effective schools in Victoria.

These results all indicate that there are changing attitudes about the value of what is occurring in Victorian schools, with Principals and school councillors, those people most closely involved with policy decisions and implementation, becoming much more aware of the partnership approach and of the need for strengthening local input. It may well be assumed that with further time to work within the system, that these attitudes will be strengthened even further.

## FUTURE DIRECTIONS

One of the difficulties faced by schools with the rapid changes to the decision making powers of parents and teachers working together as school councillors is the lack of training and support services necessary to enable people to improve their skills in decision making. So far, there is a lack of a statewide strategy to improve the skills of people at school level. The gap has had to be filled by parent groups such as Victorian Council for State Schools Organisations and the Victorian Parents Federation, both of which have limited resources for this type of activity. However VICSSO has now undertaken to provide training and informational programs to people on school councils right across the state.

A further difficulty to be faced by local communities in the future is the movement towards performance indicators which seems to be one of the products of the move towards an "effective" school system by the bureaucracy. Some of the rhetoric of the effective schools movement has rubbed off onto bureaucrats who see it as an excellent political hobby-horse because of the emotional appeal that it will have for communities. The danger of this is that effectiveness will become a centre piece for school operations, and will be used by the bureaucracy as a means of centralised control over school decision making.

Ministry officials have moved some distance towards the establishment of a framework "of school level evaluation and accountability" (Marshall, 1988) that incorporates performance indicators into that framework. The real difficulty with performance indicators is that they can only judge things quantifiably, and yet effectiveness is often a measure of quality. Marshall (1988) provides a framework of "contributing factors" within a school,

Effective  =  Effective   +  Effective school   +  Effective resource
School        curriculum      climate                use

$$(1988, p.14)$$

361

It is easy to find an example of the difficulties arising from the performance indicator way of determining whether a school is effective or not Marshall identifies "Community Involvement" as one of the indicators of effective school climate, and his method of testing this within a school would be to identify "the percentage ofparents at school events" (1988,p.15). The problem is the inability to distinguish between the quality of input between schools. Thus a school where ninety percent of the parents attended a school fete would be seen as more effective than one that had sixty per cent of the parents fully active in the life of the school. In the same paper "equity" would be tested in terms of retention rates. This kind of use of the school effectiveness literature to generate levels of accountability is not only educationally regressive, it is damaging to over fifteen years of positive inputs at the local level. If the results discussed are any indication of statewide concerns about schools then it is obvious that further studies of community perceptions of what constitute effective schools need to be undertaken on a statewide basis before any great movement towards performance indicators based on academic achievement is taken.

## CONCLUDING REMARKS

In summing up the situation in Victoria, the past twenty years has seen an enormous move towards local control of government schools. From a position in 1970 where the local community had no say as to what went on in the local school we have now reached a position where decisions made at the school site have a real impact on the day to day program in the school. Parents at the school site are now involved in the determination of school policy, school curriculum and in the employment of senior staff who will implement that curriculum; in short local communities are almost back to where they were in the early history of education in this state. But at this point it must be accepted that there is a far more knowledgable community involved in the activity.

Piece by piece the movement is towards further local control at the school site level, and piece by piece the local community is adopting strategies to assimilate the new changes. Gradually, parents are becoming more involved in the determination of what will happen at "their" school and are starting to develop a real affinity with the learning process and a greater degree of commitment to the school as a local institution, resulting in an increasing number of people becoming involved.

In a state that is desperately trying to raise retention rates and the community's attitude towards education in general, the School Council direction and the increasing involvement of parents in the decision making processes of education is a movement in the right direction. In less time than it took for a child to complete the formal and compulsory schooling program, the retention rate has more than doubled.

It seems that the main difficulty with the movement towards "effective schools" relates to the difficulties of testing. Although at this stage we in Victoria continue to shy away from the standardised academic achievement tests, the movement towards performance indicators based on the effective schools literature, which relies heavily on standardised tests, is fraught with danger. In the long run a truly effective school may be that way because of the elements that can't be tested rather than because of those that can. It is not possible to test things like quality, equality, leadership and participation with any form of standardised test yet devised, because all of these things depend on the situation, the people involved and their interactions for success. And it may well be that in the long run we value these qualities higher than academic achievement anyway. Until communities determine what effective schools are for themselves, the chances of achieving truly effective schools are marginal.

In the end it is the people involved at the school site, the children, the parents and the teachers, who are in a position to determine whether a school is effective or not. And that determination will rely heavily on what they, the participants in the education activity, hope to achieve. When the children in school now become the next generation of parents, Victoria could have a great example of an effective system of education at work. We can only wait......

# REFERENCES

Aglinskas, A. et al. (1988). *Perceptions of School Effectiveness.* Unpublished Thesis, Chisholm Institute of Technology, Frankston.

Angus, L.B. (1986). The Risk of School Effectiveness: A Comment on Recent Education Reports. *The Australian Administrator,* 7 (3).

Ashenden, D. (1987). *An Odd Couple? Social Justice. Performance Indicators.* A Public lecture sponsored by the State Board of Education, Victoria.

Bartollotta, A. & Finn, P. (1980). *Community Expectations of Education.* Unpublished Thesis, State College of Victoria at Frankston.

Cotter, M. (1981). *An Evaluation of Parents and Teachers Expectations of Primary School Education: A Case Study of a Semi-Rural Environment.* Unpublished Thesis, State College of Victoria at Frankston.

Critchley, R.D. (1982). *An Investigation of the Difference in Attitudes and Opinions of Rural and Urban School Parents Towards Parental Participation in Schools.* Unpublished Thesis, Chisholm Institute of Technology, Frankston.

Downer, B.J. & Maunder, B.H. (1982). *A Study of Community Attitudes and Opinions Towards Primary Education in the Longwarry and Drouin Districts.* Unpublished Thesis, Chisholm Institute of Technology, Frankston.

Dunmall, E.M. (1980). *Parental Opinions on Curriculum Relevancy - A Case Study conducted at Mentone Primary School.* Unpublished Thesis, State College of Victoria at Frankston.

Education Department (1933).General Course of Study for Elementary Schools, 1934. In the Education Gazette and Teachers Aid, Vol XXXIII, October, Victoria.

Fantini, M. (1986). *Regaining Excellence in Education*. Columbus, Merrill.

Fordham, R. (1985). *Ministerial Papers 1-6*. Education Department of Victoria, Melbourne, Australia.

Hawkesworth, J.V. (1980). *A Study of Principal's Attitudes to Community Involvement*. Unpublished Thesis, State College of Victoria at Frankston.

Jefferson, R.E. (1980). *Perceptual Differences in the Role of the School*. Unpublished Thesis, State College of Victoria at Frankston.

Marshall, G. (1988). *The Application of Performance Indicators at the School Level to a Program Planning and Evaluation Cycle*. A paper presented to the National Conference on Performance Indicators in Education, Sydney.

McAlpine, L.R. (1981). *A Study of Principal Acceptance and Understanding of Community Education Concepts*. Unpublished Thesis, State College of Victoria at Frankston.

Ministry of Education (1987). *Improving Victorian Schools: Implications of Data on the School Improvement Plan*. Victoria.

Phillips, R.N. (1981). *An Investigation into the Role of the Primary School Councils as perceived by a selected Sample of Council Members - A Case Study in the Frankston Region*. Unpublished Thesis, State College of Victoria at Frankston.

Purkey, S.C. & Smith, M.S. (1983). Effective Schools - A Review. *Elementary School Journal, 83*, (4).

Rosander, G.A. (1984). *Characteristics of Effective Schools*. San Diego County Office of Education, San Diego.

Skidmore, R.G. (1982). *Parental Participation - An Evaluation of the Strategies Applied to a State Primary School to Promote Substantial Parent Participation 1980 - 1982* Unpublished Thesis, Chisholm Institute of Technology, Frankston.

State Board of Education (1986). *Improving Schools: Some Policy Issues*. Victoria.

The Commonwealth Schools Commission (1971). *Schools in Australia. (The Karmel Report)*. Canberra.

# SCHOOL IMPROVEMENT: SECOND GENERATION*

## ISSUES AND STRATEGIES

Frederick I. Renihan

Saskatchewan Education, Regina

and

Patrick J. Renihan

University of Saskatchewan, Saskatoon

## INTRODUCTION

For almost a decade now, the research findings of school effectiveness researchers on both sides of the Atlantic have provided the impetus for identifying common characteristics differentiating between what Goldhammer et al, (1971) referred to as "beacons of brilliance" and "potholes of pestilence." Throughout the world, the research has clarified, time and again, several common facets behind school success. Notable among these facets were *leadership, climate, academic focus, high expectations, joint decision making, sense of mission, positive motivational strategies, and feedback on academic performance.* The studies served their purpose, and widespread initiatives were undertaken, feeding at first upon the effective schools literature, and later upon each other, to foster school improvement. The subsequent groundswell of improvement projects (in some locations characterized as "school reform") demonstrated the versatility of the "model" in a variety of school contexts; large and small, rural and urban, old and new. The effective schools research has paid off, if for no other reason than that it has been the catalyst for school improvement efforts, together with an unprecedented level of introspection among school professionals.

---

* The term "second generation" has been borrowed from the discussion of second generation issues in the human resources approach to management by Miles and Rosenberg, which appeared in the Winter, 1982 edition of Organization Dynamics.

In a previous article, we identified common characteristics of successful school effectiveness projects (Renihan et al., 1986). However, as we will argue, school improvement as a "movement" has matured to the point that retrospective views of improvement efforts are now possible. This constitutes a "second generation" with an entirely new set of questions, problems and issues which need attention if the concept of school effectiveness is to be institutionalized as a continuing focus of activity, and if entropic forces (waning motivation, changing priorities, fatigue) are not to be allowed to render the school improvement movement no more than a memorable bandwagon.

The second-generation questions, therefore, are not "Can we build more effective schools?" or "What can we do in order to improve our schools?" The question now is "What can we do to sustain and expand them?" The answers to the first two questions had their sources comfortably couched in the school effectiveness literature. The answers to the latter, however, are less clear, partly because they pertain to phenomena unanticipated in first generation school effectiveness work, and partly because they involve variables such as morale, motivation and commitment which have their roots in social-psychological factors, many of which are, by nature, ambiguous and elusive.

In this article, therefore, we will describe the notion of second generation in the context of school-improvement, stating why we believe it to be a significant problem deserving serious attention among those involved in school improvement. We will also describe, on the basis of our own experience with school improvement efforts, what we perceive to be the most significant second generation issues. Finally we will make an effort to prescribe approaches for dealing with these issues, and postulate several crucial cornerstones of effective school improvement.

## THE NOTION OF SECOND GENERATION

First generation school improvement efforts have taken their thrusts, largely from the school effectiveness literature, and many such efforts have resulted in considerable gains in the quality of teaching and school life. However, several additional questions come to the forefront as school improvement projects reach a point in their maturity when a number of serious issues, some anticipated but many unanticipated, present themselves. As we have noted, the answers are not available for most of these conundrums in the school effectiveness literature. Consequently, educators are forced to explore further afield in search of adequate coping strategies. Some projects have been more successful in this regard than have others, but, for many, the existence of new problems without answers tends at first to considerably weaken the improvement effort, threatening, in time, to kill it. This point is probably the most powerful argument in favour of a discussion of second-generation school improvement issues. *An understanding of such issues can assist educators in more effectively and proactively planning a school improvement effort with adequate consideration for later eventualities which can make or break it.*

# SECOND GENERATION ISSUES

The inherent difference between first generation and second generation concerns, as we perceive it, is that the first are concerned with *initiating* the process, the learning, the commitment, the support and so on, while the second are concerned with *sustaining* the process by whatever effective means can be employed. The identification of second generation issues emerged from our consultations with professionals involved in school improvement projects in Manitoba and Saskatchewan, Canada, between 1982 and 1988. Two broad themes emerged from analysis of these consultations. They relate to a) the organizational structure associated with the school improvement effort, and b) the actors involved in the school improvement effort, their individual readiness and their relationships with one another.

## *The Structure of School Improvement*

### a) *Maintenance*
Typical school improvement thrusts are characterized in their early life-cycle, by a period of high motivation, optimism and a feeling of accomplishment. This stage is one in which commitment, productivity and involvement are carried along at a high level on a spirit of novelty and an aura of change. Among school communities, particularly those which had been previously less active, the feeling is one of "At last we're getting somewhere."

A large part of this enthusiasm may be attributable to a sort of "Hawthorne effect," where fervor, morale, involvement and the general ethos of the school are heightened more by the feeling that something is being done, than by the specifics of what is being done. The primary concern, therefore, is maintenance. How can we sustain the improvement efforts and continue practices which have been put in place? In considering this question, several concomitant issues require attention: What do we do when enthusiasm flags? Who takes charge? How do we cope with feelings of failure, futility, and strained relationships when progress slows down or problems resurface? The level of this type of feeling, and its basis in actual improvement, has serious implications for the time when initial enthusiasm wanes, as it most certainly will.

## b) *Goal Accomplishment*

The school effectiveness literature is seductively simple. It portrays school organizations and the vehicles for improving them in terms which are eminently sensible and which are easy to comprehend. While this has largely contributed to the widespread following it has received, it must also rank as one of its most serious drawbacks, creating the misleading representation of organizational change as a simple process. Kilmann (1985) in his prescriptive text on how organizations can go beyond the "quick fix," put the idea this way:

> It is time to stop perpetuating the myth of simplicity. The system of organization invented by mankind generates complex problems that cannot be solved by simple solutions.

Success, according to Kilmann represents high performance and high morale *over an extended period of time,* and we most certainly concur with that definition when applied to the school setting. In fact, short term school improvement efforts can at best only hope for short term benefits. Unfortunately, many schools, lured by the seductive simplicity of the rhetoric and the apparent ease of bringing about successful change, approach school improvement with unrealistic expectations for what dividends the project will pay. Ultimately, however, several common questions assert themselves: What are the tangible indicators of improvement? How will we know when an objective has been reached? How do we decide what to do next? When and how should we conduct further reviews or audits of school operation?

## c) *Monitoring*

The establishment of a process for monitoring a school improvement thrust is a first generation concern, yet three factors combine to make it a common second generation issue:
a) its actual use as an appendage, rather than a planned, central activity;
b) poorly defined roles, responsibilities and actions relating to monitoring;
c) unplanned provision for using the results of evaluations.

Loosely applied evaluation, or overuse of informal evaluation, in a school improvement effort is, in itself, a serious inconsistency when considered in the light of the effective schools literature which elevates such factors as feedback, high expectations, and monitoring in the overall scheme of things. Consequently, several planning questions emerge as vital considerations in this area: What aspects of the project will be evaluated? Who will be responsible for the monitoring function? Who will report progress? To whom? Who will have responsibility for taking action regarding suggested changes?

We are not suggesting that informal monitoring does not have a place in school improvement. We are suggesting that, without carefully laid-out

368

strategies (perhaps including informal information), evaluation and its related roles in the improvement effort will, at best, be an uncertain process
subject to the sometimes capricious and arbitrary whims of those who may
be responsible for implementation.

### Actors and Responsibilities

a) *Leadership*
The type of leadership required for effective *initiation* of school improvement may not necessarily be the type required for *maintenance* of school
improvement efforts. In fact, we suggest that, once a school improvement
project is underway, a new range of leadership responsibilities, demands and
skills is called into play. The principal having responsibility for a school
involved in school improvement can expect:
- a decrease in self-initiated tasks and an increase in other directed tasks
- an increase in role-set (more people involved)
- a heightened public relations role
- greater pressures on time available during working day
- a changed time-use pattern
- greater involvement in committee work
- greater involvement in promoting and planning self-development
- heightened involvement with students
- greater need for personal administrative upgrading
- an increased monitoring responsibility
- an increased "brokerage" function (finding the physical, financial and human resources to make the program viable)

b) *Key Actors*
The gap left by the departure of key individuals in a school improvement
effort presents a problem, particularly in instances where school improvement is personality driven rather than institutionalized. The removal of leaders in the process can be traumatic, and survival of initiatives depends upon
several factors the most significant of which are the availability of energetic,
committed individuals to continue the work, and more important, the success
with which previous changes had been incorporated into the fabric of school
life, rather than being vested in, and heavily dependent upon, key personali-
ties.

c) *Staff Development*
School effectiveness and school improvement bring significant implications
for adult education among various constituent groups in the school. Two sets
of second generation issues emerge in this area.
The first pertains to staff professional development. Areas chosen as
themes for school improvement bring with them implications for staff in-

service. In turn, demands are made at the school system level for support in the form of finances and time for inservice related to the improvement theme. Leadership, therefore, has to be given to the development of relevant professional development programs. The dilemma for school administrators is that content and related resources can not be planned, in many instances, well in advance because areas of inservice are identified, understandably, at that time when school teams identify action plans for school improvement. Consequently, the nature of related inservice can only be identified when the school is well into the process of school improvement.

The second aspect of adult education relates to the impact of the education and resultant sophistication of various publics concerning school matters. In order to bring about such worthy objectives as "team ethos," "effective communication," and "a structured system of involvement," a considerable educative process has to take place. With this process comes a higher level of maturity. Consequently, there will be more people in the school community with ideas (and concerns) to share regarding educational matters, there will probably be more "experts," more committees and, concomitantly, a greater need for vigilance on the part of those responsible for the school, to ensure that ideas are listened to and that committees continue to serve a useful and constructive purpose.

Contrary to popular opinion, the work-load of administrators increases dramatically rather than lessens when a philosophy of involvement is promoted in the school organization. The subsequent "participative jungle" can create problems which can spiral proportional to the number of interest groups and individuals brought into the mainstream of the school environment by improvement thrusts.

### d) *Dissonance*

The stakeholder approach to organization is one which gives prominence to a) identifying key constituent groups with a vested interest in the organization and b) meaningfully involving them in the life of the organization.

A common second generation problem in school improvement stems from the underinvolvement (intentional or non-intentional) of key stakeholders.

Where the professional staff of a school are caught up in the throws of school improvement, other publics in the community can become very much out of touch with the internal knowledge base. The internal staff become a self-congratulatory and self-sustaining "quiet priesthood." The problem, of course, becomes manifest when the support of one or more of the 'external' partners is called for in the form of involvement, or in the injection of material resources.

It is easy to give the advice that educators should involve key publics to as great an extent as possible in school matters. Such advice, however, does not consider the constituents who are apathetic, neither does it take into consideration the periodic infusion of new lay people into the system as parents,

370

new trustees, etc. Some level of dissonance between professional and publics must exist. The task, for school leaders, is one of keeping such dissonance as minimal and potentially nondisruptive as possible.

# THE CHALLENGE

Second generation issues present challenges for those vested with the mandate of reaping the greatest possible benefits of school improvement efforts. Success in dealing with related concerns will hinge largely upon the outlook of those who shape the programs. The more pessimistic would doubtless suggest that some of the serious emergent concerns will bring about a paralysis, causing the school to revert to an "as you were" status after its brief foray into school improvement. One might even speculate that, where a project is abandoned prematurely, the resultant deflation in morale will bring a school to a status inferior on some dimensions to that which was enjoyed before the project was conceived.

A much more optimistic scenario implies some ability among school professionals to identify, and grapple with, the second generation issues as they translate into problems. The more successful teams will have some ability to approach these issues proactively, and will have strategies in place to anticipate eventualities and to effectively intercept potential problems.

We have approached the strategies outlined below with the above point in mind. Most of them should have some relevance to the process of proactive planning in school improvement. There will always, however, be some aspects of second generation issues that will be impossible to anticipate or predict clearly.

## Second Generation Strategies

For some of the issues we have identified, specific approaches are readily available, and been applied successfully in school contexts. Many others are not resolvable through the application of handy nostrums. The following suggestions therefore combine our experiences in school improvement with our speculations as to what might be useful possibilities for dealing with troublesome second-generation school improvement issues.

## Maintenance

How do successful school improvement efforts counteract the negative impacts of progress decline and the failure syndrome? In our experience, the strategies having most impact on the longevity of the project are those which *institutionalize* the school improvement effort, embedding it in the fabric of the school and its operation. This is done in several concrete ways:

- the provision of system-level support in the form of a school system philosophy of school improvement, clearly articulated and known throughout the school system
- the reinforcement of school improvement through the activities and decisions of school administrators and elected officials
- the deliberate and active solicitation of involvement of representatives of key publics, planned and structured to ensure sustained participation in activities
- the establishment of clear monitoring procedures (through a committee including representatives of teacher, student and parent groups, and involving at least one external person), structured to periodically review progress and report to staff
- the provision of deliberately scheduled times at regular intervals during the year, at staff meetings, board meetings, principals meetings, etc. to provide for discussion of schoo improvement an school progress
- the provision of school improvement – related staff development, and the provision of periodic "refresher sessions" to review school effectiveness literature, discuss ideas in the research and to keep the central messages of school effectiveness in the forefront of thinking at the school level

These activities and others like them can create over time a "culture of improvement" which can assume a life of its own in the school environment. This idea is reflected further in recent literature on the creation and nurturance of healthy school cultures, and the point is particularly well made by Saphier and King (1985) who note that, if certain norms of school culture are strong, improvements will be significant, continuous and widespread, and if they are weak, improvements will be at best infrequent, random and slow. "In short," they add, "good seeds will not grow in weak cultures."


### Goal Accomplishment
We consider it vital to the success of a school improvement project that "goal achievement points" are carefully identified to give a positive feeling that the school is going somewhere, rather than drifting aimlessly toward some nebulous and elusive "effectiveness" nirvana.

Under school improvement, periodic goal-setting compatible to the mission of the school is a central activity. The product need not be, nor should it be, a series of general platitudes about school operation. In order to improve the product and the value of the process, four criteria (which we have adapted from Ivancevich et al., 1978) may be usefully employed:

a) *Clarity*
How clearly understood is the stated goal to all parties? How easily can action plans for the school be developed from these goals?

b) *Participation*
To what extent have key constituents been involved in the process of goal-setting? 14

c) *Relevancy*
How relevant is the goal to the specific circumstances of the school? How are goals tied to reviews (audits) of school operation which may have been conducted?

d) *Weighting and Priorities*
Has some consideration been given to what matters most? What facets of school life require earlier attention than others? What facets require more attention than others? What facets require the input of more people?

*Monitoring*
The effectiveness of the monitoring function will depend upon whether or not it is seen as an appendage to, or a focal activity in, school improvement. Whatever the label given to the process, we see it as integral. This implies that formal and deliberate provision should be made for obtaining clear, periodic readings of progress and for guiding future decisions. This is most effectively accomplished by a standing monitoring committee, the membership of which is not solely restricted to professionals.

In making formal provision for monitoring and evaluation, the outline provided by Caldwell and Spinks (1986) serves as a useful guide for proactive school improvement planning. Their "evaluation plan" consists of four elements:
a) aspects of the program to be evaluated
b) kinds of information to be gathered in the evaluation
c) methods of collection of information
d) people who will be involved in gathering and providing information

An additional consideration pertains to the use to which evaluations are put. Feedback which is hidden under a pile of correspondence on a principal's desk will not only be of limited use to the school, it will, in the long run, frustrate and alienate those who provide the information. Consequently, we would expand the above evaluation plan to include consideration of how the data, once received, will be used.

*Leadership*
From our discussion to date, one point concerning leadership can be made: school improvement requires team leadership, not leadership vested in one individual. This point builds upon the definition of leadership as a property of the group. Consequently, an evaluation of leadership in the school improvement context is, to a significant extent, evaluation of the collaborative team.

Of course the individual who has the formal responsibility and ultimate accountability for, the school needs to periodically review his own skills as demanded by the new and sometimes unanticipated tasks associated with maintaining the school improvement effort. In turn, in school administrators need support, not only of the team, but also of system-level administration in the form of relevant administrative development relevant to second generation concerns.

### Key Actors

One measure of the success of a school improvement initiative lies in the extent to which it can take on a "life of its own." People and leadership are important components of the process. However, good planning and clear procedural mechanisms are required if overdependenceupon one or two key leaders in "making the program tick" is to be avoided. One approach to this is described in the text by Caldwell and Spinks (1986) in which the approach to effectiveness is couched in terms of collaborative school management and a policy-making framework emphasizing goal-setting, planning and budgeting, implementing and evaluating. The theme of this work leaves the strong message that leadership in the context of school improvement is predominantly systematic and "policy driven," rather than predominantly "personality driven."

### Staff Development

Accompanying the new and varied demands for professional development of staff is a two-sided demand for support: support from the board and administration in legitimizing and sponsoring relevant professional development activities and, more important, support from within the professional group in the form of commitment to professional development related to school improvement.

In regard to the natural outcomes of having a more educated set of publics, school administrators need to be aware of the implications of this for their own roles. *Good schools do not encourage silent partners.* The implications of involvement point to an escalating need for new and creative ways of tapping the resources of these partners. Those charged with the formal responsibility for the school, therefore, need to give serious attention to the questions of how and to what extent people need to be involved in educational matters. One old "standby," which has been a useful guide to decision makers in the past, is the application of tests of a) relevance and b) expertise in considering the nature of involvement. In other words, the nature of people's involvement depends upon how keenly interested and affected they are by the decision area, and how much understanding they have on matters relating to the issues inherent in it (Bridges, 1967).

374

# DISSONANCE

Keeping the variety of publics in touch with the affairs of the school enlarges the area of responsibility of school personnel. It calls for a well-planned program of public relations which, according to Knezevich (1984) aims at keeping the public better informed about the school, earning community acceptance of the school, and reducing the incidence of uniformed criticism. This calls for serious efforts at maintaining a high level of partnership among school publics, and in identifying and socializing those new to the system. The beginning of the public support for what goes on in the schools rests in its understanding. This would seem to be a major justification for conscientious efforts on the part of school professionals to establish and maintain a deliberate and active public relations program.

# CONCLUSION

In this discussion of second generation issues, we have advocated anticipatory approaches to school improvement as far superior to quick fix efforts. Conscious attention to second-generation concerns pays significant dividends in terms of success, longevity and levels of satisfaction with the improvement project. School improvement is not a quick fix, it is a long-term proposition; it is not personality-driven, it is team-driven; it is not simple, it is a complex process demanding an extraordinarily high level of professional involvement and commitment. Most important of all, it calls for proactive planning which takes cognizance of second generation issues, and it calls for the collaborative efforts of a diversity of school publics.

# REFERENCES

Bridges, E.M. (1967). A model for shared decision-making in the school principalship. *Educational Administration Quarterly, 3,* 51.

Caldwell, B.J. & Spinks, J.M. (1986). *Policy making and planning for school effectiveness.* Tasmania: Department of Education.

Goldhammer, K., et al. (1971). *Elementary principals and their schools: Beacons of brilliance and potholes of pestilence.* Eugene OR: Center for Advanced Study of Educational Administration, University of Oregon.

Ivancevich, J.M., McMahon, T.J., Streidl, J.W. & Szilagyi, A.D. (1978). Goal setting: The Tennaco Approach to personnel development and management effectiveness. *Organizational Dynamics, 6* (3).

Kilmann, R.H. (1985). *Beyond the Quick Fix.* London: Jossey-Bass.

Knezevich, S.J. (1984). *Administration of public education,* (4th ed.). New York: Harper and Row.

Renihan, P.J., Renihan, F.I. & Waldron, P. (1986). The common ingredients of successful school effectiveness projects. *Education Canada, 26* (3), 16-21.

Saphier, J. & King, M. (March, 1985). Good seeds grow in strong cultures. *Educational Leadership*, 67-74.

# POSTSCRIPT

# THE FUTURE DEVELOPMENT OF SCHOOL EFFECTIVENESS AND SCHOOL IMPROVEMENT

Bert Creemers
RION, Institute for Educational Research, University of Groningen

and

Dave Reynolds
University of Wales, Cardiff College

## INTRODUCTION

The greatly increased number of people taking part was the most striking thing about the Second Congress in Rotterdam, as against the First Congress in London: in Rotterdam there were over 350 people and in London around 120. The greatly increased number of people present who were involved in school improvement or school development was obvious also. However, the number of countries involved stayed at roughly the same figure (14 or 15), suggesting that some countries' involvement may be difficult to obtain - Italy, Belgium, France, Spain, Japan and the Latin American countries, for example, were not represented at either of the Congress meetings. Most important of all, we have so far had no representation at all from Third World countries in spite of the commitment to educational excellence and to equity issues that is obvious in the political discourse of so many of them. The absence of such countries does not help the countries themselves and unfortunately leaves the body of knowledge that is being established as heavily restricted in its empirical base to the industrialized nations.

## SCHOOL EFFECTIVENESS RESEARCH

### Research Design
If we proceed to look at the school effectiveness research that was on offer in Rotterdam, then it is clear that major improvements in research design have occurred over the last few years. Studies are increasingly using multiple

indicators of the quality of school intakes, as opposed to the use of one or two measures of pupil achievement and/or parental social class that was so common. A higher proportion of studies are also utilizing a 'cohort' design rather than a 'cross-sectional' one, whereby the increments for the same children in different schools can be studied over time. Most important of all, it is clear that multi-level methods of analyses which permit complex analyses of individuals, sub-units within schools, schools and local education systems are becoming widely accepted as being simply essential to capture the complexity of educational matters and essential in order to move away from the notion that schools are equally effective or ineffective for all their various subgroups of pupils.

### School Processes

Our assessment of the adequacy of the research designs for measuring the 'process' characteristics of effective and ineffective schools is more sanguine. It is clear that very few contemporary researchers include the factors of resource levels, expenditure per head or the adequacy of educational facilities amongst their variables to measure the quality of the school environment, presumably because of the negative research findings of the 1960's concerning these factors and also because of the general change in the context of educational policy discussion away from the quantity of education provided for pupils towards a concern with quality issues. However, in situations of cut backs, reductions in expenditure and probably greatly increased inequality in funding between different schools (as in the United States and Britain for example) it may be that the neglect of the resources variables are significant omissions.

Other issues concerning processes are also important. We are unaware from all published research (including that reported in this volume) of the relative strength of the various process factors or most importantly of the *order of influence* of the variables, in the sense of which variables actually precede others causally. For those using 5, 7, 11 or 13 factor models of 'effective schools' for example, it is clearly important to know which factors precede others, yet the path-analytic methods necessary to do this have not been employed, leading to an impoverishment of the school improvement initiatives.

Teacher effectiveness, and the literature concerning it, has also not received the attention it deserves. Such concepts as 'high expectations' feature frequently as school level variables but since they are likely to operate through teacher/pupil interactions in classrooms, we do not get from the literature the detail on what effective teaching at a classroom level actually goes on in the effective schools. Since research in this volume shows that classroom level variables greatly exceed the school level variables in the proportion of variance they explain, the neglect of the classroom needs to be urgently dealt with.

380

Our last observation on the school process issues that were evident in Rotterdam concerns the difficulty of making any observations about the factors that are associated with 'effectiveness' independently of the local or national context of the schools concerned. This volume reports findings that suggest the characteristics of 'what works' to be different in different local settings, dependent upon the socio-economic composition of the community the particular school is serving. Most important of all, it seems that one of the most robust findings from the North American literature on school processes concerning the strong instructional leadership role of the principal may not be universally applicable, since there is research reported in this volume which suggests that this factor may be of much less importance in determining the effectiveness of schools in the Netherlands. Whilst the explanations for differences such as these may not be immediately clear but may be concerned with the *universal* practices of principals in school leadership in, the notion of a 'blueprint' for effective schooling or of 'recipes' for school improvement needs urgent reappraisal.

### School Outcomes

Only one factor continued to concern us in this area and that was the continued concentration upon exclusively academic outcomes that was still evident in most of the papers at the Congress. Social outcomes from schools in terms of students' social development, views of themselves, capacity to make relationships or non-racist/non-sexist attitudes are important things in themselves and there is of course much evidence that it is individual's social attributes rather than only their academic development which has an increasingly important effect on such areas as occupational level through the lifespan. Given that we also have some evidence that the social development levels of schools and their academic levels of development obtained may be partially independent, the continued use of academic development measures as if they reflected all areas of students' development can no longer be defended. Other objectives are important in themselves and they are also important because they determine academic achievement.

### Research Findings

Looking at the body of knowledge as outlined in Rotterdam and as it has accumulated over the last decade, we are struck by how much doubt remains over many substantive issues of theoretical and practical importance. Questions remain as to:
- The consistency of school effectiveness over time, since studies differ in the extent to which schools effective at one time are so two or three years later.
- The consistency of effectivenss across outcomes, since those studies which have used multiple outcome indicators have often shown a surprising degree of independence.

- The consistency of effectiveness across different groups of pupils, since research (some of which is reported in this volume) shows that school effects may be different for different groups of pupils (e.g. for low/high ability, for low/high SES etc.).
- The size of school effects, since research reported in this volume shows rather smaller between-schools size effects and rather larger between-classroom size effects than expected from the literature thus far. The school effects are in policy terms still worth having, but do not justify some of the more Messianic postures of some school improvers!

# SCHOOL IMPROVEMENT

Although we have our doubts about aspects of the school effectiveness literature as above, our major concerns - having listened to or read papers from virtually every Congress symposium and plenary session - must centre on the adequacy of the school improvement initiatives that are increasingly springing up in at least ten countries known to us around the world. Many of the initiatives use simplistic five, seven, or nine factor theories derived from school effectiveness research that is itself now over a decade in age. Many improvement initiatives are not adjusted to the local circumstances of the individual school, the school district or the larger national context, in spite of the research evidence we noted earlier which suggested that different factors may be important in different contexts or areas.

School improvement efforts relate poorly to what is the focal concern of most teachers, namely the curriculum, a neglected area for contemporary improvement work which if developed would begin to make the same link between classroom and school at a policy level that is needed at a research level. Evaluation of the effectiveness of the improvement attempts is also rudimentary in certain instances, especially where studies are conducted in the British qualitative tradition. Many of the improvement attempts are also 'dropped in' to schools, rather than growing naturally out of a school reviewing itself and its organization.

Perhaps the most important concern we have is that school improvement is usually built on an inadequate model of the ineffective school. Studies usually assume that the school to be improved or made more effective is lacking some of the factors of the more effective school, such as positive teacher expectations or strong principal leadership for example. The aim is a transplant of factors from effective schools into the ineffective schools but this strategy is inadequate if the ineffective schools that are being improved themselves have factors operating that are distinctive from those in the effective schools. For example, an ineffective school may have inter-staff relationship problems, projections of its failure onto its catchment area and many 'deep structural' problems that are simply never seen in more effective schools. Rather than study the effective and then attempt to change the ineffective schools on the dimensions where they score low by comparison with the effective, we need to study more 'closer' schools to see where they may possess factors unknown elsewhere. The improvement of ineffective educational practice could then proceed on the basis of a realistic and sound understanding of the schools to be improved.

# CONCLUSIONS

In terms of numbers attending, then, and in terms of the quality of the research on offer, we see substantial progress being made, a progress which we hope to see in evidence in the area of school improvement studies too. The major task of relating the findings of research and improvement studies to the lives of policy makers and practitioners in schools still remains though and it is a matter of increasing regret to us that more progress has not been made in this area by the Congress.

Perhaps it is the image of 'school effectiveness', which smacks for some of a back to basics orientation and to others of a narrow concern for excellence rather than equity, which is responsible for this state of affairs, since there seems to be a pervasive belief that school effectivenss is associated with right wing perceptions about quality monitoring, evaluation of performance and the like. This image clearly reflects our inability to explain the strong equity dimensions of the work in effectiveness and improvement and that equity issues were the most important for the early school effectiveness movements.

If policy makers and practitioners' perceptions of school effectiveness and improvement can be changed and if further intellectual progress can be made, then there is no doubt that the school effectiveness and improvement movement that the Congress represents will have a bright future. Effectiveness and improvement of schools can appeal to people of very different political and social persuasions and, hopefully, to the three distinctive audiences of researchers, academics and policy makers in ways that few other educational traditions can manage. In the long run, this ability to appeal to a wide variety of people will perhaps prove to be a weakness, since issues such as the goals of improvement and the issue of effectiveness for what wait unresolved to generate dissent and disagreement, at least potentially. For the moment, members of the International Congress for School Effectiveness can be genuinely proud of what is being done and can simply vow to enjoy what is happening for as long as it lasts!